With Respect &c
John Clement

SKETCHES

OF THE

FIRST EMIGRANT SETTLERS

NEWTON TOWNSHIP,

OLD GLOUCESTER COUNTY,

WEST NEW JERSEY.

BY JOHN CLEMENT, OF HADDONFIELD, N. J.

Southern Historical Press, Inc.
Greenville, South Carolina

This volume was reproduced
from a personal copy located in
the Publishers private library

Please direct all correspondence and book orders to:
SOUTHERN HISTORICAL PRESS, Inc.
PO Box 1267
Greenville, SC 29602-1267

Originally printed Camden, N.J. 1877
Reprinted By: Southern Historical Press, Inc.
          Greenville, SC   2022
ISBN #978-1-63914-037-4
Printed in the United Sattes of America

TO

MY FATHER'S MEMORY

THIS WORK IS DEDICATED, THE MERITS OF WHICH, IF ANY IT HAS, ARE DUE TO HIS
INTEREST IN A CORRECT

HISTORY OF THE FIRST SETTLERS

ABOUT HIS NATIVE PLACE, WHICH INTEREST HE SO FAITHFULLY SOUGHT TO
IMPART TO

THE AUTHOR.

PREFACE.

THE collection and preservation of facts illustrative of the early history of West New Jersey have always been, to the author of this volume, a pleasing task. The little interest manifested in these events which are so rapidly passing from memory, and which hitherto have attracted so little attention, has prompted this purpose and given it greater importance. The arrangement of the material here presented to the public, it is hoped, may not be entirely without value, for the reason that, by this means, some facts may be saved from oblivion, inquiry assisted, and new light shed upon a subject too long neglected, and too much mystified by time. The method of reference which has been adopted will enable the reader to consult the authorities used, and thus any particular line of inquiry may be the more fully pursued.

It is not claimed that these Sketches are a complete history of the times to which they relate, although much effort has been made in that direction; nor that they are entirely free from error; yet, if any interest shall be excited, or any one stimulated to examine the subject still more critically, their purpose will not be wholly defeated.

INTRODUCTION.

THE first Dutch, Swedish and English settlements on the Delaware river have been so comprehensively considered by various writers within the last half century, except those included within the limits of Newton Township, Gloucester County, West New Jersey, now embraced in the city of Camden and Haddon Township, Camden County, and places adjacent thereto, that, to recite their history here, would be a needless repetition. Upon that subject little uncertainty now remains, since nearly all the leading facts that, for many years, appeared contradictory or doubtful, have been reconciled and settled, so that no reader, however particular or inquisitive, need go astray.

But the persons who, separately or collectively, made up the English colonies upon the New Jersey shore of the Delaware should not pass unnoticed; nor can they be lost sight of, however prominently the results of their undertaking may be presented. They were men of decided views and positive characteristics, of clear and discerning minds, able to consider a subject in all its bearings, and endowed with courage to overcome obstacles apparently insurmountable.

Feeling that the abuse of power had not only made their property insecure, but was also destroying the quiet of their firesides, they naturally looked for some other land in which these troubles could be avoided. With the warmest attachment to the fundamental principles of the government under which they lived, they were forced to seek a new home, where these principles could be enjoyed in their original purity. Adhering to their religious belief with a tenacity that could not be shaken, and in that belief finding nothing that encouraged resistance, the "Plantations in America" were the only asylum in which the proper administration of law could be assured, since these colonies were too distant, and of too little importance, to attract the attention of those in authority at home. Not long did it take to put these conclusions into shape, and the unanimity with which they were accepted gave force and character at once to the movement.

Here was a novel and responsible enterprise; one new in its inception, new in its development and uncertain in its results; dependent for its success upon the business capacity and persistence of those who had enlisted in the cause; yet little time elapsed before such as were equal, or unequal, to the task began to appear. Among the original projectors, the timid were soon replaced by others more sanguine, and such as hesitated, at once found those who were glad to accept their positions.

With a common object, no radical difference of opinion delayed its consummation; hence a general outline of procedure was soon adopted, and the leaders found themselves clothed with responsibilities hardly anticipated. Their object was a declared and open one, to be obtained without bloodshed, yet through privation, suffering and sacrifice. They were not mere adventurers in search of wealth to be procured by rapine and the sword, regardless of the rights of others; nor did they endeavor to seduce the unsuspecting into their scheme by plausible or specious promises. Their purpose was to secure a new home in the wilds of America, and, in so doing, to lay the foundations of a government that would give to themselves the enjoyment of liberty in its legally restricted sense, and would perpetuate the same blessings to their descendants. How well they did this needs no answer from the present generation, which now reaps the full fruition of the labors of these pioneers in their efforts to obtain civil and religious liberty. In this light it is proper to regard them, and to admire their fidelity in laying so broad and deep the fundamental principles of human rights, so that these have come to us, after two hundred years, as pure and inspiring as when first published to the world. Nor did they hesitate when they found themselves in a strange land, surrounded by difficulties even greater than they had looked for. Without a dwelling, save such as could be made of the sails of their vessels; without an acre of land prepared for culture, and without a friend to welcome or direct them; they at once established their religious meetings, organized their form of government, and put in operation their code of laws, the liberality of which is felt to the present time. Nothing shows their intention to abandon the undertaking, or to yield to the discouragements that met them; but each successive day proved the wisdom of their plans, and strengthened their belief that success must ultimately follow.

The influence of female example also deserves to be commended. Taken from their homes and from the circle of relatives and friends where the refinements, if not the luxuries, of life could be enjoyed, and where the strongest ties of human nature exist—the courage and the faithfulness of the wives and daughters of the first comers to the soil of New Jersey must excite the admiration of every reader. The trials and exposures through which they passed cannot, in our day, be fully appreciated. In the midst of a wilderness where even shelter was an object, these women are found, showing by word and deed that no complaint of theirs should bring despondency upon the little company. Resolute in the discharge of every duty, and unceasing in their efforts to contribute to the comfort and encouragement of their companions, they displayed those traits of character which belong to the sex alone, and which always accomplish so much when brought into action. Having shared every sacrifice and met every requirement, their position in the first endeavor to settle our State with English colonists should be made a prominent one and must ever command respect.

From these small beginnings at Salem, at Burlington, and at Newton, can be traced the development of West New Jersey; and to the families who made the first adventure, many of its citizens can follow their direct line of blood.

The letters O. S. G., used in the foot notes, refer to the records in the office of the Surveyor-General of West New Jersey. All other references, except those specially noticed, are made to the records in the office of the Secretary of State, at Trenton, N. J. Those indicated by letters contain records of deeds, and those by numbers contain records of wills.

Many of the wills, probates and letters of administration of the first settlers in Burlington and Gloucester counties—part of Mercer county then being in Burlington, and Atlantic and Camden counties being part of Gloucester—are on file and not recorded. The like documents, however, of Salem county—then embracing what now form Salem, Cumberland and Cape May counties—are entered in the Salem books in the same office at Trenton. The records of many marriages of early times will be found in the court minutes of Salem and Burlington counties; some also will be found in the book of "Licenses of Marriages," of later date in the same office.

ROBERT ZANE.

ROBERT ZANE was the pioneer of the settlement at Newton. He was the first of that colony who left the shores of his native land to seek a new home in an unknown and unsettled country.[1] He did not wait the tardy movements of his associates, but took advantage of the first opportunity by which he could become acquainted with the place in which his life was to be spent, his children to be reared and his bones to be laid. With the vigor of youth and a fondness for adventure, he entered upon his purpose with a determination that could not be foiled. He was too young to be the victim of religious persecution, yet his sympathies were with those whose estates were being wasted, and whose persons were at the caprice of unrestrained authority. While these abuses excited his indignation, riper minds than his had convinced him that new homes, new laws and new rulers were the only hopes for security and peace. The records of his time follow so close upon his footsteps that he is seldom lost sight of, and, from the first to the last, no question arises as to his identity under so many different aspects.

Thomas Sharp, in his Memorial, refers to him as coming from the city of Dublin to Salem four years before he, Sharp, came to Newton; and all authorities agree that he was one of the members of the first Friends' Meeting established at Salem in 1675. He probably was in the ship with John Fenwick, among many other emigrants who arrived at Elsinburg in September

---
[1] Hazzard's Annals of Pennsylvania, 422.

of the year named, this vessel being the first which came to Salem under the auspices of that remarkable man. There is abundant evidence that his stay at Salem was designed to be but temporary, although his name frequently occurs in the proceedings of the Friends' Meetings of that place, from the year 1678 to the time of his removal. His name is not among those signed to the agreements made by the planters with the chief proprietor; nor was he of those who located lands in the Salem Tenth, and received their title from the same person with a view to permanent settlement. He does not appear to have participated in the government of the colony, or to have been a party to the troubles between Fenwick and his Dutch and English rivals. His only purchase of real estate during the four years of his residence there, was that of a town lot, which he subsequently sold to William Royden in 1689, several years after he had settled at Newton.[2] Thus the whole course of his actions, previous to the coming of Thomas Thackara and of the others with whom he associated, shows that his departure from home with John Fenwick was made in expectation of being followed by them, and of their forming a united settlement within the bounds of the Irish Tenth, many miles from the place of his first arrival. The limits of the territory in which this settlement was to be made, were shown to him soon after the arrival of the London and Yorkshire commissioners, as lying between Penisaukin and Timber creeks, two large and well defined streams. Beside these, but two others, at all navigable, found their way into the Delaware within the bounds fixed; upon any one of which the selection could be made. No one can doubt that Robert Zane traversed each of these to examine locations, test the soil and discover the most eligible place "to settle down by." Opposite to where the Swansons had made their farms, and where now stands the southerly part of the city of Philadelphia, the mouth of Newton creek opened into the river and was in full view from the spot where their houses stood. Near their dwellings a few scattered huts were already built, which gave the place some pretensions to a town, whose inhabitants, however, at that time, were all Swedes.

---

[2] Salem Deeds No. 4, 168.

About this time William Penn arrived at Shackomaxin, and the prospect was that a town would be laid out, extending along the river front from the last named point down to the little Swedish village; and including it. To be near this growing place, Robert no doubt, considered desirable ; and, when his friends arrived from Ireland, he called their attention to these advantages, and, through his representations, the place on the north bank of Newton creek was fixed upon, and an embryo town soon built.

These friends and associates, to whom reference has before been made, may be known through two separate and distinct papers, bearing widely different dates, and made for entirely different purposes. The first is a deed, dated April 12th, 1677, made by Edward Bylinge and his trustees to Robert Turner, of Dublin,[3] "*Robert Zane, of Dublin, Serge Maker,* and others for one whole share of Propriety in West New Jersey;" and the second is the Memorial of Thomas Sharp, dated in 1718, in which a history is given of all their proceedings down to the writing of the same, covering a space of forty-one years, and until after the death of several of those in the first interested. Taking these papers together, the one as the first and the other as the last, the coincidence of names, dates and localities are remarkable, and puts at rest any question touching the persons participant in that adventure.

As an artisan, Robert Zane was a worker in wool, manufacturing a kind of material that bears the same name to this day, and which is used for the same purpose.[4] It is probable that he brought his looms with him, but he found no use for them here for several years after his coming, for the reason that the required material was not produced until agriculture had been somewhat advanced, and the people had made themselves farms from lands where before had stood an unbroken forest. A majority of his associates were educated to the same kind of labor, and, although producing a different stuff from their looms, yet all came under the general head of "Weavers," and were thus known among their neighbors.

---

[3] Lib. B-1, 52.
[4] Lib. B-1, 52.

In 1679 he married Alice Alday, of Burlington, in the Friends' Meeting at that place. Alice was, in all probability, an Indian maiden. A faithful search among the names of the early settlers reveals none similar to hers; and it may fairly be concluded that Robert became enamored of the bronzed beauty in one of his perambulations among the natives of the soil. Perhaps some hunting expedition found him at night-fall, hungry and foot-sore, near the hospitable wigwam of an Indian chief, by whom he was invited to rest and accept the good cheer set before him; and, while the assurance of welcome delayed him for the night, he may have noticed a daughter of his host, of artless ways and graceful movements.

"What though the sun with ardent frown,
Had slightly tinged her cheek with brown,"

he could see in her a comely, and, to his youthful eye, an attractive person. To the talk by the evening fire, during which the old chief questioned him about "the story of his life," the dark-haired damsel would listen, and with "a greedy ear devour up his discourse," and thus give him an opportunity to watch her interest in his words, and to draw from her, at least, a look of sympathy. In relating the sad story of the wrongs that drove him, and those who were soon to follow, from their homes, he enlisted her pity, and thus won her love.

In settling the preliminaries of the marriage, a name known in the English tongue must be agreed upon; this trouble was easily overcome by those whose hopes and wishes now so closely assimilated. A due regard for the discipline of the church required that her ideas of religious belief should conform to the notions of Friends; this being made satisfactory, and a name having been fixed by her parents, nothing remained but the consummation of the nuptials.

This marriage doubtless brought together a strange assemblage within the tent in which the meetings at Burlington were then held. Beside the plain and unpretending dress of the Quaker might be seen the gaudy and warlike costume of the aborigines, and while the one was characteristic of non-resistance and peace, the other bespoke resentment and revenge. In the one, humility and a patient waiting for results were apparent; a bold and defiant expression could be seen in the bearing of the other. The restraining influence of civilization was strikingly contrasted with unlettered barbarism.

The arrival of his friends from Dublin in 1681, and their purpose to take up their abode in the Irish Tenth, made it necessary that Robert Zane should remove from Salem in order to carry out the original agreement formed before his coming to New Jersey. This may be inferred from Friend Sharp's history of that event, as well as from the deed before named.[5] In the search "up and down," he doubtless was the leader, and pointed out the advantages and disadvantages of the different points, and gave them his knowledge of the surrounding country. His right was one-tenth of a whole share, and this, under the several dividends, gave him the privilege of making surveys, of which he and his sons took advantage, as appears by the records of that time.

In the division of the original survey of one thousand seven hundred and fifty acres, as made in 1681,[6] he took for his share, the upper part which extended from Newton creek to Cooper's creek, and which now includes the Collings estate, the Barton farm, and the plantation formerly held by Amos Haines, with other sub-divisions. He was the owner of property at Gloucester, which he disposed of previous to his death.[7]

With the political matters of the colony he had somewhat to do, being elected to the first Legislature in 1682, and returned in 1685.[8] During these sittings many important laws were passed, their necessity arising out of the new order of things, and being based upon a new charter of rights. The most of these were found to be salutary, and but little complaint arose among the people.

In 1684 and also in the following year, he filled the office of constable ; but what executive duties he had to discharge when the inhabitants were so few, it is hard to understand. Each tenth appears to have had an officer of this character, appointed annually by the Legislature, whose authority was confined to the bounds of the same, while the sheriff, who was also

---

[5] Thomas Sharp's Memorial.
[6] Revels' Book, 52,
[7] Lib. W., 59, O. S. G.
[8] Leaming & Spicer's Laws.

appointed by the same power and for the same time, had his duties enlarged to the vaguely defined boundaries of the counties, which boundaries in after years led to much trouble and litigation.

Although his name does not appear among the records of the Newton Friends, yet he was an active member in that meeting and sought to maintain and advance their religious principles. In his day and generation opinions were well defined upon those points, and men were advanced in accordance with their views expressed or understood.

In the year 1686, Robert Zane fell into a difficulty with a female, formerly a servant in his family, touching some obligations on his part not complied with. The trouble assumed such proportions that it got beyond the control of the meeting, and found its way to the courts of justice, in which it became a matter of public record. The minute book of the court sitting at Gloucester explains the dispute, and the entire copy, as found and extracted by Isaac Mickle, Esq., is its best history.[9]

"Upon ye complaint of Rebecca Hammond against her late master, Robert Zane, for want of necessary apparel, as also his failure in some covenants that he was by his Indenture to perform; it was ordered yt ye said Robert Zane before ye first day of ninth month next, shall find and give to ye said Rebecca Hammond apparel to the value of three pounds seven shillings and sixpence. And also fifty acres of land to her and her heirs forever. And in case ye said Robert dislike this order, then to stand and abide by ye act of Assembly in ye like case provided. Whereupon the said Robert Zane did at last declare that he would comply with ye aforesaid order and answer ye same."

This appears to have been an act within the power of the court upon complaint of the servant, under the law passed in 1682, which gave authority to examine into and settle such controversies between master and servant.[10] The law required that the servant should have, at the end of the term, ten bushels of corn, necessary apparel, two horses and one axe. The fifty

---

[9] Mickle's Reminiscences of Old Gloucester, 39.
[10] Leaming & Spicer's Laws.

acres referred to were known as "head land," to which able bodied servants were entitled, and which the court directed to be conveyed. Friend Zane was not lessened by this suit in the good opinion of his neighbors, for his name is found in connection with many positions of trust after that time.

His house stood fronting Newton creek, near to, and perhaps a short distance above, the place where the Camden and White Horse turnpike crosses that stream, and on the farm lately owned by the heirs of Edward Z. Collings, deceased. Like all others of its day, no taste was displayed in its construction, but, being surrounded by the primeval forest, and near a beautiful, living stream of water, its wild and romantic appearance would be attractive to an artist's eye. The clearing of the land, at that day, was a slow process, accomplished with few laborers and poor implements, while, to add to the difficulty, heavy timber had to be felled and removed; yet these people soon began to write to their friends at home of the prolific soil, the favorable climate, and the plenty that pervaded the land.

With all such flattering accounts, however, it is to be supposed that much of the means for the comfort and sustenance of the first settlers was derived from the forest and streams that teemed with game and fish of many kinds, which kept the wolf from the door in more than a single sense.

An incident that occurred during the career of Robert Zane, showing the care with which the Society of Friends regarded the disputes among their members, and how much scandal was avoided by the settlement of such troubles within the pale of the church, may be noticed here.

John White, a resident of Newton, died, leaving his brother Joseph, William Bates, Thomas Thackara and Robert Zane, executors of his will. The property which he left to be managed by his executors for the benefit of his children, was, for those times, considerable. In the progress of the settlement, a difficulty arose between Joseph White and the other executors, which found its way into both the Newton and the Salem Meeting, causing much discussion and ill feeling. A committee of six members from each meeting was appointed to settle the matter. This committee met at the house of Thomas Gardiner, Jr., at Woodbury creek, to hear what could be said by each party. A conclusion was reached, and an award signed by eleven of the committee, Richard Darkin of the Salem Meeting dissenting. This award was laid before the Salem Meeting upon the 26th day of the eighth month, 1691, and by it approved. Joseph White appealed to the Quarterly Meeting, which confirmed the act of the Monthly Meeting. In these proceedings, Richard Darkin gave his reasons for not signing the award, which were considered by each meeting in its review of the same. In regular order, the parties took the matter to the Yearly Meeting, held at Burlington, and, on the 29th day of the second month, 1693, Richard Darkin on the one part, and Thomas Sharp, one of the signers of the award, on the other part, were heard by Francis Davenport, Alexander Brearley, Samuel Carpenter and James Fox, the committee appointed by the meeting. After due consideration, the meeting confirmed the award aforesaid in all things. Much dissatisfaction still existed, but, on the 24th day of the fourth month, 1695, the decision of the committee of the Yearly Meeting was reported to the Salem Meeting, and the controversy abandoned so far as regarded the trouble among the executors.

John Hugg subsequently became the guardian of William White, son of the said John White. He also fell into difficulty with Joseph White, the contentious executor, about the payment of money due the ward, which was in his hands. In 1698, the guardian made complaint to the Salem Meeting of this default, and, in the next year, Edward Shippen, Anthony Morris and Isaac Norris were appointed a committee to adjust the same. This committee reported against Joseph White. In 1703, the matter makes its appearance again at the Yearly Meeting in Salem. At this meeting Joseph White is rebuked for his neglect in the premises. In the twelfth month of that year, however, he appeared before the meeting at Salem, and showed that a settlement had been made between himself and William White, thus putting an end to this tedious controversy.

Robert Zane's will was executed in 1694, the year in which he departed this life. This paper is a ragged, damp-stained manuscript, in the files of the office of the Secretary of State, where it has probably escaped the eyes of searchers, for a century past. It contains much valuable information about his real estate, and also gives some facts concerning his family. Elizabeth, a second wife and mother of several of his children, was made executrix. She died in 1700, before a settlement of the estate was effected.[11] She was a daughter of Henry Willis, of Hempstead, Long Island, who was appointed by the court to close up the executrix's accounts. The posthumous child, as named in his will, was a daughter, and was called Rachel.

Nothing appears upon the papers to show who were the children of the first wife, so that the native blood can be traced to the later generations of the family. They were Nathaniel, who married Grace Rakestraw, of Philadelphia, in 1697; Robert, who married Jane ———; Elnathan, who married ——— ———; Simeon, who died without children; Mary, Esther and Sarah. Nathaniel died in 1727; his children were Joseph, Jonathan, Ebenezer, Isaac, William, Margaret, Abigail and Hannah.[12]

Robert deceased in 1744; his children were Robert, who married Mary Chattin; Joseph; William; Simeon, who married Sarah Hooten; Isaac, who married Asuba Wilkins; Rebecca, Rachel, Elizabeth, Esther; and Sarah, who married James Whitall.[13-14]

Elnathan died in 1732. He was a shoemaker, and resided in Haddonfield. In 1703, he, Elnathan, sold 127 acres of land to John Fisher, the same being part of the estate owned by his father, lying next to Cooper's creek. John Fisher sold to Arthur Powell in 1716, who conveyed to William Cooper, of Philadelphia, in 1730.[14] The same property passed through a branch of the Burroughs family to Amos Haines, who, in 1804, devised it to his son Amos. Two of the children of Elnathan Zane, Nathaniel and Elnathan, also lived in the same place; the last named of whom married Bathsaba Hartley, in 1761, a daughter of Roger and Rebecca Hartley,

---

11 Gloucester files, 1700.
12 Lib. No. 2, 510.

13 Lib. AB, 152.
14 Lib. No. 3, 138. Lib. K, 1.

and half-sister to Mathias Aspden. This person was a son, by a second marriage, of the widow of Roger Hartley with Mathias Aspden, in 1756. As a shipping merchant, he accumulated a large estate and, upon the breaking out of the Revolutionary war, sympathized with the Crown and removed to England. In 1779, he was attainted of treason, and his property sold. In 1786, the attainder was removed, and damage awarded for the waste of his estate. He never married, and died in London, August 9, 1824. His estate followed the direction of a will made by him in 1791, and went *to his heirs at law.*[15] These few words occupied the courts for more than twenty years, at an expense of thousands of dollars; the English heirs being claimants on the father's side, and the American, being claimants in the maternal line. In 1833, Judge Baldwin decided in favor of the first named. An appeal was taken, and a new trial granted. In 1848, the verdict of a jury, before Judge Grier, in Philadelphia, was in favor of the American claimants, which virtually put an end to the suit. The estate amounted to $600,000, and was distributed accordingly.

It will be seen that the male branch predominated in the Zane family; but many of them, having a spirit of unrest, incident to the blood in the maternal line, wandered into the West, far beyond the line of civilization, and the original estate passed out of the name in a few decades after the death of the first owner. By his, Robert's, will, one-third of the estate went to his son Nathaniel, and the same proportion to his son Robert. Nathaniel died in 1727, and devised his part to his son Joseph, who also bought his uncle Robert's share in 1740. Joseph deceased in 1759, and gave this estate to two of his children,— Esther, wife of Richard Collings, and Rhoda, wife of Thomas Heppard.[16] The last named sold the undivided half-part to Richard Collings, in 1762, whereby the latter became owner of the original estate, as before named.[17] A portion of the same is still held in the family; but much the larger part has passed to other owners.[18]

This Richard Collings (who was one of the descendants of Francis Collins), on account of the numerous family of that

---

15 Supreme Court of the United States, No. 160. 17 Lib. W., 59, O. S. G.
16 Lib. No. 9, 238.   18 Lib. B, 316, Gloucester Records.

name in this region, and for the purpose of distinction, changed the spelling of his name, by introducing the letter *g;* this has led to some confusion in genealogy; yet the tradition is generally accepted, and is looked upon as correct.

James Whitall, who married Sarah, one of the daughters of the second Robert Zane, settled on a farm which he purchased of Samuel Shivers, in 1725. This property fronted Cooper's creek, in Haddon township, and was formerly known as the "Ann Burr Farm." James Whitall must have died a few years after, for, in 1729, his executors sold the same to John Eastlack. In 1742, it became part of the estate of Elizabeth Estaugh (by her husband's will), who deeded it to her nephew, Ebenezer Hopkins, in 1752; one of whose children was the before-named Ann Burr.

Isaac Zane, a grandson of the second Robert, in his wanderings among the early settlers of the Western States, was captured by the Indians, and remained with them for many years. The contradictory statements made in regard to this person have lead to much doubt as to the truth of the story; and, with some, ne is placed in a different family and connected with a different history. DeHass, in his history of the Indian wars of Western Virginia, published in 1851, says that the family is of Danish origin, that it first moved to France, thence to England, and finally emigrated to America; and that one branch settled in New Jersey, nearly opposite to Philadelphia, and the other in Virginia. From the Virginia branch, this historian traces the pioneers of the Western wilds, and places Ebenezer Zane at the head of these brave men. His first cabin was built where the city of Wheeling now stands, and there he erected a stockade for the protection of his family, in 1777. He was employed by the United States government in various positions of trust and responsibility, and always discharged his duties to satisfaction. From this man the name and family have become numerous in Western Virginia. He died in 1811.[19]

Reference is made to Jonathan and Silas Zane, brothers of Ebenezer, who were his companions in arms against the Indians. Jonathan was considered the most expert hunter in

---

19 DeHass's History of Indian Wars in Western Virginia, 331.

his day, and often aided in the capacity of a spy in the troubles with the red men. Reference is also made to Isaac Zane, who, the account says, was captured when about nine years of age, and, becoming thoroughly Indian in habits and appearance, married the sister of a Wyandotte chief. By her he acquired a large landed estate, and had a family of eight children. He remained true to the whites, and, by timely information, saved them from many bloody visitations. In consideration of these services, the government granted him ten thousand acres of land on Mad river.

The remarkable coincidence of Christian names in this narrative with those of the descendants of the first-comer to Newton, would suggest some error on the part of DeHass in fixing the location of their settlement, and would lead to the supposition that he had been misinformed in this respect.

Letters and other memoranda now in possession of the family in this part of our State, place the identity of Isaac beyond a question. In 1798, an account of his captivity, marriage and position among the Indians, was published, and a visit which he made to his friends and relatives about Newton, goes to show that he was of the New Jersey family, and that Robert Zane was his ancestor.[20]

The family is numerous in most of the Western States; it has sprung from the hardy, brave men whose love of adventure and fondness for the solitude of the wilderness, kept them in advance of civilization. About the old homestead plantation, no one bearing the name has owned any of the soil for many years; and, but for the titles and traditions that are inseparably connected therewith, they would have long since been forgotten.

---

20 Family Papers.

THOMAS SHARP.

OF the few colonists who settled in Newton in 1681, Thomas Sharp was the master spirit. He infused his energy and good judgment into the whole company; was their adviser and guide, and was, no doubt, as he deserved to be, their leader in all important undertakings. He was an Irishman, and by occupation a "woolstead comber,"[1] but appears to have had better opportunities for education than most persons at that time, or, certainly, than those with whom he was associated.

Although, as he says, a young man, he had the entire confidence of his companions, and the end shows that this confidence was not misplaced or abused. He was a nephew of Anthony Sharp, a wealthy merchant of Dublin, who became the owner of several shares of propriety; part of which he conveyed to Thomas, who also acted as his agent in the sale of the remainder. Under this conveyance he made all his locations, and took part in the government of the Province.

A faithful sketch of the life of this man, from the time of his arrival in New Jersey until his death, would be a history of Gloucester county for that period, and would be the most reliable basis upon which the writer could found his statements. His thorough knowledge of the country, his acquaintance with the settlers, and his truthful accounts of the progress of the colony, as by himself recorded, have made him an authority not to be questioned.

---

[1] Lib. G-3, 36.

Touching the first settlement at Newton, no better account can be given than his own, so that future generations may have the evidence of a participant therein. Although written thirty-seven years after that event, yet it contains an exact statement of facts, and embodies everything necessary to an accurate knowledge of that undertaking. Every reader will peruse it with interest, and may thank Friend Sharp for doing so good a work for those coming after him. It is here presented entire, as copied from Liber A, of Gloucester county deeds, page 98, in the office of the Secretary of State, at Trenton, New Jersey:—

"Let it be remembered yt upon ye nineteenth day of September, in ye year of our Lord one thousand six hundred and eighty-one, Mark Newby, William Bates, Thomas Thackara, George Goldsmith and Thomas Sharp, set saile from ye Harbor belonging to ye city of Dublin, in ye Kingdom of Ireland, in a pink called '*Ye owners adventure,*' whereof Thomas Lurtin, of London, was commander, and being taken sick in ye city, his mate, John Dagger, officiated in his place ; in order to transport us, and yt we might settle ourselves in West Jersey, in America. And by ye good providence of God we arrived in ye Capes of Delaware ye eighteenth day of November following, and so up ye bay until we came to Elsinburg, and were landed with our goods and families at Salem, where we abode ye winter. But it being very favourable weather and purchasing a boat amongst us, we had an opportunity to make search up and down in yt which was called ye Third tenth, which had been reserved for ye proprietors dwelling in Ireland, where we might find a place suitable for so many of us to settle down together, being in these early times somewhat doubtfull of ye Indians, and at last pitched down by yt which is now called Newton creek, as ye most invitingist place to settle down by, and then we went to Burlington, and made application to ye commissioners yt we might have warrants directed to Daniel Leeds, ·ye Surveyor General, to survey unto every of us, so much land as by ye constitution at yt time was aloted for a settlement being five hundred acres, or yt we had a right to, for a taking up it under, which accordingly we obtained.

"At which time also Robert Zane, who came from ye city of Dublin, and had been settled in Salem, four years before, joined in with us who had a right to a tenth. Mark Newby to a twentieth, William Bates to a twentieth, Thomas Thackara to a twentieth, Thomas Sharp (out of his uncle Anthony Sharp's right) a twentieth, and George Goldsmith (under ye notion of Thomas Starkey's right) a tenth; all which of us, excepting William Bates who took his on ye southerly side of Newton creek, we took our land in one tract together for one thousand seven hundred and fifty acres, bounding in ye forks of Newton creek and so over to Cooper's creek, and by a line of marked trees to a small branch of ye fork creek and so down ye same as by ye certificate of it standing upon record in ye Secretary office it doth appear. And after some time finding some inconveniency in having our land in common together being at ye time settled at ye place now called Newton in ye manner of a town for fear as aforesaid at which being removed we came to an agreement to divide. George Goldsmith he choose the head of the creek, Thomas Sharp the forks or lower end of the land next towards the river, by which means the rest kept to their settlements without any disadvantage to themselves.

"And so ye land was divided according to every man's right. But it is to be understood as I have so much hinted before, that by ye constitution of ye country at yt time, no person, let his right be never so great, should survey and take up above five hundred acres in one tract to make one settlement of, and yt within six months, or otherwise, it was free for any other person that had rights to land to survey it to himself as if it had never been taken up for any other person. Whereupon many were obliged in order to secure good places to themselves to give one hundred acres to secure the rest; and many were deterred from taking up their land yt could not find means to secure it leaste they should spend money to no profit. Now ye state of ye case touching George Goldsmith (having a full and certain knowledge thereof) is this wise. Thomas Starkey did desire and order George Goldsmith to take up some land for him in West Jersey; when it is reasonable to suppose he had a right, but brought nothing with him to make it appear, and ye commissioners at yt time gave way by ye credit of the report of ye rest concerned that he might take up five hundred acres, but it never was returned in Starkey's name.

"George Goldsmith being uneasy under ye circumstance he lay, writ several times to Thomas Starkey, giving him to understand he had taken up five hundred acres of land for him provided he would allow him one hundred acres of it for settling the same as ye general custom then was. The letters either miscarried or otherwise the demand being ungrateful to him he answered them in silence. Supposing as it may be supposed yt ye land being taken up for him could not be taken from him, it could not be allowed.

"Now this put George upon further thought what to do to secure himself, whereupon he made application to Robert Turner and layeth his case before him, signifying if he would allow him one hundred acres of yt land whereon he had made his improvements, he would suffer him to take up yt five hundred acres in his own right. Robert taking the matter in due consideration and searching the records at Burlington about it, and finding it so to be recorded in George Goldsmith's name, who had no right at any time to take up any land in yt province, agrees to survey it to himself, and accordingly did, and records it as such in ye Secretary's office; conveys one hundred acres of ye same, according to agreement, to George Goldsmith, and unto his heirs and assigns forever. The other four hundred acres he sold unto Isaac Hollingsham.

"The foregoing is a true relation of yt settlement of Newton, as also a true and impartial account of ye foregoing tract of land, settled by George Goldsmith. Given under my hand the 3rd month, 3rd, 1718.

"THOMAS SHARP.

"Allowed by John Kay, the 3rd month, 4th, 1718."

In addition to the one thousand seven hundred and fifty acres located as before named, there were also one hundred acres of meadow land taken up at the mouth of Kaighn's run, and fronting on the Delaware river. This was done for the purpose of procuring hay for their cattle through the winters; and it shows how careful they were in obtaining lawful possession of the soil before they applied its products to their own purposes.

In many of the old papers this stream is called Little Newton creek, but, like others, this title has been lost and that of an adjacent owner substituted.

Like the larger tracts, the meadow was soon divided into lots, showing that their being held in common led to trouble among the owners.[2] The map here given is the only history of that transaction, but is sufficient to show the manner in which it was accomplished.

For some reason not explained, the bounds of the county of Gloucester were not defined by Legislative enactment until the year 1694, although the judicial limits thereof seem to have been recognized as early as 1682, in which year Thomas Sharp was appointed constable of the third tenth,[3] which same became part of the said bailiwick. This executive office, although defined as that of constable, must have extended to that of sheriff, since, in the same year, Burlington and Salem counties each had a sheriff appointed under the same authority, yet no such action was taken in regard to the third and the fourth tenth. As suggested by Isaac Mickle, Esq., in his notice of this matter, the confusion caused by Edward Byllynge in the colony, and the long adjournment of seven years of the Legislature, may be accepted as the reasons, but nothing satisfactory appears of record in regard to the matter. The inhabitants of that region of country, however, did not wait the tardy movements of their law makers, but proceeded with all due solemnity to establish a county for themselves—a faithful record of which action, made by Thomas Sharp at the time, is still preserved in the Clerk's office, of Gloucester county, at Woodbury. It runs as follows:—

"Gloucester, ye 28th of May, 1686. By ye propyetors, freeholders and inhabitants of the third and fourth tenths, (alias, County of Gloucester,) then agreed as followeth: Imprimis— That a courte be held for the jurisdiction and limits of the aforesaid tenths or county, one tyme at Axwamus, (alias, Gloucester,) and another tyme at Red Bank.

---

[2] Revel's Book, 50-59.
[3] Leaming & Spicer's Laws,.

Item:—That the four courts for ye jurisdiction aforesaid, be held in one year at ye days and times hereafter mentioned, viz: Upon ye first day of ye first month, upon ye first day of ye fourth month, upon ye first day of ye seventh month, and upon ye first day of ye tenth month.

Item:—That ye first courte shall be held at Gloucester aforesaid, on ye first day of September next.

Item:—That all warrants and summons shall be drawn by ye Clerk of ye courte, and signed by ye Justice, and soe delivered to ye Sheriff or his Deputy to execute.

Item:—The body of each warrant, &c., shall contayne or intimate the nature of ye action.

Item:—That a copy of the declaration be given along with ye warrant by ye Clerk of ye courte, that soe ye defendants may have the longest tyme to consider ye same and prepare his answer.

Item:—That all summons, warrants, &c., shall be served, and declarations given at least ten days before ye courte.

Item:—That ye Sheriff shall give ye jury summons six days before ye courte be held on which they are to appear.

Item:—That all persons within ye jurisdiction aforesaid, bring into ye next courte ye mark of their hoggs and other cattell, in order to be approved and recorded."[4]

With these novel proceedings, clerk Sharp had much to do, and, in all probability, prepared the paper as recorded; which in after years was received as legitimate, and so recognized by the Legislature of the colony. After that time the records were regular, and, all such as had occasion to appear at courts, either voluntarily or otherwise, submitted to the action thereof without protest. Isaac Mickle, Esq., author of "The Reminiscences of Old Gloucester," has copied many interesting things from these ancient books into his valuable work, which show Thomas Sharp to have been an efficient recorder and master of his duties. In view of the much labor and the poor pay, our clerk facetiously gets off the following lines, doubtless after a hard day's work:

"The clerks of this county I think I may proclaim,
Will not at present the owner of it load with much gain.
T. S."

---

[4] Lib. A, Court Minutes, Woodbury.

More truth than poetry is certainly here contained, yet nothing appears to prove that any duty was neglected, or further complaint made by that worthy man. After the machinery of the new county was fairly adjusted and found to run smoothly, Thomas Sharp withdrew from the duties of clerk, and was succeeded by John Reading, who served the people for many years after.

Being the only surveyor in these parts, his time was much occupied in that kind of business. In addition to the recording of deeds for the county, he kept a private book of all his proceedings, in which he placed maps and memoranda, showing his great care in such matters and his ability as a practical man. He also made other books containing plans of houses, calculations of the movements of the sun and moon, and many other things in accordance with his taste and leisure. One of these volumes was left in the hands of Hannah Ladd, after his decease, and was deemed so valuable, that an act of the Legislature was passed to have the same placed in the office of the Surveyor-General at Burlington, N. J.; thus it was made a lawful record, and has been so recognized to the present time. His money accounts, settlements and charges, will be found scattered through them. An occasional extract from them may prove interesting. In the year 1720, he paid several subscriptions for John Estaugh, towards the building of the meeting house at Haddonfield, of fifteen pounds each; he, at that time, having charge of much of that person's estate, in the collections of rents, &c. In the discharge of these duties, he traveled to Amboy in one direction, and to Cohansey in another, at each of which places John Estaugh had landed estate. In 1686, he appears to have paid the expenses of transporting Isaac Gooden and family from England, which he itemized in the following manner:

	£	s.	d.
Passage for self and wife,	11	00	00
Lost,	2	03	.00
For carrying goods,	00	15	00
For burial of his wife,	1	16	00
For nursing child,	00	06	00
Expenses from home to ship,	2	00	00
In shors, [chores?]	00	05	06
	18	05	06

These charges are light when compared with like expenses of the present day, and show about the average cost of removal from the one country to the other at that time.

Perhaps the most curious part of these books is the poetry therein. Among the multifarious duties of this man as Surveyor, County Clerk, as Judge of the Court, weaver, dyer, and others not known, he found time to woo the muse, and has left in rhyme somewhat of the history of his times, of the trials that vexed the church, and of other things to be gathered by the reader.

Part only is here given—not to be criticised too severely—but to show the character of the man, and the various occupations in which he engaged. Like many of the old records, much has been defaced, and parts entirely obliterated by damp, but, perhaps, enough has been secured to show the meaning of the author.

> "By way of introduction—
> The settlement of Newton and its state,
> As then it was, and now, I do relate,
> Because my knowledge thereof was most true;
> As by what follows here doth plainly shew.
> An introduction doth this work begin
> Like silken clew for guide of strangers in,
> That in time to come it may plainly be,
> And they that know not, may be made to see.
> The matters here contained, as thou may find,
> Have been with pressure some years on my mind;
> But now, at last, I have thought it well,
> And to Posterity, its good to tell.

1681.

> In eighty-one, in Salem we did arrive,
> At which time then the People began to thrive,
> And had in store for to supply our want,
> Which, otherwise, would have been rather scant.
> If to Burlington had gone, as we were bound,
> We should be lost and disadvantage found
> It would have been most surely unto us,
> And must have pinched and punished ye purse.
> Now being settled on this wise, I say,
> The winter mild, and nothing in the way,
> We had ye advantage for to try and find
> A place that was agreeing to our mind.
> After some time and labor spent, we agreed on
> The Creek, ye seat and place now called Newton.
> The persons yt thus had ye care to fix,
> Did, in ye whole, amount to number six.
> So in ye Spring we made our settlement,

> And lived so as that we were content;
> Although somtimes we were hard bestead,
> Yet the Lord in kindness did afford us bread.
> In Newton then there did shine
> Some yt were zealous and divine;
> They largely did with care provide
> For those yt come from ye true guide,
> To direct their minds to stand in truth,
> They had received in they er youth;
> Yet in a while some youth did show
> That they in goodness did not grow.
> But now poor Newton is decayed;
> The youth not zealous, I am afraid,
> Nor don't endeavor with ye care
> Their forfathers took a larger share.
> I shall be glad I live to see
> Their zeal increased and better be,
> And they endeavour to remove
> By real action in true love;
> Then I am in hopes ye case will mend,
> And be far better in ye end;
> But, if they careless do remain,
> Then will ensue both loss and pain.
> The love I have yt they may come,
> And with true drawings really won
> And settle in ye lasting truth
> Their forfathers set in their youth,
> That in ye end they may obtain
> That which will be their lasting gain,
> And leave yt odour unto theirs,
> As did their fathers who are in their.
> —By T. S., the 14th of ye 12th mo., 1718."

To return to the practical regarding the subject of our sketch,—he may be again found in the discharge of a good work, the keeping of a town book, commenced in 1723. This contains the record of the proceedings of the town meetings of the people of Newton, the entries being made in his quaint, odd manner, with a style of penmanship peculiar to himself. This duty he continued until 1728, inclusive, when his son Samuel succeeded him. Thus, in every new undertaking, he was the pioneer, laying down the general outlines of proceedings, and giving up the duties when the same went forward properly.

His map of the land in Newton township, made in 1700, and here given, is a paper that must interest every resident within its bounds, not only for the information therein contained, but also as showing the labor which he was willing to bestow upon a subject purely for the public good. This is but part of the valuable records of that nature which he has left,—records, extending over a large amount of territory in West New Jersey, in which he was commissioned as a deputy surveyor. The compass and protracting instruments used by him were of rude construction, compared with those of our day, now so nicely and accurately adjusted by machinery; yet, laboring as he did under these disadvantages, his field work and maps are not behind the best of the present time. In 1689, he laid out the city of Gloucester, designed, no doubt, as a rival to Salem and Burlington, which were already villages of some pretension. These towns had even start with Philadelphia, but they have, many years since, lost all comparison in present or prospective importance.

By appointment of the Legislature in 1684, with Henry Wood, Francis Collins and William Bates, he became one of the commission to lay out highways, which same appointment was continued the next year.

In 1685, he was returned as a member of the Assembly, the session of which commenced May 12th, and sat for one day.[5] At the November session in the same year, his name does not appear, which would seem to imply that two elections, preceding each sitting of that body, were had in each year.

The trouble among the people settled about the Penisaukin creek, concerning the line between the counties of Burlington and Gloucester, appears to have existed for several years, and led to many wordy combats and considerable legislation. The Grand Jury of each county took action in the premises, and assumed a belligerent attitude toward each other, seeming to lay aside, for the time, the element of forbearance and non-resistance so prominent in the early days of Quakerism. In 1689, the courts of Gloucester county appointed a Commission to run and mark the said boundary line, and Thomas Sharp was the Surveyor.[6] The people of Burlington county were notified, and, if they chose, could have appeared and seen the work performed. Three years after the Legislature appointed four of its number to report upon this difficulty, but, their decision being unsatisfactory, the law was repealed

---

5 Leaming & Spicer's Laws.
6 Minute Book, Woodbury.

at the next session. In 1694, an act was again passed, defining the boundaries of Gloucester county, but still leaving the cause of the difficulty an open question, by not fixing upon which branch of Cropwell river, or Penisaukin creek, the said boundary was to run. In 1709, however, an end was put to these differences by a law clearly naming the south branch; and this has remained as then fixed to the present time.[7]

In 1700, Thomas Sharp was appointed one of the judges of the several courts of Gloucester county, and, if practical knowledge has any merit, he was eminently qualified for that position. That he took an interest in the advancement and prosperity of the religious denomination of which he was a member, may be seen from the frequency with which his name occurs among the proceedings of that society. He was one of the trustees of the Newton Meeting, and, no doubt, assisted in the erection of the first house that was set apart for religious worship. With Elizabeth Estaugh he selected the site for the meeting house at Haddonfield, surveyed the lot, wrote the deed, and put the same on record in his private book, after she returned from England with it, having the signature of her father thereunto attached. In this paper he has again shown his odd style of description. It reads thus:

"As they shall see convenient to lay out from the tract of land settled by John Estaugh, lying in ye township of Newton, any where on ye north side of ye road yt leads out of ye King's road to Newton, as far from ye west corner of John Gill's fence as where ye said road intersects the same."

Upon the deed he placed a map of the lot conveyed, by which all vagueness and uncertainty of description are corrected. This remarkable man has left other interesting memorials and writings—generally of a religious character—not here copied for want of room. He participated in every political movement in and about the colony, and his name will be oftener found among the records at Burlington, Trenton or Woodbury, than that of any other man of those early times.

---

7. Leaming & Spicer's Laws.

In the division of the original survey as jointly held under the location, he says: "I took the forks or lower end of the land next toward the river."[8] There he settled, cleared a farm and improved some meadow. He owned property in other parts of the county, although not the holder of much real estate.

Thomas Sharp was also appointed ranger for Gloucester county. The duties of this office cannot be better understood than by copying in full the commission and instructions to the appointee.

"PROVINCE OF NEW JERSEY, {SEAL} WESTERN DIVISION. To Thomas Sharp, of ye county of Gloucester, greeting:

Thou art hereby authorized by ye power and order of ye Councill of Proprietors to be Ranger for Gloucester County. In all things well and faithfully discharging thy said office, and ye trust in thee reposed, according to ye instructions herewith sent. And from time to time and at all times, to give an account of thy proceedings in ye said office to ye President of ye Councill for ye time being, when, and so often as thou shalt by him be thereunto required, and make good to him ye effects due to ye Proprietors forth of ye Royalty of rangeing.

"Given under my hand and seal, ye fifth day of November, Anno Dom., 1708."

Attached to the commission is a copy of instructions to rangers, explaining at once the purposes of the office, their duties and authority. These instructions are as follows:

"INSTRUCTIONS FOR RANGERS.

"1st. All unmarked horses and mares above ye age of thirty months shall be accounted wild, and none others.

"2nd. It shall be lawful for ye several rangers within their respective limmitts to take up such horses and mares, and shall give notice thereof, by fixing of papers ffor discovery of ye same in three of ye most publick places in ye County where they shall happen to be taken up.

---
8 Revel's Book, 50.

"3rd. After such publication ye same not being owned within ye space of four weeks, they shall be appraised by two honest men, indifferently to be appointed by ye Constable of that jurisdiction, and after that exposed to sale by public vendue, ye one half part of ye price thereof to be paid into ye hands of ye President of ye said Councill for ye time being, and ye other halfe to ye ranger.

"4th. Any such horses, mares or other cattle which shall be found unmarked and taken up, being claimed by any person, and its appearing by ye oaths or affirmations of two witnesses taken before one justice of ye peace within ye time above limited, that ye said creatures do belong to ye persons claiming ye same, and it happening yt ye owners and ranger cannot agree about ye reward, they shall choose, each of them, one indifferent and substantial man of ye same County to allot and award ye said ranger his fees and reward, ffor taking up ye same."

His first wife and the mother of his children was Elizabeth Winn, whom he married in 1701. In 1729, he departed this life, and was, no doubt, buried in the old Newton grave yard. He left a will, executed in the year of his death, in which he named his children and disposed of his property.[9]

Five years before his death, he probably married Judith Potts, the widow of Thomas, and daughter of ———, Smith. From this marriage there was no issue. His children were Thomas, who married Catharine Hollingham; Isaac, who married Margaret Brathwill; Samuel, who married Martha Hall; Joseph, an idiot; John, who married Elizabeth Paine; Elizabeth, who married John Hallowell; Mary, who married ——— Smith; and Sarah, who married ——— Pearce.

In 1723, Thomas Sharp gave by deed part of the homestead property to his son Samuel, who settled thereon; and in the same year, he conveyed another part to his son John, who, in 1731, sold to his brother Samuel. At that time John resided in the parish of Christ's Church, London, and carried on the business of a weaver.[10] He was the youngest son; but why he

---
9 Lib. No. 3, 56.
10 Lib. DD, 358, O. S. G.

took up his home in the mother country does not appear. Seven years after the death of his father, Samuel sold his land to Tobias Halloway, and probably removed from the neighborhood. In these latter days this estate is known as the "Burrough Farm," now part of the property of Samuel C. Champion, deceased.[11] As the holders of any land, none of the name have been residents hereabout for many years. John Hallowell, who married Elizabeth, was a resident of Darby, Pennsylvania, and the ancestor of a large and respectable family in that section of the state. Mary and Sarah may also have left this part of the country after their marriages, as they cannot be traced with any certainty at this date. It is remarkable that the descendants of a man who played so prominent a part in the first settlement of Gloucester county, and who, more than any other, was careful to have the history of his time preserved to coming generations, should so soon be lost sight of, and not known among the families of the present day.

---

[11] John Burrough's Re-survey, 1810, O. S. G.

MARK NEWBIE.

THIS man was an Englishman, a resident of the city of London, and a tallow chandler. He was a member of a Friends' Meeting, whose house of worship was in a street of that city, called "Barbican." Some of the antiquarians say that it derived its name as follows:

"Barbican is a street near Smithfield, London.[1] The Barbican, originally a Roman watch tower, lay little north of this street; it was an appendage to most fortified places, and from it the street took its name." Another says: "Barbican is a good, broad street, well inhabited by tradesmen."[2]

In 1681, the persecutions that were carried on towards the religious society of which he was a member, led many Friends to remove to Ireland, where the rigor of abused law was not so keenly felt, and where for several years this class of citizens enjoyed comparative peace and quiet. Among them was Mark Newbie, who disposed of his property in London, and had a temporary residence in Dublin, with a view to settling in America and making it his permanent home.

The question of removal, was, at that time, and for the reasons before stated, very gravely considered among Friends, and, in fact, with some communities had already assumed a practical shape. The movements of William Penn in this matter were watched with interest, for he had a controlling influence in the Society, and his steps therein were ready to be

---
[1] Smith's Antiquarian Rambles, Vol. 2, 170, &c.
[2] Murry's Hand Book, 31.

followed. His opinions soon became known, and these influenced others accordingly. In this movement Mark Newbie saw an opportunity to assist in carrying out his previously settled purpose, for, in the same year, he joined with William Bates and a few others, to make the adventure which ended in their settlement at Newton.[3] The history of this has been well related by Thomas Sharp; it combines the reasons, facts and incidents thereof, better than any other account given, or that could be gathered at this late day. There are many reasons for supposing that Mark Newbie was a man or considerable estate, and, although he lived but a short time after his arrival, yet he became the owner of several tracts of land, and had valuable personal property. The situation of his house in the settlement (which was an humble and unpretending habitation,) is a question of more than ordinary interest to antiquarians, and to all such as care to preserve the history of the times in which lived these brave men, who planted the seed of civil and religious liberty now enjoyed by the millions occupying the soil.[4]

Upon an old map left by Thomas Sharp, designed to show the several tracts of land owned by Robert Turner, within the bounds of Newton township, this faithful historian has marked the position of several houses, as they were placed the year after the arrival of the settlers, and after their separation. This map fixes it near the north side of the main, or middle branch of Newton creek, opposite to where William Bates had placed his cabin, a short distance below the old grave yard, but above the late residence of Samuel C. Champion, deceased. Upon consulting a later map made by Friend Sharp, in 1700, much change may be seen as to the situation of the dwellings of the inhabitants; but the house designated as Mark Newbie's has the same position as on the first paper showing its locality. At the last date, Stephen Newbie owned that part of his father's land extending from the main branch to fork branch, and occupied the old homestead; while his brother Edward had erected buildings upon the part of the paternal estate that lay

---

3. Lib. A, 98, Gloucester Records.
4. File T, O. S. G.

north of the last named stream, and there lived. This division of the original property of Mark Newbie has been the cause of some doubt as to the true position of his residence, but the comparing of the two maps aforesaid places it beyond cavil.

In one of the accounts of this colony left by Thomas Sharp, in his quaint manner he says : "And immediately there was a meeting set up and kept at the house of Mark Newbie, and in a short time it grew and increased, unto which William Cooper and family that lived at the Point resorted." This clearly proves not only where the house was situated, but also that within its walls was established the first Friend's Meeting in Gloucester county, and, after Salem and Burlington, the first in West New Jersey. In this dwelling, built of logs, with the earth for a floor and a bark roof for a ceiling, were the doctrines of a revealed religion first proclaimed upon our shores by those who had left their homes and friends, to enjoy this privilege that was denied them there.

The lapse of time has swept away from us every appreciation of this privilege, for no attempt has since been made to abridge the rights of citizens in the enjoyment of religious opinions. No change of government or political excitement, for the last one hundred and ninety years, (save the abortive attempt by Lord Cornbury,) has sought to infringe this fundamental principle, so plainly and broadly laid down in the concessions and agreements of 1676. In this building assembled the families, in all not more than twenty persons, (attended, perhaps, by a few friendly Indians, who must have observed the similarity of these silent sittings to their own dignified and quiet assemblages,) who had come to take up their abode in the wilderness, and build for themselves and their posterity a government free from intolerance and persecution.

Who among them, no matter how enlarged their views or speculative their notions, could foresee the nation which was to rise out of such imperfect beginnings ? That the latent powers embodied in their simple form of government should spread to the limits of a continent, and be the pride of a free and independent people ? That these elements, based in justice and founded in right, would be the centre whence would radiate civil and religious liberty, to be enjoyed and appreciated by all who should come within its influence?

This was the initial point whence originated the many religious communities according to the order of Friends that are known in various parts of the country, some of which have gone to decay, and to the present generation are unknown.

Mark Newbie was also the founder of the first bank in the State of New Jersey, having a charter granted to him by the Legislature,—the words of the act running in this wise:

"And for the more convenient Payment of small Sums, be it enacted, by the Authority aforesaid, that *Mark Newbie's* half-pence called Patrick's half-pence shall, from and after the said Eighteenth Instant, pass for half-pence Current pay of this Province; *provided*, he, the said *Mark*, give sufficient Security to the Speaker of the House, for the use of the General Assembly from Time to Time being. That he, the said *Mark*, his Executors and Administrators, shall and will change the said half-pence for pay Equivalent upon demand; *and provided also*, that no Person or Persons be hereby obliged to take more than *five shillings* in one Payment."[5]

This law was passed at the session of May, 1682, and doubtless went into effect as soon as the said Mark had entered the proper security as required under the act.

The history of this bank may be readily followed through the records of those days, and enough gathered to show its beginning, progress and end. As security to the people of the Province, and as required by law, Mark Newbie conveyed to Samuel Jennings and Thomas Budd, as commissioners, a tract of land in Newton township containing three hundred acres, located by the said Mark.

When a settlement was made between the administratrix and the commissioners, a deficiency of thirty pounds was discovered in the banking operations, which was, however, made good out of his personal estate, thus releasing the land before named. By request of the widow, Hannah, Samuel Jennings and

---

[5] Leaming & Spicer's Laws.

Thomas Budd conveyed the same to Thomas Holmes, William Bates and Thomas Jenney in trust for Edward Newbie, the second son of Mark, in 1685; "but, if Edward die before he attain his majority, then to his brother and sister, Stephen and Rachel."[6]

Edward, however, lived to become the owner in fee, and by his will gave said land to his two sons, Nathan and Gabriel. Nathan died single and intestate, and his estate was merged into that of his brother Gabriel, who devised the same to his son John.[7]

On March 14th, 1764, John Newbie conveyed all the unsold parts of said tract to Isaac Cooper, in whose name and family the larger portion remains to this day.

The deficiency before named was doubtless caused by the death of the banker, the time being too short for him to perfect his arrangements in relation thereto. Had he lived, its usefulness might have been much enlarged, accommodating the community around him, and proving a profitable and commendable enterprise.

This half-penny was a copper coin struck by the Roman Catholics after the massacre in Ireland in 1641, and was generally known as St. Patrick's half-penny; it had the legend FLOREAT REX on the obverse, and on the reverse, ECCE GREX.[8] In 1680, half-pence and farthings were coined by royal authority, with the national symbol (the harp) and the date.[9] The worth of the half-penny was about one cent of our currency, but, on account of the unsettled standard of values, varied from that according to circumstances.

Struck without the authority of law, and, perhaps, only to commemorate some event in the history of that unfortunate people, this coin never obtained circulation in the old country. Through the foresight of Mark Newbie, it was bought in quantities at a slight discount, brought to West New Jersey, and made to answer the wants of the settlers, which wants were recognized by the Legislature in the act before named, and it answered their purposes for several years.

---

6 Lib. B, 126.
7 Lib. Y, 78.
8 Humphrey on Coins, Vol. 2, 511.
9 Vol. 2, 686.

In these latter days this coin is not in circulation, and can only be found in the cabinets of those that are curious in such matters, and fond of studying the progress of artistic mechanism in this particular line. Numismatics has, for many years, attracted the attention of persons of taste and leisure, by whom large sums of money have been paid for rare specimens of coin. Their interest and enthusiasm has done much to develop the progress of art through the various ages of the world as connected with civilization, with the advance of commerce and the spread of the human race.

As a legal tender among the colonists, the act made a strange provision, if the value was as before stated; for, by that act, no person was required to receive more than a certain number of pieces toward the discharge of a debt. As a matter of convenience, this part of the law was perhaps a nullity, since the settling of accounts and all other ordinary money transactions would necessitate the use of various amounts.

[10]Previously to the passage of the act regulating the value of Mark Newbie's money, the Legislature established the standard of Old England shillings and New England shillings, and also in 1693, did the same thing in regard to the Spanish coin, which by that time had come to be in circulation. For many years after the first settlements in New Jersey, there was much trouble among the people concerning the standard value of the various coins as established in the several Provinces. The colonial government attempted to remove this trouble, but it seems to have utterly failed. Paper money, the first of which was issued in New Jersey in 1709, had a double value, that in East Jersey, regulated by the worth of a guinea in New York, and that in West Jersey controlled by the worth of a guinea in Pennsylvania, thus leading to confusion and loss among the inhabitants.

The chapter styled "Currency of New Jersey," attached by Judge Elmer to his history of Cumberland county, is interesting and instructive, being an exhaustive dissertation upon that subject, and showing great labor and research.

It is not to be supposed that Mark Newbie had any authority under the law, to make this coin for the purpose of keeping

---

10 Leaming & Spicer's Laws.

up the circulation, and to enlarge his credit, whereby to get gain and establish his name as a successful financier; but he was careful to keep the amount circulated within proper bounds, for the very cogent reason that part of his estate was pledged, to make good any short-coming in this regard. Without these restraints, the influence of the church of which he was a member, and the watchful care of those around him to prevent a hazard of his credit, made him what in these days would be called a careful banker, too slow to make money and altogether behind the age.

In this connection the historian of the banking system of America, in his researches to discover where it originated, will fall upon the act of the Legislature of New Jersey, of 1682, and at once seek to discover where this institution was situated, how constructed, what its success, and what its end.

The action of the Legislature showed the foresight of our law-makers, even at that early day, in securing the people against imposition or fraud, and proves that they had a correct view of banking privileges, when they required a specie basis with real-estate security. To emulate this in these latter days would have saved much loss that has fallen upon innocent persons, and would have prevented the scandal now surrounding this class of corporations.

Within the same township, therefore, on the same spot, and in the same building, originated the first religious denomination according to the order of Friends in Old Gloucester county, as well as the first banking corporation in New Jersey,—*perhaps, in America*.

If the early associations of the settlement of a neighborhood have any interest; if the wide spread good of any institution, be it religious, political or financial, can be felt in a community and traced to its beginning, be that beginning ever so humble and unpretending; such associations, such incidents, and such history deserve some record, so that those who make inquiry hereafter, may not consider *this* an ungrateful generation.

> " Here, the dawn of reason broke
> Upon the trampled rights of man;
> And here a moral era woke—
> The brightest—since the world began."

The selection of Mark Newbie's house in which to hold the first meetings of Friends, shows him to have been a leading man in the church, and one who had much influence in matters ecclesiastical. In the political affairs of the colony he took a prominent part, and filled several positions of trust and responsibility.[11] At the May term, in 1682, of the Legislature, he appeared as a member, and was selected by the Governor as one of his council. He was made one of the commissioners for the dividing of land, and one of the committee of ways and means to raise money for the use of the government, at the same time. The amount of money assessed upon the third tenth for that year, which consisted of what is now Gloucester, Atlantic and Camden counties, was *forty shillings*, a sum of money that contrasts strangely enough with the large amounts paid for taxes by the people in the same territory at the present time.

At the September session of the same year, he again appeared and sat as one of the Governor's council, and participated in the making of many important laws, and was again appointed one of the commissioners to divide land.

In this year, the question whether the Proprietors had the right of government seems to have been mooted; a question of serious import to the purchasers of the soil, and one which they considered as involving their success as a colony, and materially affecting their privileges in religious toleration.[12] It assumed such a shape that a committee was appointed to draft a number of queries touching the question, to be submitted to the home government, and to Edward Byllynge, in order to know whether any difficulty in this regard really existed. Mark Newbie was one of the persons selected to discharge this important duty, but he died many years before the question was settled.

In the proceedings of the May term, 1683, the minutes say that Thomas Olive was appointed as one of the Governor's Council, "in place of Mark Newbie, Dead," thus showing that he deceased between the two terms of the Legislature; and this corresponds with many of the records relating to his real estate.

---

[11] Leaming & Spicer's Laws.
[12] Leaming & Spicer's Laws.

He died intestate, but no steps were taken to settle his estate until the 4th of the 7th month, 1684, when administration was granted to his widow, who proceeded with the appraisement, which amounted to one hundred and eighty pounds together with a large real estate.[13]

So far as can be discovered, his family consisted of two sons and two daughters, all of whom were born before the parents' settlement here.[14] They were Rachel, who married Isaac Decou, in 1695; Stephen, who married Elizabeth Wood, in 1703; Edward, who married Hannah Chew, in 1706; and Elizabeth, who married John Hugg, in 1714.

Hannah, the widow of Mark Newbie, married James Atkinson in 1685. After this marriage it is probable that meetings continued to be held at the house in which Mark had deceased; as the records refer to several marriages that were consummated there. It does not appear there were any children by this marriage.

Stephen and Elizabeth Newbie had but two children,[15]—Mark who died single, in 1735, and Hannah, who married Joseph Thackara.[16] Stephen deceased in 1706.[17]

Edward and Hannah Newbie's children were Nathan,[18] Gabriel, Rachel, and a child unborn at the time of Edward's death in 1715.[19] Nathan died single; Gabriel married and deceased, leaving one child, John.[20]

It will, therefore, be seen that, after two generations, the family name was confined to one person, perhaps the last in this region of country. Hereabout, the blood may be traced through the Huggs and the Thackaras, although in some lines with trouble and doubt.

Among the children of Joseph and Hannah Thackara[21] were two sons, Stephen and Benjamin.[22] Stephen deceased in 1767, having lived on part of the original estate.[23] He had three sons, Joseph, Thomas and James, and perhaps other children.

---

13 Gloucester files 1683.
14 Lib. B1, 126.
15 Lib. Y, 78. Lib. No. 1, 169.
16 Lib. No. 4, 129.
17 Lib. No. 1, 169.
18 Lib. Y, 78.
19 Lib. No. 2, 104.
20 Lib. Y, 78.
21 Lib. No. 11, 106.
22 Lib. No. 4, 129.
23 Lib. W, 22, O. S. G.

Benjamin owned and lived on that part of the property lately held by Samuel C. Champion, and there he died in 1785. His wife Mary and twelve children survived him. They were Isaac, Abigail, Ann; Hannah, who married Joseph Jones; Mary, who married Joseph Elfreth; Mark; Margaret, who married John Tuft; Benjamin, who married Hannah Horner; William; Rachel, who married Francis Bilderback; Jacob; and Elizabeth, who married Abraham Reeves.[24]

Persons of this and other branches of the family settled in Salem and Cumberland counties, but among them the name of Newbie has never been known. The fatality that seems to have attended the Huggs, has left but little opportunity to follow the line in that direction, yet full access to the papers of the family might develop the whole connection of the descent to the present day.

The tracing of genealogies, or the knowledge of families, has not yet, in this country, become an attractive feature in its history; and the meagre scraps that happen to be gathered already can only be hoped to make the beginning of a more careful and successful research. Labor under endless discouragements, is the only means of attaining the proper end in this regard; and, until better compensated, it will not enter a field where profit is so seldom known to follow. As, among the descendants of Mark Newbie, there are many with whom the name has become extinct; so, in others, it has spread so rapidly that quite as much trouble attends the arrangement of the one as the other; a difficulty seldom appreciated and never repaid.

---

[24] Lib. No. 17, 461.

WILLIAM BATES.

IN the year 1670, this person lived in the county of Wickloe, Ireland, where his occupation was that of a carpenter.[1] The county town, which has the same name, is situated on the coast of the Irish sea, about thirty miles south of the city of Dublin, at which place considerable trade is carried on with other parts of Great Britain.

Here, also, all the courts are held for that district, and here may be found the common jail for the security and punishment of offenders within its limits.

In this, and in several different previous years, Parliament passed acts to prevent and suppress conventicles within the kingdom. These acts were made especially oppressive toward the Quakers, and under them many outrages were committed upon their persons and property.[2] If the policy of the government, the administration of its laws and the condition of its people, be any evidence of the progress of civilization; then England stood in no enviable light, during the few years before and after the date above named, in respect to religious toleration within her borders.

Loathsome prisons crowded to suffocation, courts busy with the trials of unoffending citizens, and arrogant officials robbing the people of their hard earnings to sustain a voluptuous and wicked clergy, are dark spots scattered through the history of a nation that boasts of the rights of her citizens.

---
[1] Lib. B1, 52.
[2] Besse's Sufferings, Vols. 1 and 2.

During these days a meeting of the religious Society of Friends was held at the house of Thomas Trafford, in the town of Wickloe, at which place William Bates was a regular attendant.³ Neither the small number that assembled there, nor the sanctity of a private residence, saved them from annoyance by the soldiery, for they were soon dragged to the jail, and there confined for several weeks, away from their homes and families. At the next sessions they were indicted, and, upon refusing to enter into bonds for their subsequent appearance at court, were sent immediately to prison. No regard was paid to sex or condition in life while under confinement, and so obnoxious were the dampness and foul air, in which they were forced to exist, that many died and the greater number suffered in health. In 1671, a declaration suspending the penal laws in ecclesiastical matters was signed by Charles Second, at that time king. This was a great relief to this class of citizens; but, on account of jealousy towards the Papists, the declaration was withdrawn the next year, and Friends again felt the displeasure of those in authority.⁴ Laboring under these disabilities, it was most natural that all such as sympathized with George Fox and his doctrines, should seek for a new country where toleration, to a degree at least, existed, and where they could enjoy their religious opinions in quiet.

During these persecutions the settlement of the land in America was much talked of, and some few colonies had been successful in getting a foot-hold, and had sent back to their friends in England flattering accounts of the country and climate. In the adjustment of the trouble between Edward Byllynge and John Fenwick, the attention of William Penn and other prominent men in the Society of Friends, was attracted to the territory, through which the river Delaware flowed, and very soon the initiatory steps were taken to secure a title for the same, and,—which was most desirable,—to have the right of government to follow in the same channel.

The books of record of that date are full of the deeds made from Byllynge and his trustees to persons wishing to get away

---
3 Besse's Sufferings, Vol. 2, 479.
4 Besse's Sufferings, Vol. 1, 27.

from the abuses that surrounded them, and to remove to a wild and unknown land, rather than to remain.

Among these is a deed, dated April 12th, 1677, from William Penn and others to Robert Turner, linen draper, of Dublin ; Robert Zane, serge maker, of Dublin ; Thomas Thackara, stuff weaver, of Dublin ; *William Bates, carpenter, of the county of Wickloe*, and Joseph Slight, tanner, of Dublin, for one whole share of Propriety in West New Jersey.[5]

Touching William Bates, it is very safe to say that his conclusions in regard to this step were reached in the common jail at Wickloe, where many dreary days were passed while his family was suffering at home. However vague and indistinct his ideas of the rights of persons were, in the form of government under which he lived, or how much such rights could be abused by authority of law, we cannot at this time judge; but we may suppose that they had come to be practical questions with him, placed beyond discussion and without the chance of amendment. The decision to remove to New Jersey was made under much deliberation, and after considerable inquiry in regard to locality, since it was important that the colonists should be near each other for fear of the Indians.

This deed shows the place of residence and the occupation of each grantee, and doubtless is a faithful record of these facts at the time therein named, which, taken in connection with the memorial left by Thomas Sharp, shows conclusively who were the persons that originated the settlement at Newton. Mark Newbie became a subsequent owner, while Thomas Sharp and George Goldsmith represented the interests of others, which six persons were the founders of that settlement.

During the four years that elapsed between the date of the deed and their coming, Joseph Slight disposed of his interest, and Robert Turner, having acquired a large amount of property in Pennsylvania, turned his attention to that in preference to his West Jersey estate, and did not become a direct partner in this enterprise.

It is readily seen that Robert Turner was the merchant through whom Robert Zane and Thomas Thackara disposed of

---

[5] Lib. B1, 52.

their manufactured goods, and that their business relations brought them frequently together, whereby the partnership here presented was created.

Although the county of Wickloe is some distance south of the city of Dublin, yet William Bates had business or religious intercourse with Robert Turner, and was influenced by him to be a participant in this novel and important movement. Of all the callings, his was likely to be the most useful, and his services to be the most in demand, when once they had arrived at their place of destination, for the first thing to be done was to provide some kind of shelter for their families.

This was in the shape of rude huts made of poles, placed partly in the hill side, and covered with the skins of animals or the bark of trees. Without any other floor than the earth, with no windows, a stick chimney and a single apartment, it needs no sketch of fancy to see, how inconvenient and uncomfortable the habitations of these first comers must have been.

On March 10th, 1681, being the time of the survey made to the other partners on the north side of the middle branch of Newton creek, for some unexplained reason, William Bates took his two hundred and fifty acres on the south side of the same stream, opposite the upper end of that tract, and there he built his house.[6] Two years after he made another survey adjoining the first and of like number of acres, and made a subsequent purchase of Robert Turner of other adjoining land, which extended his estate from the Graysbury line to William Albertson's boundary.[7] Much of this is included in the farms now owned by Jeremiah Ridgway and the heirs of Joseph Eldridge, deceased. His habitation stood by the creek, just below the mouth of Bates's run, and near the house on the Ridgway farm.

In common, however, with the other owners, he had an interest in the meadow land at the mouth of Kaighn's run, whence he obtained the hay for his cattle for the winter months, a necessary provision, as no other means of sustaining their stock was obtainable at that early day.[8] As the master

---

6 Revel's Book, 25.
7 Revel's Book, 53.
8 Revel's Book, 25.

mechanic, there can be no doubt, who planned and built the first meeting house at Newton, in 1684; who constructed the rude seats and erected the plain unpretending galleries, in which sat the forefathers of this people, who were faithfully carrying out the belief and the form of religious worship as brought with them across the sea.

To the descendants of William Bates this is a reminiscence worthy to be remembered, and to be told to their children, becoming more interesting as the lapse of time increases.

In 1683, he was one of the representatives from the Irish tenth in the Legislature of the Province, and was the same year appointed constable.[9] The next year, he was again returned as a member, and was appointed one of the commissioners for laying out highways, which last office he held for two years. That he was a useful man, both as a mechanic and a private citizen, is evident, and in each position he commanded the respect of those around him. He died in the year 1700, leaving a will, now on the files of the office of the Secretary of State, but never placed on record. His children were born in Ireland, some of whom were married in a few years after their arrival here. They were Jeremiah, who married Mary, a daughter of Samuel Spicer; Joseph, who married Mercy Clement in 1701; Abigail, who married Joshua Frame in 1687; William, who married an Indian girl; and Sarah, who married Simeon Ellis in 1692.[10]

Jeremiah settled on part of the original tract, as conveyed to him in 1693 by his father, who occupied it as a farmer.[11] Although his father left a will, yet the records say that he died intestate as to another part of his real estate, of which Jeremiah, as the oldest son, became seized. This is possible, but a closer inquiry may explain the difficulty, if necessary, and show that the will covered all the real estate. This last named tract, however, was given by Jeremiah Bates in his will to his son William, who re-surveyed the same in 1731; and upon this land the said William lived at that date.[12]

---

9 Leaming & Spicer's Laws. 11 Lib. G3, 348.
10 Lib. G3, 257, and Newton Meeting Records. 12 Lib. No. 6, 331. Lib. M1, 165, O. S. G.

Jeremiah and Mary Bates were the parents of four daughters and one son:[13] Martha, who married James Wall; Abigail, who married Thomas Thackara; Mary; Sarah, and William.[14]

William Bates married and had three children—two of whom died in infancy—leaving but a daughter, Mary, who married William Harry, of Philadelphia.[15] Jonathan Zane was her guardian in 1750, her father having died two years before that time.[16]

In 1759, Mary and her husband conveyed to Daniel Cooper a part of the land of which her father died seized, intestate; in this deed her connection with the first William Bates is apparent. In this branch of the family, the name was lost in the third remove from the first comer.

Jeremiah Bates deceased in 1723, leaving a will, in which document he named his progeny, and disposed of his landed and personal property.[17] He sold part of his land in 1700 to Elias Toy, a Swede, who probably settled on the same.[18]

In the year 1706, Joseph Bates settled on a tract of land which he purchased of Joseph Thorne. This lay on the south side of the south branch of Cooper's creek, in Gloucester township, near where the White Horse tavern now stands. Part of this is now owned by Jacob Lippincott.[19-20] His home was, in all probability, a cave in the hill fronting the creek, where his children were born and his family reared. At that time, he was beyond the line of settlements that were extending from the river towards the east and south, but was not far from the trail that went on the south side of the creek past where Long-a-coming (or Berlin) now stands, towards the sea coast. His wife was a daughter of James and Jane Clement, who had come from England and settled on Long Island. She was the first of the name within the bounds of Gloucester county; at the time of her marriage she lived with the family of John Hinchman, in Newton township, with whom she doubtless had come from Long Island. This marriage took place according to the order of Friends, at John Hinchman's house, as was

---

13 Gloucester Files of Wills.
14 Lib. S, 275.
15 Lib. S, 274.
16 Lib. No. 6, 375. Lib. No. 7, 97.

17 Gloucester Files of Wills.
18 Lib. G3, 321.
19 Lib. A, 84.
20 Lib. A, 47, of Divisions, Woodbury.

sometimes the practice in those days, owing to the distance from meeting houses and the bad condition of the roads.

The difficulty in tracing this branch of the family is the same that often occurs in others; it arises from the continuance of one Christian name from father to son and grandson, complicating the distinctions beyond the possibility of solution.[21] The records show that Joseph Bates died in 1731, and that Elizabeth Bates became his administratrix.

Among the children was a daughter Abigail, who married Samuel Lippincott, a son of Freedom and Elizabeth.[22] They resided in Pilesgrove, Salem county, N. J., with the following children: Joseph, Samuel, Joshua, Mercy, Abigail and Elizabeth. Many of the descendants of this branch of the family still reside in that section of the State.

In 1734, another Joseph Bates died, leaving a will; but which of these was the subject of this sketch, it is difficult to determine.[23] The last named had a daughter, Abigail, who married John Hillman, and other daughters.

His sons were Benjamin, Thomas and Jonathan. Jonathan's wife, Elizabeth, survived him, and died in 1765, leaving several children. The estate passed out of the family in 1767, by deed to Jonathan Aborn, and, after several conveyances, became the property of John Cathcart in 1794, who built the present brick mansion standing on the premises.[24] He had also a park for deer on part of his estate, for deer-hunting was one of the manly pastimes, fashionable at that day. The advance of agriculture has done much to change the habits, amusements and prejudices of our people, for, where once the hunter's horn and the music of the hounds were heard at nearly all seasons of the year, now the generous soil may be seen yielding its fruits to the husbandman. Where once were the well known haunts of bears and burrows for foxes, are now spread out green pastures and growing crops, the assurance of reward to thrift and industry.

Abigail Bates, who married Joshua Frame, removed to Pennsylvania with her husband, whose descendants at this day have

---

21 Lib. A, 47, of Divisions, Woodbury.
22 Lib. No. 3, 140.
23 Lib. No. 3, 432.
24 Lib. A, 47, of Divisions, Woodbury.

no knowledge of the pedigree of their maternal ancestor; neither is anything known of her in this region of country.

William Bates settled on the east side of a tributary of the south branch of Cooper's creek, known as Tyndall's run, about two miles east of Haddonfield. His house was near the residence of Joseph Browning, and within the bounds of a small survey which he made in 1687.[25] In March of the same year, he purchased of Robert Turner an adjoining tract of land containing two hundred and fifty acres, and increased his boundaries by subsequent purchases.[26] His place was near an Indian settlement, where this people raised their corn and pumpkins, and made their homes through the winter, when not away upon their hunting expeditions.

It is possible that William Bates married an Indian girl, like many of the early settlers; this would account for his making his home in one of the villages of the nation, and thus securing the title of the land to himself.

It is unfortunate that the records of the marriages of the first comers to West New Jersey, with the native females have been lost, in so many instances, and that so few are now known, and they only through a vague and uncertain tradition. Like John Randolph of Roanoke, those who are sure of this kind of connection with the aborigines, boast of the purity of their lineage, and are proud of this line of ancestry. In very many families, even at this late day, may be discovered the strain of Indian blood thus originated, unmistakably cropping out in feature or form, and showing the peculiarity so distinctly as to place it beyond controversy.

As in all newly settled countries, the scarcity of females among the emigrants made it rather a necessity than a choice to seek marriages among the natives. At the same time there were among these many comely and attractive maidens, who, being to "the manor born," were much better suited to the situation than those unused to the hardships and trials of a frontier life. In these marriages the consent of the swarthy girl was not the only difficulty to be overcome, for she stood

---

25 Lib. G1, 23.
26 Lib. G2, 131.

in all her native beauty, without a *name* known to the English language, and this defect had to be supplied before the ceremony could be performed in accordance with the law, then, as now, in existence.

Our ancestors being Friends, and using the language as they wore their clothing, pure and simple, would very naturally cast aside all romantic or suggestive names, and attach to the bride one after their own style, thus increasing the difficulty of discovering her nativity.

The enchantment lent by distance, has much to do with the romance that has always surrounded these associations, and, although the hand of the artist may favorably impress us with the beauty and grace of the female aborigines, yet an introduction into real life has invariably changed the notions of such as have thus ventured.

So far as good housewives were concerned, the little opportunity for display in this regard among the first settlers, placed all upon a level, and, as the improvement in dwellings and the surrounding comforts increased, the chances were that the Indian wife and mother kept pace therewith, and at last came to be as cleanly and economical as the best.

In this branch of the family somewhat more certainty can be reached, yet the knowledge of much that is desirable has been lost.

William Bates, the second, died intestate, and his estate descended to his son Joseph, who also dying intestate, the same estate, by the same law, became the property of his son Thomas.

It is a fair presumption that there were other children of both William and Joseph, but, at this late day, no means exist whereby they can be discovered, by reason of the law which regulated descents of land and carried the entire real estate to the oldest male heir.

Thomas Bates deceased in 1783, having devised nearly all this estate to his son Joseph, who lived where his ancestor made his first settlement, near Tindall's run. At that time he owned about four hundred acres of land in one tract, extending from the farm now owned by Abel Hillman, on the west, to

Peterson's mill stream on the south, now divided into several plantations.

In the year 1786, Joseph Bates made a re-survey of these lands, in which his title is fully set forth.[27]

Sarah Bates, who married Simeon Ellis, resided with him at Springwell, which place was near where Ellisburg now stands. She survived her husband several years, and dealt somewhat in real estate after his decease. Her children were Simeon, who married —— ——; Thomas, who married Catharine Collins, in 1722; Jacob, who married Cassandra Albertson, in 1750; Jonathan, who married Mary Hollingshead, in 1737; William, who married Sarah Collins; Joseph, who married Mary ——; and Sarah, who married John Kay, in 1730.

It will be seen that from Joseph and William, the sons of the first emigrant of this name, must the family be traced, which, in the lapse of one hundred and ninety years, has spread through nearly every State of the Union.

[27] Lib. U, 66, O. S. G.

THOMAS THACKARA.

THIS man was probably a native of Yorkshire, England, where the family suffered much religious persecution, by reason of their adherence to the opinions and practices of George Fox. In 1656, Thomas Thackara was taken from a religious meeting at Leeds, and confined for several weeks in York Castle. In the same year, Daniel and Christopher Thackara were sent to the Wakefield prison in Yorkshire, and, in 1660, Thomas and Daniel were again confined in the same jail.[1] At a later date, in 1683, Hannah Thackara with several others was taken from the meeting at Leeds, and confined in the Moothall prison at that place, during cold weather without fire, and there kept for nine weeks. From this kind of records it can be safely concluded that in and about Leeds in Yorkshire, the family of this name may claim their nativity, and from the records thereabout may trace their origin.

The first information that can be discovered of the subject of this sketch, is traced to Dublin, Ireland, where he was engaged as a "stuff weaver," in the year 1677, and became one of the grantees of the deed made to Robert Turner, William Bates, and others, for real estate in West New Jersey.[2] It may be too broad an assertion to say that he was the same Thomas Thackara who was imprisoned in York Castle, in 1656, although the lapse of time between that occurrence and the

---

[1] Besse's Sufferings, Vol. 2, 1.
[2] Lib. B1, 52.

date of the conveyance may be reconciled, supposing him to be but a middle-aged man, when a resident of that city. This is a question that can only be settled by access to private family correspondence, very little of which has been preserved through the several generations that have lived since the coming of the first adventurers; being considered as worthless material by most of tidy housekeepers, and therefore committed to the flames.

The deed before named calls him a "stuff weaver," one having something to do with the manufacture of flax; large quantities of which were cultivated in Ireland at that time, and made into the linen material so useful and so much admired, even at the present day.

Robert Turner was the merchant who sold the manufactured article; being a man of large estate, he was in intercourse with traders in other localities. This gave him the opportunity of knowing the inclinations and purposes of Friends in other parts, and by this means, those in his neighborhood were also advised in regard to their removal to America. Of these were the persons joined with him in the deed aforesaid, and thence their intentions may well be inferred. Thomas Thackara was a man of some estate; this is evidenced by the original purchase, as well as by the many surveys made after his coming; he was also a married man with family before he left the shores of his native land to make his home in the wilds of America. Whether he was a creditor of Edward Byllynge, or had made the purchase for the purpose before named only, and, like many of the same religious persuasion, had determined that no change could be for the worse, does not appear.

Enough has been left on record, and enough therefrom written, to show where and how originated the settlement of Newton in 1681. Thomas Sharp, then a person just coming to manhood, and filled with the spirit of adventure, gives much by his memoranda, and the various writings left behind him. Imagination may readily carry us back to some humble dwelling in the city of Dublin, in which these persons would meet from time to time, to consult as to the best means to carry out their purpose, as well as to know how many were bold enough to follow their example. Anthony Sharp and Robert Turner, both Quakers, and both men of fortune, were the guides in this, and not only gave their advice as to the detail of the movement, but also covered the doubtful points by contributions of their means. Friends all, thus there was but a single channel wherein ran their opinions, as to the necessity of the thing, and, as the sequel proved, all other difficulties were forced to give way to the object before them. These meetings of business, like many of their religious sittings, were secret, and the conclusions arrived at were known only among their own sect. Robert Zane was the pioneer, and came with the Fenwick colonists to accomplish the necessary explorations, and to fix upon some place where to make their homes. The difficulties existing between Byllynge and Fenwick, and the period occupied in their arrangement, gave Robert Zane ample time to examine the country and write home to inform those of his partners who were to follow him, of his opinions and success therein.

By some agreement among the Proprietors, and for reasons not known, the third tenth was set apart for such of the emigrants as came from Ireland, and within the limits of this tenth it is apparent that the searchings for a site for a town were made. These limits were Penisaukin creek on the north, and Timber creek on the south, extending back into the woods an indefinite distance; and the point was not finally settled until 1765, when Samuel Clement first ran and fixed the head lines of the townships within the bounds of old Gloucester.

To return with our sketch to Dublin, where the receipt of letters from Robert Zane was looked for with much anxiety, and where these were read before the little meeting of such as were closing up their affairs to take a final leave of home and friends,—it can be well understood what attention was given to their import, their advice and their direction. What arguments arose out of their different constructions, and how the hopes and the fears of those present predominated as conclusions were reached! How the sanguine temperaments were checked by the more prudent and older heads, and how the opinions and suggestions of some were modified and directed by those of more experience, but of no less decision of character! How wives, mothers and daughters attentively listened to the expressions of opinion, made on such occasions, and now and then participated, when *their* comforts were made part of the conversation! How they encouraged the doubtful, and restrained the impulsive, smoothing over the rough points of the stronger sex, and healing the differences of opinion by soft words! How prolific a subject, and how beautiful a theme for the pen of the novelist, who desires to have his story based upon fact, and conform to the truths of history!

"It was on the nineteenth day of September, 1681, from the harbor belonging to the city of Dublin, in the kingdom of Ireland, that Thomas Thackara with his family set sail in the pink "Ye Owners Adventure," with other persons of like intent for the capes of the Delaware; where they arrived on the eighteenth day of November following, and so up the bay until they came to Elsinburg, and were landed with their goods and families at Salem, where they abode the winter."[3] Their arrival was anticipated by Robert Zane, who had come four years in advance, and who in that time was familiar with the country and the difficulties that surrounded them. The condition of these was not so desolate as that of many others, for, upon their landing, they were welcomed by friends and provided with shelter at once. Although not at the end of their journey, yet the exposure to an American winter was avoided by this arrangement, and opportunity given for the men to pass judgment upon the action of Robert Zane, and to decide where to fix their permanent abode. The winter, however, was mild, and their traveling about was done in a boat which they purchased at Wickaco, of the Swansons, and with which the several creeks within the third tenth were explored before a conclusion was reached.

This done, and they having submitted their title deeds to the commissioners at Burlington, Daniels Leeds, the surveyor-general, came in person to set apart their lands by metes

---
[3] Lib. A, 98.

and bounds, in accordance with the requirements as laid down by the Proprietors. In all these operations Thomas Thackara doubtless took a leading part, and was familiar with every step made to secure a clear estate and to have the boundaries well defined. The survey bears date March tenth, 1681, and appears to have a discrepancy when compared with the time at which they set sail from Dublin, (September nineteenth), in the same year, which, according to the present chronology, would make the taking up of the land some six months before their departure from home.[4] This trouble is reconciled when it is understood that, under the old style, March was the last month in the year, and that the last day of the year was the twenty-fourth of that month, thus making the twenty-fifth of March under the old system correspond with the first day of January under the present.

The first survey of 1,600 acres Mark Newbie, Thomas Thackara, Thomas Sharp, Robert Zane and George Goldsmith held in common; but it was soon found that this kind of estate would lead to difficulty, and Thomas Thackara was the first to separate his interest by taking two hundred and fifty acres as his share, and receiving a title therefor from the other owners.[5] In 1695, he purchased an adjoining tract of two hundred acres of Isaac Hollingsham, and this purchase extended his landed estate from Newton to Cooper's creek. These tracts lay between Robert Zane's share above, and Mark Newbie's below, including the farm, now the property of John Campbell, the old Newton grave yard and some other adjoining lands. He erected his first house near where the present farm buildings of John Campbell stand, and there he continued during the remainder of his life. Excepting sixty acres that he gave to his son-in-law John Whitall, Thomas Thackara retained the whole until his death; all then descended to his oldest son Benjamin.

Benjamin conveyed fifty acres to his brother-in-law, John Eastlack, and by his will gave the remainder to his son Joseph, who re-surveyed the same in 1760. Stephen, the son of Joseph,

---

[4] Revel's Book, 25.
[5] Revel's Book, 59.

inherited this estate under the will of his father, and, by his own, gave parts of it to his sons Joseph, James and Thomas. In connection with this, Stephen held considerable land in Newton township, coming to him through his mother; but this, like the other property, passed out of the name many years since. The election of Thomas Thackara as a member of the first Legislature that sat at Burlington to frame and adopt laws for the province of West New Jersey, shows him to have been a leading man, and one on whose good judgment his neighbors relied. It was a responsible position; for these new comers found themselves the inhabitants of a land without law, except so far as generally promulgated through the original concessions which did not enter into detail, or through the practical application of the principles therein embodied. This had to be done to put the government in operation and make it what was promised by the owners of the soil. It is needless to write of their success in this regard, for they gave to the world the evidence of sound morality, unflinching justice and a faithful regard for right, that has been the admiration of all lovers of liberty from that time to the present.

Together with Mark Newbie and William Cooper, he was appointed one of the judges of the court for the third tenth in the year 1682, and was continued in that place until 1685, inclusive.[6] The authority, in all probability, only extended to that of Orphans' Court, Quarter Sessions and Common Pleas, and was held for the judicial division as named in the law, until the year 1686, when the third and the fourth tenth were made one bailiwick by the inhabitants, and thereafter so recognized by the Legislature of the province. It does not appear that any records of their proceedings were kept; if they were, some careless person has long since committed them to the flames. How great the pity, that such valuable memoranda as these are not appreciated by every one into whose hands they may fall; so that all like papers might be saved to coming generations! Where these courts were held; what the business; who the litigants, and whence the advocates; tradition does not give any knowledge, and we are left to surmise and speculation

---

[6] Leaming & Spicer's Laws.

upon a point of much interest in the early history of our neighborhood. The records commence, however, in 1686, and are carefully preserved in the clerk's office of Gloucester county; curious and instructive documents, to such as care to be familiar with the doings of our ancestors.

Thomas Thackara was also one of the land commissioners, the discharge of which duty was important and responsible; he had to examine titles, direct the deputy surveyors in locating land, and prevent the interference of adjoining surveys, which duty required discretion, good judgment and firmness, but withal very often was liable to censure, and frequently to personal abuse.

Perhaps there was no one thing that proved the regard in which this person was held, in the religious denomination of which he was a member, and of the community at large, so much as his selection to sign the address of the Newton meeting to the yearly meeting of London, protesting against the conduct of George Keith, in his differences with the Society of Friends. To defend the opinions and practices of the society against the subtle reasoning, and ingenious arguments of such a man, required a thorough knowledge of the tenets upon which it stood, and much talent, coupled with forbearance, to successfully guard them against overthrow. William Cooper was his associate in this, and the paper forwarded to the Friends in London, proves them to have been equal to the occasion.

The first Friends' meeting house built at Newton, stood upon lands conveyed by him to the trustees of the society, and doubtless without compensation. The original deed for this has been lost, nor is it of record, but enough remains of memoranda and recitals, to settle any doubt in this matter.

In the year 1702, administration was granted upon his estate, which is evidence of the time of his decease.[7] His first wife probably died after his settlement here, as in 1689 he married Hepzibah Eastlack, a daughter of Francis, also a resident in these parts.

---

[7] Gloucester Files.

His children were Benjamin, who married Mary Cooper, a daughter of William, and a grand-daughter of the first William; Thomas, who married Ann Parker, and Abigail Bates; Hannah, who married John Whitall; Sarah, who married John Eastlack, and Hepzibah (perhaps a child by the last wife), who died single. Benjamin married Mary Cooper in 1707, according to the order of Friends, and, the record says, at John Kay's house.[8] This may appear strange, but there is reliable information for asserting that a meeting was held there for several years, for the convenience of Friends at Evesham and Penisaukin, alternating each first-day with one held at Penisaukin for the same purpose. John Kay's house stood on a farm now owned by the heirs of Joseph W. Cooper, deceased, near Ellisburg; but no vestige of it can be discovered at this day. He, Benjamin, settled on the property where his father deceased, and, being the oldest male heir, inherited the whole estate; but, with that fairness so commendable in all like cases, he gave his brother and sisters a proportionate share of their parents' property. He died in 1727, leaving his widow and three children,— Joseph, Hannah and Mary.

Joseph married Hannah Albertson in 1731, and Hannah Newbie, a daughter of Stephen and grand-daughter of Mark Newbie, the first of the name hereabouts.[9-10] Hannah married Peter Champion in 1740; Mary married Thomas Wright. It is through this branch of the family that the present generation must trace their connection with Thomas Thackara, the emigrant from Ireland.

In 1699, at the Newton Meeting, Thomas Thackara and Ann Parker were united in the bonds of matrimony. She was a resident of Philadelphia, where she probably lived with her parents. Jeremiah Bates, in his will, dated 1728, mentions that his daughter Abigail is the wife of Thomas Thackara.[11] By these records, the matrimonial affairs of this son can be understood with some certainty, and they show in what line the descendants may look for their pedigree. Thomas Thackara, perhaps a son of the second Thomas, who married Elizabeth

---

8 Lib. No. 1, 479.
9 Lib. No. 2, 462.
10 Lib. No. 4, 129.
11 Gloucester Files.

———, removed within the limits of the Salem Meeting in the year 1759, where that branch of the family still remain. Their children were Hannah, born 1754; William, born 1756, and dying in 1776; Stephen, born 1760; Jacob, born 1763; Joseph, born 1765; and Thomas, born 1771.

John Whitall and Hannah Thackara were married according to Friends' rules, in 1696, at the house of the bride's father in Newton township; and, on the first day of March in the same year, (perhaps at the time of the marriage,) Thomas Thackara presented his son-in-law a deed for sixty acres of land, the same being part of his homestead estate. This piece of property lay in the northern part of his survey, and is now included in the estate of the late John C. Decosta, deceased. On this John Whitall made his home, and there he resided until his death in 1718. The immediate position of the house cannot at this time be discovered, but, probably, it stood near the residence of the present owner, an unpretending, comfortless habitation.[12] The issue of this marriage, so far as can be discovered, was three children: Mary, who married John Wood; Hannah, who married Henry Wood; and Job, who married Jane Siddon. Job settled at Red Bank, in Gloucester county, and from him the name may be traced, which at this time is spread through every State in the Union. He deceased in 1722. John Eastlack, who married Sarah, another daughter of Thomas Thackara, also settled on part of his father-in-law's estate.[13] This was fifty acres, conveyed to his wife by her brother Benjamin, in 1706; it lay adjoining the land owned by John Whitall, but no vestige of the house can be traced at this time.[14] Thomas Sharp, on his map made in 1700, marks one hundred acres as owned by John Eastlack, which had been previously held by George Goldsmith. Part of this tract is now owned by John Stoy, whereon he now resides. It was taken from the northwest portion of Richard Mathews' survey, which afterwards became the estate of John Haddon. Whether this was the land mentioned by Thomas Sharp, as given to George Goldsmith, to settle the difficulty

---

12 Lib. No. 2, 257.
13 Lib. No. 2, 202.
14 Lib. A, 107.

about his locating Thomas Starkey's rights, does not appear; yet its situation on Newton creek, about "as high as the tide flows,"'would seem to answer the calls of the deed, and fix the place of his first settlement.

By an agreement with the widow of John Whitall, John Eastlack became the owner of this property in 1724, and so continued until his death in 1736, at which time his son John was seized of both tracts by the will of his father; and upon this estate he lived and died.[15]

In 1760, he made a re-survey of the said two tracts of land, thereby settling the boundaries and showing the antecedent title. This may, at some future day, prove to be a very important record, now spread out in the books of the Surveyor-General's office of West New Jersey. In 1718, he purchased a farm of John Wright, in Newton township, lying on the south side of the main branch of Newton creek, which estate remained in the family for many years after.[16] John and Sarah Eastlack had six children: Sarah, who married James Mickle, in 1732; Samuel, who married Ann Breach, in 1733; John, who married Mary Bolton, in 1737, and Patience Hugg, in 1741; Daniel, who married Mary Cheesman, in 1740; and Esther, Elizabeth and Hannah.

In the immediate neighborhood in which Thomas Thackara made his first home, none of the name have lived for many years; and the land which he selected as his choice of the estate, having been held in common, passed into the ownership of strangers before the third generation from himself had died.

As in some other families, the female branches have predominated, and the day may soon come when the blood must be traced among other names.

---

15 Lib. No. 5, 131.
16 Lib. A, 100, 111.

GEORGE GOLDSMITH.

THOMAS SHARP, in his memorial of the settlement of Newton, says that George Goldsmith was one of the persons who came with him in the pink called "Ye owners adventure," of which Thomas Lurtin, of London, was commander. In another paper, also left by Friend Sharp, he says George Goldsmith "is an old man,"—an expression rather indefinite, but supposed to mean a middle-aged person without family. It may also be inferred that he came without any estate, since, in the location of land, he represented a tenth of one whole share owned by Thomas Starkey. Although he had no written authority from Thomas Starkey, yet Thomas Sharp had knowledge of his desire that Goldsmith should make selections of land for him; and, upon these representations, the commissioners allowed a survey to be made, extending from Newton creek to Cooper's creek, containing about five hundred acres of land. Upon further investigation, it was discovered that Thomas Starkey did not furnish the "rights" necessary to complete the title to said survey, and, as George Goldsmith found himself in a "strait," he (Goldsmith) induced Robert Turner, of Philadelphia, to return the location in his own name, the latter allowing Goldsmith one hundred acres of land, in view of his trouble in the premises.

The one hundred acres which Robert Turner allowed to George Goldsmith, were conveyed by deed, dated the thirtieth of the ninth month, 1687, but in separate tracts, one of eighty acres and one of twenty acres, lying some distance apart.[1]

[1] Lib. G, 31.

The larger piece was part of the survey as made by Goldsmith; it fronted on the main branch of Newton creek, and adjoined the upper line of the first general survey of the *Newton peoples*, as expressed in one of the old deeds. The exact position of this piece of land has been lost sight of through the various alterations of boundaries, and the many changes of titles since that date.

The smaller tract was situated near the forks of the main and the north branch of the last named stream, adjoining Thomas Sharp's and Stephen Newbie's lands.

George Goldsmith made his improvements on the upper or larger piece of land, for he conveyed the twenty acres to Stephen Newbie the next day after he had procured his title.[2] On the same day on which he sold the twenty acres to Stephen Newbie, (tenth month first, 1687,) he purchased a like quantity of land of Francis Collins, adjoining the upper lot; thus making his plantation of one hundred acres at one place on the creek, "about as high as the tide flows."[3]

The map showing Robert Turner's lands in Newton township marks the residence of George Goldsmith as on the twenty acres in the forks of the creek; but this is probably an error, since the records prove the conveyance of that piece of land as before stated.

This is further proved by the writings of Thomas Sharp in this relation, in which mention is made of the agreements between Turner and Goldsmith to have his land, *where he had made his improvements*, referring no doubt to the five hundred acres' location.

But little importance, however, attaches to this, except to show where the first comers erected their humble habitations and removed the forest to plant their crops. The instances are but few where such first settlements are known to have been made, as later generations found more eligible spots, and had little regard for the places where the old homes stood. Even with the original proprietor, such were only temporary buildings, and were changed as soon as time and circumstances would permit,— forgotten before the second generation had passed away.

---

[2] Lib. G, 25.
[3] Lib. G, 28.

Robert Turner kept the remainder of the five hundred acres' location until 1693, when he sold it to Isaac Hollingsham, whose son Isaac, a few years after, conveyed the same to Sarah Ellis, widow of Simeon; and in her family, parts thereof remained for many years.

Joseph Ellis, a son of Sarah, settled on these lands, which in progress of time passed to the female branches of his family, and, consequently, out of the name.

Although the name of George Goldsmith enters much into the documents and papers of the times in which he lived, yet of himself or family, if any he had, but little can be discovered. He was a member of Friends' meeting, but the only notice of his participation in religious matters is the minute of the Salem Meeting in 1681, when Richard Robinson and George Goldsmith were appointed a committee to speak to Thomas Smith "about his disorderly walking," &c.

This was during the first winter after his arrival from Ireland and before the settlement at Newton, showing that, although a stranger among the Salem people, yet he was soon called upon to discharge a delicate and important religious duty. If the first books of records of the Newton Meeting had been preserved, perchance his name would have occured therein, and have shown something of his standing among his neighbors and the interest he took in the advancement of the church in America. He appears to have been something of a land jobber, for, in 1693, he sold "rights" to William Albertson.[4]

In 1694, he conveyed to Nicholas Smith twenty-four acres of land in Newton township, situated on the north branch of the creek of that name, and, in the next year, conveyed one hundred acres near the last named tract to John Iverson, who, in 1697, sold said one hundred acres to Margaret Ivins.[5]

He appears to have kept clear of the political troubles that surrounded him, and avoided all the religious controversies then being carried on in the colonies. His name is not mentioned among the appointments of colony, county, or township officers, nor in any of the paper warfare so diligently waged among the religious zealots of the times.

---

4 Lib. G3, 199.
5 Lib. G3, 41, 242.

The records of the Friends' meeting of Philadelphia in the year 1696, show that George Goldsmith and Ellen Harrison were married according to the good order of that Society, after the several "passings" then customary on such occasions. As all means of identity (except the name) have passed away, some doubt exists as to whether the two names mean the same person; or whether the George Goldsmith, of Newton, in the colony of West New Jersey, is the same George Goldsmith that married Ellen Harrison in Philadelphia in 1696. Such marriages frequently occurred, and often mystify the genealogy of families, sometimes to the entire defeat of the searcher.

It has happened that persons were supposed to have died single, and the family tree has so been made up, when the truth is, that such had gone from their particular meeting and contracted matrimony in other places.

If, as Thomas Sharp says, George Goldsmith was an old man in 1681, the fifteen intervening years could not have added anything to his youth, or his inclinations toward matrimony; and the fair presumption is that the subject of this sketch was not the person named in the records of the Philadelphia Friends' Meeting, in connection with the aforesaid marriage.

The little that is known of him in after years, leads to the inference that he removed from this region of country, disposed of his real estate, and left none of his blood or name behind him. In Pennsylvania, and in other parts of New Jersey, the name sometimes occurs; but, in Old Gloucester, since the beginning of the eighteenth century, and, in fact, since the departure of this man, but few of like surname have resided.

This, however, is speculation, and not intended to lead any one astray, for his descendants may be traced through the female branches of his own blood, as definitely and as correctly as in any other manner, if such theory be a proper one, and the starting point be beyond a doubt.

Such difficulties in genealogy add much to the interest of the search, provided always that success attends the labor, and a knotty, troublesome question is solved.

FRANCIS COLLINS.

FRANCIS COLLINS was a son of Edward and Mary Collins of Oxfordshire, England; he was born January 6, 1635. His father was the owner of considerable landed and personal property in that county, which, after his decease, passed to the control of his widow. Francis was apprenticed to a bricklayer, and subsequently removed to London, where he was convinced of the correctness of the religious principles of George Fox, and at once became one of his followers. In 1663, he was married to Sarah Mayham, at the Bull and Mouth Meeting of Friends, and settled at Ratliff, in the parish of Stepney, county of Middlesex, which parish was, at that time, within the built up portion of the city of London. In an account book of his, still in existence, he made the following entry: "Francis Collins, his book, this 25th day of the first month, 1675, now living at Ratliff Cross, next door to the Ship Tavern;"—fixing his place of residence at that time beyond a question.

His adherence to the Quakers was obnoxious to his family, as is shown by the will of his mother and also by that of his sister Elizabeth.

In the book before named are many curious things, written in a style hard to decipher at this late day. Among these are the names and dates of the births of his children by the first marriage; the names of many persons with whom he had business relations; also the account of moneys paid to him for rebuilding the Friends' meeting house at Stepney that had been destroyed by a mob a few years previous to that time. This book also shows that he was a bricklayer and builder, and kept a store, evidently seeking for gain in various ways, yet adhering strictly to his religious opinions and example.

After rebuilding the meeting house in 1675, no other disturbance appears of record in that section, much to the credit of the authorities and much to the peace of Friends. The parish of Stepney, like many other ancient places in and around London, has its own legends,—told to this day among the superstitious, as no less wonderful than true. This parish being by the side of the river Thames and a resort for seafaring men, a tradition still exists among the English sailors, that all who are born upon the ocean belong to Stepney parish, and must be relieved in case of distress by the authorities thereof.

Francis Collins was among those who were imprisoned and fined for their adherence to their religious principles; and this doubtless had much to do with his coming to America, where his opinions could be enjoyed in peace.

For the first two years after his arrival, his movements are somewhat uncertain; he was employed, perhaps, in searching to and fro through the primitive forests for a suitable location for himself and family.

In 1682, he erected the first Friends' meeting house in Burlington, and, in the next year, he received two hundred pounds, and one thousand acres of land from the Legislature for building a market house and court room at the same place.

There may be another reason for his coming to New Jersey, disclosed in a deed from the trustees of Edward Byllynge, made in 1677, to Francis Collins, of Ratliff, of the parish of Stepney, in the county of Middlesex, bricklayer, Richard Mew, of Ratliff, aforesaid, merchant, and John Bull, of London, merchant,[1] for certain shares or parts of shares of propriety. The deed says that Edward Byllynge was indebted to Francis Collins in the sum of two hundred pounds, to Richard Mew one hundred pounds, and to John Bull fifty pounds; to

---
[1] Lib. B2, 681.

discharge which this conveyance of real estate in New Jersey was made.

The first taking up of any land by him was on the 23d day of October, 1682, when he located five hundred acres in Newton township, bounded on the west side by the King's road; upon which land part of the village of Haddonfield now stands.[2] Two days after, he made another and adjoining survey of four hundred and fifty acres, lying on the southwest side of the first and extending to the south branch of Newton creek.[3] Perhaps no better selection for soil and situation could have been made, showing that he acted deliberately and understandingly in this the first step towards a settlement in a new and unknown country.

"To secure a landing," he made a survey of one hundred and seventeen acres, bounded on the south side by Cooper's creek; most of which is now owned by John E. Hopkins and Joseph C. Stoy.[4] Francis Collins sold this survey to Richard Gray, whose son John conveyed the same to Ebenezer Hopkins in 1746.

Francis Collins built his house on the hill south of the village, where formerly resided John Gill, perhaps where he found a few acres cleared of the timber, and ready for him to cultivate his summer crop.

He styled his new place "Mountwell," that being according to the English custom of having some particular name for each person's estate; which name often follows through the various conveyances from one generation to another for many years. The frequent changes in the ownership of land in New Jersey may be the cause of the disappearance of these names, yet the examination of old deeds and dilapidated records often discovers curious things in this regard. The Mountwell estate, at this day, is divided among many owners, and, if each were tenacious of the old title, much confusion would ensue.

Being here some years before Thomas Sharp and his companions, he, in connection with others, did something by way of advice in their selection of a place "to settle down by;"

---
2 Revel's Book, 39.
3 Lib. G2, 25.
4 Lib. GH, 360.

giving them his experience in the wild woods, and his intercourse with the aborigines, a subject of much interest to these new comers.

His residence was isolated, some five miles from the little village at Newton, and without any intermediate settlements ; for, in 1700, Thomas Sharp places but five houses on his map between Mountwell and Newton, thus showing how slowly the country filled up in the intervening eighteen years.

The Salem road marked out as passing near where the village of Haddonfield now stands, could have been nothing more than a bridle path, and but seldom used except by the Indians.

His dwelling, in all probability, was only a rude wigwam surrounded by many other like habitations, the homes of those who were becoming more and more familiar with the pale faced intruders, in whom they could discover nothing but peaceful intentions. Although of slow growth, the confidence once established was never impaired by any act of emigrant, or of aborigines.

With the political affairs of the colony Francis Collins had much to do. In 1683, he was returned as a member of the Assembly to represent the interests of the third tenth, and at that session was appointed one of the commissioners for dividing and regulating land. In the difficulty between the proprietors and Edward Byllynge about the government having passed with the fee to the soil, he was one of the committee to adjust the matter among those interested.[5] A long epistle was prepared, in which several queries were submitted to some Friends in London touching this important question; but no conclusion was arrived at until the surrender in 1701, when all the rights of the government were given to the Queen.

On the eleventh day of the third month, 1683, Samuel Jennings was elected Governor, and named Francis Collins as one of his council, showing that his Excellency, considered him worthy of that honorable and responsible position.

In 1684, he was again elected to represent the third tenth, and, at that session, was made one of the judges of the several courts of that division of the territory of West Jersey, it being

---

5 Leaming & Spicer's Laws.

before the bounds of Gloucester county were defined and settled. In 1685, he was appointed to the duty of laying out highways, a task which seemed to have been easily discharged, since the Indian trails were generally adopted for roads, and so remained for many years after that time.

May 28th, 1686, the "Proprietors, Freeholders and inhabitants" of the third and the fourth tenth, agreed to call that territory the county of Gloucester, and they established all the political and judicial machinery necessary to set the bailiwick in motion. In September following, the first court was held at Arwamus, *alias* Gloucester, at which Francis Collins acted as one of the judges. In this position he continued for several years, discharging his various duties acceptably to the people. Some mystery surrounds this, as he had removed into Burlington county soon after his second marriage; yet his name appears as one of the judges of Gloucester county, and as participating in all the business thereof. He was a public man in many other positions, as the ancient records conclusively show.

In religious matters he doubtless took much interest. He was one of the leading members of the Newton meeting, then the only place of public worship in this region of country. Among the few marriage certificates preserved from those early times, is one stating that Thomas Shable, of Compton house, in ye province of West Jersey, was married to Alice Stalles, of Newton township, in ye same province, twelfth month, twenty-third, 1686, at Newton meeting. The autographs to this, prove that all the daughters of Francis Collins were present, thus displaying the curiosity of the sex, and leaving evidence that this characteristic is not of modern growth.

Their hand writing shows them to have been young ladies of more than ordinary education, which was procured while they were residents of the mother country, since no opportunities for learning existed here at that time. Glad of any excitement about their quiet forest home, it was most natural that they should take advantage of such an interesting event, to break the monotony that surrounded them. Their dress, made to conform to the plainness of the sect, did not destroy their graceful movements, or the comeliness of their persons. The only means of travel, except by water, being on horseback, they doubtless from long practice were admirable equestrians, which exercise detracted neither from health nor from beauty.

They drew around them many admirers, and, in the progress of time, left the parental home, and became the heads of families, and the maternal ancestors to long lines of descendants.

Mary, the wife of Francis Collins, died soon after his settlement here, leaving him six children,—Joseph, who married Catharine Huddleston of Mansfield, Burlington county, N. J., in 1698;[6] Sarah, who married Robert Dimsdale, M. D., of Chatteris in Cambridgeshire, England, in 1713; Rebecca, who married Thomas Briant, in 1698; Priscilla, who married John Hugg; Margaret, who married Elias Hugg; and Elizabeth, who married Josiah Southwick.

Doctor Dimsdale was a prominent man in his day, and deserves notice here. He was confined in the prison in Hertfordshire, for practicing medicine without a bishop's license; whether he refused or neglected to obtain one, does not appear. He was a man of much talent in his profession, and was the inventor of some popular nostrums that brought money to his purse and notoriety to his name.[7]

He came with William Penn to Pennsylvania, but, in 1683, surveyed a large tract of land, south of Mount Holly, in Burlington county, lying on both sides of a stream that falls into Rancocas creek at Lumberton, called Dimsdale's run.[8] He was owner of one-third of a whole share of propriety, bought of Nicholas Lucas, in 1682.[9] On this tract he erected a brick house, and, being a man of wealth, dispensed a liberal hospitality to his friends and visitors. He was somewhat interested in the political questions of the day, and sat as one of the judges of the courts of the county, wherein he lived.[10] In preparing for his return to England in 1688, he appointed John Tathen and others, his attorneys to manage his estate in America. In 1699, he revoked this, and made Francis Davenport, John Shinn and John Scott, his agents,

---

6 Friends' Records.
7 Burlington County files, 1720.
8 Revel's Book, 33. Basse's Book, 231.
9 Lib. GH, 533.
10 Leaming & Spicer's Laws.

with like powers.[11] His property here increased in value, but he did not return to look after it. The records show many of the transactions concerning his land in New Jersey, but may never get beyond the iron doors of the building where now preserved, except as some enthusiast be curious enough to disentomb them. In 1688, he returned to England, and settled at Theydon Garnon, near Epping, in Essex, where he died in 1718. By a previous marriage, he had two sons, John and William, neither of whom came to this country. Their estate in West New Jersey passed, in 1746, to Richard Smith (the younger), and Ebenezer Large.[12]

His widow, Sarah, by whom there was no issue, returned to New Jersey, and resided in Haddonfield during the remainder of her life, taking an active part in the religious society of which she was a member, and being frequently associated with Elizabeth Estaugh in her christian labors. In these persons, the intimacy of the families, as it existed in England, was here represented, keeping alive the kindly feeling there so closely united, by reason of the trials and persecutions passed through in the early days of their religious profession. The name of Elizabeth Estaugh as a witness to her will, proves that their friendship, ended only by her death. She died in 1739, distributing her estate among the children of her brothers and sisters, by her last will and testament.[13] By a deed from her father in 1714,[14] she became the owner of a tract of four hundred and sixty acres of land in Newton township, being the second survey made by him—now owned in part by the Hinchmans, Samuel Nicholson, Jeremiah Willits and others—extending from near Haddonfield, southwesterly to the south branch of Newton creek. Upon the first day of April, 1725, Sarah Dimsdale sold the whole tract to Simeon Breach and Caleb Sprague, who held it in common until April 30th, 1726, at which date they made division thereof. By this deed of partition, Caleb Sprague took two hundred and fifteen acres in the northerly part of the tract, and Simeon Breach took two hundred and forty-five acres next to King's run. None of the

---

[11] Lib. B2, 487, 546, 669.
[12] Lib. GH, 542.
[13] Lib. No. 4, 208.
[14] Lib. A, 11.

papers touching this transaction are of record; a circumstance which may lead to much trouble in days to come, should some sharp-scented lawyer insist on knowing the titles to these lands from the first taking up. Such difficulties must often occur in relation to the land in West New Jersey, by reason of the frequent neglect of owners in this regard.

Joseph Collins, the only son of Francis by the first marriage, settled on the homestead farm, and there remained during his life. Upon the second marriage of his father, this estate was involved in a trust to Robert Dimsdale and John Budd, for the use of such children as might be the issue of that connection.[15] This was done to guard against the operation of the law of descents in force at that day, which gave the oldest male child all the real estate of which the parent died seized. This trust was defeated in 1716,[16] as the father and his second wife, in connection with the trustees, conveyed Mountwell to Joseph in fee, and, in 1717, the children by the second marriage released all their right in the same to their elder brother.[17]

Joseph died in 1741,[18] leaving the following children,— Benjamin, who married Ann Hedger; Sarah, who married Simeon Ellis; Catharine, who married Thomas Ellis; and Rebecca, who married Samuel Clement.[19]

Benjamin was a carpenter, and lived in Haddonfield. Joseph Collins and his wife Catharine executed to Benjamin a deed for a portion of the Mountwell tract fronting on the south side of the main street of the village, retaining to themselves a life estate therein. Part of this was sold by the parties interested, in 1734. Benjamin died in 1756, leaving two children, Joseph and Priscilla, both minors at that time.[20] It will be noticed that the name in this branch of the family is only perpetuated by two persons, Benjamin, the son, and Joseph, the grandson.

Previously to his death in 1735, Joseph Collins and Catharine, his wife, conveyed to Samuel and Rebecca Clement a part

---

15 Lib. A, 76.
16 Lib. B2, 572.
17 Basse's Book, 138.
18 Lib. No. 4, 294.
19 Lib. No. 8, 395.
20 Lib. No. 8, 395, 544. Lib. No. 4, 294.

of the Mountwell tract, for considerations which showed them to be in favor with the parents. These were the sums of one hundred pounds, and sixteen pounds, annually, during the life of the said Joseph and Catharine and the survivors of them.[21]

Rebecca, who married Thomas Briant, lived with her husband on his estate near Mount Holly, Burlington county, where he owned a large tract of land. In an affidavit made by this man in 1733, in relation to the identity of George Elkinton, who came to New Jersey as a servant of Daniel Wills, he says that he was born at Shippen Warden, Northampshire, England, and in that year was sixty-eight years of age, and married Rebecca Collins. He was, in all probability, a servant of Daniel Wills, as Daniel appears to have brought several persons with him in that capacity, the most of whom became valuable and influential citizens.

In the year 1704, Francis Collins conveyed to Thomas Briant and his wife Rebecca, a tract of land containing four hundred acres situate in the "forks" of Timber creek, a short distance west from Chew's Landing. Rebecca survived her husband and died in 1743.

Her children were Elizabeth, wife of Daniel Haines; Sarah, wife of John Fennimore; Ann, John, Abraham and Benjamin. The descendents of this woman are, at this day, connected with some of the most respectable families in West New Jersey, who, with a little care, may trace their lineage to one of the first settlers of the colony.

John Hugg, who married Priscilla, had considerable estate and resided at Gloucester, (now Gloucester city,) to whom the family now scattered over the country may trace their ancestry. His death is thus noticed by Smith in his History of New Jersey:

"In this year (1730) died John Hugg, Esq., of Gloucester county. He was about ten years one of the council. Riding from home in the morning he was supposed to be taken ill about a mile from his house; when getting off his horse he spread his cloak on the ground to lie down on—and having

---
[21] Liber EF, 65.

put his gloves under the saddle and hung his whip through one of the rings, he turned the horse loose, which going home put the people upon searching, who found him in this circumstance speechless; they carried him to his house and he died that evening."

In 1695, Francis Collins conveyed to John Hugg and his wife Priscilla a tract of land lying south of Haddonfield, and bounding on Little Timber creek, which they in a few years afterward sold to John Hinchman.[22]

It is to be regretted that nothing conclusive can be discovered in regard to the children of Priscilla, as she had deceased, and John Hugg had married a second wife, by whom there was issue also. His children were numerous, but he made no distinction as to their mother. In regard to the children of Margaret, a like difficulty occurs, which may never be solved, except by some persevering genealogist interested in tracing his own blood.

Josiah Southwick, who married Elizabeth, the youngest daughter by the first marriage, was a resident of Mount Holly, and interested in an iron foundry established at that place. He was a man of considerable estate and left some descendants, who still reside in New Jersey.

The children of Josiah and Elizabeth were Josiah, James, Ruth and Maham.[23] This family name never became extensive in New Jersey, and now is confined to but few persons.

The marriage settlement, as before named, between Francis Collins and Mary, his second wife, bears date December 21st, 1686,[24] about which time this marriage took place at Burlington meeting. She was the widow of John Goslin, a practising physician and merchant of the town of Burlington, and the daughter of Thomas Budd, one of the largest proprietors and earliest settlers in the colony, who became a prominent man in the religious and political troubles of that day.

The one son by her first marriage is the ancestor of the name in New Jersey. Upon the consummation of this mar-

---
[22] Liber A, 183.
[23] Census of Northampton Township, 1709.'
[24] Liber B2, 572.

riage, Francis Collins removed to Northampton township, Burlington county, where he resided during the remainder of his life. Perhaps no more reliable information of this man and his family can be had than from a copy of the census of Northampton township, made in 1709, and preserved by the Historical Society of New Jersey. Among those there noticed are these:

Francis Collins, aged 74; Mary Collins, aged 44; John Collins, aged 17; Francis Collins, aged 15; Mary Collins, aged 11; Samuel Collins, aged 9.

John died in 1761.[25] His wife was Elizabeth, a daughter of Benjamin Moore of Burlington county. They had a numerous family, of whom, according to the best data to be obtained, the following are the names and marriages: Sybilla, who married Samuel Gaskill; Susanna, who married Daniel Garwood in 1737; John, who married Patience ———; Francis, who married Ann Haines (widow), and Elizabeth ——— (he dying, the latter afterwards married Ishmael Kent); Joseph, who married Diana Pritchett; Charity, who married Charles Kain; Sarah, who married Samuel Bates; Lizzie, who married Samuel Hugg, Robert Friend Price and Daniel Smith; Mary, who married James Budd, and Priscilla, who married Joshua Evans (his second wife). Joshua Evans was a preacher among Friends, and of that society there was no more exemplary or self-denying member. He adhered strictly to the spirit and letter of his belief, yet was not intrusive or objectionable in so doing. He saw the evils of intemperance, and, by his example and precept, induced many members of the same society to abandon the use of liquor, even at that early day. He resided on part of the estate now owned by Joseph O. Cuthbert, near the centre of old Newton township. A history of his labors as a public Friend, published several years after his decease, shows him to have been an acceptable member of his church, faithful in his duties and a consistent Christian.

It may be seen that the blood of John Collins is distributed among so many collateral lines, that its tracing would be almost impossible.

---

25 Lib. No. 10, 346.

Francis settled on land (which his father conveyed to him by deed of gift,) on the north side of Cooper's creek, lately Aaron Moore's.[26] The house, a brick one, was burned in 1866. It had some pretension to size and style in its day, but was both small and unsightly, when compared with those of the present time. He sold part of this land to Jacob Horner in 1718. His children were Joshua, who married ——— ———; Job, who married ——— Haines and Elizabeth Ballinger; John, who married Ruth Borradale; Priscilla, who married James Mulock, M. D.; Charles, who married Ruth Starkey, and Sarah, who married Ephraim Haines.

Mary, the only daughter by the last wife, married Thomas Kendall, and settled in Burlington county.

Samuel, the youngest child of Francis and Mary Collins, married Abigail Ward in 1721. Their children were Samuel, who married Rosanna Stokes; Mercy, who married Samuel Thomas and Solomon Haines.

Samuel and Rosanna settled at Colestown, where his business was that of a blacksmith. He purchased land of Thomas Cole on the west side of Penisaukin creek, and built a house and resided there during his life. This property was since owned and occupied by George T. Risdon, now deceased.

Their children were Abigail, who married John Lippincott; Rachel, who married Joseph Champion, and Hannah, who married Enoch Allen.

The children of Samuel and Mercy Thomas were Samuel, who married Hannah Bishop, and Hannah, who married ——— Clyne. Mercy's child by the last marriage was Elizabeth, who married Isaac Mullen.

Much speculation has arisen in regard to the first Samuel here named, as to his being a son of Francis and Mary Collins. That they had a son of that name is beyond cavil, and his marriage appears in the proper order of time. In 1728, Mary Collins, as executrix of Francis Collins, deceased, conveyed to this person a lot of land at Gloucester and a portion of a share of propriety, part of which share of propriety Samuel conveyed to his son Samuel, the blacksmith. This, in connection with

---

[26] Lib. H, 52. Lib. BB, 104.

other like data, seems to identify this person with Francis and Mary Collins in a manner sufficiently conclusive as to such relationship.

John (the son of John) settled in Waterford township, near Glendale. His residence, a large brick house, not now remaining, stood upon the farm now owned by John Stafford. He had considerable real estate in that region, and deceased in 1768. His wife survived him, and his child Mary, who was then the wife of Samuel Hugg, of Gloucester.[27]

He gave his land to his daughter during life, and to her children (if any she left), in fee after her death; and, in default of such issue, the same was to pass absolutely to John and Job Collins, sons of his brother Francis.

The daughter Mary died without children "her surviving," and the land became the property of John and Job, who occupied it for several years; but, at this present time, none of it is held in the name or blood of the family.[28]

In 1720, and but a short time before his death, Francis Collins executed his will (which remains on file in the proper office), expressing his desire in regard to the remainder of his property.[29] To his children, as they arrived at their majority, he conveyed portions of his land,—a circumstance which decreased the amount of property that passed by his will. He was probably a man of wealth and active business capacity. Much known through the colony, he commanded the respect of all. He lived to see his descendants increase in a remarkable degree, and occupy much space in the land of his adoption. He took part in all the changes and troubles of the colony, from the beginning until the government was fixed upon a solid basis, and the people contented and prosperous.

He could not but notice its advancement in all material interests, beyond the expectations of the most hopeful, and, in his declining years, observe the many changes that had been wrought since he set his foot upon the soil. Where had been but a few Indian huts, towns and cities were coming into existence; and, where miles of forests once extended, the

---

27 Lib. No. 13, 297.
28 Gloucester County Records, 1805.
29 Burlington County Files, 1720.

plantations of the settlers now gave evidence of progress and prosperity. The doctrines of George Fox had spread abroad in the land, and the fruit thereof was a religious, moral, and law-abiding community.

In his visits to his son Joseph at Mountwell, where he first broke the virgin soil to test its productiveness, he could see how rapidly the country was filling up, and that already an embryo village had made its appearance, on the King's road near his place.

A site for Elizabeth Estaugh's meeting house had been selected. John Gill had fenced the land near the same, and a few mechanics had settled hard by, each extending his business as the folk increased in the neighborhood.

At Gloucester also, where his daughters then lived, a marked change was observable since his first passage up the river to Burlington; and Philadelphia was already a place of growing importance, the centre of trade for West New Jersey and Pennsylvania.

Nearly two hundred years have passed away; generation after generation has followed since that time, each increasing in numbers, and each augmenting the breadth of cultivated acres, until the primeval forests have disappeared before a teeming population, and the aggressive spirit of the age.

The little companies who settled at Salem, Philadelphia, Burlington and Newton, formed but the centres from which have radiated those energies, that till the soil, fill the workshops and crowd the cities.

From these have gone out the multitudes that have made the waste places to bloom, and the generous land to yield its increase; that have changed our rivers into great highways of commerce, and forced the mountains to give up their treasure; that have founded a government, which has become the pride of its citizens and the admiration of the world.

WILLIAM COOPER.

WILLIAM COOPER and his wife Margaret, before their emigration to New Jersey, lived at Coleshill, in the parish of Amersham, Hertfordshire, England. This town lies about twenty-six miles northwest of the city of London, in which he was born in 1632. After he attained his majority, his occupation was that of a blacksmith. They were Friends and members of the Upperside Monthly Meeting, in whose minutes the records of the births of their children may be found, which are as follows:

William was born ninth month, 26th, A. D. 1660;
Hannah was born ninth month, 21st, A. D. 1662;
Joseph was born seventh month, 22d, A. D. 1666;
James was born third month, 10th, A. D. 1670;
Daniel was born first month, 27th, A. D. 1673.

James probably died young, as no mention of his name appears in any papers relating to the family; the others came over with their parents, and afterwards were the ancestors of the family in these parts.

Like others of the same religious persuasion, William Cooper suffered, both in estate and person, from those who considered that they were doing God's service, in molesting such as chose to differ from them in opinion and practice,—despoiling him of his horses and cattle, and dragging him to prison from the place where he was attending religious service.

Samuel Smith, in his history of New Jersey, does not fix the time of the arrival of this person with his family; which was probably not for a year after the first emigrants had come to Burlington. Neither is the name of the vessel given, the place of landing nor the names of those who came with him. Among persons tracing their family from the one continent to the other, this break in their history is always a regret; it is an omission that Samuel Smith might, perhaps, have filled, but, at that period, he did not attach much importance thereto. The time has passed, however, to remedy this defect, except in a few cases, a defect which always leaves a shade of doubt as to identity, and, sometimes, a breach that nearly destroys it. In this particular case no question exists, since the documents of a religious and legal character follow each other so closely and so continuously, that the William Cooper of Coleshill, of 1660, was the William Cooper of Pyne point, in 1682, beyond a doubt.

The first is the certificate of the Monthly Meeting at Coleshill, which is as follows:

"WHEREAS, William Cooper, of Coleshill, in the parish of Amersham, and the county of Hertford, hath signified unto us that he hath an intention, if the Lord permit, to transport himself with his wife and children unto the plantation of West New Jersey, and hath desired a testimonial from this meeting for the satisfaction of Friends there or elsewhere, unto whom he may be outwardly unknown;

"We, therefore, whose names are here underwritten, do hereby certify all whom it may concern, that the said William Cooper and Margaret, his wife, having lived in these parts for many years, ever since the first of their convincement, have walked conscienciously and honestly among us, agreeably to the profession and testimony of truth, according to the best of our observation and knowledge of them.

"In witness whereof, we have hereunto set our hands, this, the fifth day of the twelfth month, 1678."

This fixes his nativity (the previous record showing the names and ages of his children), and also proves that he contemplated coming to "the plantation of West New Jersey." He could not have arrived here before the middle of the year following, the twelfth month being February, and not a proper season for ships to start upon long voyages. He could not, therefore, have come with the first adventurers.

The next act of William Cooper, as the records show, was one for the purpose of locating lands in New Jersey; this, doubtless, occurred soon after his arrival here, and bears the date of October 5th, A. D., 1680.[1]

At that date, he selected fifty acres within the town bounds of Burlington, and had the same surveyed and returned to himself. It is possible that there was some delay in having the bounds defined, and in putting them on record.

There can be but little doubt, however, that on this piece of land he erected his first house and made a home for his family. The troubles between the London and Yorkshire commissioners in regard to the parts of the territory each were to take, hindered the fixing of the boundaries of individual settlers, and may account for the difference in the known arrival of some and 'the return of their surveys; yet, in the the case of William Cooper, the fact that the time of his arrival was not exactly known, leaves the taking up of his first location and his coming still an open question.

In a short time it was found that the lines of the fifty acres interfered with those of an adjoining tract, owned by the "widow"[1] Perkins; this trouble was afterwards settled by John Woolstan, unto whose wife William Cooper conveyed the same in 1695,[2] she being his only daughter. Whether he continued his business after his settlement here, and attended to the necessary wants of the inhabitants, which, in his particular line, were important, there is no record, for the worker in iron of that day was skilled in many other branches of mechanism, now in no way connected therewith.

He probably had knowledge of the coming of the settlers at Newton, some perhaps being known to him in the mother country, as they had secured the title to their land but fifteen

---
[1] Revel's Book, 7.
[2] Lib. B2, 500.

months before he accomplished the same for his property at Pyne Point, to which place he soon removed from Burlington. The intimacy so soon established between them warrants this conclusion; so do many other incidents scattered through the history of the times, showing that the intercourse here was but a continuation of that begun before this adventure was undertaken. The survey of three hundred acres at Pyne Point bears the date of June 12th, 1682.[3] Within its bounds was a large Indian settlement, and in this William Cooper with his family made his abode. The position was well taken, being one of the most commanding in this section of the country, and a good location for a town. The point of land made by the junction of the creek (afterwards called by his name) with the Delaware river, was selected as the site for his house, this site now being under water by the encroachment of the river upon the shore.

Before William Cooper selected this land, however, William Roydon had made a survey lower down the river, with which the boundaries of William Cooper's tract was found to interfere. It is evident that much controversy grew out of this trouble, and that it was not settled during the life of William Cooper. In 1723, William Cooper, the son of Daniel and grandson of William, became the owner of much the larger part of Roydon's survey;[4] and, being seized of his father's adjoining real estate at the same time, this difficulty may be said to have ended there.

William Roydon located other tracts of land in New Jersey, and crossed the ocean several times between the arrival of the commissioners at Burlington and his death. In his will he styles himself "citizen and grocer of London," in which city he died during the year named.

If tradition be correct, he was a shrewd business man, and did not always heed the precepts laid down by Friends, when his own interest was involved. Although he speaks in his will of William Cooper as "his trusty friend," yet the trouble about the bounds of their adjoining land did not make the same

---

3 Revel's Book, 32.
4 Lib. D, 456.

impression upon the mind of William Cooper. Nearly one hundred years after his death a copy of his will was brought to Philadelphia and recorded in the proper office, being a necessary link to the title to some of his real estate in America. His family, if he had any, did not settle here. He had a brother Robert and a sister, Esther Wright, both of Essex, and a sister Eve, wife of Richard Crews of London.

The Indians were not molested, and, although Arasapha, their king, conveyed to William Cooper all the estate that they had within the bounds of his location, yet no claim was set up by the grantee, and no trouble appears to have taken place between the old and the new inhabitants. The consideration in the deed between the aborigines and the settlers was made up of rum, match-coats, beads, guns, pots, kettles, pans, and such articles of general utility and fancy as satisfied this simple-minded people and always prevented any trouble in the future. This town was opposite a similar Indian settlement on the river called Shackomaxin; between these places a ferry was already established, as to the beginning of which "the memory of man runneth not to the contrary." Here the adventurers under the patronage of William Penn landed, and set up the first Friends' meeting in his colony. In the third month, 1681, a meeting was fixed at the house of Thomas Fairman; and it was thus kept for more than a year, until the Friends united with those in Philadelphia.

It is interesting to observe the religious intercourse that was maintained between the Quakers on each side of the river, an intercourse which lead to many marriages among the younger members, and to some complicity in tracing the genealogies of such.

In 1682, a six-weeks' meeting of business was held alternately between Shackomaxin and Pyne Point, which was maintained for several months; the said meetings being held at the house of Thomas Fairman of the one place and at that of William Cooper of the other. This custom appears to have been established by the yearly meeting held at Salem, for the convenience of Friends; but it did not long continue, for a place of worship was soon built at Philadelphia, and also one at Newton, thus avoiding the necessity of using private dwellings. The meeting at Mark Newbie's house, to which William Cooper of the Point resorted, had been kept before he removed from Burlington, showing where the principles of George Fox were first promulgated in this section, and making it a point of interest to such as care to inquire thereinto.

The intercourse of William Cooper with William Penn and the other trustees of Edward Byllynge was frequent, by reason of the large amount of land which he purchased for himself, and also as agent for others, still residents of England or Ireland. He was present at the celebrated treaty of Penn with the Indians, and doubtless gave that great man the advantage of his experience among this strange people. The similarity of the conduct of each toward them, and the continued and lasting amity preserved from the first, show the same element of kindness and fair dealing to have actuated and controlled both. The same principles of justice and of right, so much extolled in the conduct of the Patroon of Pennsylvania, were no less rigidly adhered to by the Proprietors of New Jersey, always accomplishing the same end and deserving the same measure of praise.

In the progress of time, the children of William Cooper took upon themselves the responsibilities of matrimony, and set up their own establishments. Hannah married John Woolstan in 1681, and before her father removed from Burlington. This was his second marriage, the first wife being a sister of Thomas Olive, at that time governor of the province. He came in the same ship as the commissioners, and at his house were held the meetings of worship for Friends in the early settlements. He was a worthy citizen, and the ancestor of numerous and respectable descendants. By the first marriage he had a son John, who, in 1683, married Lettice Newbold. In 1698, he (the father), died, disposing of a large landed estate by will.[5] His children by Hannah Cooper were Samuel, who died single; Jonathan, who married Sarah Pearson in 1707; Hannah, who married George Nicholson in 1706; Sarah, who married Edward Borton; Mary, who married Samuel

---

5 Burlington County Files.

Bunting in 1713; Joshua, who married —— ———; Michael; Elizabeth, who married Daniel Wills in 1714, and Rebecca, who married Francis Smith in 1714.

Jonathan removed to Bucks county, Pennsylvania, where he resided in 1715.[6] The daughters settled in their native State, and became the maternal ancestors of some of the most respectable families hereabout.

The name of John Woolstan occurs among the Friends in England who suffered persecution for religious opinions. His house was the first erected in Burlington, and in it, the first monthly meeting of Friends was held after their arrival.

Hannah, his widow, married John Surkett of Burlington, as her second husband; he deceased in 1709,[7] and she then married John Wills, son of Daniel, one of the commissioners, and father of Daniel, who married her daughter Elizabeth. There was no issue by either of the last marriages.

William Cooper married Mary, a daughter of Edward Bradway of Salem, N. J., in 1682. He died in 1691, leaving a will, in which he names his father, William Cooper, his father-in-law, his wife Mary, and three children, John, Hannah and Mary.[8] He probably died at Pyne Point, and perhaps unexpectedly, as Samuel Spicer and Henry Wood, both residents near that place, were witnesses to his will.

The inventory of his personal property discloses that he was a resident of Salem, and a blacksmith.[9] His children married as follows: John married Ann Clark; Hannah married John Mickle, and Mary Benjamin Thackara. As may be seen, William was about twenty years of age at the time of his coming to New Jersey. He was employed by his father in his own calling; this made him a useful man among the adventurers. He died young, and by his will left the care of his children to Edward Bradway and John Kay.

John deceased in 1730, leaving his widow Ann and the following children, James, John, David, Mary, Ann, Sarah, Hannah, and a child unborn.[10]

---

6 Lib. A, 38.
7 Lib. No. 1, 337.
8 Lib. A, Salem Wills, 85.

9 Lib. A, Salem Wills, 65.
10 Lib. No. 3, 118.

Joseph Cooper married Lydia Riggs in 1688. This female was of Irish parentage, but at the time of her marriage was a resident of Philadelphia. It is probable that, in 1695 (in which year the ferry and adjoining land were given to Daniel), William Cooper conveyed, by deed of gift, to Joseph, a tract of land bounded by Cooper's creek, east of his father's residence, where he, Joseph, settled. On February 18th, 1708, William Cooper conveyed two hundred and twelve acres to Joseph. The words of the deed are, " William Cooper, late of Cooper's Point, in Newton, Gloucester county, New Jersey, to Joseph Cooper, of the same place, for his house, land and farm called Cooper's Point, where he lately dwelt." [11]

He had previously erected a house and out-buildings on a tract of land which he had located on the north side of Cooper's creek, in Waterford, now Delaware, township. A portion of this house is still standing, it being part of the homestead of Benjamin B. Cooper, deceased, about one mile from Ellisburg toward Camden; and it is now one of the land marks of early times. To this place he removed, but not long to remain, as he died in 1710.

In 1697, Joseph Cooper purchased of Abraham and Joshua Carpenter four hundred and twelve acres of land, in Newton township, bounded by Cooper's creek,—now constituting the most easterly part of the Cope estate.[12] This he conveyed to his son Joseph in 1714, just as he had purchased it of the Carpenters. He owned much other real estate. He died in 1731, disposing of his property by will.[13] His children were Isaac, who married Hannah Coates; Joseph, who married Mary Hudson and Hannah Dent; Benjamin, who married Rachel Mickle and Elizabeth Burcham (widow); Lydia, who married John Cox; Hannah, who married Alexander Morgan; Sarah, who married Joshua Raper; and Elizabeth, who married Samuel Mickle.

The most noticeable of these was Joseph, who erected a large brick house on the Carpenter tract, and there lived. There were several children by his first marriage, all of whom

---
11 Lib. AAA, 382.
12 Lib. A, 08.
13 Lib. No. 3, 173.

died young, except Mary (and she before her father), who married Jacob Howell. She left two daughters, Hannah, who married John Wharton, and Mary, who married Benjamin Swett in 1762. Joseph Cooper, in his will, gave a tract of land, situated on the south branch of Cooper's creek, in Water ford, now Delaware, township, to these children, subject to the life estate of his second wife, Hannah, which, after her death in 1754, was divided between them. This tract of land, in the old papers called the "Wharton tract," many years since passed out of the family; it is now divided into several valuable farms, among which is one owned by the widow of Charles H. Shinn, deceased; and on it stands the old mansion, built before 1728, at which time it was occupied by George Ervin, a tenant of Joseph Cooper, the son of the first settler.

Hannah Dent, the second wife of Joseph Cooper, whom he married in 1735 in Philadelphia, was a minister among Friends, and came from England to New Jersey in 1723. The memorial published by the monthly meeting of Haddonfield, after her death in 1754, shows her to have been held in much esteem by that religious society. There were no children by this marriage.

Joseph Cooper died in 1749.[14] During his life he was an active business man. He was a member of the Legislature of this State for nineteen consecutive years, which shows that he represented the people of Gloucester county in a manner satisfactory and acceptable, and, although more than one hundred years have passed away since that time, yet no like confidence has been extended to any representative of the constituency of this region. He held other official trusts in the county, which he discharged with fidelity; and he seems to have been universally respected. The Haddonfield Monthly Meeting also noticed his death, and left on record evidence of the estimation in which he was held by the Society of Friends.

Daniel Cooper, the youngest son of William, came to New Jersey when about seven years of age. There was no portion of his life of which his recollections were so vivid as that occupied in coming here. Alive to every object about him,

---

14 Lib No. 6, 274.

in the novel position in which he then was, he could never forget them, and he doubtless in after years could enter more into the details of the voyage, than any other who shared it with him.

Without a regret, he looked happily forward, and, amid ever changing scenes, did not share the sorrow of his seniors in parting from friends and home. Of an age to attract attention, he doubtless made the acquaintance of all on board, ventured into every part of the ship, and was soon on social terms with the crew. Their odd dress, wonderful sea stories, and quaint ballads, excited his childish curiosity, and impressed upon his plastic mind things there to remain as long as he should live.

Daniel was twice married. In 1693, to Abigail Wood, a daughter of Henry and Hannah, who lived near by his father's place, but on the opposite side of Cooper's creek. At that time he took possession of the Roydon ferry, previously purchased by his father, and continued the same under the license granted to Roydon by the court sitting at Gloucester.

The license, as granted, is a curious document, but it embodies everything necessary to be said, either by way of explanation or for the exercise of authority in exacting tolls. No better history can be given of it than an entire copy from the record.

"WHEREAS, at a court held at Gloucester upon ye first day of ye first month in ye year one thousand six hundred and eighty-seven it was presented to ye Bench that a constant and common ferry was very usefull and much wanted from Jersey to Philadelphia, and also that William Roydon's house was judged a place convenient, and ye said William Roydon a person suitable for that employ; and therefore an order from ye court was then granted for ye establishment and fixing of ye same. Whereto ye bench did then and there assent, and refferred to ye Grand Jury ye methodizing of ye same, and to fix ye rates thereof, which was by them agreed and concluded upon as hereunder follows:

"Therefore we permit and appoint that a common passage or ferry for man and beast be provided, fixed and settled in some convenient and proper place between ye mouths or entrances of Cooper's creek and Newton creek, and that ye government, managing and keeping of ye same be committed to ye said William Roydon and his assigns, who are hereby empowered and appointed to establish, fix and settle ye same within ye limits aforesaid, wherein all other persons are desired and requested to keep no other common or public passage or ferry.

"And ye said William Roydon shall prepare and provide good and sufficient boats, with other conveniences suitable to ye said employ, to be in readiness at all times to accommodate people's actions, and shall take no more than six pence per head for such persons that shall be by him ferried over ye River, and not more than twelve pence for man and horse or other beast, and so not exceeding twelve pence per head for any sort of beast so ferried over, as above said; except swine, calves and sheep, which shall pay only six pence per head and no more.

"Given under our hands and seals at ye Court held at Gloucester for ye Jurisdiction thereof, this ye first day of ye first month, in ye year of our lord one thousand six hundred eighty and eight.

FRANCIS COLLINS,   CHRISTOPHER WATKINS,
ANDREW ROBESON,   SAMUEL SPICER.
JOHN WOOD,

"Entered, Examined and Recorded this 24th day of April, Ano 1689,

per me, JOHN READING, Recorder."[15]

The accommodations at this ferry were nothing more than open boats fitted with oars, and occasionally with sails, which occupied much time in crossing, to say nothing of danger and exposure to passengers. A few trips each day were all that could be made in fair weather, and during a storm communication ceased altogether. Abigail Cooper, the wife of Daniel, died in a short time after their marriage, and without children, for, in 1695, he married Sarah, a daughter of Samuel and Esther

---
15 Lib. G1, 110.

Spicer, who also lived on the north side of Cooper's creek near Pyne Point. On the 6th day of the second month, 1695, William Cooper conveyed to Daniel, the ferry, with one hundred and fourteen acres of land attached, and by the same deed other real estate in Gloucester county.[16] Daniel and Sarah Cooper's children were three sons,—William, who married Mary Rawle, of Philadelphia; Samuel S., who married ———— ————, and Daniel, who married ———— ————.

Daniel Cooper died intestate, in 1715.[17] The appraisement of his personal property amounted to four hundred and fifty pounds, including two ferry boats, showing that he resided at, and kept the ferry at the time of his decease. His real estate was large, and he was, no doubt, one of the wealthiest men of his day. In 1730, William Cooper, the son of Daniel, petitioned Lord Cornbury, then Governor, for a license to keep a ferry "where one had been kept for more than forty years;" which license was granted, "with the exclusive right of ferry for two miles above, and two miles below, so long as he accommodated the people, upon the payment of one shilling yearly on the fast day of St. Michael the Archangel."[18] This charter was certainly a liberal one, extending beyond the limits of the present city of Camden, without any time fixed for its termination, and with a tax that, by the face of the document, was to be but nominal. It was a monopoly so far as regarded these privileges, within the distance named, but in after time it became modified, and finally was abandoned. The exact position of this ferry upon the river front is not now known; it was probably between Cooper street and Market street, as Royden's survey extended but a short distance above the first named street.

The amount of business done at this river crossing may be inferred from the number of inhabitants in this region in those days. The census of Gloucester county, taken in 1737, shows a population of three thousand two hundred and sixty-seven, including one hundred and twenty-two slaves.[19] A large proportion of these lived near some navigable stream, depending

---

16 Lib. A, 39.
17 Gloucester Files.
18 Lib. AAA, 249.
19 Lib. GH, 1.

upon boats as a means of travel; and, in going to Philadelphia, they would use their own transportation and not cross either at Gloucester or Cooper's ferry. Also it has been seen that, in 1715, Daniel Cooper had but two ferry boats, no doubt of ordinary size and without capacity for carrying many people; which kind of evidence goes very far to prove that the means, though scanty, were sufficient for the wants of the public.

Daniel, the youngest son of Daniel, in 1728, settled near the head of the north branch of Cooper's creek, on the farm lately owned by William Hooten, deceased. He was a farmer, but was sometimes called a drover. This latter occupation was only occasionally indulged in, to procure cattle from along the sea shore for himself and neighbors. These were bred upon the meadows, and in the endless forests abounding there in those days. Wild and nearly unmanageable, it required much tact, patience and woodcraft to control them.

The first William Cooper deceased in 1710, leaving a will, in which he named his children and disposed of the remainder of his property.[20] His personal estate amounted to upwards of seven hundred pounds sterling,—a large sum for the times, but of small account in these days of wealth and pretension. Under the residuary clause of his will, parts of the estate passed to his grandchildren, who, at the time of his death, were John Cooper, Hannah Mickle, Mary Thackara, Joseph Cooper, Benjamin Cooper, Isaac Cooper, Lydia Cox, Hannah Thackara, Sarah Raper, Samuel Cooper, Daniel Cooper, Jonathan Woolstan, Samuel Woolstan, Mary Bunting, Sarah Borton, Elizabeth Wills, William Cooper, Rebecca Smith, Hannah Nicholson, and Elizabeth Mickle.

It is scarcely necessary to say that William Cooper was an eminent member of the Society of Friends, and participated in everything that went to the advancement and stability of the church whose tenets he had espoused. He was a preacher among them, and lived at a time when the expounders of such doctrines were especially obnoxious to the mass of the people of Great Britain; he, therefore, like others, suffered much thereby; but, before his death, he saw the success of these

---

20 Lib. No. 1, 260.

doctrines and their free development in the land of his adoption. He had much to do with the political management of the colony, being a member of the first Legislature that sat for the framing of laws. This was a work of great labor, but, in the end, it showed good judgment and practical common sense.

Adopting the statutes of England as the basis, they made the new features of their system conform thereto, so far as was consistent with the rights of the settlers. Inducements were held out for emigration, and the system of jurisprudence made as liberal as possible to accomplish that end. Through the several sittings of this session William Cooper was present, and participated, no doubt, discharging his duties acceptably. He was appointed one of the commissioners to divide land, and also one of the committee to devise means for raising money for the use of the colony. The next year he was continued a member. In 1684, when the trouble with Edward Byllynge in regard to the government was taken up, and Samuel Jennings and Thomas Budd sent to England as commissioners therefor,[21] the sum of one hundred pounds was allowed to each for expenses; and to William Penn was to be paid a like sum for services in the same matter. To assure the payment of these several sums, William Cooper, with nine others, joined in a bond as security therefor.

In 1685, he was again returned as a member of the Legislature, and also continued commissioner for the division of land. In 1696, he was appointed one of the judges of the several courts of the county of Gloucester; he also filled many other minor appointments in a township capacity.

The remaining part of his original survey, being a small tract of land fronting on Cooper's creek and adjoining William Roydon's survey, William Cooper conveyed to two of his grandsons, John Cooper, son of William, and Joseph Cooper, son of Joseph;[22] this was the last of the real estate held by him in Newton township. He had made other surveys in different parts of Gloucester county, some of which he conveyed, and some passed by his will.

---

21 Leaming & Spicer's Laws.
22 Lib. A, 28.

Parts of this real estate, particularly those within the city of Camden, still remain in the family, and have followed the blood of the first owner, under the proprietors, from generation to generation, for nearly two hundred years.

This is remarkable where the laws regulating the descent of real property are so liberal, and where the third generation seldom hold the land of their ancestors. Ability to possess, and a desire to perpetuate, family estates, are commendable traits; they deserve emulation and should become to a greater extent characteristics of Americans. Yet, in our haste to get gain, all things else become secondary, and the exceptions are among those who are not willing to venture the paternal acres in fortune's lottery.

WILLIAM ALBERTSON.

THE name of Albertson, or Albertsen, as it is sometimes written, may be found among those of the earliest Dutch emigrants to New Amsterdam, who came here to barter with the natives for furs and the few other commodities which they had among them for trade.[1] As early as in 1650, the records of births and baptisms in New York, indicate that Albert Albertson had a child baptized in the church of that place, and that others of this name had the same rite administered to their offspring. Other records of that date show this family to have had several representatives in the colony, some of whom were men of considerable estate and influence.

At this period a few small dwellings of the humblest character stood close around the fort at the outlet of Hudson river, where the Hollanders had a small garrison for protection against the natives, and where also were collected the articles of exchange that made the little commercial trade about that spot.

It was at the time when each Dutchman had his farm or bowery, somewhere within the busiest part of the present city of New York, and drove his cow to pasture along the tortuous paths leading to his lot; some of which same paths are now among the most crowded thoroughfares of the metropolis of America. It was in the good old times of sour-krout and wild tobacco, when a promising cabbage patch and a small quantity of smoked herring, rendered each inhabitant happy for the

---

[1] Manual of Common Council, N. Y., 740, Library N. Y. His. Soc.

coming year at least; and these were the days when the ancestors of the Knickerbockers sought the Battery to enjoy a quiet smoke, and to listen to the merriment of the negroes at Communipaw.

As the town enlarged, the family in question also increased, and their names may be found in various relations as time went on. True to their native blood, litigations and difficulties grew out of their stubbornness; and the court minutes show how tenaciously any supposable right was adhered to, and how often these troubles ended in a law-suit. The Dutch settlements upon the Delaware would naturally be the cause of more or less intercourse with those upon the Hudson river; and persons and families can be traced from the one to the other, they, doubtless, changing their abodes to improve their condition and advance their estate.

In 1656, Hans Albertson purchased a patent for a tract of land at Fort Casimir, on South (Delaware) river, whereon he settled.[2] In 1672, Derick Albertson had built a mill near the same river, one-half of which was claimed by William Toms. This claim had to be settled by a suit at law.[3] This was previous to the establishment of any court on South river, and, as a consequence, the parties were forced to appear before their High Mightinesses at New York, taking thereto all their witnesses and proofs at much expense, a practice yet characteristic to the last degree. By this it may be seen that members of this family found their way to the colony on South river, and made permanent settlements; yet there can be no question of their nativity, or of their arrival on the shores of America.

In the progress of events William Penn became the owner of the territory of Pennsylvania, which included all the Dutch and Swedish settlements on the west side of the Delaware river. The doctrine of ethics, laid down by him as the basis of his government, destroyed very much of the litigious element that formerly existed, and produced a new state of things among the inhabitants. Quarrels and disputes that previously had ended in court, were now disposed of in a manner much less conspicuous, and more satisfactory to those interested.

---

2 Dutch Manuscripts, 383.
3 Dutch Manuscripts, 350, Library N. Y. His. Soc.

Differences of opinion that often led to estrangements between families and among neighbors, were settled within the quiet precincts of the church, where the outside world was prevented from meddling, and where good advice and restraining influence prevailed.

Gradual, yet positive and well defined, was the progress of the teachings of Quakerism among the older settlers; and its footsteps may be discovered from time to time, until the new dispensation pervaded the communities within its bounds, and but slight traces of the old order of things could be seen.

On May 2d, 1682, William Albertson located a tract of land in Newton township, between the south and the middle branch of the creek that bears that name, and settled thereon.[4,5] It does not appear whence he came, but the probability is that he was of Dutch extraction, as before named, and that his parents were among the Hollanders of New York. The house which he built—no doubt, a small one—stood by the middle branch, and nearly fronting the little settlement called Newton; but in a few years it entirely disappeared. He was a married man with a family when he came there; shortly after he removed to Byberry, Pennsylvania, and gave the possession of the estate to his son William. This occurred before 1692, for, in that year, he purchased a tract of land in the town bounds of Gloucester, the deed for which names him as then a resident of the place above mentioned.[6]

Upon the setting apart of a lot of land at Newton whereon to build a meeting house, he was one of the persons who accepted the trust therefor, and no doubt took an active part in the erection of that place of worship.[7] This trust was continued until 1708, when other and younger men were called to occupy the same position.

He made several locations and purchases of land, while a resident here; but his removal so soon from this neighborhood leaves but little of his history among us, yet, so far as his record goes, he was a person much respected in his day and generation. In 1685, he was returned as a member of the

---

[4] Lib. T, 355, O. S. G.
[5] Lib. G3, 141.
[6] Lib. S6, 405, O. S. G.
[7] Sharp's Book, 50, O. S. G.

Colonial Legislature; he also held other minor county and township offices during his settlement here.[8]

His children were William, who married Esther Willis, daughter of Henry and Mary, of Westberry, Long Island, N. Y., in 1695;[9] Abraham, who married Hannah Medcalf;[10] Rebecca, who married Joseph Satterthwaite; Ann, who married Walter Forrest[11] and John Kaighn; Cassandra, who married Jarvis Stockdale; Benjamin, who married —— ——; and Josiah, who married Ann Austin of Evesham, Burlington county, N. J.

At the time of his decease, he resided at Poquesin, in Bucks county, Pennsylvania, where he owned grain and saw mills, and considerable other property. He died soon after the execution of his will (1709), survived by his widow Hannah, and by all his children except Ann.[12]

To his son William, in the year 1698, he deeded the homestead property, whereon he remained until his decease in 1720.[13] This was a valuable estate, and he improved it by enlarging and banking the meadow attached to the property, which, at that time, was the only soil from which hay and pasture were derived. The artificial grasses now used upon the upland, had not then attracted the attention of agriculturists, for which reason the meadow and marsh lands along the streams commanded much the higher price, and were considered as a necessary appendage to every farm. The meadow land on each of the branches of Newton creek, was, no doubt, the attraction that brought the settlers first to this place, and was, in fact, the only means they had for sustaining their cattle.

To avoid expense and to secure the land from the overflow of the tide, William Albertson placed a dam across the south branch, and reclaimed much of the marsh above the same. In this dam there were tide gates, the construction and utility of which need not be explained here.[14] These were kept in use until the dyke was put across the mouth of the creek, at the river, in 1786, when all the improvements on the several

---

8 Leaming & Spicer's Laws.
9 Friends' Records, Long Island.
10 License Book, 25. Lib. No. 7, Salem Records, 156.
11 Lib. No. 6, Salem Records, 32.
12 Philadelphia Records. Lib. M, 75, O. S. G.
13 Lib. A, 104. Lib. G3, 139. Lib. No. 2, 139.
14 Albertson Papers.

tributaries of the same were abandoned. The utility of this manner of making meadow, in a sanitary point of view, is very questionable; the miasma arising from the stagnant water and from exposed vegetable matter, incident to the system, is unavoidable; it spreads disease through the entire neighborhood, and very much lessens the value of property within its baneful influence.

The owner erected a substantial brick house, which, at the time it was built, ranked among the best in this section; but, when compared with the present system of architecture, it appears insignificant enough. This house still stands, and shows at a glance the many years that have passed away since its erection.

In front of and at a short distance from it, may be seen the ditch and bank that surrounded the park for deer, which covered many acres of land and extended to the south branch of the creek. On the bank stood a high and substantial fence, that effectually prevented the game from escaping when once within its bounds; and there the owner and his invited friends could find excellent sport at any season of the year.

Connected also with the place was a race course, where the speed of the pretentious horses in the neighborhood could be tested, and where, doubtless, the conceit was often taken out of various owners and backers, who resorted thither to fleece a jockey disguised as a greenhorn.

All these prove not only that the owner was a man of wealth, but also that, in its enjoyment, the drift of his inclination brought around him a class of associates that had similar tastes.

William Albertson was an active man in the affairs of the colony, and, besides holding other positions of public trust, was returned as a member of the Assembly in 1685.[15] He was for several years a member of the council of proprietors, and at a time when men of the best judgment were called upon to act in that capacity.[16] In the affairs of the township his name is often seen, which shows that he looked after the interests of his neighbors as well as the enjoyments of his own estate.

---

15 Leaming & Spicer's Laws.
16 Minutes of Council, O. S. G.

He died in 1720, leaving a widow and the following named children: John; Abraham, who married Sarah Dennis; William, Jane, Mary and Esther.[17]

Part of this estate descended under the name of William Albertson through four generations to a daughter Sarah, the only child of the last William, who married David Henry, in whose name a portion of the same still remains; thus continuing part of the original property in the line of blood for nearly two hundred years; one of the rare occurrences of lineal inheritance touching landed property in New Jersey.[18]

Abraham settled on the tract of land which his father purchased of Andrew Robeson in 1692, situated in the town bounds of Gloucester and on the south branch of Newton creek, which his father conveyed to him in 1698.[19]

He died in 1739, leaving the following named family:[20] Isaac; Jacob, who married Patience Chew; Abraham, who deceased without children; Ephraim, who married Kesiah Chew; Joseph, who married Rose Hampton; Aaron, who married Elizabeth Albertson; Levi, who married Kesiah Roberts; Jonathan; Rebecca, who married —— ——; Beverly, and —— ——, who married Richard Chew.[21]

The estate, as held by the father in 1757, belonged to four of the sons, Jacob, Joseph, Isaac and Ephraim, among whose descendants parts of it were held for many years, but at this writing it has passed out of the name and blood.

Of Rebecca, who married Joseph Satterthwaite, nothing is known; as families after two or three generations are apt to forget the maiden name of their maternal ancestors, and it is probable that all traces of her as the daughter of William Albertson have been lost.

Ann, the wife of Walter Forrest, settled with her husband in Salem county as early as in 1686. They were married at Newton meeting, according to the order of Friends, to which they adhered as long as they lived. Her husband, in connection with his brothers Francis and John, purchased a large tract of land in that county, in 1678, on Salem creek, of

---

17 Lib. No. 2, 139.
18 Lib. T, 355, O. S. G.
19 Sharp's Book, Lib. S6, 405, O. S. G.
20 Lib. No. 5, 136.
21 Family Papers.

John Fenwick, and there they erected a corn mill, called the "Brothers' Forrest," perhaps the first of the kind in Fenwick colony.[22] In the same year, they purchased other lands of John Fenwick, and afterwards became the owners of adjoining tracts.

At the time of the first purchase they were residents of Burlington, and doubtless came over among the first emigrants. When Walter Forrest died in 1692, he was a resident of Byberry, Pennsylvania, where he had some estate.[23] There was no issue by this marriage.[24] About two years after his death the widow married John Kaighn, who was a carpenter and resided at Byberry, where it may be supposed the marriage took place.[25] They soon after removed to Newton township, and settled on a tract of land which he had purchased of Robert Turner, fronting on the Delaware river.[26] At this place she died, leaving one child, Ann, who died in 1715, unmarried, thus ending this branch of the family in the second generation.[27]

By the will of his father, dated December 17th, 1709, recorded in Pennsylvania, Josiah Albertson received a tract of land in Gloucester township, bounded on the south side by Otter branch, and thereon he settled and cleared a farm.[28] In 1727, he married Ann, a daughter of Francis Austin, of Evesham, Burlington county, N. J. Her father was one of the first settlers in that neighborhood; and many of this name are still to be found thereabout. There the first habitation of Josiah and Ann was built, on the land given him by his father, at a short distance south of the old Salem road, where he both plied his calling of shoemaker, and at the same time removed the timber from the soil.

He enlarged the breadth of his acres by purchase and location until his possessions were double those left him by his father. In 1743, he built a large and substantial brick house, perhaps on the site of his log cabin; part of which is now standing and is occupied by his lineal descendant, Chalkley Albertson, who owns much of the original estate. Whether

---

22 Lib. B, 16. Salem Deeds.
23 Salem Wills, A, 69.
24 Salem Wills, No. 5, 98.
25 Salem Deeds, No. 6, 32.
26 Lib. G3, 127.
27 Lib. No. 2, 162.
28 Lib. M1, 75, O. S. G.

Josiah continued his business of making shoes, tradition does not reveal, but the chances are that his farming interests and lumber operations consumed all his time, and that the business of his youth was soon forgotten.[29]

The children of Josiah and Ann Albertson were eight daughters and one son; Hannah, who married Jacob Clement; Mary; Cassandra, who married Jacob Ellis and Jacob Burrough; Patience, who married Isaac Ballinger; Elizabeth; Josiah, who married Eleanor Tomlinson and Judith Boggs; Sarah, who married Samuel Webster; Katurah, who married Isaac Townsend, and Ann, who married Ebenezer Hopkins and Jacob Jennings.[30] These daughters were remarkable for their healthy look and comely appearance. In their attendance at meeting, they rode on horseback, presenting quite a cavalcade when several were together.

Their attractive appearance abroad and substantial qualities at home, made them desirable wives for those of the same religious denomination in search of such, and the records show that such qualifications were understood and appreciated; none of those that arrived at suitable age were left as "single sisters."

In the collateral branches of this part of the Albertsons, it may be seen how many families can trace their lineage to them; and how widely spread may become the connections of a particular stock, when the families are numerous and change their names, localities and associations.

---

29 Lib. T, 310, O. S. G.
30 Family Papers.

ELIZABETH ESTAUGH.

THE life and character of Elizabeth Estaugh are especially interesting to every resident of Newton township and its neighborhood, since her name and example will always command the respect and admiration of any one at all familiar with her history. Although only the collateral ancestor of a large family in this region, yet her name in this connection is always spoken of with commendable pride and deserving reverence.

The passing away of one generation after another has not blunted the interest felt in her good deeds, nor has the lapse of time obliterated the traditions handed down from parent to child. One hundred and fifty years have not destroyed the attractions that surround the romance of her early life, and no mention can be made of the history of this neighborhood, that is not connected with the acts and associations of Elizabeth Estaugh.

She came to New Jersey a young, unsophisticated girl, comparatively alone. Fresh from the care of solicitous and affectionate parents, she left a home in which she had been surrounded by friends and by all that rendered life attractive, to cast her lot in the midst of an unbroken forest, at some distance from her nearest neighbors—a stranger in a strange land.

Whatever may have been her youthful fancy of a life in the wilds of America, separated from her parents and friends, the realities of her situation must have occasionally pressed heavily upon her spirits, and caused her almost to regret the strange and responsible position which she had assumed. Perhaps at no period of her eventful life, did the leading traits of her character appear to a better advantage than thus early in her career.

Self reliance and decision of purpose, based upon conscientious motives, were here developed, and these in the hour of trial did not desert her.

She was a daughter of John Haddon, a Friend, who lived in Rotherhithe, in the parish of St. George, borough of Southwark, county of Surrey, England, then a suburb of the city of London, and on the east side of the river Thames.[1]

The long crooked street of Rotherhithe, lying, as it does, near to and parallel with the river, remains to this day the same narrow thoroughfare as when John Haddon resided there.

The old Horslydown meeting near by, where Friends assembled for worship, has long been abandoned, and it is now used as a carpenter's shop. The Southwark meeting house has also given way to modern improvements, and the ground where once lay the remains of deceased members, is now occupied by the foundation of a railroad bridge, leaving no vestige of this place, of so much interest to such as care to visit the homes of their ancestors.

John Haddon was a blacksmith, extending his business to the making of anchors, and had his shop between the street before named and the river.[2]

Diligence and economy produced their legitimate ends, and, in the course of time, brought to him a large estate, which he used with discretion during life, and disposed of judiciously at the time of his decease.

The ancestry of this man may possibly be traced to the manor of Haddon in Derbyshire, now part of the estate of the Duke of Rutland.

The old baronial mansion of Haddon Hall is still standing, and is one of the points of interest to be visited by tourists. Although abandoned as a residence by the owner, yet everything remains as used and occupied many centuries since. As its name indicates, it was, perhaps, the seat of the Haddon

---

[1] Lib. AAA, 61, 245. Lib. A, 203. Lib. D, 413, 419.
[2] Lib. G3, 458, O. S. G. Sharp's Book. 43, O. S. G.

family before the conquest; but, in the arbitrary distribution of territory by William, this estate was given to his son, and the original owners were driven from the soil, or degraded by their Norman rulers.

John Haddon lived in the times of the persecution of Friends, and suffered, in common with others of like persuasion, from the tyranny and oppression of those in authority.[3]

His children were born during this abuse of power. They heard and, perhaps, saw much of the distress that was brought upon their friends, and had impressed upon their youthful minds the feelings and sentiments of the parents, which early impressions no doubt adhered to them through life. Whatever of forbearance and forgiveness may have been instilled into their riper opinions and judgment by the teachings of a true religion, the remembrance of these wrongs done to an unoffending and law-abiding people could never be obliterated.

He was not among the first that became interested in the lands of West New Jersey, but no doubt knew of, and perhaps participated in, the advancement of the little colony, hoping that it might prove to be an asylum for those of like opinions who were, at home, borne down by the fanaticism of others.

Although the plan of settlement was novel, and the system of government contained elements that were especially attractive to this class of professing Christians, yet it was no matter of money speculation among those who originated it, and did not in the end accrue very much to their pecuniary advantage. The inception and carrying out of the whole plan were in good faith, and, although difficulties subsequently occurred, yet these were from no fault of the principles adopted by the Proprietors.

The success of the scheme in its various phases was canvassed on many occasions at the home of John Haddon, by those already interested, and in the presence of his children; they thus became familiar with its workings, and the progress which it was making among the people. Various circulars and pamphlets were published, and letters also were written home by those already emigrated, which attracted much attention; and the daughter Elizabeth could not have been indifferent to the movements made by her friends in that direction.

---

[3] Besse's Sufferings, Vol. 1, 126, 485.

He does not appear to have been a creditor of Edward Byllynge, and, like many others, to have accepted an interest in the land to save a debt likely to be lost; but he purchased of Richard Matthews one-eighth of a right of propriety in the year 1698, some twenty-four years after the acceptance of the trust by William Penn and others for the purpose of paying Byllynge's debts.[4]

John Haddon had but two children, Sarah, who married Benjamin Hopkins, a wine merchant of the city of London, and Elizabeth, who was born in 1682 and married John Estaugh.[5]

In the year of the purchase above named, another was made of Thomas Willis, a son of John Willis, of a tract of land in Newton township, bounded on the north side by Cooper's creek, containing about five hundred acres of land.[6] In view of these purchases, John Haddon may have contemplated removing to New Jersey with his family and settling among his friends, many of whom had already preceded him, intending to make it their permanent home. There was some restraining influence, however, that prevented the carrying out of this purpose, which cannot be explained, except that the daughter Sarah was already married and settled in the city of her birth, whom the mother was not willing to leave behind, perchance never to see her again. If intended, the idea was abandoned before Elizabeth left her home, for her father executed to her a power of attorney to become his agent in New Jersey for the location, purchase and sale of lands; this he would not have done, had he expected to come here in person.[7]

In 1701, being in the nineteenth year of her age, Elizabeth Haddon left the home of her parents, in company perhaps with a few friends, and came to New Jersey to occupy and look after the possessions of her father. In this act were first manifested that courage and decision of character, of which so much was seen in after years. At that age, to attempt such an adventure showed a great sacrifice on the part of the parents, and much self-reliance on the part of the child. In man nothing is so

---

[4] Lib. G3, 458.
[5] Lib. No. 3, 58.
[6] Lib. A, 80.
[7] Lib. G3, 347.

much admired as high-toned moral courage, with a disinterested and unselfish purpose to accomplish; and no less will be accorded to this young female who assumed responsibilities that many of the other sex would avoid, even with much greater attractions than those that lay before her. Perhaps a motive, as yet undeveloped, may have had something to do with this act, a motive to be explained by what occurred within a year after her arrival and settlement in her new home.

A short time before this voyage was undertaken, a young man of much talent—a native of Kelvedon in Essex, afterwards a resident of Rotherhithe, in Surrey[8]—had appeared among the Quakers of London, and attracted considerable notice as a public speaker. He had scarcely arrived at man's estate, yet he stood an accepted minister in expounding and defending the religious belief of the Society of Friends.

An acquaintance and frequent visitor at the house of John Haddon, an intimacy grew up between himself and the daughter Elizabeth, which very naturally ripened into a stronger feeling.

This young man was John Estaugh, born upon the second month 23d day, 1676, at Kelvedon, a small town about fifty miles northeast of London. He became convinced of Friends' principles by hearing Francis Stamper of London preach at the funeral of a neighbor; and he appeared in the ministry when about eighteen years of age. He was a member of the Cogshall Quarterly Meeting, in the county of his birth.

He received a minute from that meeting, dated seventh month 28th, 1700, allowing him to go to America on a religious visit. He was accompanied by John Richardson, and arrived in the river Patuxent, Maryland, in the first month of the following year.

They travelled in Virginia together, visiting many meetings, and returned through Pennsylvania to Philadelphia. It was at this time that John Estaugh first met Elizabeth Haddon after her arrival, while she remained among her friends, and before she took up her abode on the estate of her father in New Jersey. Perchance a mutual pleasure was manifested when

---
8 Lib. A, 03.

they met, that betrayed a latent feeling common to both; and, although taught from childhood to avoid expressions of joy or grief, yet, upon an occasion like this, such expressions were pardonable in those whose hopes so closely and warmly sympathized.

While in Philadelphia, on this occasion, John Estaugh thought it his duty to go back to Virginia, "not feeling his mind clear of that province."

Some doubts existed in the minds of John Richardson and John Estaugh, as to the propriety of separating, and several of the elders were convened and made acquainted with their prospects in this regard, and, after proper deliberation, the wishes of John Estaugh were granted. He therefore separated from John Richardson, and spent considerable time in Virginia, preaching among the people scattered through those "wilderness countries."

In the meantime, Elizabeth Haddon was making preparations to occupy her new home; and the appearance among them of so young a female, who had crossed the ocean without her parents, attracted the attention of the hardy pioneers. The scenes before her must have contrasted strangely with those that surrounded her home in the suburbs of the great city of London. Here the prospective streets of the town were only defined by marks upon the trees of the forest, and the few scattered houses showed but little of the large city that now occupies the soil. The hill-side upon the Delaware front was yet full of caves, where lived the emigrants who had not means or opportunity to erect better dwellings; and the strange appearance of the natives must have filled her mind with misgivings as to the security of the new settlers.

Francis Collins, the friend and companion of her father, who had settled at "Mountwell," extended to her the hospitalities of his house, and, by his direction and advice, controlled her in much of her future conduct. In going to his residence, they crossed the river at the ferry kept by Daniel Cooper, and performed the remainder of the journey on horseback, as nothing more than a bridle path led from one settlement to another. This road passed through a continuous forest, save the few settlements at Newton; there she was greeted by those who had preceded her to this new country, and who listened to such information as she might give them of friends left behind.

The surroundings to her were all new and strange. Every thing being in a state of nature, she at last came to realize the privations through which her associates had already passed, and the difficulties that must beset her in this novel undertaking. In passing along they turned away from the road to look at the land purchased of Thomas Willis, where this "youthful emigrant" was to make her home in the future, and where she expected to dispense the hospitalities of her household, in a manner consistent with her condition in life and her liberality of spirit.

Two miles beyond, they reached "Mountwell," where the yet single daughters of her escort gave her that welcome which she, in her lonely condition, could well appreciate; and the kind regard for her comfort that was extended to her in their humble dwelling, was proportionate to that which she, in after years, fully and gratefully returned.

It has been generally believed that she erected the first house on this tract of land, bringing with her much of the material from England. This is an error, as a map of the land made by Thomas Sharp in 1700 (which was before her arrival), proves that buildings were already on the land; and it is supposable that she occupied those already there.[9] John Willis, the locator of the survey, no doubt, put the dwelling there and lived on the premises some time, for fourteen years had elapsed between the date of the taking up and John Haddon's title. She probably enlarged and improved the house, so as to accord with her notions of convenience and comfort, and to receive her friends in a proper manner; for it is known that she never turned the stranger away from her door, or suffered her acquaintances to look for entertainment elsewhere.

This house stood on the brow of a hill on the south side of Cooper's creek, at Cole's landing, about two miles from Haddonfield, in a commanding situation, and near that stream,

---
9 Lib. A, 80.

which in those days was much used as a means of travel; and, according to the custom of the times in giving a name to such settlements, it was called "Haddonfield."

This name was retained until the building of the new house in 1713, erected still nearer the village as it now stands; after which it was called "Old Haddonfield," in order to distinguish it from the more modern and extensive settlement last mentioned.[10]

Mrs. Maria Child, in her story which she called "The Youthful Emigrant," of which Elizabeth Haddon is the heroine, says that John Estaugh did not visit her until the winter following her arrival and settlement here. That John cultivated forbearance as one of the Christian virtues, and attended closely to his Master's work, there can be no doubt; but the fair authoress has little knowledge of human nature, if she supposed that so great a temptation as a visit to this new home of Elizabeth (which home, by the way, was not the greatest attraction to this place in the forest) could be resisted. The many associations that surrounded their friends in England, furnished subjects for conversation, interesting and agreeable, to say nothing of the new and wonderful things that met their observation at almost every step in their present situation. The meeting at Newton needed some one to minister spiritual things to its few attendants; and who could blame him for being present occasionally at their sittings? and, after these, for accompanying his friend to her residence, to continue their conversation over her plentiful board?

Again, in weaving together the threads of her romance, Mrs. Child presents the scene in which these two persons are depicted as adjusting the saddle girths of the horse upon which Elizabeth rode, as taking place while on their way to attend the Quarterly Meeting of Friends at Salem; and, while this is being done, she represents the fair damsel as breaking to John a subject, that she believed she was directed in this manner to approach, regardless of the conventionalities which generally govern in like cases. Without any desire to criticise or destroy the drift of this well told story, we must

---
10 Lib. No. 11, 113.

suggest that the probability that these long journeys were accomplished by water, must interfere somewhat with the romance thrown around it, and mar the certainty of the facts involved, which, there can be no doubt, the authoress designed to observe. For many years after the settlement of the country, no extended journey was attempted, except by water, where the place to be reached was near a navigable stream; and, in the case in question, the facilities for traveling from Philadelphia to Salem by packets were sufficiently attractive to avoid horseback riding for so long a distance. Upon the last point, the deliberate conduct of Friend Estaugh may have been rather slow for Elizabeth's impulsive nature, and, although something had been evasively said upon the delicate subject, yet their probable separation for a time rendered it excusable on her part to wish to have the matter settled. It was a commendable proceeding; and how many suitable companions by either sex might be secured, if more speed were observed by the one, and more courage by the other!

Whether John performed this part of the courtship awkwardly, or whether Elizabeth showed her courage and good sense by acting as before mentioned, matters not, for the marriage was accomplished at her residence on the first day of the eighth month, 1702, in the presence of a committee of Friends, and of a few invited guests.[11] Among the guests several of the aborigines might have been seen. Their knowledge of the bride was attained by hearing the story of her life from her own lips, which excited their admiration for her courage— among them a leading virtue; and she commanded their regard and respect ever after. They were dressed after their peculiar style, in garments made especially for the occasion, displaying upon these the rude taste of their people, and their interest in the present event.

Their apparent indifference to the scene before them was much like the calm demeanor of the rest of the company; yet they were keen observers of all that passed, and supposed the ceremony had but commenced, when they were told that

---
11 Friends' Memorials.

"the brave pale-face girl" and John Estaugh were husband and wife, until death should separate them.

The solemnizing of marriages in public meetings was not generally observed in early times; for what reason does not always appear, yet such was the fact, as is seen in the record referring to those dates.

Soon after this marriage had taken place, John Estaugh became the attorney of John Haddon, and took charge of his landed interests in New Jersey; which had become large by location and purchase, and required much of his time and attention. He, however, continued an acceptable minister among his people, and made many religious visits during his life.[12]

He was also, for several years, agent for an association in London, known as the "Pennsylvania Land Company," the last settlement with the society having been made by his widow as his executrix two years after his death.

As the country filled with settlers, mechanics became more plentiful, and building materials were more readily obtained; the erection of a new house was contemplated, more suitable for the accommodation of their many friends and consistent with their wealth and position in society. Another site was selected, and, in 1713, a brick house was built, a short distance from the village of Haddonfield, where the present residence of Isaac H. Wood now stands. This was on a tract of land which John Haddon purchased of Richard Mathews, and, after the house was finished, it was called "New Haddonfield."[13] In a few years, however, the name was lost to both places, and attached to the village which stands partly on the last named tract of land.[14] The house was substantially built, and bore the evidence of wealth and taste in the owner; it was designed to secure the comfort of the occupants, so far as the knowledge of architecture and convenient arrangement went at that day.[15] Among other things, and what would seem strange at this time, a distillery was attached to the premises, and the smith shop which was there before the purchase by John Haddon, was kept up, and the tools were

---

12 Lib. G1, 203. Lib. AAA, 245.
13 Lib. Q, 460.
14 Lib. B, 44, Woodbury.
15 Lib. No. 11, 113.

disposed of by Elizabeth Estaugh in her will.[16] This stood near the junction of Tanner street and the turnpike road, and was in existence within the memory of some now living.

The garden was surrounded by a brick wall, part of which is standing at this time. In the yard are the yew trees, planted by the hands of the first residents; they are the admiration of every visitor to this interesting spot. One hundred and fifty years leave them as almost the only monuments of the liberality and taste of those who originated this place, and, fortunately, they have stood through successive generations to connect the present with the past. The yard and garden show the care and judgment exercised by this remarkable woman; and, what is commendable in the present owner, everything that is known to have originated with her, is preserved with scrupulous care. The old house was destroyed by fire in 1842. To the antiquarian this place has much that is attractive, for here may be found those relics of by-gone days that have escaped the too often vandal hand of progress—relics which grow more interesting with their age.

The neighborhood of New Haddonfield was gradually being occupied with new comers, most of whom were Friends, when the propriety of establishing a new meeting was considered among them; the Newton Meeting being several miles away, with miserably bad roads to travel most of the year.[17] About 1720, and perhaps earlier, a meeting house was built near the King's road, and meeting was regularly continued there. The energy and liberality of Elizabeth Estaugh were again shown in putting this meeting on a permanent basis, for, in 1721, she went to England, and procured from her father a deed for one acre of land, and on this stood the new building, as a place of public worship.[18]

The quaint description of the boundaries no doubt originated with Thomas Sharp, who prepared the deed before it was taken across the ocean for the signature of the donor; and, as one of the witnesses to this document, stands the name of Elizabeth Estaugh, in her own peculiar style of penmanship. The trus-

---

16 Lib. No. 11, 113.
17 The Friend, Vol. 4, 206.
18 Sharp's Book, 43, O. S. G.

tees were William Evans, Joseph Cooper, Jr., and John Cooper. In this way and at this time, originated the Friends' Meeting at Haddonfield, where it has until the present continued; it being, until the year 1818, the only place of public religious worship in the village.

By deed of gift, in 1722, John Haddon conveyed all the land which he had purchased of Richard Mathews, to John and Elizabeth Estaugh, and in the deed called the tract "New Haddonfield;" in 1732, they conveyed one and a quarter acres adjoining the lot where the meeting house stood, to John Mickle, Thomas Stokes, Timothy Matlack, Constantine Wood, Joshua Lord, Joseph Tomlinson, Ephraim Tomlinson, Joseph Kaighn, John Hollinshead, Josiah Foster and William Foster, as trustees to and for the use of the Society of Friends.[19]

In 1763, the trust was continued by deed from Ephraim Tomlinson, Josiah and William Foster, to John Gill, Joshua Stokes, Nathaniel Lippincott, Samuel Webster, John Glover, James Cooper, John Lord, John E. Hopkins, John Brown, Isaac Ballinger and David Cooper, as trustees for the same purpose.

In 1828, all these trustees were dead, and Samuel Webster, as the oldest son of Samuel Webster (one of the trustees aforesaid), continued the trust to other members of said meeting for like purpose.[20] The first meeting-house was built of logs; it was much larger and more confortable than the old house at Newton, but every part of the work was scrupulously plain, and without paint or ornament of any kind. It stood upon the site of the brick house that was erected in 1760 and taken down in 1852, and, when the brick house was built, the old one was removed to the opposite side of the Ferry road and used as a stable. If some person, curious in such things, had made a faithful sketch of the old log meeting-house, as it appeared in its latter days, and the sketch were in existence at this time, some enterprising photographer would find for the duplicates a ready sale in this region of country.

---

19 Lib. B, 44, Woodbury.
20 Lib. VV, 322, Woodbury.

John Haddon died in London, in 1723. In his will he mentions that his wife had just died, with whom he had lived for forty-seven years—a remarkable clause in such a document, but placed there to perpetuate his affection for her, the companion of a life time.[21]

By his will he devised his entire estate (except a few small legacies) to his two children, and made them executrixes. The estate, however, was to vest as a joint tenancy; to defeat which, Benjamin and Sarah Hopkins, and John and Elizabeth Estaugh conveyed said real estate to John Gill (who was their cousin and resided at Haddonfield), in 1726, in trust for certain uses.[22]

In this act, that regard for each other which existed between Elizabeth Estaugh and her husband, and which had been shown from the first, was again manifested; for, in the deed of re-conveyance from John Gill to them in 1727[23] for one-half of the same land, the estate was made to vest in the survivor, thus showing that any advantage that might be derived from the law regulating the descents of land, should not defeat the wishes of the owners.[24].

The husband, however, died first, and the entire estate passed to Elizabeth Estaugh in fee simple, as if the deed had not been executed.

John Estaugh had some skill in chemistry and medicine, which he made useful in his neighborhood, especially among the poor. He traveled in the ministry, beside writing many letters to meetings in other parts; and, while in London in 1722, he addressed a long epistle to the Quarterly Meeting of Salem and Newton of which he was a member. His writings were collected and printed in 1744, by Benjamin Franklin in Philadelphia.

He died in Tortula, one of the West India Islands, on the sixth of the tenth month, 1742, while on a religious visit there.[25] The brick tomb erected by order of his widow over his remains which lay at that place, has long since gone to decay.

---

21 Liber No. 3, 58.
22 Lib. D, 413, 415.
23 Lib. D, 419.
24 Liber W, 254.
25 Lib. No. 4, 357. Friends' Memorial.

he being only known by the people there as a stranger, who, in the course of events, was soon lost sight of and forgotten.

No better evidence need be had of the respect in which he was held by the community in which he lived, than the memorial set forth in the minutes of the Monthly Meeting at Haddonfield, immediately after his death. While mourning his loss to themselves as a valuable member, it bears witness of his consistent religious life and usefulness among them, and added to this is the testimony of his widow, recording the confidence of a companion who knew him as a man and a Christian in the every-day walks of life. This sincere, but subdued expression, coming from a bereaved wife, proves that the traits of a true professor, had controlled and governed him in all his intercourse with his fellow men. By his will he gave all his estate to his widow.

Elizabeth Estaugh survived her husband some twenty years, and lived in the house built in 1713, in the same manner as during his life, entertaining Friends in their visits to the various meetings in the neighborhood. Her consistent Christian profession showed itself in many ways, not the least of which was her kindness toward the poor of the surrounding country, observing the Bible injunction of secrecy in this regard.

The farm, of which about one hundred acres were arable land, was under her own care, and received her personal attention. Having no children of her own, she adopted Ebenezer Hopkins, a son of her sister Sarah, who came to this country, was educated by, and resided with, his aunt at New Haddonfield, and who, in 1737, married Sarah, a daughter of James Lord, of Woodbury creek, and died intestate in 1757.[26]

In 1752, his aunt conveyed to him a tract of land fronting on Cooper's creek, in Haddon township, generally known as the "Ann Burr farm," which adjoined other lands owned by him at that date, and derived from the same source.[27] On this estate he probably resided, and, in addition to his agricultural pursuits, turned his attention to the surveying, the laying out and the conveying of land.

---

26 Lib. No. 9, 38.
27 Lib. S, No. 6, 124, O. S. G.

His wife survived him, and the following named children: John E., who married Sarah, a daughter of William Mickle; Haddon, who married Hannah, a daughter of Joshua Stokes; Ebenezer, who married Ann, a daughter of William Albertson; Elizabeth E., who married John Mickle; Sarah, who married Caleb Cresson; Mary, who married Joshua Cresson, and Ann, who married Marmaduke Burr. From these came the Hopkins family that is now spread through many parts of the United States; one branch of which still remains in the neighborhood of the first settlement, owning, however, but little of the original estate.

After the death of her husband, Sarah Hopkins removed to Haddonfield, and occupied a house and lot, purchased in 1752 by Elizabeth Estaugh of the estate of Samuel Mickle, deceased.[28] The house stood on the westerly side of the Main street, on the site of the present residence of Sarah Hopkins, the widow of a lineal descendant of Ebenezer and Sarah. It was removed some years since, and now stands on the north side of Ellis street, owned and occupied by Mary Allen. It is a small, hipped-roofed building, and, although somewhat altered, yet retains much of its antiquated appearance.

No other building is now left that can be associated with Elizabeth Estaugh. Here, doubtless, she made daily visits to the widow and her children, looking closely after the comfort of the one, and the moral training and education of the others. It is evident that she took much interest in them, since in these orphans she saw the perpetuity of her large landed estate in her own blood, and the tone of her will indicates a long settled intention in this regard.

In this house resided her only collateral descendants, and those who were to her the continuation of her family in America.

There was perhaps no act of Elizabeth Estaugh during her life, that showed more of her business qualifications than her last will and testament, which bears date November 30th, 1761.[29] In this is exhibited a thorough knowledge of her estate, both

---

28 Lib. Q, 480.
29 Lib No. 11, 113.

real and personal; and in her disposition thereof is manifested consummate judgment and sound discretion. She provided for her nearest relatives, but did not forget the humblest of her servants.

Her real estate was principally given to the children of her deceased nephew, Ebenezer Hopkins, while some portion of her personal property she gave to others of her connections. In disposing of some of her personal estate to the single daughters of her nephew, she provided that they should marry in accordance with the order of Friends, or the legacy should follow another direction, a contingency that might press hard upon some of these young girls, yet it showed the bent of her mind, and the strength of her prejudices in favor of her religious belief.

This remarkable woman died March 30th, 1762, in the eightieth year of her age.[30] It is unfortunate that she did not, near the close of her life, prepare or dictate her autobiography, so that the incidents of her eventful career could have been preserved, as she would not then have left the most interesting and romantic parts of her life to vague and uncertain tradition.

Of men's characters much can be gathered from their participation in public affairs, from their conduct in the purchase and sale of real estate, from the more general knowledge of them in the community, and, finally, in the disposition of their property by will; but of females, whose sphere of action is more limited, whose duties are quite as important yet less conspicuous, and whose influence may be observed in all classes of a community, but not always acknowledged by the stronger sex, the chances of securing a faithful history are at best uncertain and perhaps erroneous. This may be said of the subject of this sketch, who, although forced to assume responsibilities that many men would shrink from, still always exhibited the characteristics of the true woman. The estimation in which she was held, appears in the notice taken of her death by the meeting of which she was a member; in which her valuable services are acknowledged, and by which it is shown that she was adorned with every Christian virtue. Her remains were

---

30. Friends' Memorials.

interred in the yard at Haddonfield, but nothing marks the spot of her burial.

Who, at this day, would not be gratified if some monument, however rough the stone or rude the letters, had been erected to show where were laid the remains of Elizabeth Estaugh, whose life was spent in contributing to the good of those around her, and whose labor in well-doing is felt and appreciated unto the present day.

> "Is it not a noble thing to die
> As dies the Christian with his armor on!—
> What is the hero's clarion, though its blast
> Ring with the mastery of a world, to this?"

JOHN GILL.

JOHN GILL came to New Jersey under the patronage and guardianship of Elizabeth Estaugh. The blood relationship that existed between these two persons may be inferred from expressions that occur in the various papers of Elizabeth Estaugh, in reference to John Gill, and in her will, particularly, she names him as *"her kinsman."* His parents resided in or near London, and his mother was probably a sister of John Haddon, father of Elizabeth.

Some of the name lived in Cumberland, others in Cornwall, Devonshire and Huntingdonshire; being Friends they were subjected to fines and imprisonments, for refusing to pay tithes, or attend the national church, and to do other things required under the laws then in existence.

Henry Gill lived at Godalming, in the county of Surrey, London, in 1670, and was fined on two occasions for not attending church at Guilford. This was in the same part of that city in which John Haddon resided, and this Henry Gill was probably the father of John.

This, however, is but conjecture, and, until a faithful search be made among the records of the meetings in that part of London, may so remain. The instances are but few in which the genealogies of families in America can be properly connected with those in England, a defect always to be regretted.

John Gill was a young man of considerable education, which was the exception at that day; he certainly had the confidence and good opinion of his uncle and cousin, this good opinion being assured by the gift of a tract of land made to him by John Haddon, which gift was bestowed, in all probability in order that he might participate in the political affairs of the colony, then in much confusion.

The time of his coming over is in doubt, and that of his age at such coming; yet enough may be seen upon the records to prove that he must have followed his cousin very closely.

In 1709, he was appointed administrator of the estate of William Higgs, deceased, of Newton township,—conclusive evidence that he had arrived before that date, and also had attained his majority. So far as noticed, this is the first record of his name, and has much to do with settling the question here mooted.[1]

In connection with John Estaugh, the management of John Haddon's estate here was controlled by him, and, no doubt, many of the locations returned to John Haddon were selected through his advice and observation.

John and Elizabeth Estaugh, and Benjamin and Sarah Hopkins conveyed all their landed estate to him in 1726, that which was in New Jersey being large and valuable. It was done to defeat the joint tenancy created under their father's will, and to place each share within the absolute control of its owner.[2-3] After the decease of John Estaugh, he became the attorney and adviser of his widow, and managed her large estate in a proper and acceptable manner. It is needless to follow this line to prove the confidence that existed between Elizabeth Estaugh and John Gill, for, during his life, she took no step in the disposition of her estate, without some act of his appearing in connection therewith.

As to his position as a church member, he may also be judged by the intimacy between his cousin and himself; for it can be accepted as a truth, that Elizabeth measured every one according to the religious tenets to which she so rigidly adhered, and which were laid down by the great prototype and leader in her belief, George Fox.

---

[1] Gloucester Files, 1718.
[2] Lib. D, 413, 415.
[3] Lib. D, 419.

JOHN GILL.

In 1723, commences the record of the proceedings of the town meetings of Newton, in a book which Thomas Sharp says that he was ordered to purchase, and for which he paid nine shillings. The first entry is this:

"At a town meeting held at Newton for the township, the twelfth day of the first month called March, 1723, in order to choose officers for the ensuing year, Joseph Cooper and John Gill were continued Overseers of the Poor, and having made up their accounts there is found to remain in bank for ye service the sum of six pounds fourteen shillings and ten pence."

The overseers of the poor appear to have had charge of all the moneys of the township at that time, paying out the same and rendering a yearly account of such disbursements. This was continued for several years, which made the office one of the most responsible and important in the township. But John Gill withdrew from that position after the next year, the reason for which appears in a minute made in the book. The discharge of this duty he, no doubt, considered outside of his office, and that the best way to avoid a repetition thereof was to resign. The entry, as made, is as follows:

"At said meeting it was agreed yt Jonathan Bolton give some hay and corn to Ann Morris's horse, in order to make him capable to carry her to ye place from whence she came, and that she stay but until the seventeenth day of this instant; and after that the overseers of the poor force her away if she refuse to go; and that what charge is expended in ye perfecting of it shall be allowed by this meeting."

What became of Ann Morris or her horse, does not appear from the record; but, it being a new feature in the duties of the overseers of the poor, neither Joseph Cooper or John Gill accepted the position for several years after that time.

When John Gill died, in 1749,[4] his son John was old enough to take his place in the several positions which he, the father, had been called to fill, and, more particularly, in the management of the estate of Elizabeth Estaugh, which was constantly

---
[4] Lib. No. 6, 231.

increasing, and which required his personal attention and good judgment; and, although Ebenezer Hopkins, her nephew, had married in 1737 and settled near her residence, yet John Gill, the son, appears to have had the same oversight of her estate that his father had during his life time.

He was a much more active business man than his father; this appears by his location, purchase and sale of lands in various sections of the country, by his participation in political affairs, and by the discharge of many duties involving the confidence of his neighbors and the public. He was one of the persons selected by Elizabeth Estaugh as executors of her will, which trust, thus bestowed, evidenced her regard for his capability and honesty.

The first grant of land made by John Haddon to John Gill was in 1714; it was for two hundred and sixty acres of the survey which he had purchased of Thomas Willis, a son of John, in 1698.[5] This land was situated in Waterford township, now Delaware, on both sides of the Haddonfield and Berlin road, and near the head of what was formerly known as Swett's mill pond, now owned by Joseph C. Stafford, and others. The conveyance says that the land was then in the occupation of John Gill, the inference of which is that he resided thereon; if so, he lived in a small, hipped-roof frame house, which stood on the north side of the stream that falls into the mill pond—a house many years since torn down. It was surrounded by locust trees, some of which yet stand and mark the spot where his dwelling was situated. Although this place was in the midst of a forest, yet he was not entirely without neighbors. William Bates had settled on Tindall's run, about one mile west, where he was living with his Indian wife. George and Timothy Matlack, who purchased land the same year, had their plantations about two miles south; and Joseph Cooper had cleared some of the land given to him by his father, and had built a house on the opposite side of the stream, not far from the residence of John Gill. This was before his marriage, but the comforts of his bachelor home were, no doubt, looked after by some elderly female unknown to the present generation.

---

[5] Lib. A, 13.

Previously to the year 1739, this tract of land passed into the possession of Bartholomew Horner, who, with his wife Elizabeth, conveyed it to their son Jacob. Jacob died intestate, and it descended to his oldest son, Isaac. He conveyed to his two brothers, Nathan and Jacob, and the first conveyed his interest to the last in 1771. In Jacob's family it remained for many years, but it now has passed out of the name.

The next residence of John Gill in Waterford township was near the north side of the south branch of Cooper's creek, where the King's highway crossed the same, and where the road leading to Edward Clemenz's landing turned to the westward from that thoroughfare. This property is now owned by James H. Billington.

It was a public place at that time, the landing being the highest on the creek; and thither all the wood and lumber in the region round about, intended for the Philadelphia market, were taken to be transported in vessels. The remains of the old wharf may yet be seen near the forks of the creek; and this place in the days of our ancestors was the scene of much business activity, occasioned by the teams in bringing, and the boats in taking away the only articles of sale and exchange among the people at that time. After 1715, it was known as Axford's landing, and it still retains the name; but some of the oldest inhabitants must be found, before the inquirer can know where to look for that place.

In a deed from William Lovejoy to Thomas Kendall, in 1697, a tract of land was conveyed, situated at a place called Uxbridge, "lying on the south branch of Cooper's creek on the road leading from Salem to Burlington."[6]

This tract of land was near where John Gill lived, and the name was probably given in expectation of a town springing up at that point, several years before there was any thought that Haddonfield, as a village, would have a name or an existence. The description in the deed is conclusive as to the locality, and, although affixed twenty-five years before the present name was attached to the village, yet it never obtained any notoriety, and seems to have no history except in the old

---
6 Lib. B2, 645.

conveyance above referred to. Although the name may more particularly apply to the land on the north side of the stream, yet, if a few houses had been built in 1697, and the improvements extended to the south side of the creek, the chances are that our forefathers would have adhered to the original title given at that period, and that the name of Haddonfield would never have been known, except as attached to the two residences of Elizabeth Estaugh. From this it may be inferred that William Lovejoy came from the town of Uxbridge, which is in Middlesex, England, about twenty miles from London, and that he wished to keep the name of his native place in remembrance, like many of his associates who came to New Jersey about the same time.

In 1718, John Gill married Mary Heritage, a daughter of Joseph and granddaughter of Richard Heritage,—the first of that name in these parts.[6] Richard was a carpenter, and came from Brayle's Inn, Warwickshire, England.[7] He purchased rights of Edward Byllynge, in 1684, and, upon his arrival here, made a location of land on the north side of the south branch of Penisaukin creek, in Burlington county, and called his new home "Hatten New Garden."[8] He purchased other rights and made other locations in that region. None of the land, as originally held by him, has been owned by the family for many years; and none of the name reside in that section of the country at the present time.

Richard Heritage died in 1702, without a will, and such parts of his land as he had not previously conveyed to his children, passed to his oldest son John, as his heir at law.[9] His children were John, who married Sarah Slocum in 1706; Joseph, who married Hannah Allen in 1697; Sarah, who married William Clark in 1687; and Mary.

John died intestate in 1716, leaving two daughters,[10]—Mary, who married Hasker Newberry, and Naomi, who removed to Blanden county, North Carolina, and died a single woman. He lived on the homestead property after his father's death and until his own decease, but his descendants never occupied it.

---

6 Lib. No. 8, 358.
7 Lib. G2, 69.
8 Lib. G1, 141.
9 Lib. AL, 456.
10 Lib. No. 2, 82.

Joseph's father conveyed considerable land to him, much of which he sold.[11] It lay on both sides of the creek, and, at the present time, it is divided into several valuable farms. The part which he occupied, was in Burlington county, and was bounded by the creek. He died in the year 1756, leaving a will.[12] His children were Richard, who married Sarah Whitall and Sarah Tindall; Joseph, who married Ruth Haines; Benjamin, who married Kesiah Matlack; John, who married Sarah Hugg; Mary, who married John Gill and John Thorne; and Hannah, who married ——— Roberts.

John and Mary Gill had but two children,—John, who married Amy, a daughter of David Davis of Salem county, in 1741, and Hannah, who married Thomas Redman of Haddonfield in 1737. John Gill died in 1749, and his widow married John Thorne in 1750.

In 1728, John and Elizabeth Estaugh conveyed to John Gill two tracts of land, one in Haddonfield, and the other (meadow) lying in Waterford (now Delaware) township.[13] The first named tract was bounded by the westerly side of the King's road, and extended from Cooper's creek nearly to the Methodist church and contained eighty-seven acres. Four years after, the same persons granted John Gill three other lots, the largest of which joined the last named on the southwest; it is now divided by Grove street into nearly equal parts.[14] The second of these is owned by Rennels Fowler and the devisees of John Clement, deceased, on the front; but nearly all the original lines have been obliterated. The third lot passed into the possession of his daughter, and upon it the old Thomas Redman mansion formerly stood.

These grants were "for love and affection," which the grantors bore the grantee. Part of this estate still remains in the family, and is now owned by John Gill, whose lineage can be readily traced to the first of the name in this region.

The first tract of land, as herein named, John Gill sold in a short time. He soon after came within the bounds of Newton township, where he made his permanent residence upon the

---

11 Lib. G3, 182.
12 Lib. No. 8, 358.
13 Lib. E, 373.
14 Lib. E, 375.

estate conveyed to him for a nominal consideration by John and Elizabeth Estaugh, between whom and himself there existed the pleasantest social intimacy.

This tract of land, or a large part thereof, was an open field, covered with wigwams and cabins of the natives. Prior to 1720, John Gill had enclosed part of it, and had the land under cultivation; for, in the description of the lot of land conveyed by John Haddon to Friends for the meeting-house lot, John Gill's fence is named as part of the boundary, which fence stood near where the turnpike road leaves the main street of Haddonfield.[15] On this field, and perhaps at John Gill's house, were held the elections for members of the Assembly, annually. These elections were conducted in accordance to law, but they would appear strange to us of these latter days. By the act of 1682, the freeholders could meet at any place which they chose, and elect the members in any manner thought best at the time. The time, however, fixed by law, was the fourteenth day of the second month (being the 14th day of April) of each year. This law was changed, and the sheriff, or some other person appointed by the governor, was authorized to take the ballot box from place to place within the county, with two other persons selected by the candidates to act as officers of election. The consent of the candidates to remove from the place last selected, was required, but the rule generally required two days; at the end of that time, the polls were changed to some other desirable locality, within the county and convenient for the people. To accomplish an election therefore, several days were consumed, as the territory of Gloucester was large, Atlantic and Camden counties then being within the bounds of the old bailiwick.

Another curious feature of these elections was the few votes then polled. In 1737, there was but nine hundred and thirty white male persons above the age of sixteen, within the limits of the county; it may readily be seen how light the canvass was, and how few the inhabitants, even after some fifty years from the first settlement. The voting was done by voice, and not by ballot, as now; the name of the voter and that of the

---

15 Sharp's Book, 43, O. S. G.

person voted for, were recorded and copied for any person willing to pay for the same; publicity thus being given to the act of each person,—a peculiarity that would not be allowed at this time. The penalties against bribery and corruption were severe; but it is supposable that chicanery and deception were winked at among the electors, and that every kind of expedient was used by one party to defeat the other, each arguing, no doubt, that, unless their opponents were defeated, the country would be utterly ruined.

George Fox, the founder of Quakerism, during his travels in America in 1672, in going from Maryland to New York, passed through West New Jersey, and was, on several occasions, entertained by the Indians. It is well known that the Indian trail, first traveled by the whites from Salem to Amboy, crossed Gloucester county near where Haddonfield now stands, and that the same trail was used for many years after the earliest settlements. Along that path George Fox and his associates must have traveled, and it is no stretch of fancy to say that they were entertained by the natives who lived at the "Great Fields," now the town aforesaid. In his journal he says:

"We came one night to an Indian town and lay all night at the king's house, who was a very pretty man. Both he and his wife received us very lovingly, and his attendants (such as they were) were very respectfull to us. They laid mats for us to lie on; but provisions were very short with them, having caught but little that day."

Whether the king, whose fine appearance and noble bearing attracted the attention of this remarkable man, resided here or not, cannot be known at this late day. It is, however, a pleasant incident in the early history of the village to associate his movements in this connection.

In the year 1740, John Gill, as attorney for the heirs-at-law of Joseph Elkinton, deceased, went to England to recover an estate claimed by them, and at that time remaining unsettled. This property was situated in Oxfordshire and Warwickshire, where suits at law were prosecuted for obtaining possession thereof; which, after several years of litigation, proved successful. The children of Joseph Elkinton, who was a son of George, the first comer to New Jersey of that name, were Mary, the wife of David Stratton, of Evesham, Burlington county, N. J.; Ann, the wife of Stephen Brooks, of the same place; Elizabeth, wife of John Lippincott, also of the same place; Frances and Amy Elkinton. Numerous affidavits were taken here and appear on record, showing whence and when George Elkinton emigrated to New Jersey, whom he married, and many other particulars necessary to connect the claimants here with the family remaining in England.[16] The matter was fiercely contested in the courts, consuming much time and money before its conclusion. The account book of John Gill relating to this transaction, is still preserved in the family, showing the care and precision observed by him in rendering a statement of his proceedings in the premises.

During his absence, his wife Mary and son John, acting by letters of attorney, sold a lot of land in Haddonfield to Timothy Matlack (1744), and had general oversight of his affairs hereabout. While living there (1746), he purchased a tract of land of John Cox, also a resident of London, lying on the south side of the south branch of Cooper's creek about two miles from Haddonfield. The next year after the purchase, he deeded this survey to his son John, a part of which has remained in the family and name to the present day. The old Salem road passed through this tract, and the second John sold most of that which lay west of the same. Like many other such pieces of land, the old lines, owing to the division, sale and exchange of property, have become entirely unknown to this generation.

The account book before mentioned shows that John Gill, while residing in London, frequently paid his *brother William* for "diet and lodging," proving that there were others of the name and family in that city. He never returned to the land of his adoption, but died in London.

The children of John and Amy Gill were Mary, who married Jacob Roberts; Sarah, who married Job Whitall; Amy, who married Joab Wills; Elizabeth, who married Jacob Burrough;

---
16 Lib. AAA, 229.

John, who married Anna Smith ; and Mercy, who married Samuel Abbott.

Amy deceased, and, in 1767, he married Abigail Hillman, widow of Daniel and daughter of Samuel Nicholson. She died without issue, and, in 1781, he married Sarah Pritchett, widow of Josiah and daughter of John Cowperthwaite. There was no issue by the last marriage. John died in 1794. A noticeable feature in the genealogy of this family is that, for several generations, there has been but one son, to whom has always been given the christian name of the first comer, which has limited the surname of the branch of the family hereabout to but few persons.

Thomas Redman, who married Hannah, should be noticed in this connection. He was a son of Thomas. one of the first settlers in the city of Philadelphia, and one of the leading mechanics at that time. In 1712, he was a member of the city council, and participated much in the affairs of the colony during William Penn's residence there.

The son was apprenticed to a druggist, and, upon attaining his majority, removed to Haddonfield, and continued the same business. He was held in great respect among Friends, and traveled much as a minister in that religious denomination. Hannah, his wife, died, leaving three children,—Mary, who married Mark Miller; Thomas, who married Mercy Davis in 1747, of Salem county; and John, who married Sarah Branson.

He married Mary ———, a second wife, and died in 1766, leaving a will, in which he disposed of a large amount of real and personal property;[17] the appraisement alone amounting to more than five thousand pounds, sterling. There was no issue by the last marriage.

The third Thomas Redman was also educated as a druggist, and continued the same calling, but was more of a public man, politically speaking, than his father. He was a careful business man, and, as a conveyancer, had the confidence of the entire community. Although he adhered to the detailed and elaborate forms of English titles, yet plainness of penmanship and clearness of intention characterized all his legal papers. His

---

[17] Lib. No. 12, 363.

correctness in copying was proverbial, and Chief Justice Kirkpatrick of this State, on one occasion, paid him the compliment of not comparing documents prepared by him, saying that "papers from the hands of Thomas Redman needed no such scrutiny."

He was a valuable man in the society of Friends, and did much to sustain the church in this region of country. Many anecdotes are related of him, showing that he was an upright business man, plain of speech, consistent in his profession, faithful in his trusts, and scrupulous in all his dealings.

Among the several positions of public trust which John Gill was called upon to fill, was that of commissioner of loans, he being one of the three appointed for Gloucester county. The object of the law, and the duty of the commissioners, appear to have been to loan bills of credit issued by the State, to such persons as could give satisfactory security for the repayment of the same; and this security had to be in the shape of mortgages on real estate, of the value of which the commissioners were to be satisfied by personal view.

These commissioners were constituted bodies politic and corporate, in succession, in fact, and in law, to sue and be sued, and with various other powers in the act named. No greater sum than four hundred pounds, nor any less than fifteen pounds, could be loaned to one person for the space of twenty years, at five per cent. per annum. This system of supplying the country with money was in operation for several years, but at last fell into disuse, and the law finally repealed. While John Gill was thus acting as commissioner, and had charge of the securities during the revolutionary war, his house was pillaged by a party of British soldiers, and, among other things, these were carried off and not recovered. By an act of the Legislature of New Jersey, in 1779, he was idemnified from any loss concerning the same.

Although many of this name may be found in New Jersey, yet they do not appear to have originated with the family herein mentioned.

ARCHIBALD MICKLE.

THIS man was an Irish Quaker. The records of Friends in Philadelphia indicate that he came from Lisbrun, a town in the southern part of the county of Antrim, Ireland, and that he arrived at that city on the second day of the sixth month, A. D. 1682.

He probably was among the adventurers that followed William Penn to his new colony, bringing with him considerable estate and a full supply of implements to continue the business of a cooper, in which calling he had served as an apprentice in the land of his nativity. This was worth much to him among the settlers, who generally arrived with but little housekeeping material, and had to be supplied with their wooden ware of home manufacture, when a new establishment was to be set up. Coopers were also in demand along the sea coast, as whale fishing occupied much of the time of the people, and barrels were necessary to carry away the oil. This was the most lucrative business among them, and more capital was invested in it than in any other branch. In a letter from the West New Jersey Society to Jeremiah Basse, their agent, then residing at Cape May, dated December 24th, 1692, he is directed to secure the services of a French cooper at Plymouth, skilled in making casks. The letter further says: "In the season let him make a little wine and brandy, and send us the wine in casks and the brandy in bottles."[1] Much is also

---
[1] Lib. B2, 423.

said about barrels for the fishing season, and the quantity required would certainly employ several persons, and among them it is possible that Archibald Mickle was one.

The next notice made of him was in 1686, when he married Sarah Watts, at the same meeting at which his certificate of membership and the date of his coming had been recorded.

Four years after that time, he purchased a tract of land of Robert Turner in Newton township, Gloucester county, containing two hundred and fifty acres.[2] This survey was situated near the head of the south branch of Newton creek, adjoining lands located by Francis Collins. This tract afterward became the property of Joseph Lowe, who occupied the same.

At the date of this purchase, Archibald Mickle was still a resident of Philadelphia, but he soon after came to Newton township and settled, and there remained until his decease in 1706. In 1697, he made another purchase from the same man, of five hundred and ten acres, which survey fronted on the river Delaware and extended eastward towards Cooper's creek.[3] This deed excepted several meadow lots, and is valuable as showing the antecedent title of the grantor.

He did not make the first improvements there, for a man named Thomas Spearman lived in a house on the tract at the time of his purchase, which house stood near the river shore and near where the former residence of Isaac Mickle, deceased, is situated.

He was the owner of considerable other real estate in the neighborhood, and the inference is, therefore, that he was a man of more means than most of his neighbors, and, excepting William Cooper, of any other in the township. In the political affairs of the colony, his name does not appear, but the fact of his being a Quaker and a strict adherent to his sect, may be drawn from that clause of his will which directed that any one of his children marrying without consent of Friends was to only have one-half of his or her share of his estate. This is certainly a significant expression, and places his religious proclivities beyond a doubt.

---

2 Basse's Book, 119.
3 Lib G3, 133.

His will was dated in 1706; in which he gave his real estate to eight of his children.[4] His widow Sarah survived him, she being the mother of all his children. After the father's death, the estate was conveyed to the widow, and she, by her will (1718), gave the property to three of her sons, Archibald, James and Joseph,[5] who divided the same by quit claim in 1727.

Seven sons and three daughters were the representatives of this couple, as follows: John, who married Hannah Cooper (daughter of the second William), in 1704; Samuel, who married Elizabeth Cooper daughter of Joseph, in 1708; Daniel, who married Hannah Dennis, in 1711; Archibald, who married Mary Wright in 1719; Isaac, who married Sarah Burrough, daughter of Samuel; Joseph, who married Elizabeth Eastlack in 1723; James, who married Sarah Eastlack in 1732; Sarah, who married Ezekiel Siddon; Mary, who married Arthur Powell; and Rachel, who married Benjamin Cooper in 1718.

John Mickle, the oldest son, was an active man in the political matters of the colony in his day, and also dealt much in real estate. By Thomas Sharp, as his deputy surveyor, he located several tracts of land in different parts of West Jersey. In 1733, he was appointed one of the judges of the several courts of Gloucester county, and filled other offices of public trust and responsibility.

In 1703, "for natural love and affection," his father conveyed to him a farm containing one hundred and fourteen acres, bounded on the south side by the south branch of Newton creek, and being within the town bounds of Gloucester.[6] On this farm he settled, and there remained during his life. He deceased in 1744, his wife and the following children surviving him: William, who married Sarah Wright in 1732; John, who married Mary Stockdale, of Burlington county, in 1741,[7] and deceased in 1765; Samuel, who married Letitia Matlack in 1742 (he having deceased in 1750, she married Thomas Hinchman); and Hannah, who married John Ladd in 1732.

---

4 Lib No. 1, 149.
5 Lib No. 2, 95.

6 Lib. A, 184.
7 Lib. No. 5, 63.

Samuel Mickle was one of the first settlers in the village of Haddonfield. He became the owner of a lot next adjoining the tavern property, lately belonging to John Roberts, deceased, and there he erected a dwelling. Timothy Matlack, his wife's father, owned the Roberts's estate and another lot to the east, fronting on the street. Timothy was a shopkeeper, and was so taxed by the township.

Of John Ladd, the father, and John Ladd, the son, much appears in the various records and traditions of their times, which proves them to have been conspicuous persons. They were prominent in the political and religious matters that surrounded them, and the subjects of much hard talk, for which some of their defamers appear in no very enviable position.

As early as 1690, Samuel Taylor puts himself on record, admitting that he had been uttering falsehoods about the elder John Ladd and Sarah his wife, but upon what particular subject these words originated, does not appear. He, however, made a clean breast, and admitted that all his assertions were slander, and, in the form common in those days, the retraction thereof has come down to the present generation. The entire record is copied here to show the manner of so doing,—a practice that has no existence now. It runs as follows:

"This may certify all persons whom it may concern; that, whereas, I, Samuel Taylor, of Gloucester river, within the Province of West Jarsey, Sawyer, have of late publicly reported several false, scandalous, reproachful and detracting speeches, of and concerning John Ladd, of ye same place aforesaid, Yeoman, and Sarah his wife, which were of infamous import, and tending to prove ye said parties to be of unjust dealings and evil and dishonest lives and conversations; therefore I, ye said Samuel Taylor, being moved to ye said report by my precipitate and unadvised passion and anger against ye parties above said, do hereby certify that I herewith repent of, and am unfeignedly sorrowful for my speaking, declaring and publishing any report of such evil tendency aforesaid, and do freely and voluntarily own and acknowledge that I have grossly abused, traduced and wronged ye said John Ladd and Sarah, his wife, by means of ye' false, slanderous and defaming reports and speeches above said.

"In testimony whereof, I have hereunto put my hand this 24th day of June, Anno Domini, 1690.

"SAMUEL TAYLOR.

"Recorded by order of Court, this ye 10th day of August, 1690.

"JOHN READING, Recorder."[8]

The father was a practical surveyor, and assisted in laying out the city of Philadelphia for William Penn. The compass and chain used by him in this work are now in the possession of the Historical Society of Pennsylvania, at its rooms in Philadelphia; they are preserved as a valuable relic of those early times. In compensation for his services, the Patroon offered him thirty pounds, or a square of land, within the limits of his town, but John decided to take the money.

William Penn, surprised at this, said: "Friend John, thou art Ladd by name, and a Ladd in comprehension. Dost thou not know this will become a great city?"

In measuring the distances over the rough soil, and in marking the lines of the streets upon the trees, John could not realize the assertions of Friend William, and concluded that his expectations had gotten the better of his judgment.

While wading about the swamps of Dock creek, and fixing the intersections of Market and Chestnut streets with those of Third and Fourth streets in that vicinity, our surveyor doubtless reflected much upon what had been suggested, and thought the whole scheme was a huge castle in the imagination of his employer.

Time, however, as in all similar cases, has shown which of these entertained the better notions; and, although the one was considered as hazardous in his ideas, yet the other acted as a prudent man, and was influenced by the opinions of those around him. But few of the men that accompanied William Penn to America comprehended the extent and importance of his undertaking. This may account for many of the hindrances

---

[8] Lib. G2, 72.

which he met with in carrying out his proposed plans. Not understood in his purposes, he soon became the object of censure and abuse; but, as a Christian and a philanthropist, he has long since come to be appreciated. That he was actuated by the purest of motives and governed by the desire to promote the welfare of his people, at this day, is not questioned.

After the lapse of another half century, John Ladd the son, appears to have been traduced by one of his neighbors in some of their political or religious controversies, and, not resting very comfortable under the same, he required of William Ives a legal admission that he had said some ugly and untruthful things about him. This admission was spread upon the records over his own signature, done in open court, and witnessed by the judges thereof.

"A Knight of the Post" implied that John had been convicted of some petty offence, and been punished at the whipping post, or set in the stocks, a means much in use at that time to vindicate the honor of the commonwealth and to preserve its dignity.

The insinuation that he could not be trusted as a sworn witness, perhaps touched John's pride quite as much as the first charge, and led to the arrest of William Ives and his admission to the falsity of the whole.

This means of the vindication of the character has passed out of use many years since, and to the present generation is unknown. Like the first, the entire record is copied that the reader may draw his own inference therefrom.

WILLIAM IVES'S ACKNOWLEDGMENT, MADE IN OPEN COURT AT GLO'STER.

"WHEREAS, I, William Ives, of the township of Gloucester, in Gloucester, in the province of West Jersey, yeoman, in the presence of divers creditable persons, inhabitants of the said county, sometime since did falsely and without any cause or reason, speak and say that John Ladd, of the said county was a Knight of the Post, and that I did not know but I might sue one Henry Sparks, but that I could not trust to the said John Ladd's testimony, and I acknowledge likewise, that I spoke and said sundry false, scandalous words touching and concerning the reputation and character of him, the said John Ladd.

"Now I do hereby acknowledge and publickly declare that I have wronged and injured the said John Ladd's character by the uttering and speaking the said false scandalous words and sayings, having not the least shadow, colour or foundation for the same; and I do hereby desire forgiveness of the said John Ladd, for the injury done.

"Gloucester, ye 28 October, 1744.

"WILLIAM IVES.

"Witnessed by Ja. Hinchman, one of ye Judges of the Court of Common Pleas at Gloucester, Wm. Harrison, Daniel Mestayer.

"Recorded February 8th, 1744.

"CHARLES READ, Sec."[9]

Hannah Ladd survived her husband, and, being in possession of his papers, she discovered that one of the books left by Thomas Sharp was among them. It was one of his private records as surveyor and conveyancer, and was considered of such value that an act of the Legislature was passed, that it might be made part of the public records of the Surveyor General's office, where it has remained since that time.

Daniel Mickle deceased in 1712, leaving a will. In that document he mentioned his wife and a child unborn.[10] This posthumous child was a boy, and was named Daniel. His grandmother, Sarah Mickle, provided for his maintenance and education; and also anticipated the needs of the widow.

Archibald Mickle died in 1735, without children; his widow survived him,[11] and, in 1736, married Blackinston Ingledon of Philadelphia, to which place she removed with her second husband.

James Mickle deceased the year following the death of Archibald, leaving his widow and two children, Rachel and Jacob.[12]

Ezekiel Siddon, the husband of Sarah, was a butcher, and resided upon a property which he had purchased of Jacob Coffing

---

9 Lib. GH, 41.
10 Lib. No. 1, 406.
11 Lib. No. 4, 52.
12 Lib. No. 4, 65.

in 1709. This fronted on the river in Newton township, and is now part of the Mickle estate.[13] He was the owner of other real estate near his homestead. He died intestate, and but little is known of his family at this time.

Arthur Powell, the husband of Mary, was a son of Arthur Powell, who first settled on Penapaca creek, in Philadelphia county, Pennsylvania.

He came thence from the town of Flushing, Long Island, in the State of New York, where his name, that of his wife Margaret, and those of two sons are set down in the census list made in 1698. According to that record he was of French extraction.

In 1692, he (the father) purchased of Thomas Chaunders, one hundred acres of land in West Jersey, at Mulberry Point, on the sea coast, near Great Egg Harbor.[14] In the same year, he purchased a like number of acres of Robert Turner, at the same place, and thereon he probably settled. The value of the whale fisheries, which were so attractive to the new comers in that region, may have induced his removal from Pennsylvania. He had two sons, Arthur, a carpenter, and Richard, a shoemaker. He died intestate in 1718.[15] In 1716, Arthur (the son) purchased a farm of John Fisher, in Newton township, bounded by Cooper's creek, being part of the original estate of Robert Zane, the first settler, and there he, Arthur, made his home.[16] John Fisher purchased said land of Elnathan Zane, a son of Robert, in 1703, who became owner thereof, by the will of his father, and sold the same when he attained his majority. Arthur and Mary Powell had but three children (two of them daughters): James; Rachel, who married ———— Lewis; and ————, who married ———— Kent. In 1730, he purchased a large tract of land on Timber creek, of John Brown, and also became the owner of other real estate.[17] He died in 1749.[18] In Newton township the family was never very large, yet in other parts of old Gloucester county the name often occurs.

Rachel, who married Benjamin Cooper, died in a short time without children. Benjamin subsequently married Elizabeth

---

13 Lib. A, 144.
14 Lib. G2, 133, 134.
15 Lib. A, 178.
16 Lib. A, 100.
17 Lib. G2, 26.
18 Gloucester Files, 1749.

Burcham, widow of Jacob, and daughter of Samuel Cole. The issue of this marriage was numerous, and as follows: Joseph, who married Elizabeth Haines; James, who married Sarah Ervin and Hannah Saunders; Samuel, who married Prudence Brown; Benjamin, who married Elizabeth Hopewell; William, who married Ann Folwell; Isaac; and Elizabeth, who married George Budd.

Benjamin Cooper was a son of Joseph, and a grandson of the first William; which William conveyed to the first Joseph, two hundred and twelve acres of land in 1709, who also conveyed the same to his son Benjamin in 1728.[19] This included the ferry at Cooper's Point, which Benjamin conveyed to his son Samuel, with about thirty-eight acres of land adjoining, in 1769.[20]

Of the division of Archibald Mickle's original purchase, as made between Archibald, James and Joseph in 1727, Joseph's portion passed into the Kaighn family; and Isaac Mickle, senior, in later years, became the owner of Archibald's share and James's also, and conveyed them to his nephew, Isaac Mickle, junior, in 1780.

The land between the south line of the original Mickle estate and Newton creek was located by Robert Turner (in 1687), and by Richard Arnold (in 1702). Richard Arnold purchased of Robert Turner, and conveyed the two tracts of four hundred and twenty acres to Martin Jarvis in 1700.[21] In 1702, Martin Jarvis sold two hundred and eight acres from off the eastern part of the tract to John Wright, and four years after conveyed the remainder to Jacob Coffing. After various conveyances, too numerous to name in this connexion, the larger part of the Turner and Arnold surveys became, in 1790, the estate of Isaac Mickle, junior, who re-surveyed the same in that year.[22]

In tracing the genealogy of this family, the want of heirs in the male line is constantly occurring, which frequently leads to doubt, and occasionally to error. Like the Coopers, they remained upon the original estate, and held tenaciously to the acres of which Archibald first became the owner; in some

---

19 Lib. AE, 205. 21 Basse's Book, 26.
20 Lib. AE, 213. 22 Lib. U, 443, O. S. G.

generations increasing the family name, and, in others, finding it reduced to but few persons; until, within the last decade, it has passed entirely away. No portion of the land at this time remains in the blood of the Mickles; and already the old estate is in the hands of strangers, traversed by avenues, and divided into town lots. Another decade may see the fishing grounds covered with piers and docks, the busy mart of commerce, and without a vestige of its present rural beauty.

Isaac Mickle, deceased, author of the "Reminiscences of Old Gloucester," was a descendant in the paternal line of this family. That he was a zealous and reliable antiquarian, no better evidence can be adduced than the book just named. In this work, his industry and good judgment are manifest; he has condensed and arranged many facts touching the early history of West New Jersey, not before noticed. Accepted as reliable on all subjects there treated, no library intended to illustrate the history of our State, is complete without it, and, as the desire to become better acquainted with this subject increases, so will this book become more appreciated. With all such as are seeking knowledge in this direction, the name of Isaac Mickle will be held in grateful remembrance.

JOHN KAIGHN.

IN the year 1694, John Kaighn was a resident of Byberry, in Bucks county, Pennsylvania. He was a carpenter, and the husband of Ann, the widow of Walter Forrest and daughter of William Albertson.[1] Walter Forrest came to Burlington in 1678, and very soon purchased a large tract of land in Salem county, bounded by Salem creek; in connection with his brothers, he erected a mill thereon, the first in that section of the State.[2] Before his decease, however, he had removed to Byberry. This occurred in 1692. By his will he gave considerable property to his widow's brothers, situated in Salem, which they in a few years disposed of.[3] There was no issue by this marriage. Ann, the widow, so remained for two years, when she married John Kaighn. By this marriage there was one child, a daughter, who bore the mother's name.

The daughter was born June 24th, 1694, and the mother died July 6th, of the same year. The daughter, who died single in 1715, gave by her will her property to her two half-brothers by the father's second marriage.[4]

In 1696, John Kaighn married Sarah, the widow of Andrew Griscom and sister of John Dole, then a resident of Newton township.

The blood of the Albertsons, therefore, was not connected with this family any longer than till the death of Ann, the daughter

---

[1] Lib. No. 6, 32, Salem Records.
[2] Lib. B, 16, Salem Records.
[3] Salem Wills, A, 69.
[4] Lib. No. 2, 162.

of Ann and John in 1715, leading those who wish to follow the maternal line in another direction.

As a carpenter, John found abundant business, for every ship that arrived was crowded with emigrants, whose first purpose, after landing and selecting sites, was the erection of dwellings. These, in most instances, were rude and unpretending, yet the services of a mechanic were necessary in some parts; hence the constant employment of the carpenters of that early period in providing shelter for the new comers.

The nativity of John Kaighn is easily traced through a letter in possession of the New Jersey branch of the family, dated August 26th, 1702, endorsed "To Mr. John Kaighn—Linener, in West New Jersey, nigh on Delaware river side, opposit to Philadelphia city, in America." It was from his mother, Jane Kaighen. It was written from her residence, at that time, in Kirk Andrew, a town in the north of the Isle of Man, where she lived with her daughter and son-in-law, Daniel Lane.

She informs her son that his father died the November previous to her writing; that his sister Ellen, born after he left the Isle, was married and settled in the parish of St. German, on the west coast of the island; that, for a short time after the decease of her husband, she had lived with her son Charles, at Ballacragga, on the south-east coast, but, not being happy there, had removed to Kirk Andrew. On the same sheet of paper, John Kaighn has left an unfinished letter, without date, in reply to his mother, generally of a religious character.

In this she is told that he had "lost two good and loveing wives, in a few years time—and left alone with young babes;" that these were two boys and one girl, "the youngest yet at nurse."

Sarah Dole came with her father's family from Wales, but from what part cannot be traced.

The first purchase of real estate by John Kaighn in Newton township, was on the fourteenth day of ninth month, 1696, when Robert Turner conveyed to him four hundred and fifty-five acres of land, fronting on the Delaware river and extending from Line street to Little Newton creek.[5]

---

[5] Lib G3, 127.

Like many of the old English deeds, this discloses the whole of the original title as vested in the grantor, at once valuable and interesting to such as care to push their inquiries thus far.

In 1699, John Dole purchased two hundred and twenty acres of this tract from John Kaighn, and settled thereon.[6] He was a shoemaker, and came from Long Island, N. Y., where he had married Mary Jessup, of Jericho, in 1688. He died in 1715, and by his will gave this land to his two sons, John and Joseph.[7] Joseph Dole married Hannah Somers, a sister of Richard, in 1714, and removed to Great Egg Harbor, where he died in 1727, leaving a will.[8] His children were Hannah, who married Daniel Ingersoll; Sarah, who married John Scull; Rebecca, who married Joshua Garwood; Mary and Servia.

John Dole also removed to Great Egg Harbor, and died in 1748, without a will.[9] What family he left, if any, is not known.

John Dole conveyed his undivided part of the tract of land in Newton township, devised to him by his father, to his brother Joseph, who conveyed part thereof to John Kaighn in 1723,[10] and the remainder to Joseph Cooper in the same year.[11]

Andrew Griscom was the owner of a tract of land adjoining that of John Kaighn's and part of Samuel Norris's survey; but from whom purchased, and the exact locality of the land, are not known.

Andrew Griscom, by his will in 1694, gave the same to his wife and two children, Tobias and Sarah, and, upon certain contingencies, to John Dole in fee. At the time of John Kaighn's death, he was the owner of this land, but in what manner does not appear.[12]

Tobias Griscom, a son of Andrew, married Deborah Gabitas, at Burlington meeting, in 1711, and settled in Newton township, where he remained until his decease.

He dealt considerably in real estate, and made several locations in his own name under "rights" which he purchased in 1716 and 1717. In the last named year, he purchased of

---

6 Lib. G3, 240.
7 Lib. No. 2 of Wills, 08.
8 Lib. No. 2 of Wills, 430.
9 Lib. No. 6 of Wills, 331.

10 Lib. D, 52.
11 Lib. D, 436.
12 Lib. A, 83.   Lib. D, 52, 54.
   Lib. C, 240.   Lib. G3, 240.

Hugh Sharp, several tracts of land in Gloucester county, near the sea shore, valuable for the cedar swamps, some of which still retain the name of the former owner.[13] In 1721, and after his death, his widow as executrix of his will, re-conveyed the same properties to the original grantor.

Tobias Griscom deceased in 1719,[14] leaving his widow and the following children: William, who married Sarah Davis, and who was a saddler and lived in Haddonfield; Tobias, who died a minor; Andrew, who married Susanna Hancock, and who was a blacksmith and settled at Tuckahoe; Mary, who married Tobias Halloway; and Samuel, a house and ship carpenter, who resided in Philadelphia. The latter assisted in the erection of Independence Hall, and lived for many years on Arch street between Third and Fourth in that city.

John Kaighn had much to do with the settlement of the estate of Walter Forrest, the deceased husband of his first wife. A large part of the real property was purchased by him, among which was the mill called the "Brothers Forrest," and three hundred acres of land attached. This was conveyed to him in 1701, but he sold it the next year to Isaac Pearson.[15] With this sale his interest ended in that section of West Jersey, but he continued to increase the borders of his land in Newton township until he found himself one of the largest owners in this section.[16] On March 7th, 1708, he became one of the trustees of the Newton meeting with Benjamin Thackara, William Cooper, William Albertson, Thomas Sharp, Joseph Cooper and John Kay. He is thus shown to have been an active member of the religious Society of Friends; and his remains doubtless lie buried within the walls that now surround part of the first estate dedicated to such purposes in this region of country. In 1712, Benjamin Thackara conveyed a small adjoining piece of land to the same trustees for the same use. In 1771, it was discovered that all the trustees had died; and to continue the property in the right channel, Josiah Kay, the heir at law of John Kay, who was the last deceased, made a deed in the same year to John Gill, Joshua Stokes, Nathaniel

---

13 Lib. A, 87, 208.
14 Lib. No. 2, 132.

15 Lib. No. 6, 32, Salem Records.
16 Lib. No. 7, 156.

Lippincott, James Cooper, John Brown, David Cooper, Joshua Lord, John E. Hopkins, John Evans, Isaac Ballinger, Samuel Webster and John Glover.[17]

In 1808 again, the trustees were dead, except Samuel Webster, who, in that year, made title to Joseph Glover, Joseph Burrough, Jr., John Albertson, Abel Nicholson, Josiah Webster, Joseph Kaighn, Joseph Sloan and Benjamin Cooper.

From about the year 1797 to 1811, much trouble existed between the trustees of the Newton Meeting house property and James and Joseph Sloan, in relation to the boundaries of the same. James and Joseph Sloan had become the owners of part of Thomas Thackara's estate, which adjoined the Friends' property, and claimed a portion of the land by them occupied, in fact, that portion on which the old meeting house stood. This particular lot, measuring sixty feet in width and forty-five feet in depth, with another lot adjoining, was conveyed by Joseph Sloan to James Sloan in 1810, and by him held until 1819, when he released his interest therein to Samuel Eastlack and others, who had charge of one part of the burial ground.[18] In 1811, Joseph Sloan abandoned his claim by his deed to the trustees of the Haddonfield Monthly Meeting, which extended to the old grave yard within the brick wall, and some adjoining lands.[19] The removal of Friends from the neighborhood, and the erection of other places of worship, gradually decreased the interest of the society in these premises; and the destruction of the old meeting house by fire on the night of December 22d, A. D. 1817,[20] was the end of any further assembling upon the spot made memorable by the many associations that surround it. The disputes before named, which at that time were considered a scandal to the church, may be the means of identifying where stood the *old meeting house*, where, at some future day, a suitable monument will be placed in remembrance of its purposes, and to point out its locality.

In 1699, John Kaighn was appointed by the Legislature, one of the judges of the several courts of Gloucester county, and was so continued for three years thereafter. Upon the first

---

17 Lib. M, 172, Gloucester Co., Woodbury. 19 Lib. O, 597, Gloucester Co., Woodbury.
18 Lib. W, 585, Gloucester Co., Woodbury. 20 Joseph Hinchman's Journal.

entry of his name, the clerk of the joint meeting, spelled it "Cahaen," which doubtless surprised Friend John, when he came to look upon the record and found the orthography of his name so sadly tortured, yet, when pronounced, so near correct.[21]

The duties of the judges of the courts at that day had not been well defined, and the minutes of their proceedings contrast strangely enough with those of the present. In township affairs he, no doubt, took part; but, as Friend Sharp was not authorized to buy a book until 1723, which was near the time of his decease, no record of such transactions has come down to the present generation.

In 1710, he sat as a representative from Gloucester county in the Legislature, only a few years after the surrender of the government by the proprietors to Queen Anne, and in the midst of the most troublesome times of the people.

John Kaighn's will was proved June 12th, 1724, in which he gave a house and lot in Philadelphia, to his wife Elizabeth, and, after a life interest in some other parts of his property, the remainder to his two sons, John and Joseph.[22]

These sons were by the second wife, and were born as follows: John, December 30th, 1700, and Joseph, December 4th, 1702, each taking the blood of the Doles, and basing the maternal origin in New Jersey upon the same line as that of the Griscom family.

His third wife was Elizabeth Hill, of Burlington, at the meeting in which place they were married in 1710. By this marriage there was no children.

The inventory of his personal estate amounted to two hundred and thirty-five pounds, sterling, showing him to have been one of the substantial men of his day. The next year after their father's death, Joseph conveyed to John all his interest in the real estate devised to them, consisting of much valuable property, with fisheries and meadows attached;[23] and, soon after, John re-conveyed the entire homestead property to Joseph, who so held the same until his death.

---

[21] Leaming & Spicer's Laws.
[22] Lib. No. 2, 267.
[23] Lib. C, 19.

In 1727, Joseph Kaighn married Mary Estaugh, of Philadelphia, a daughter of James and niece of John Estaugh, of Haddonfield. This fact is proved by various expressions used by Elizabeth Estaugh, in her will, wherein she names the children of Mary Kaighn, and places them among her legatees.

Joseph Kaighn was an active man in the affairs of the township. He was initiated therein by his election as one of the surveyors of highways, in 1723. His associates were Jacob Medcalf, Samuel Shivers and Thomas Dennis. What the duties of these officers could have been, may always remain a mystery, as, at that date and for many years after, the roads were simply the widening of the Indian trails, without regard to the shortest distance or the best location; yet these officers were annually elected, and, no doubt, had some important labors to perform. The year of his marriage, he was promoted to the position of overseer of the poor, then the most responsible office of the township. As such officer, he received and disbursed all the funds raised for public purposes, as appears by the annual report spread out on the pages of the township book.

From the year 1736 until his death (excepting the year 1738), he was assessor, and also held other minor positions among the people. His will bears date May 7th, 1749, in which year he died,[24] having carefully described each tract devised to his children by metes and bounds,—a precaution too often neglected when a large real estate is thus to be disposed of.

The old brick house near the Kaighn's Point ferry, was probably the residence of Joseph. It has lost its identity with the past, as the march of improvement has destroyed its proportions, and left but part of the original building.

The box and yew trees, which were planted when the dwelling was being erected, are the only land marks to show where one of the ancestors of the family had his home. The centre building was two stories high, and ornamented by various colored bricks, with a wing on each side built of stone. The site was well chosen, since a good view was had of the river, and of William Penn's "brave town," which, for many years, did not reach as far south as Dock creek.

---

24 Lib. No. 7, 05.

The farm and meadow land are now traversed by paved streets, and covered by the habitations of a thrifty population, separated only by such political divisions as are incident to all good governments, aiding in every respect the advancement of the people.

Joseph Kaighn's wife survived him, and the following named children: Joseph, who married Prudence Butcher, widow of —— Butcher, and daughter of —— Rogers; John, a physician who died single, about forty years of age; Isaac, who died in his minority; James, who married Hannah Mason; and Elizabeth, who married Arthur Donaldson.

In 1753, Mary, the widow of Joseph, married Robert Stevens, a resident of Newton township, who died in 1759; and before his last wife. By this marriage there was no issue.

Robert Stevens's first wife was Ann Dent, whom he married in 1739. She was an English lady, and sister of Joseph Cooper's second wife. They came from Yorkshire, the last named being a minister among Friends, a testimony from Haddonfield Monthly Meeting, showing that she was acceptable as such.

At the time of the death of Joseph Kaighn, all his children were minors. The real estate devised to the daughter, was to be hers, "if she married with her mother's consent," a restriction mostly disregarded by parents as well as children. Joseph and Prudence Kaighn had four children, William, Mary, John and Joseph. The first three named died in their infancy, and Joseph married Sarah Mickle, in 1795, a daughter of Joseph.

In 1732, John Kaighn married Abigail Hinchman, one of the children of John Hinchman, the first of that name who settled in Gloucester county. He deceased in 1749, leaving a will.[25] He was a blacksmith, and followed his business in Haddonfield for several years; but afterwards he removed to a farm on Newton creek, where he died and was buried in the old grave yard at the meeting house near his residence. The property in Haddonfield he gave to his daughter Sarah, subject to the use thereof by the mother during her life. His children

---

25 Lib. No. 6, 230.

were Sarah, born 1733; Elizabeth, born 1736; Samuel, born 1737, who married Mary Gerrard; John, born 1740, and Ann, born 1744.

The widow Abigail afterwards married Samuel Harrison, and resided near Gloucester. The issue of this marriage was a daughter, Abigail, born 1751, who married Richard Edwards in 1768. They had ten children, all of whom died single, excepting Samuel, who married Martha Heulings, and Sarah, who married Joseph Collins. Abigail Harrison survived her last husband, and died in 1795, at Taunton iron works, Burlington county, where lived her son-in-law, Richard Edwards.

Like his brother Joseph, John was somewhat of a township politician, for in 1725 he was elected freeholder, and, at different times thereafter, held the same position. His name is found upon the town book almost every year from 1725 to the time of his decease. He acted as clerk from 1732 to 1741, when he was succeeded by Samuel Mickle.

This family name is oftener associated with others of like pronunciation and different spelling than any other in this section; which has frequently led to trouble and difficulty. One family writes the name Cain, another Kain and another Kane, and they are in no wise related to each other.

The descendants of John Kaighn, the subject of this sketch, never became numerous in this part of the State of New Jersey, but some of his descendants have adhered to portions of the original landed property to the present time. The increase in the city of Camden has covered the larger portion with substantial improvements; and another half-century will find the entire estate thus occupied.

THE GRAYSBURYS.

IN the year 1692, James, Joseph and Benjamin Graysbury, brothers and ship carpenters, came from the island of Bermuda, to Philadelphia.[1] It does not appear whether they were Friends, banished from England, or whether they were natives of the said island. The opportunity for getting ship timber to carry on their business was certainly an attraction in these parts, and may have been the secret of their settlement here. They had their place of business in Philadelphia, and probably, Joseph and Benjamin there remained during their lives. The next year after their arrival, they joined in a purchase of five hundred acres of land, of Robert Turner, which land was situated in Newton township, and on the south side of the main branch of Newton creek.[2]

At that time, Robert Turner was a merchant in the city of Philadelphia, but owned much land in New Jersey, and particularly in the neighborhood of the above named tract. From a map made by Thomas Sharp, showing his lands lying on Newton and Cooper creeks, the amount appears to have exceeded two thousand five hundred acres within the township; he therefore was much the largest owner of real estate in this region. This map also indicates that Robert Philips, planter, had already settled thereon; but where his habitation was, does not appear. After this man, James Graysbury made the first

[1] Lib. G2, 174.
[2] Lib. G3, 426.

improvement on this purchase; but where his cabin stood, is also in doubt. He probably cleared considerable land, looking somewhat to agriculture for the maintenance of his family. This man was the son of James, so far as the records can be digested; yet the vague manner of expression used in many conveyances and wills, renders a proper understanding of them almost impossible.

James (one of the brothers) died in 1700, leaving one son, James, his two other children being born after his decease. In anticipation of this, he made provision in his will that his share of said tract of land should belong "to his child or children yet to be born," and it proved that the issue was twins, named by the mother, Elizabeth and Annie.[3] In the progress of time the second daughter here named married Daniel Martin, a resident of Philadelphia. In 1722, the sisters conveyed the said land to James, upon which he resided until his death.

Benjamin (another brother) died, seized of his share of said five hundred acres, leaving two children, Margaret, and Mary, who married Richard Kelley, also a resident of Philadelphia. They conveyed their interest to James, their cousin, in 1720.[4]

Joseph (the last brother) died intestate and without children. His undivded interest of said land descended to his nephew, James, he being the eldest son of James, who was the eldest brother of Joseph.[5]

The law regulating the descent of real estates in force at that time, deprived the children of Benjamin and the sisters of James, of all right in the property of their uncle Joseph, although standing in the same blood relationship as James. The rule of "the oldest male heir" is in this case clearly exemplified, and shows how unjust was the application of the law of primogeniture,—a law that has long since, in the State of New Jersey, given way to a more rational, just and equitable distribution of real estate. For many years the English code obtained, contrary to the progress and spirit of the age, and at variance with the liberality and intentions of our law makers.

---

3 Sharp's Book, 03, O. S. G.
4 Lib. D, 253.
5 Lib. M, 110, O. S. G.

The infringements on this were gradual, but always in favor of the female heirs, until every barrier was swept away, and the daughters of an intestate had the same rights of inheritance.

Immediately upon obtaining the title to his property, James Graysbury proceeded to perfect the same and to establish the boundaries by a re-survey; which was accomplished in 1721.[6]

It will be noticed, that, after the death of the three brothers, there was but one person to represent the family name; thus became centered in James, the son of James, the genealogy of future generations, as well as the title to most of the original estate, as by them purchased of Robert Turner.

The only severance from the first purchase was that of fifty acres sold to John Willis, a ship carpenter of Philadelphia, in 1696; which land fronted on the creek. There John Willis erected a house.[7] This, however, after several conveyances, became the property of Caleb Atmore, and in his name it remained for many years.

James Graysbury conveyed said estates to two of his sons (James and Joseph), and they immediately after conveyed the same to their brother Benjamin, who then resided on the premises. In 1783, Benjamin bought of Caleb Atmore the fifty acres that had been sold to John Willis in 1696, by his grandfather and great uncles, and became therefore owner of the original tract. This now includes the farm lately Joseph FewSmith's, deceased, on the east, and that of Edward Bettle, on the west, and all the intermediate property, showing it to have been one of the best locations made in the township, whether soil or situation be regarded.

On the farm first named is the old family graveyard, where rest the bones of the earliest generations of the Graysburys, and of some of their descendants. In the same neighborhood lived Simeon Breach, Joseph Low, Caleb Sprague, John Hinchman, and others, who, in all probability, were also there interred, with many of their descendants. Nearly all were slave-holders, as appears by the wills of several; this part of their personal property found a final resting place in Hinchman's, now gener-

---

6 Lib. M, 110, O. S. G.

7 Lib. A, 189.

ally known as Hurley's graveyard. For many years the memory of the forefathers was held in respect, but the presence of strangers has left no trace of the immediate locality of the old Graysbury graveyard.

> " Perhaps in this neglected spot is laid
> Some heart once pregnant with celestial fire,
> Hands, that the rod of empire might have sway'd,
> Or waked to ecstacy the living lyre."

It is unfortunate that the genealogy of the three brothers who originated the family in New Jersey, cannot be traced with more accuracy, the greatest difficulty being that the female branches so largely predominated, the name thus soon disappearing in subsequent marriages. The will of James Graysbury was executed in 1760, but he lived for some years after that time. His wife, Mary, survived him; also the following children: James; Joseph;[8] Mary, who married John Franklin; Ann, who married —— Warner; and Benjamin. The number of Benjamin's marriages involves the maternal line of his progeny in much doubt. His first wife was Elizabeth, a daughter of Samuel Sharp, and granddaughter of Thomas Sharp (the first surveyor in Newton).[9] His second was Lydia Matlack, daughter of John; next he married Letitia Shivers, and, after her death, he married Ann Morton. Ann survived him and married Jonathan Morgan.

In 1783, it will be seen that Benjamin Graysbury was the owner of the original estate, and was the only one of the family that remained in the neighborhood. He probably built the house, part of which is still standing on the farm lately owned by Joseph FewSmith, deceased, now by William Bettle; and there he resided during his life. He acquired much other real estate, and was classed among the wealthy men of his day. A shade of romance connected with the third wife of Benjamin may not prove uninteresting here.

· By the will of John Tomlinson, who died a single man, in 1760, he devised to Letitia Shivers nearly all of his estate,— "out of regard to her."[10] These are significant words, when

---
8 Lib. No. 12, 282.
9 Lib. AR, 359.
10 Lib. No. 10, 387.

used in the connection in which they here stand, and the most rational conclusion must be that marriage was contemplated between them, but that death prevented its consummation. Fifteen years after that time she became the wife of one of the most respectable citizens of Gloucester county, and, perhaps, the mother of some of his children. Doubtless many of the grandmothers of the last century could tell over the sad romance connected with this affair; having knowledge of the particulars, and always remembering it as one of the incidents of their younger days.

Benjamin Graysbury died in 1747.[11] His children were Benjamin; James, who married Beulah Warrick; Mary, who married Isaac Kay; and Abigail, who married John Branson. Whether these were the children of one mother or of more than one, does not appear, and may never be disclosed, unless some enthusiast indulge in a waste of time and labor never repaid and seldom appreciated. Although the collateral branches of the family have become extensive in West Jersey, yet the name has never been much known except in the neighborhood of the first settler.

On the south side of Newton creek and near the end of Atmore's dam, not many years since, stood a small antiquated house, built partly of brick and partly of frame, one and a half stories high, with hipped roof, small windows and low, narrow doors. In early times this was kept as a tavern, and stood beside the public road leading from Philadelphia to the seashore. It was probably built by John Willis, the ship carpenter before noticed, as it was on the land which he purchased of the Graysburys. The dam being the easiest means of crossing the stream, all the travel passing between the points before named was centred here, making this "hostelry" a desirable stopping place, since here the greatest number of folks could be seen in a given time. It was enlarged until its ancient form was entirely lost to the later generations, who did not know it as a resting place for travelers.

Being the head of navigation, all the trade carried on with Philadelphia by water in that neighborhood started from that

---

[11] Lib. No. 38, 40.

point, and, perchance, a packet left every day tor the city to accommodate the people, being a much easier means of communication than travel over the circuitous and, no doubt, bad roads that led to the ferries. If the owners of the property were the keepers of the inn, then Joseph Kirlee succeeded John Willis, and John, the son of Joseph Kirlee, followed, who, in 1718, sold to Thomas Atmore. About the year 1773, Thomas died, and his son Caleb took possession, and by this name it has been known among the people of later times. The situation being near the middle of the township, it was a suitable place for business meetings, and there the politicians of that, day "most did congregate," to discuss the affairs of the colony. Here, for many years the few inhabitants elected the various officers to carry on the machinery of their little municipality, and, here, personal rivalry and political prejudice cropped out, just as in these days of ambition and greed for office. Before the days of mails, this was the place where news from the city or county could be gathered, and whence correspondence could be forwarded to various parts of Gloucester and Salem counties by the few travelers going to and from their several homes. The name of this inn has passed into oblivion. No doubt, some high sounding title from the mother country was emblazoned on the sign that hung before the door, and informed strangers that they approached the Bull and Mouth, the King and Cross, or some other names that, in these days, are not attached to such public resorts, but are regarded as antiquated and out of date.

Inside, the low ceilings and ill arranged rooms told that ventilation and convenience were not regarded; yet the well sanded floor and the bright pewter dishes betrayed the good house-wife and thrifty matron. The bar-room opened by a double door, cut horizontally, and within might be seen the crib which screened the liquors and protected the dealer.

The immense open fire-place, arranged with a bench on each side, made sitting-room for guests by day, and beds for dogs at night,—to say nothing of the straight-backed slat-bottomed chairs that stood around the walls. The visitors were mostly rude, uneducated people, unused to the refinements of society, and contending with adversity in its many ugly shapes. The means of comfort, as now understood, were not at hand, and several decades passed away after the first adventurers arrived, before anything beyond the necessity of their conditions was attempted.

At this old tavern might occasionally be seen a party of hunters, pledging their good opinion of each other in a bowl of whiskey-punch, or "stone-fence," and enjoying in their peculiar way the last of a successful chase. Wrestling, running and jumping were indulged in, when a few of the neighbors met; and every man that participated, was soon graded as to his ability in each. The fare was abundant, and such as epicures of the present day would revel in. It was dried venison, bear's meat, fresh fish, and wild fowl, with corn bread or hoe cake, well prepared, and made inviting by the tidy appearance of the surroundings. The liquors, also, though drawn from wooden casks, and drank from horn tumblers, imparted an invigorating, healthy effect; and, when evaporated by a good night's sleep, left no suspicious feelings after them.

Of this ancient house, not one stone rests upon another, as it stood in the days of our forefathers; and nothing but a slight depression in the ground shows its place. In the midst of a quiet, agricultural neighborhood, the visitor now cannot appreciate the busy scenes that formerly surrounded it. The creek, once a beautiful, living stream, from being dammed at the mouth, was, for many years, only a muddy ditch; and, where once spread the sails of the graceful water-craft, nothing remained save a miasmatic bog, affecting the health of the neighborhood, and the value of adjacent land as well. Of late years, however, the tide is allowed to flow, and the many advantages incident thereto will follow in due time.

The highway that took its tortuous course through the grand old forests, passing around the heads of streams, avoiding the hilly places, and extending for miles into the country without a habitation near it,—this road, that brought the few travelers past the door, is scarcely known and is, in many places, entirely obliterated.

Wealth, enterprise, and the increase of population, have changed these routes into straight, well cared-for thoroughfares, while the Indian trails at this day cannot be remembered by the oldest inhabitant. When this tavern at Atmore's dam opened its doors to the public, or when ended the days of its usefulness, no record can be found; but, like many other places of interest to the seeker after ancient things, enough has been gathered through tradition, that deserves a faithful search the more thoroughly to know its history.

Around the broad, open fire of the bar-room, the legends, the arguments or the songs, will never be renewed; nor, upon the green before the door, will the wrestlers ever again join hands.

> "Thither no more the peasant shall repair
> To sweet oblivion of his daily care;
> No more the farmer's news, the barber's tale,
> No more the woodsman's ballad shall prevail:
> No more the smith his dusky brow shall clear,
> Relax his ponderous strength, and lean to hear;
> The host himself no longer shall be found,
> Careful to see the mantling bliss go round;
> Nor the coy maid, half willing to be prest,
> Shall kiss the cup to pass it to the rest."

JOHN KAY.

AMONG the leading men of the times, the name of John Kay occurs as often as that of any other person. He was a son of Garvis Kay, and came to New Jersey about the year 1680. The history of this family in England is worthy of notice in this connection, and may not prove uninteresting to those of the name in this region of country, Lower, in his Dictionary of Family Names, says: "The family of Kaye is of great antiquity in the county of York, being descended from Sir Kaye, an ancient Britton, and one of the Knights of the warlike table of that noble Prince Arthur, flower of chivalry! The truth seems to be that, at Woodsome in Yorkshire, there resided in very early times a family of Kaye, the head of which, some centuries later, was created Baronet by Charles I. The patent expired in 1810, but was revived shortly afterwards in favor of the reputed son of the fifth Baronet."

Some of the family may be found in Durham and Berkshire, but it is more numerous in Yorkshire than in any other county in England. Many of them were Friends, and consequently suffered persecution at the hands of those in authority, in the shape of fines and imprisonments. At the court of quarter sessions, held at Wakefield in Yorkshire, in 1661, John Kay, Baronet, was the presiding judge, and committed sixty Quakers to prison. Ten years after, John Kay was fined for attending meeting at York in the same shire. It is possible that the latter was the same person as the former; and that, while the committing magistrate, he became convinced of the truth of the doctrines preached by George Fox, laid aside his titles, and suffered with the Friends in person and estate.[1]

In 1675, Garvis Kay of Holmforth, in the Parish of Kirk-Burton, Yorkshire, was prosecuted for tithes, committed to prison for contempt, and there kept for two years. He was released for some flaw in the indictment, but again committed by proceedings against him in the ecclesiastical courts.

Although it would be a venture to say that the two Kays here named were the same that came to New Jersey, yet the dates and incidents may be reconciled, and such suggestion really may be a fact. This, however, must be left for some one in the blood, and curious to trace the family beyond the ocean.

The first of the name hereabout was John Kay, who purchased one hundred acres of Francis Collins, in 1684, situated on the north side of the north branch of Cooper's creek, adjoining a tract of land which he (Francis Collins) afterwards sold to Simeon Ellis.[2-3] These one hundred acres are now part of the farm lately owned by Joseph W. Cooper, deceased, and lie about one mile east of Ellisburg, in Delaware township. In 1696, Jarvis Kay located one hundred acres of land situated on the southerly side of the south branch of Cooper's creek; but, from the vague and uncertain description, its exact position cannot be discovered.[4] This tract is probably now included in the landed estate of John Gill, and lies about one mile south of Haddonfield in Centre township, bounded by the stream aforesaid. Whether the Jarvis Kay here mentioned was the father of John, or whether he lived on the survey before mentioned, is unknown at this late day, and without much trouble and bootless research, may always so remain.

There is a tradition in the family that the first habitation of John Kay on the tract of one hundred acres was a cave in the hillside near the creek, and that there he and his family resided. This is probable, as many of the first settlers adopted this mode of shelter, until time could be had to clear a portion

---

[1] Besse's Sufferings, Vol. 1, 14.
[2] Lib. A, 01, Gloucester Deeds.
[3] Basse's Book, 236.
[4] Lib. A, 32, O. S. G.

of their land and erect log cabins, which were universal in the first settlement of the country. Were the dwelling a cave or a cabin, there is much of interest surrounding the place where it stood; and it deserves a faithful search in order to discover its true locality.

In 1685, a religious meeting was established by consent of Burlington Friends, at the house of John Kay, in connection with one of the same character to be held at the house of Timothy Hancock, at Penisaukin, on alternate first-days, for the accommodation of Friends in Evesham, and about Penisaukin and Cooper's creek.[5] These meetings were continued until 1707, at least, as the records show marriages to have taken place there as late as that time. William Clark and Mary Heritage were married there in 1696. Benjamin Wood and Elizabeth Kay, and Benjamin Thackara and Mary Cooper, were married there in 1707, as were doubtless many others, the record of whose marriages has been lost.

At that date (1685), the settlers in Evesham, or the Vale of Evesham, as the neighborhood is called in some of the old titles, were but few, and wide apart.[6] Among them were William and Elizabeth Evans, who lived in a cave near Mt. Laurel, on a tract of land which William had located in 1682; and here were born their children. Noel Mew and his Indian wife had settled on part of a large tract of land located by his father, Richard Mew. His habitation was on the farm lately owned by James Wills, and near a stream of water called Noel's run, which doubtless received its name from him. Thomas Evans, a brother of William, also settled in that neighborhood; his family was small, however, he having but a wife and one daughter.

John Inskeep resided east of Marlton, in a small cabin surrounded by Indians, with whom he lived on excellent terms. Thomas Eves lived near by, as well as Henry Ballinger, Francis Austin, and others, who were known in those days as the "Evesham Friends," and attended the meeting at John Kay's house. Elizabeth Evans, the wife of William, was a public

---

5 Asa Matlack's Mem.
6 Revel's Book, 72.

Friend, and doubtless followed closely in the footsteps of the founder of her profession, and, in their meetings at this place, frequently exhorted those around her to do likewise.

John Kay's house was several miles from where these people lived, but it proved how much they were attached to their religious principles, and what difficulties they were willing to overcome in order to observe the requirements of the society.

In this connection it may be proper to notice another meeting of Friends, held at the house of Thomas Shackle, from the year 1695 to 1721. Some one who has had access to the minute book of the Friends' Meetings in this section, has made the following extract therefrom:

"The Monthly Meeting of Gloucester from the year 1695, was held alternately at Newton and at the house of Thomas Shackle, until the twelfth month, 1721, at which time it was held at the meeting house at Haddonfield, which was built in the fore part of that year, on ground given by John Estaugh, for the accommodation of the Monthly and Quarterly Meetings. After some time, two meetings a week for worship, were constantly kept there, which are still continued, excepting when that on the first-day is held at Newton.[7] The Monthly Meeting is now constantly held at Haddonfield, and the Quarterly Meeting alternately there and at Salem. The Quarterly Meeting was first set up by order of the Yearly Meeting at Burlington, to be held alternately at Salem and Newton."

The house of Thomas Shackle stood upon the farm now owned by Amos Kaighn, in Delaware township, a short distance northwest of the Haddonfield and Moorestown road, and about one mile from Ellisburg.[8] The land Thomas Shackle purchased of Francis Collins in 1689, and, in 1735, it became the property of John Burrough.[9]

This extract fixes the year in which the meeting house at Haddonfield was built, the erection of which centred all the meetings at one point, much to the comfort and convenience of the people.

---

7 "The Friend," Vol. 4, 206.
8 Lib. G1, 97.
9 Lib. X, 14.

Proud, in a foot note to his History of Pennsylvania, says "that John K*e*y was the first child born of English parents in Philadelphia, and that William Penn gave him a square of ground. He was born in a cave long afterwards known by the name of Penny Pot, near Sassafras street." He remembers him to have been in the city about six years before his death, which occurred in 1767. He was buried at Kennett, in Chester county, Pennsylvania, where he had previously resided.

The subject of this sketch and the person named by Proud cannot be the same, although the name is frequently spelled differently, which sometimes leads to doubt.

John Kay became the owner of many tracts of land near his first purchase, some of which he located, and some of which he bought of the settlers. One of the old deeds calls him a clothier, which implies he was a manufacturer of, or a dealer in cloth. Whether this had reference to his calling before or after his settlement here, does not appear.

The coloring matter for his goods was not one of the troubles in manufacturing, for our Quaker ancestors were careful to avoid anything in dress that pertained to style or pretension. Of the few changes that have made any inroads upon the practices of primitive Friends, this is the most radical. In England, the members of this sect cannot be distinguished by their dress, and such may soon be the case in America.

In 1710, John Kay purchased the Lovejoy survey, partly covered by the village of Haddonfield, which purchase included the mansion house and corn mill built by Thomas Kendall in 1697, now part of the estate of Josiah B. Evans, deceased; both of which buildings stood on the south side of the creek, and within the bounds of Newton township. To this place John Kay removed, and he there resided until his death.[10]

This "corn mill," in the days of our ancestors known as the "Free Lodge mill," as then constructed, would be a curiosity to the mechanics of the present time.[11] The driving of one run of stone was, perhaps, all that was desired, the machinery being so heavily and clumsily made that it would contrast

---

10 Basse's Book, 237.
11 Basse's Book, 62.

strangely with the perfect application of power, the avoidance of friction, and the nice adjustment secured by experience and ingenuity to the same uses at the present day.

The mill stood some distance below the dam, at the end of the race-way cut in the bank, which secured additional head and fall without increasing the expense. The remains of this race-way may yet be seen, but the site of the mill is entirely obliterated. That it literally was a corn mill there can be no question, as no other kind of grain was raised here for many years after its erection, nor was bolting apparatus introduced after other cereals were cultivated, but our forefathers ate their bread made of the dark flour, taken up with the bran still remaining therein; which, although it detracted from the appearance, yet aided materially in the digestion.

A story is still extant, much to the scandal of our worthy ancestors, that, in going with a "grist" to the mill, they always put a stone in one end of the sack, the better to balance the grain in the other, when hung across the horse or ox that carried it, not understanding that, with grain in place of the stone, a double portion could be thus transported. If this be true, then the improvement in the mode of getting a grist to and from the mill is quite as discoverable as the advantage derived from modern well adjusted machinery. This was probably the first grain mill in Gloucester county, and, if it stood now as in the days of its usefulness, many would be the visitors to examine its arrangement and inspect its odd construction.

In 1685, John Kay was elected a member of the Assembly of the province of West New Jersey, and, in 1703 and 1704, again filled the same position.[12] During this time he was also appointed one of the justices of Gloucester county, which, under the laws of the State, then existing, made him one of the judges of the several courts of the same. He held several local offices, and discharged their duties to the satisfaction of the community.

In 1710, he was again elected one of the members of the Provincial Assembly from Gloucester county, which was part of the fourth session of the Legislature after the surrender

---

[12] Minutes of Assembly, State Library, Trenton.

made to Queen Anne, and in the ninth year of her reign. Upon the meeting of this body at Burlington, he was chosen speaker, which appointment at that time was sufficient to mark him as a man of more than ordinary ability. Robert Hunter was governor, holding his commission from the Queen, and, by her instructions and authority, striving to settle the difficulties then existing between the colonies, but now united under his administration. Much depended on the discretion and good judgment of the Legislature in making the surrender acceptable to the people, and John Kay was a prominent man during all these difficulties. He was continued speaker through the sessions of 1711-12 and 1713.

Upon the meeting of the Legislature in 1716, Daniel Coxe was returned as a member of the Assembly in place of John Kay, and was chosen speaker. The proceedings of that body, however, show in what way this occurred; for William Harrison, sheriff of Gloucester county, was arrested and brought to the bar of the House by the sergeant-at-arms, and reprimanded "for adjourning the election poll from the "great field" near John Kay's house, to William Cooper's, several miles distant, without the consent of the candidates, which was contrary to law."[13] By this transaction, the defeat of John Kay was brought about, which led to the censure of the principal executive officer of the county. What sheriff Harrison's explanation or apology was, does not appear upon the record, yet it is evident that he was in sympathy with Dr. Coxe, and enlarged his authority to carry out his wishes. John Kay at that time resided at the corn mill, and the "great field" was part of John Haddon's estate, bounded by the King's road and part of the village of Haddonfield.

Although several years had passed away since the assumption of the government by Queen Anne, yet the participants in the political troubles previous to that had not forgotten their animosities, as was evidenced in the foregoing transaction. Daniel Coxe made himself obnoxious to Governor Hunter, and, at the next session, absented himself from the Assembly, at which time John Kinsey was elected speaker in his stead. Coxe was afterward reprimanded and expelled from that body.

---

13 Minutes of Assembly, State Library, Trenton.

Another peculiarity about this election was the returning of Daniel Coxe for the counties of Salem and Gloucester; so, upon the organization of the Assembly, he was called upon to decide which of the two counties he would represent. After much controversy, in which he manifested considerable ill feeling, as well as his ignorance of the laws, he concluded to serve for Gloucester, considering doubtless that the influence of John Kay would hinder the consummation of his plans, if sitting as a member at that time. This made it necessary that a warrant should issue for a new election in Salem; upon its return it was found that William Clews was elected; but delay was caused in his taking his seat by reason of his scruples in regard to the necessary oath. After considerable explanation, this trouble was overcome, and the hindrance caused by a factious and unprincipled man removed.

Among the colonial records in the state paper office in London, England, notice of his election is entered; it is there imputed to the "inundation of the Swedes,"[14] reference being had to such of that nationality as were inhabitants of Salem and Gloucester counties.

Daniel Coxe was the son of Dr. Daniel Coxe of London, who became the owner of twenty-two whole shares of propriety in West New Jersey, and was governor of the province from 1687 to 1690. In 1691, a number of persons, residents of London, formed themselves into what they called the "West New Jersey Society," and purchased of him the above named shares, he reserving, however, surveys already made, being large tracts in Salem county, then including both Cumberland and Cape May. This deed also contained grants for two hundred thousand acres, called the "Merrisinbes Province," contiguous to West Jersey; two shares of propriety in East Jersey; three whole shares in Merrimack, New England; ten thousand acres in Pennsylvania; a dwelling house and pottery house with all the tools, in Burlington; town-lots at Perth Amboy, and Town-lots at Gloucester and Egg Harbor. The society consisted of forty-eight persons having a common seal, with, perhaps, a charter from the King. Many large surveys

---

[14] Publications of the New Jersey Historical Society, Vol. 5, 93.

were made and sold, realizing considerable money to the association; but the troubles with their agents here, and the dissensions among themselves at home, finally reduced the number of persons to but few, who eventually sold the entire estate to Benjamin B. Cooper, of Gloucester county, N. J. Even at this date large sums of money are held by the treasurer, waiting the lawful owners; who may have some trouble in making the legal connection, after such a lapse of time, with those who constituted the original society.

Daniel Coxe (the son) was bred to the law, and was a man of good education and many redeeming traits of character, but of an erratic and impetuous temperament, which was continually getting him into difficulty with those in authority. He was a member of Lord Cornbury's council, and sympathized with him in many of his arbitrary and illegal acts done under the color of law; this rendered him especially unpopular with the Quakers of the province.

In the year 1734, he was appointed one of the associate justices of the Supreme Court of New Jersey, and discharged his duties with much satisfaction to the people; age and experience having tempered his composition and made him a valuable and exemplary member of society. He remained on the bench until his death, which occurred in 1739. Judge Field, in his History of the Provincial Courts of New Jersey, says of him:

"His early career in New Jersey was clouded by his connection with Lord Cornbury, and his difference with Governor Hunter, but he lived to enjoy the confidence and respect of the community, and his judicial duties appear to have been discharged with ability and integrity."

At the election which occurred in November, 1716, John Kay was again returned as a member of the Assembly and, although not elected speaker, he took a prominent part in all the proceedings of that branch of the government. Among other matters of importance, he was chairman of the committee to procure the settlement of the boundary line between New York and New Jersey, then a subject of much controversy and ill feeling.

He was also chairman of the committee to prepare a law to fix the partition line between East and West Jersey,—a matter that interested the council of proprietors of each division; that has found its way into every tribunal in the State, and that remains to this day a subject of trouble and litigation. At this session he also procured the passage of an act to make perpetual an act entitled, "An act that the solemn affirmation of the people called Quakers shall be accepted instead of an oath in the usual form, and for qualifying and enabling the said people to serve as jurors and to execute any place of trust in the province." From this may be dated the law that relieved Friends from the many difficulties that grew out of a legal formality, and which had been a source of annoyance to them since the surrender of the government to Queen Anne, and, particularly, since the arrival of Lord Cornbury, her first executive officer. He was in advance of his times in discerning the necessities of the people and the interests of the province. He grew up with the emigrants, had knowledge of all the political difficulties through which they passed, shared all their privations, was participant and assisted in the settlement of all the leading questions of the day in which he lived, and enjoyed the confidence of his constituency until the last. He was a member of the Society of Friends, and one of the trustees of the Newton meeting from 1708 until his death.

As one of the members of the Council of Proprietors of West New Jersey, he was also a prominent man, sought out many abuses incident to the location of land, and had the same corrected during his continuance in that office. It does not appear that he was a practical surveyor, yet his thorough business qualifications placed him on an even footing with the deputies; by which means he understood the whole manner of procedure in the laying on of rights according to the rules, and, sometimes, to the discomfiture of that class of men.

John Kay died in 1742, a wealthy man, leaving a widow (Sarah), who survived him several years. Their children were John, who married Sarah Langstone in 1707; Sarah, who married James Norris; Mary, who married Benjamin Wood in 1707; Isaac, who married Mary Ann Gregory in 1738; Josiah, who married Rebecca Davenport in 1713, a daughter of Francis, one of the first settlers at Burlington, N. J., who came from Whittington, Derbyshire, England; Benjamin who deceased, single, in 1732; and Joseph, who died in 1721, leaving a widow, Elizabeth, and children.

At the time of his death, John Kay owned all the land on the east side of the main street in Haddonfield, extending from Cooper's creek to Ellis street (excepting a few lots which he had sold); also land lying between the two branches of Cooper's creek, extending some two miles up each branch, and a large tract on the north side of the north branch, beside surveys in other parts of Gloucester county. In 1727, he conveyed to his son Josiah, the one hundred acres which he purchased of Francis Collins, upon which Josiah settled, who, in 1745, conveyed the same to his son Francis.[15] It is probable that this tract of land remained in the family and name for many years after the last conveyance, but, at this writing, it has lost its identity therewith.

In the same year (1727), John Kay conveyed to his son Isaac several tracts of land, the whole containing seven hundred and thirty-four acres, situated on both branches of Cooper's creek.[16] In this deed, the grantor is called "John Kay of the Grist Mill, at the head of Cooper's creek, in Newton township, Gloucester county, New Jersey," his residence and occupation at that time thus being proved beyond a question. The only part of the original landed estate that has remained in the family and name from the location to the present time, is the farm now owned by Joseph Kay, of Haddonfield, and situated on the south side of the north branch of Cooper's creek in Delaware township. This tract has descended continuously through the blood and name for nearly two hundred years, never having passed by a deed from one owner to another in that time. Excepting a small portion of the land occupied by Sarah Norris, the son John possessed all the land owned by the father on the east side of the main street in Haddonfield, extending nearly to Ellis street. His children were Isaac, who married Hope French; John, who married Rebecca Hartley; Mathias; William, who marrried

---

15 Lib. S6, 338, O. S. G.
16 Lib. DD, 175.

Barbary Smith; Rebecca; Hope, who died before her father, single; Ann, who married Joshua Evans; and Mary, who married Abraham Heulings.

James Norris, a shipwright, who married Sarah, built one of the first houses in Haddonfield, on land then owned by her father, where he, during his life, and his widow, after his death, kept a store. James Norris deceased in 1742 intestate, leaving one child, Elizabeth, who married Isaac Smith in 1739, and John Hinchman in 1747.[17]

Sarah Norris died in 1755, leaving a will.[18] She gave Jonathan Axford two horses and the use of her house, set her slaves free, and bequeathed a sum of money to the Newton Meeting.[19] The inventory of her personal property amounted to nearly four hundred pounds. She continued her store until her death, dealing in all the various commodities incident to the trade of a country merchant. Of such of her customers who were slow to pay, she would hand over the accounts to the officers of the law, to secure the debt already in danger, and as a terror to all others in like manner offending. Her property accumulated under her management, showing that she had good business qualifications. Her daughter Elizabeth had two children by her first husband (daughters), but none by the last. She died about the year 1804, surviving John Hinchman several years. Her children were Sarah, who married Joseph Hugg in 1761, and Mary, who married Jacob Jennings in the same year.

Mary (the wife of Benjamin Wood), deceased before her father, leaving four children, namely: Abigail, who married Robert Hunt; Mary, who married Joseph Cole and Richard Matlack; Elizabeth, who married Elias Toy; and Hannah, who married Joseph Heulings.[20]

Isaac (to whom his father had conveyed land in 1727) had his residence on what is generally known as the "Fotteral Farm," now owned by Hannah, the widow of Josiah B. Evans, deceased. In the year 1791, most of the land owned by Isaac was re-surveyed by his son Joseph, and the boundaries settled.[21]

---

[17] Lib. No. 4, 376.
[18] Gloucester Files, 1758.
[19] Lib. No. 7, 390.

[20] Lib. S, 61.
[21] Lib W, 190, O. S. G.

Isaac Kay died in 1757, leaving the following children: Isaac; Joseph; Sarah, who married Abraham Bryant; Elizabeth, who married Isaac Horner; and one child not born at the time of his decease.[22] This part of the estate has not been in the name for many years.

As before stated, Josiah lived on the old homestead, where he died in 1771. His children were Francis, who married Jemima French; Joseph, who married Ann Thompson (and who, dying before his father, left children); Isaac; and Elizabeth, who married ———— Parker. This family increased rapidly. There is some doubt as to the correctness of its genealogy as here given.

Although the sons of the first settlers remained on the paternal estate, yet the second generation soon spread far beyond the limits of New Jersey, and the name may now be found in all sections of the Union.

The descendants of Mary have multiplied largely; they would find some trouble in tracing their line of blood to its source, so tortuous and so diluted has it now become.

At this day, it is probable that the family of Sarah Norris has no existence. The second generation from her was limited to two females, and, if from them it has been enlarged, no knowledge of the fact is possessed in this region of country.

---

22 Lib. No. 8, 350.

SIMEON ELLIS.

SAMUEL SMITH, in his History of New Jersey, says, "Thomas Ellis came to Burlington, New Jersey, in 1677." He came from Burlington, in Yorkshire, England, as one of the servants of George Hutchinson, who was a distiller. In reference to this class of persons, a note is appended, which says: "Many that came servants succeeded better than some that bought estates. The first, inured to industry and the ways of the country, became wealthy, while others were obliged to spend what they had in the difficulties of the improvements. And others, living too much on their original stock, for want of sufficient care to improve their estates, have in many instances dwindled to indigency and want." Thomas Gordon, in his history of this State, copied after Smith, and mentions another Thomas Ellis, who arrived a few years later; but the same person is probably meant, as, by some oversight, the name may have been repeated.

He settled on a town lot located to him in Burlington, in 1680, and died two years after, leaving a daughter Elizabeth, who was apprenticed to John Brown the same year. This was done by the judges of the court, and appears among its proceedings.[1]

William Ellis also came to Burlington county in 1683, and made a location of a considerable tract of land in Springfield

---
[1] Revel's Book, 04.

township. He was from Tunstall, in Holderness, Yorkshire, England, and, in all probability, was of the same family as Thomas.[2]

Of the nativity, or of the arrival of Simeon Ellis in New Jersey, nothing is known; and it may, perhaps, always remain a doubtful question, for the reason that very many of the emigrants of that day had no entry made of their names upon the ship's books, and also because many of these books have been destroyed through the carelessness of the owners, or of those into whose possession they may have fallen.

It is probable, however, that he was not among the first that landed here, as he did not purchase any real estate until 1691; at which date many settlements had been made in Burlington and Gloucester counties, and the city of Philadelphia had come to be quite a thrifty village.[3] This purchase consisted of two hundred acres of land conveyed to him by Francis Collins, and was part of a survey of eight hundred acres made by him, bounded by the north side of the north branch of Cooper's creek.[4] The two hundred acres lay on both sides of the King's highway, as the same had been but a short time before laid out by the commissioners appointed for that purpose.

Simeon built his log cabin near the stream, and but a short distance from the road; here he always after lived, and here were all his children born. As was the custom in those days, his place had to be designated by some title, and he adopted that of "Springwell;" but, like the position of the first habitation, it has long since been forgotten. This practice was brought by our forefathers from England, where every gentleman's "seat" had a particular name, which name is tenaciously adhered to from generation to generation by the family. The constant change of the title to land in New Jersey, and the disposition of many families to remove from the ancestral acres, are reasons why so few estates at the present day retain the names by which they were christened at the first settlement. Some, however, may so be found; also, in possession of the owners, may be seen the original title to the estate, coming

---

[2] Lib. B1, 121.
[3] Lib, G2, 127.
[4] Lib. P, 238.

down through the same blood, with the pride of family always apparent.

In 1695, Simeon bought four hundred acres of land of Elias and Margaret Hugg, adjoining his first purchase. This Margaret was a daughter of Francis Collins, who had conveyed the said four hundred acres to Samuel Jennings and Robert Dimsdale, as trustees, in 1687—part of the eight hundred acres survey before named.[5]

These first purchases of Simeon Ellis, as described by present localities, include the village of Ellisburg, in Delaware township; they are almost equally divided by the Camden and Marlton turnpike, and the Moorestown and Haddonfield road. But few of the original boundaries are left, excepting the water course, as the purchase, sale and division of land, in the space of one hundred years, obliterate very many ancient land marks.

Several other purchases were made, some of which lay on the south side of the north branch, now included in the farms of John Ballinger and of others adjoining.[6] A part of this estate is now owned by Joseph Ellis and the heirs of Josiah Ellis, deceased, lineal descendants of the first settlers. All the remainder has passed out of the name many years since.

Simeon Ellis was not a participant in the political troubles of the times in which he lived, and does not appear as an office holder upon any of the records. He was a member of the Society of Friends, and among those who made up the little assemblage at John Kay's house, a short distance from his own; where he met the few of the same sect that came from Evesham.

Simeon Ellis died in 1715, dividing his property by will among his children.[7] His personal effects, by appraisement, amounted to two hundred and fifty-three pounds, sterling, and he, doubtless, was considered a "well-to-do" farmer by his neighbors, for his estate ranged much above the average of that time. His wife, who survived him, was Sarah, a daughter of William Bates, to whom he was married, according to the order of Friends, in 1692, at the old Newton meeting house, then a short distance from the home of the bride.

---

5 Lib. G3, 71.
6 Basse's Book, 28.
7 Lib. No. 2, 05.

Sarah, the widow of Simeon Ellis, dealt somewhat in real estate after the death of her husband, as, in 1717, she bought some four hundred acres in Newton township, fronting on Cooper's creek, and extending to the main branch of Newton creek.[8] This she purchased of Isaac Hollingsham, and, the next year, her son Thomas conveyed her an adjoining tract, making her at that time one of the largest land holders in the township.

Portions of this property remained in the family and name for many years after the death of the widow, following the collateral branches to the present generation ; but they are now divided into lots and farms, parts being owned by Edward C. Knight, William P. Tatem, John C. De Costa, and others.

The landed estate of Simeon Ellis and of his widow Sarah, in her own right, was therefore large; and, lying as it mostly does, in the improved sections of Camden county, if taken as a whole, it would now be of much value.

In disposing of his property by his will, Simeon Ellis mentioned seven children, namely: Thomas, who married Catharine Collins, daughter of Joseph, in 1722; Joseph, who married —— ——; William, who married Sarah Collins, daughter of Joseph; Simeon, who married —— ——; Jonathan, who married Mary Hollingshead (the latter surviving him, and afterwards marrying Robert Stiles); Mary, who married —— ——; and Sarah, who married John Kay, in 1730.

The homestead estate, which was devised to Thomas, William and Simeon, was held by them, as given by their father, until 1754, when, owing to some trouble in regard to the boundaries, they joined in a re-survey of the same, which settled all matters in dispute with adjoining owners.[9] This proceeding also showed in what manner the three sons held the paternal estate, and on what part of which each lived at that time.

Thomas had three hundred and nineteen acres of the western part, fronting on the creek and extending north. His residence was on what is generally known as the Lewallen farm (a short distance from Stevenson's mill). The Ogden estate, being for-

---
8 Lib. A. 56, 121.
9 Lib. S, 338, O. S. G

merly the farm of Charles Collins, deceased, was part of Thomas's share; and also much other adjoining land; all this is now divided and sub-divided into plantations, the primitive forests being gone and most of the ancient boundaries obliterated. In 1766, he sold the larger part of the same to Joseph Collins, who, by his will, divided it among his sons.[10]

This Joseph Collins was, perhaps, the son of Benjamin and nephew of Catharine, the wife of Thomas Ellis, and the only person of that branch of the family who carried the name to the present generations.

William had two hundred and thirty-three acres in the most northerly part of the original tract, lying, as it now does, on both sides of the Haddonfield and Moorestown road, and mostly absorbed in the farms of William Morris Cooper and the heirs at law of Batheuel Heulings, deceased. In 1757, he lived in Newton township, at which time his occupation was that of a carpenter; but he afterwards removed to his part of his father's estate, and there died intestate, in 1759.[11] His wife Catharine became his administrator. He had but two children, namely:[12] Abigail, who married John Cox in 1744; and Ann, who married Peter Champion in 1746, John Stokes in 1751, and Samuel Murrell.[13]

The landed property was divided between the two daughters; it has many years since passed out of the name and blood.[14]

The daughter Ann, by her several husbands, had the following issue: By Peter Champion, one child, Joseph, who married Rachel Collins; by John Stokes, none; by Samuel Murrell, a son Samuel, who married —— Hubbs.

The children of John and Abigail Cox, were William, who married Phœbe Duffield; John, who married —— Tallman and Ann Dylwin; and Samuel, who married Sarah Emlen.

A short distance east of the Haddonfield and Moorestown road, and on the Heulings farm, is the spot where were buried the slaves of the Ellis family, a spot scarcely known to the present generation, but not as yet used for farming purposes. Occasionally a member of the owner's family would be interred

---

10 Lib. L, 109, Woodbury.
11 Lib. P, 459.
12 Lib. No. 9, 213.
13 Book of Licenses of Marriages, Trenton.
14 Lib. AH, 385.

at such place, and consequently be lost sight of among the after generations of the proprietor.

Simeon had the larger share in acres, as well as the homestead improvements, for his portion of the paternal property, it being three hundred and sixty-six acres, with an extensive front on the creek. He occupied the house built by his father and tilled the land, from which the latter had cleared the timber, when he made his settlement at that place. He was an intelligent man for his day, and the ancestor of the family that still retain parts of the original estate. As a tiller of the soil and one who sought to develop agriculture, he was a public benefactor; as a dispenser of the law in the guise of a country squire, he commanded that deference which in years gone by was paid to such individuals, maintaining the dignity of the realm and respect for the King.

His docket is a curious volume, interspersed with the entries of actions at law, charges for grain, credit for money paid for labor on his farm, and much other matter, foreign entirely to the purpose for which the book was intended. In the year 1742, Sarah Norris, who kept a store in Haddonfield, being out of patience with many of her delinquent customers, applied to Squire Ellis, to try *his* remedy; upon whose record her name frequently appears as plaintiff in suits there entered. To show that she was in earnest, the execution soon followed the judgment; which meant that the claim must be discharged, or the defendant be sent to jail. That a man could more easily pay his debt when fast in prison than at liberty, was one of the absurdities of English jurisprudence, brought to New Jersey by our ancestors; but the notion has been exploded, having given way to common sense and a more liberal sentiment.

The quarter sessions court, in fashion then, consisting of two justices of the peace, with authority to try petty crimes, sometimes sat at Simeon's house. Perchance some scamp, without the fear of law before his eyes, had robbed his neighbor's henroost, and he, while in the enjoyment of a meal therefrom, had been pounced upon by a constable and taken at once to trial.

The court, with all gravity, and, in consideration of the importance of the crime, would listen to the evidence; hear the story of the defendant; and, after much judicial hesitation, declare the criminal guilty. If an old offender, twenty lashes on the bare back would only be sufficient to vindicate the dignity of the law; which sentence would be passed with a hint of more, if again convicted.

To a tree near by, in the most public manner, would the culprit be taken; and there, in the presence of the crowd, tied, stripped and beaten,—a proceeding which degraded alike the victim of the law, and those whose morbid tastes could induce them to witness the sentence carried into effect.

Like the court, these scenes have become obsolete. Elements of Christianity have been infused into the corrective systems of our government, more charitable in their operation, and less humiliating to the unfortunate.

By the gracious favor of his Majesty, the peace officers of the realm were clothed with authority to solemnize marriages. Although much the larger portion of the inhabitants in West Jersey were Quakers, and careful that the young folks should adhere to their form in this regard, yet it sometimes happened that an alliance would be made in which the "beau or belle" was outside the pale of the church. In these cases, Simeon Ellis was often called upon; and he, without the presence of any one except the parties themselves, would join them in the bonds of holy wedlock. This breach of discipline was frequently overlooked; and, if a proper explanation was made, and an acknowledgment forwarded to the meeting, the erring one was retained in membership.

From the year 1727 to 1791 inclusive, a law was in force requiring a man who contemplated marriage, to file a bond under his hand and seal, with the Governor of the State, with sufficient security; the condition of which was that he had no lawful let, impediment of pre-contract, affinity or consanguinity, to hinder the same. A copy of one of these is here given, which may prove of interest to the reader. It is as follows:—

"KNOW ALL MEN BY THESE PRESENTS, That We, James Mulock of the County of Gloucester, in the Province of New Jersey, Practicioner of Physick, and Robert Friend Price, of the same Place, Esq., are holden and do stand justly indebted

unto His Excellency, Jonathan Belcher, Esq., Captain-General and Governor-in-Chief of New-Jersey, &c., in the sum of Five Hundred Pounds of current lawful Money of New-Jersey; to be paid to His said Excellency the Governor, his Successors or Assigns. For the which Payment well and truly to be made and done, We do bind ourselves, our Heirs, Executors and Administrators, and every of them,
firmly by these Presents. Sealed with our Seals, Dated this Sixteenth day of April Anno Domini One Thousand Seven Hundred and Fifty-Seven, [1757].

"THE CONDITION OF THIS OBLIGATION IS SUCH, That whereas the above Bounden James Mulock hath obtained License of Marriage for himself of the one Party, and for Priscilla Collins of Gloucester County of the other Party, Now, if it shall not hereafter appear, that they the said James Mulock and Priscilla Collins have any lawful Let or Impediment of Pre-contract, Affinity, or Consanguinity, to hinder their being joined in the Holy Bands of Matrimony, and afterwards their living together as Man and Wife: then this Obligation to be void, or else to stand and remain in full Force and Virtue.

    "JAMES MULOCK,   [SEAL.]
    "ROBT. FR'D PRICE.   [SEAL.]

"*Sealed and Delivered in*
 the Presence of
  "JOS. HARRISON."

If no other good was accomplished, the great value of the papers arising from the operation of the law is sufficient. These bonds and certificates arranged in chronological order, are well cared for in the office of the Secretary of State at Trenton; and they contain an amount of information that otherwise would have been lost. Occasionally the records show that the parties were from another state, by reason, no doubt, of an inexorable parent or stubborn guardian, whose consent to the marriage could not be had.

Weddings, in those times, frequently extended through days of hilarity and frolic. Dancing, blind-man's buff, and pawns were the usual means of enjoyment, and were entered upon with a zest that proved that every one was in search of pleasure. Like many others, these customs have passed away, and time has interposed so many generations that the present has no remembrance of them. Our sturdy ancestors on these occasions seemed boisterous and rude, but it should be considered that they had other occupations than the study of refinement and polish. Those who remove the timber and conquer the soil of a new country, seldom have time to indulge in education or luxury.

Simeon Ellis died in 1773, leaving a will. Parts of his land he conveyed to his sons, but much passed to them by devise.[15] He survived his wife, and left the following children: Isaac, who married Mary Shivers (daughter of Samuel); Benjamin, who married Sarah Bates; William, who married Amy Matlack; John, who married Priscilla Peterson (widow); Sarah, who married William Duyre; and Simeon, who married ——— Bates (sister to Benjamin's wife.)

Isaac settled on that part of the homestead now included in Ellisburg, and built part of the present tavern house.

Benjamin erected a home on a few acres given to him by his father, on that side of the road opposite the late residence of David D. Burrough, deceased, and there he lived and died.

William removed to the landed estate of his wife, near Glendale, part of which is still owned by Joseph H. Ellis; he here occupied himself as a farmer. His fondness for hunting and field sports drew around him, during the winter months, men of like tastes, and his house was generally the starting point for such as enjoyed those manly pastimes. These traits of character have not been lost in the latter generations, and only lack full development from want of deer and foxes, so plenty in days of yore.

Simeon remained on part of the original purchase, leaving but few immediate descendants.

Joseph settled on his mother's property in Newton township, and probably had his home on the north side of the main branch of Newton creek, generally known as the former resi-

---

15 Lib. No. 16, 144.

dence of Jacob Stokes, deceased. He became the owner of all, or the largest part of the maternal estate, and so held it during his life. His occupation was that of a farmer, and he does not appear to have participated in the political matters that occasionally agitated the community around him.

He died in 1757, intestate.[16] Having no sons, the estate, upon his demise, soon passed out of the name, and, except by the examination of the old titles, no trace of it can be discovered. His immediate descendants consisted of four daughters, namely: Priscilla, who married Jacob Stokes; Sarah, who married John Buzby and Isaac Mickle; Abigail, who married Caleb Hughes; and Kesiah, who married Benjamin Vanleer, M. D.[17] Excepting the descendants of Jacob Stokes, none of the family are known in this region at the present day.[18]

Jonathan lived in Haddonfield, but what his occupation was does not appear. In 1733, John Gill sold him a lot on the west side of the main street, where he built himself a house. Three years after, he sold the property to John Kaighn. He died a young man and intestate.[19]

---

16 Lib. C, 241, Woodbury.
17 Lib. O, 368.
18 Lib. T, 398.
19 Lib. Q, 460, 475.

JOSEPH TOMLINSON.

THIS person came to New Jersey from the city of London. He was a member of the Horslydown Meeting of Friends. This meeting was on the Surrey side of the river Thames, which, even at that day, had become part of the great metropolis by means of the several bridges already erected. He appears to have been in some way under the patronage of Anthony Sharp, an uncle of Thomas Sharp already mentioned. Many of this name, however, suffered persecution in England, from 1654 to 1690, for their religious opinions. These were residents of Lancashire and Derbyshire; they were fined and imprisoned for conforming to the belief of Friends, laid down at that period.[1] Whether Joseph was of the same family cannot be known at this day, except by persistent and fortunate search.

He arrived previously to the year 1686, and became an apprentice of Thomas Sharp, who had settled on Newton creek five years before that time.[2] Although his education was better than that of many of his day, yet his apprenticeship was to learn the business of woolstead comber or dyer, that being the occupation of his master when not upon some surveying expedition, or not engaged in his official duties.

In addition to this, he was further advanced in the common branches of English education, and, when he attained his

---
[1] Besse's Sufferings, Vols. 1-2, 145, 327.
[2] Sharp's Book, O. S. G.

majority, was well fitted for business of any kind, and soon participated in the political affairs of the colony. He was something of a carpenter as well; for, in 1686, he made an agreement with his master to build him a house for a specified sum, and to furnished all the material except the nails.[3] The dimensions and style of this dwelling do not appear, but the presumption is that it was small and unpretending in both; and required but little architectural skill in any particular.

It is possible that Joseph Tomlinson was one of the persons who erected the Friends' meeting house in Newton, the first building set apart for religious worship in Gloucester county, and the second in West New Jersey.

For some reason the articles of apprenticeship were set aside, and Thomas Sharp agreed to pay him five pounds per annum for his services, and four pounds at the end of the term. In a letter copied by Sharp into his book, as written by Joseph Tomlinson to Anthony Sharp in Ireland, dated Newton, May 3d, 1691, mention is made of the trouble between them; but the record is so much defaced by time, and the book so little cared for, that the matter contained therein cannot be deciphered.[4]

A copy, however, is here given, leaving blank such parts as cannot be intelligently made out, to be supplied by such as have leisure and patience to make the attempt.

"Copy of a letter sent by Joseph Tomlinson to my Uncle Anthony:

"NEWTON, May 3, 1691.

"MOST RESPECTED MASTER:—Having this opportunity good to write to thee, hoping thou together with * * my * * thy family are in good health, as I am, praised be * * * * wonder that I never received any letter from thee * * years, but only in a letter to thy cousin, wherein * * * * * to complain of us boath without just cause * * * in Ireland understand not the difficulties * * * * and thou seemest to be offended with Thomas because * * * * which I took of thee was not performed * * * he tels * * * complained to thee by letter that I was demanding performance,

---

[3] Sharp's Book, O. S. G.
[4] Sharp's Book, O. S. G.

but my writing was not for that purpose * * * you passed strange censure on my * * * say I had deserved to have my time given to me * * * not performed which I did not, for I thank God I have your charitie. God having given me my limbs to * * * * my living and if I had complayned of extraordinary * * * to thee I should not only deserved to be released * * * * I did for it would have been worse for me if it had * * * than it is, and I am very well satisfied that * * Yet notwithstanding if it had been or could have * * * * * for my parents sake and my fathers sake * * * me had I dyed on it I would have gone * * * * * * the effects that we have * * * * * * * * * * * * * * * * used and the taking up of land here is more chary * than you think of, and I myself was taken * * so dangerously that I had like to have lost my * * and have lost one of my big toes, and I was lame * * months and for the charge my master paid five pounds * * * chisurgeon which for his lost time and promise I * * paid him again before I left him * my service * * * well and truly served and computed the like * * * services of me. * * the stock would at last have been five pounds and the goods that thou sentest are merchantable. No more at present, but * * * receive a Release from under your hand that * * * wholy free from that, the which you have not * * * so remayne your friend to serve you.

"JOSEPH TOMLINSON.

"Remember my love to my father, mother, brothers and sisters, and * * * any of them be yet alive * * * a letter directed to them come to thy hands.

"Farewell."

Friend Sharp, with his accustomed particularity, made a note thereof in the same book, as follows: [5]"Joseph fell lame the 29th of July, 1688, and so continued until the 29th of November, but in as much as he found himself some parts of the time, and did some small matters of work, we reckon but

---

5 Sharp's Book, O. S. G.

three months' diet at four shillings a week, &c.," Other entries referring to him are made, which seem to show that the relations between them were not the happiest, perhaps growing out of Joseph's youthful fancies, or Friend Sharp's exacting policy towards him. There is no doubt, however, that their association was of much use to the younger person, since, in addition to the moral and religious training which he received, his education was improved and advanced through the care of his preceptor. The difficulties before named do not appear to have destroyed the friendly feeling between them, for, in after years, the kind offices of his old master are seen in several business transactions.

As time progressed, Joseph took unto himself a wife, and settled down to be a good business man and valuable citizen. In 1690, he located one hundred and seventeen acres of land on the east side of Gravelly run in Gloucester township, adjoining a tract of land which he had previously purchased of Joseph Wood, and on which he had settled and first lived after leaving the house of Thomas Sharp in Newton.[6] This stream of water, sometimes called McGee's branch, is a tributary of the north branch of Timber creek, and falls into the same on the south side about two miles above Chew's Landing. He soon increased the breadth of his acres, so that his possessions extended from Gravelly run on the north to Holly run, or Sharp's branch, on the south. These he retained through life, and gave to his sons by will after his death.

What could have been the inducement for Joseph Tomlinson to purchase and settle on land so far beyond the line of civilization, is, at this day, difficult to imagine. At that time, the settlements had scarcely reached beyond the navigable streams, and even there were but few and far apart. Yet, in his case, his abode was surrounded with miles of unbroken forest; and, was without any neighbors within half a day's travel, while large tracts of unlocated land were between Newton and the place which he had selected for his future home, the title of which could have been secured for a mere pittance. He had to go some ten miles to attend the Newton

---

[6] Sharp's Book, O. S. G.

Meeting, and, if, as a farmer, he took his produce to the Philadelphia market, the distance was still increased. True, he was within two miles of navigation on Timber creek, but it is hardly to be supposed that he kept his boat to carry his family to meeting, and himself to market in the city, or to court at Gloucester and Red Bank.

It is needless, however, to speculate upon these things one hundred and eighty years after their occurrence; and the conclusion must be that the reasons for such an isolated settlement as made by Joseph Tomlinson were sound and sufficient, unto his mind at least. His leisure hours in this secluded spot were not wasted, for he turned his attention to the reading and understanding of the laws of the community of which he deemed himself a part, and in which he was soon to fill conspicuous and responsible positions. In examining the appointments of the Legislature for Gloucester county, it is seen that he was made sheriff in 1695; and, for the year 1696, the following may be found, "King's Attorney, Joseph Tomlinson."[7]

This means that he was made the law officer of the province, to defend its honor and dignity, and for the prosecution of all offenders against the peace and tranquility of the same. That he was first examined as a law student and licensed to practice, there can be no question; and he, therefore, stands as the first attorney, according to the record, of Gloucester county. This appointment appears to have been made for three years, for, in 1700, he was re-appointed to the same position; which shows that his duties were acceptably discharged, and that he retained the confidence of those in authority. It will be seen that these duties commenced under the proprietary government, as instituted by our Quaker ancestors, and extended beyond the surrender to Queen Anne, when the courts were put upon a different basis and surrounded by much more parade and display.

In the first, the strictest simplicity was observed, both in the manner, and in the means of dispensing justice among the few litigants that sought their rights through this channel; for the judges who sat were elders in their own religious denomination, and regarded such things as essential to the purity of their

---

[7] Leaming & Spicer's Laws.

belief. It is not too much to say that their Honors remained covered while on the bench, wearing their broad-brimmed hats and their plain, uncolored coats as an evidence of their disregard of the customs of the court and the vanities of the flesh. In the jury-box, the same thing could be observed; in the dress and demeanor of the bar, the same; and, when a prisoner was charged, the style and phraseology of the language partook of all such peculiarities. Perhaps so rigid was the court on this point, that no gesture or vehemence was allowed on the part of the advocates; and, without regarding the earnestness of the talker or the extremity of his case, any breach of decorum was deemed a contempt, and punishable accordingly.

Not so after the surrender. Lord Cornbury, cousin to the Queen, and the first governor under her authority, came to the United Province, filled with the forms and ceremonies of a proud and exacting court.

In 1700, an act was passed making it the duty of the sheriff of each county to meet the provincial judges and other officers, when riding the circuit, at the verge of his county, to escort them to the seat of justice, and then remain in attendance until the court adjourned and they were again beyond his bailiwick. The costume of the judges consisted of scarlet robes with deep facings of black velvet, and powdered wigs adorned with silk bags. The lawyers wore black silk gowns and wigs, and all the attendants were dressed in a somewhat similar manner.[8] With these innovations, were brought in many new forms and rules, putting our Quaker judges completely at fault, and at once creating trouble and confusion. Obedience to those in authority was a maxim too deeply instilled to be entirely disregarded, yet the presence of cocked hats, gold lace and side arms, was almost too much for that forbearance upon which our ancestors prided themselves.

Through all these radical changes Joseph Tomlinson, as prosecutor of the pleas, attended to his duties, though, if very strict as a Friend, he saw himself surrounded with much that was inconsistent with his notions of propriety, and that taxed his patience to the utmost.

---

[8] Fields's Provincial Courts.

He probably held the position of prosecutor of the pleas until 1710; in this year he was appointed one of the judges of the several courts of Gloucester county, for which position he was well fitted, after having so much experience in the modes and procedures of that branch of the government.[9] Whether he accepted the position with its observances of form and dress, or adhered to the plainness and simplicity of his religious associates, does not appear. He remained a member of the court until his death, doubtless a useful man therein, from his practical knowledge and familiarity with its uses and purposes.

Many of these formalities were adhered to until after the Revolutionary war; in fact, within fifty years of this writing, the judges were escorted from the hotel to the court room by the sheriff, and constables bearing staves, who, in the large counties, made considerable parade. All these have gradually fallen into disuse, until the true republican simplicity of our ancestors is a noticeable feature about our seats of justice.

In the year 1719, Joseph Tomlinson died, leaving his wife Elizabeth and the following named children:[10] Ephraim, who married Sarah Corbit and Catharine Ridgway; Joseph, who married Lydia Wade, of Salem, N. J., and Catharine Fairland, of Chester, Pa., (the last in 1738); Ebenezer; Richard; John, who married Mary Fairland, of Chester, Pa., in 1736; Othniel, who married Mary Marsh, of Salem, N. J.; William, who married Rebecca Wills; Margaret, who married Edward Borton; Elizabeth, who married Bartholomew Wyat, of Salem; Mary, who married Samuel Sharp; and Ann, who married —— Gaunt.[11]

Bartholomew Wyatt came from Worcestershire, England, to Salem county, N. J., about the year 1690. His name first occurs in the Salem Meeting records in 1693, when he was appointed one of a committee to attend the Quarterly Meeting at Newton, Gloucester county, N. J. In the same year (1693), he married Sarah Ashton. They had two children, namely: Bartholomew, born 1697, who married Elizabeth Tomlinson; and Elizabeth, born 1707, who married Robert Smith. The first Bartholomew was a prominent man in the civil affairs of

---

9 Leaming and Spicer's Laws.
10 Lib. No. 2, 136.
11 Lib. No. 4, 122.   Lib. No. 5, 308.

the county, as well as active member of the Society of Friends, and one of the largest contributors to the fund for the erection of the brick meeting-house which once stood in the present graveyard in Salem. He died in 1726.

The second Bartholomew was also an active member of the same religious denomination. In 1730, he was recognized as a preacher, and much respected as a consistent and upright man. His wife, in 1732, also appeared as a public Friend, whose preaching was acceptable. Bartholomew had two children, Bartholomew. and Sarah. The latter married Richard Wistar of Philadelphia.

Ephraim, the oldest son, settled on a tract of land which his father gave him by deed, adjoining the homestead on the east, and extending towards the north branch of Timber creek.[12] In 1732, he purchased of the executors of Abraham Porter, deceased, six hundred and nineteen acres, lying on both sides of the last named stream; which extended his possessions nearly to the south branch of Cooper's creek.[13] He was a preacher among Friends, and held in much estimation. A testimony from the Haddonfield Meeting is abundant evidence of his consistent and exemplary life. He was born in 1695 and departed this life in 1780, leaving a second wife, Catharine, a son, Ephraim, and two daughters,—Elizabeth, who married Aaron Lippincott and Mary, who married James Gardiner.[14]

To the son Joseph, the father devised the homestead property, containing about two hundred acres of land, whereon he settled after the death of the testator. During his life he purchased considerable real estate.[15] He deceased in 1758, leaving a widow, Catharine, two sons, Joseph and Samuel, and three daughters.

By the will of his father, John took about three hundred acres of land higher up Gravelly run, upon which he settled and remained until his decease in 1755. His wife survived him, and also three children, namely: Isaac; Hannah; and Eleanor, who married Josiah Albertson.

William settled on a farm in Waterford township near Haddonfield, which he bought of the executors of John Lord in

---

[12] Lib. DD, 200, O. S. G.
[13] Lib. P, 230.
[14] Lib. P, 187.
[15] Lib. M2, 339, O. S. G.

1733; he lived there but a short time, as he died in 1737. His wife and three sons survived him. They were Samuel, who married Ann Burrough; William; and Daniel, who married Mary Bates.[16]

Othniel, who married Mary Marsh in 1744, first settled in Salem county, and, in the year 1753, removed to Chester county, Pennsylvania, to a place within control of the Concord Monthly Meeting. Othniel died in 1756.[17]

By this marriage there was but one child, Mary, who married Samuel Hibberd in 1770, and who had seven daughters. In 1760, the widow married Aaron Ashbridge. It is not known whether there was any issue by this marriage.[18]

It is probable that others of the sons deceased in their minority, and the daughters, following the fortunes of their husbands, have long since been lost sight of in the genealogical labyrinth built up through this lapse of years. The family has not, however, lost its identity with the first settler, and much of the landed estate owned by him still remains in the name. Of the life of the subject of this sketch, there are doubtless very many interesting incidents, which, by patient research among the musty records still extant, could be brought to light, and would show much of the history of his times, in connection with the progress of the people in their social, judicial and political condition; and which would contrast strangely with such as pervade our system at the present day. That he was a progressive man is shown by his selecting his home so far from the first settlements, in the depth of the wilderness, surrounded only by the aborigines, where nothing but industry and perseverance could procure him a farm.

In connection with these difficulties he became proficient in legal knowledge. He, therefore, attracted the attention of the community, and was called to fill the responsible positions before named. These things, when viewed from a proper standpoint, stamp him as a man whose career through life is worthy of being traced and recorded, and who deserves a much better biography than the foregoing brief and imperfect notice.

---

16 Old Deeds, not recorded.
17 Records of Salem Friends' Meeting.
18 Goshen and Wilmington Meetings, Pa. and Del.

It is perhaps proper, in this connection, to mention that John Tomlinson located and settled on a tract of land at the Indian town of Oneanickon, or Mount Carmel, in the year 1685.[19] This place was in Springfield township, Burlington county, near the old Copany meeting-house. He resided here until 1691, when he sold the same to Matthew Champion, and removed from that locality. It is likely that he was a brother of Joseph, and that he may have settled with him, on the head of Timber creek, as he sold about the time of Joseph's purchase at that place. Of his family nothing is known, and all of the above in relation to him, except the location and sale of the land, is conjecture.

---

19 Revel's Book, 77, 89.

SAMUEL COLE.

SAMUEL COLE and his wife Elizabeth emigrated from Cole's Hill, Hertfordshire, England, and landed on the Jersey shore above Philadelphia. His name does not appear among those given by Smith or Gordon in their histories of the first settlements of New Jersey; the reason for which may be that he came as a servant with but little estate.

He was a haberdasher and hatter, and, in all probability, plied his calling after his arrival here.[1] He came among the first of the emigrants, and made judicious selection of his land whereon to seat himself, but, for some reason, soon after he had erected a dwelling, he sold his first location and removed further into the country. The return of this survey bears date 3d month, 13th, A. D. 1682. It includes five hundred acres of land on the north side of the mouth of Cooper's creek and fronting on the river.[2] William Cooper, who emigrated from the same place, had settled on the opposite side of the stream in the midst of an Indian village, and "over against" the Indian town of Shackomaxin, so that Samuel Cole's plantation was not far from other habitations of man, although in the midst of the primeval forest. Being a neighbor to William Cooper at Cole's Hill, he again finds himself near by; from this it may be inferred that he was governed in his choice by the

---
[1] Lib. G2, 33.
[2] Revel's Book, 63.

advice and direction of his former associate and friend. A few settlements were made near him, bounding upon the creek and laying higher up the stream, that water course at that time being the only highway upon which the people traveled to and from the city of Philadelphia.

He was, perhaps, one of the creditors of Edward Byllynge, as, in 1676, William Penn and the other trustees conveyed to him and Benjamin Bartlet one-ninetieth part of a share of propriety; under which he claimed the title to the land by him taken up.[3,4] Although this was a small portion, yet it placed him upon an equal footing with the largest holders as touching the political affairs of the colony; under this right he was afterwards called to fill several important offices.

Samuel Cole cleared a few acres and built a house on the land which he had located, but soon after sold the buildings and one hundred acres of his survey to Henry Wood, who occupied the same.[5] In 1687, he sold the balance of the survey to Samuel Spicer, as well as a quantity of rights, which Spicer soon appropriated.[6] He had other lands at the same place, which were disposed of to settlers thereabout.

Upon the sale of his dwelling and part of his estate on the Delaware to Henry Wood, he removed to a place called Penisaukin and purchased five hundred acres of Jeremiah Richards (1685), who had previously erected buildings thereon and cleared some land.[7] This was near the settlement of William Matlack, Timothy Hancock and others, but on the south side of the creek that now bears that name. The rights under which Richards had made his survey, he purchased of Henry Stacy, who had emigrated to New Jersey, but soon returned to England, where he deceased. Like most of the settlers, he had not been long the owner, before he gave his place the name of "New Orchard," which name was remembered for many years, but has long since been lost sight of. This plantation was near the head of the south branch of the stream before named, but has years ago lost its identity by the division and sub-division, sale and transfer, incident to real estate in New Jersey. Several other adjoin-

---

[3] Lib. A, 4.
[4] Lib. G2, 33.
[5] Lib. B, 66.
[6] Lib. G, 111.
[7] Lib. B, 75.

ing surveys were made by him, and, at his death, he was the owner of more than one thousand acres of land, then in unbroken forest, but now many valuable farms.[8] The direct and collateral branches of this family are still owners of much of this land.

Samuel Cole had much to do in the political troubles of the province; among which was the settlement of the boundary line between the counties of Burlington and Gloucester, and in which he was personally interested, as his land lay on the stream of water and on both sides of the highway where the trouble existed. He was a member of the Legislature in the years 1683 and 1685, in which last year commissioners were appointed to fix the line, who settled it to be from the forks of Penisaukin, up the south branch to the Salem road; then along the road to the north branch of the same creek; thence to the head thereof; and thence upon a southeast course to the utmost boundary.[9] With this boundary the people about Penisaukin were dissatisfied, and, in 1693, the act was set aside, and the present line was agreed upon about the year 1706.

A few years after Samuel Cole had settled at New Orchard, he returned to England to arrange some unsettled business; in coming back to New Jersey, the vessel touched at the island of Barbadoes, where he was taken sick and died. At this place there was a large settlement of Friends, many of whom had been banished from England during the religious troubles, and many others of whom had gone into voluntary exile, to join their connections and to be free from intolerance and bigotry.

Samuel and Elizabeth Cole had but two children,—Samuel, who married Mary, a daughter of Thomas Kendall; and Sarah, who married James Wild.

Thomas Kendall, above named, came to New Jersey as one of the servants of Daniel Wills. Being a bricklayer, he was a useful man in the province. He built the first corn mill in Gloucester county, in 1697 (now Evans's, near Haddonfield), and became the owner of considerable real estate. As Samuel Cole died intestate, and his widow was appointed administratrix

---

[8] Basse's Book, 29.
[9] Leaming & Spicer's Laws.

ninth month, 23d, 1693, the whole of his real estate descended to his son Samuel, who occupied the same until his death in 1728.[10] He was a man of some political aspirations, having been appointed sheriff in 1710, in 1713 and in 1724. He left a will,[11] and the following named children: Samuel, who married Mary Lippincott; Joseph, who married Mary Wood; Thomas, who married Hannah Stokes; Kendall, who married Ann Budd; Elizabeth, who married Jacob Burcham and Benjamin Cooper; Mary, who married Edward Tonkins; Susanna, who married William Budd; and Rachel, who married Enoch Roberts.

In 1739, the devisees of the second Samuel Cole re-surveyed the original estate, which shows how their ancestors held it. The old house, as erected by the first Samuel Cole, is shown on the map, and is now (1877) standing, but it has been long since abandoned as a dwelling. It is built of logs, is one story high, has two windows and one door. It stands in the door yard of the farm, formerly Joseph H. Cole's, deceased. It is used for various purposes and is fast going to decay. Another generation, and it will be forgotten.

James Wild was a wheelwright, and settled on the north side of the south branch of Penisaukin creek, on five acres of land, which he purchased of John Cowperthwaite in 1712, and at but a short distance from the residence of his father-in-law. He died in 1731, leaving a will.[12] His children were James, Samuel, John, Sarah (who married Jonathan Thomas), Jonathan, Elizabeth, and Rachel. His widow Rachel, who was a second wife, survived him. In his will he speaks of Alexander Morgan as his brother-in-law, but how such relation existed, cannot at this writing be discovered. Four years after, his widow Rachel died, intestate, but leaving some considerable estate. Of this family nothing is known at the present day, as none of the name have lived in this region for many years; and the above defective sketch is only here introduced, that something may be gathered therefrom of interest to such as search with better facilities and greater success.

---

[10] Gloucester Files, 1683.
[11] Lib. No. 3, 02.
[12] Lib. No. 3, 450.

Within the bounds of the land of which Samuel Cole died, seized, on the west side of the King's road from Salem to Burlington, and about one-half mile south of Penisaukin creek, stands St. Mary's church, better known, however, as "the old Cole's Town Church," having been always under the control of the Protestant Episcopal denomination of New Jersey. The history of this church dates back into the beginning of the eighteenth century, and, in all probability, had its origination in the Keithean controversy, which separated many Quaker families from the religious doctrines as laid down by George Fox, and, as a consequence, drew them around the dissenter whose talent and eloquence made the tenets of his new belief attractive and acceptable wherever he preached.

After his separation from Friends, brought about by controversy upon doctrinal points and church discipline, both in America and before the yearly meetings of London, he came again to the colonies under the patronage of the "Society for the Propagation of the Gospel in Foreign Parts," established in London by a few members of the church of England. He traveled through most of the towns and villages from Massachusetts to South Carolina, seeking for his proselytes among the members of the society from which he had been expelled, and established churches in many places where sufficient numbers of his followers lived in the same neighborhood. In his journal, which was published before his death, he says: "September 15th, 1703, I preached at the house of William Heulings in West Jersey," which was but a short distance from where the old church stands, and this may be safely accepted as the beginning of St. Mary's church at Colestown. Although not all the requirements of a religious organization were complied with at once, yet the interest then and there commenced was never lost sight of or abandoned, simply for want of numbers; and the intervals of religious service at the dwelling houses of such adherents as resided thereabout, were never so widely separated as to destroy the connection of George Keith's preaching in 1703 with the ultimate success and establishment of the church.

The first building was erected about the year 1752, and was repaired in 1825, without any change as to the interior arrangement. In subsequent years, and after the same religious denomination had erected churches at Camden, Moorestown and Haddonfield, the old house was suffered to fall into decay, and well nigh tumbled to the ground; but a few of the descendants of the old families that worshiped there, with commendable liberality and good taste, in 1866 again repaired the old house, faithfully preserving its ancient form and antiquated appearance.

In further connection with this matter, John Rudderow, who emigrated from England about the year 1680, and who lived in Chester township, Burlington county, N. J., between the north and south branches of Penisaukin creek, and died in 1729, inserted the following clause in his will: "I give ten pounds towards the building of a church in that place to be convenient hereaway."[13] This man, who settled at the place in which he deceased, was an Episcopalian, and was, no doubt, a participant in the religious quarrel of which George Keith was the leader; around him most of the few families in that region collected, and formed the body of the church. His education (he having graduated as a lawyer in England), and influence in the neighborhood as an upright and conscientious man, would make him, next after Keith, the principal person in such an enterprise, and the devise made in his will shows clearly what was in contemplation even at that early day, and how desirous he was that such an enterprise should be carried out.

After the lapse of a few years, another incident occurred, that establishes an additional link in the history of this church, and that may be held quite as reliable as the devise of John Rudderow, before named; and is, in fact, the connecting link that unites beyond controversy its earlier and latter days. To the perseverance and care of Asa Matlack is due what is recorded of the sayings of Abigail Rudderow (widow of William, who was a grandson of the first John,) touching this matter. This lady was a daughter of Thomas and Rebecca Spicer, and of remarkable intelligence and memory. She was born in 1742, and lived

---

[13] Lib. No. 3, 308.

to the age of eighty-three. She always resided in the neighborhood, and, doubtless, was conversant with every matter of moment which occurred in that section of the country. She was married when she was about sixteen years of age, and lived to see her descendants multiplied in more than ordinary proportion, and scattered through the various States of the Union. Relative to the traditions in question, her own version of it is more interesting than any other:

"At nine years of age I was baptised at the church by Dr. Jenny, which at that time was being built, the roof being on and the weather-boarding up as high as the window sills. The ground had been previously consecrated by Dr. Jenny from Philadelphia."

This gentleman, the Rev. Robert Jenney, A. M., came to New York as chaplain in the royal army stationed in that city. In 1722, he was chosen rector of the church at Rye, in West Chester county, New York, but only remained there four years. He removed to Hempstead on Long Island, and afterwards to Philadelphia as rector of Christ church. He died in 1762, aged seventy-five years.[14]

This baptism, which occurred in 1751, and was so likely to be remembered by Abigail Spicer, fixes the erection of the church beyond a question. Its subsequent history from that time to 1825, the year of her decease, was familiar to her; and how great the regret that some person had not saved it from loss! Being placed upon social equality with the clergy who officiated there, her knowledge of their coming, time of service and removal, was reliable, and would have made the reminiscences of the old chapel of deep interest to such as emulate their forefathers in worshiping around its altar.

The births, baptisms, marriages and burials, were incidents that would naturally attract more or less attention in a rural district; and, with a person whose religious feeling was centred in that spot, they would be indelibly marked upon the memory. Although many years have intervened between the incidents connected with this ancient church, yet they are so linked

---

[14] History of Rye, 312.

together, and relate so plainly to the same object, that its history can be traced through the times of its usefulness without uncertainty or doubt; just as among the land marks of a long neglected pathway that time and circumstances have, in the lapse of years, well nigh destroyed, enough is sometimes left to trace its direction and discover its place. Events are evanescent, passing from the memory, never, perhaps, to be re-called, and, but for the care of some, to make a record thereof, would in a few decades be forgotten.

The high, boxed pulpit, the small, narrow chancel, the dark, ill arranged galleries, and the badly shaped, uncushioned benches, leave no doubt that this structure was erected long before comfort was regarded, or convenience studied. The outside appearance is plain and unpretending; without steeple or belfrey, stained windows or arched roof, it stands, the evidence of simplicity in the taste of our forefathers, and of the little means which they had to expend in such an edifice.

Around the building, and in the small burial ground originally attached, lay the remains of those who worshiped within its walls from time to time, and who, in the fulness of their days, passed to the same account as those before them, strengthening the links of fraternal regard that have connected generation with generation unto the present day.

Of the ministers who have supplied this church at various periods, there is no continuous record. All, however, have acted in the capacity of missionaries, the church standing in a thinly settled neighborhood, and being several miles from any town. William Sturgeon (the assistant of Dr. Jenny, who was then rector of Christ church, Philadelphia,) visited the people once in each month while the house was in progress of building. Nathaniel Evans, a young man of finished education and great talent, had charge also of St. Mary's and the church at Gloucester, and resided with his parents at Haddonfield. He was admitted to holy orders by Dr. Terrick of London, and came immediately to New Jersey in discharge of his duties. He was a man of much literary taste, and a volume of his poems was published after his death, a copy of which may be found in the Franklin Library of Philadelphia. He followed Mr. Sturgeon and took charge of the church when finished, and there he preached for six years. He died October 29th, 1767, at the age of twenty-five, and was buried at Christ church, Philadelphia. An interval of five years now occurred, when Robert Blackwell was selected, November 19th, 1772. He married Rebecca, a daughter of Joseph Harrison, and resided in Haddonfield. During the Revolutionary war, he became a chaplain in the army, and the church was again left without regular service.

Henry Miller, president of the college of Philadelphia, was his successor, and he was soon followed by the Reverend John Wade. He died in 1799. His remains were interred in front of the main entrance to the church, the stone that marks his grave at this day being buried beneath the soil.

Samuel Sprague, who lived in Mount Holly, and ministered in spiritual things to the people of that region of country, occasionally preached here. Andrew Fowler, next followed; in the quaint language of the recorder, "he had a wife and three children and three churches under his charge." When he was there, or how long he remained, is not known. After him came Levi Heath, of Burlington, and then Samuel Pussey, who was the cause of much trouble in the church. He was an impostor, having produced the ordination papers and their accompanying documents of a clergyman who died on the passage over with him. With these testimonials he was accepted as a minister, and so continued until the truth was discovered. In succession came Daniel Higbee in 1807, and, after him, Richard Hall.

The last named person preached there in the year 1811. Since that time, various vicissitudes have befallen the old chapel. As before stated, these facts were gathered by Asa Matlack from Abigail Rudderow, and may be relied upon as correct.

The oldest legible stone now standing in the yard is that of Philip Wallace, who was there buried in 1746, aged eighty-two years; and dated in the same year is that of Mary Wallace, his wife, aged eighty.

These were among the first English settlers about the mouth of the Penisaukin creek, and were Friends until the schism caused by George Keith, when they became his followers and were identified with the church of England. The name is sometimes differently spelled, but the family is the same.

In 1760, Humphrey Day and Jane, his wife, were buried here, the first being seventy-five, and the latter, sixty-five years of age. They lived on the north side of Cooper's creek, owning part of the estate lately held by the Shivers family. He was, perhaps, a son of Steeven Deay (as he spelled it), who was a resident of Chester township, Burlington county, in 1696.

Elias Toy was here interred in 1762, aged forty-seven years. His residence was in the last named county near the river shore, where part of his land still remains in the name. He was a descendant of one of the Swedish families who settled on the shores of the Delaware long before the English came, and whose ancestors worshiped at Tinakum and Wicaco, much after the faith and forms of the Protestant Episcopal church of the present day.

Many of the rude, rough monuments erected there to point to the resting place of friends and families have yielded to time and exposure, showing at this date only parts of letters and figures, from which nothing definite can be deciphered.

If a descendant of "Old Mortality" had chanced here a hundred years ago, wandering through the country, clad in hodden gray, with black cloth leggins and strong clouted shoes, riding upon a white pony around whose neck there hung a canvass pouch containing his tools, following the bent of his ancestor with the same sincere devotion, he would have found here abundant room to gratify his strange, but commendable vocation.

Here, day after day, could have been seen his faithful beast, tethered among the graves, to seek, as best he could, a precarious living, while his master sat upon the defaced tombstones, striving, with chisel and hammer, to restore the almost worn-out names and dates to their original freshness. Refusing any reward, save the bare entertainment of himself and beast, his acts would have been held in grateful remembrance by those who, but for him, might have sought in vain for relatives or friends in this long neglected spot. Considering it a religious duty and upon himself incumbent, nothing would have hindered him except his answers to the words of some observer curious to know his object, and then, only to clear his glasses and arrange his tools, the better to prosecute the work before him. The task completed, and his pony saddled for his departure, he, perchance, would have repeated the memorable language of his predecessor in view of the kind offices extended to him. "The blessing of our Master be with you. My hours are like the ears of the latter harvest, but your days are in the spring; yet you may be gathered into the garner of mortality before me, for the sickle of death cuts down the green as oft as the ripe; and there is a colour in your cheek that, like the bud of the rose, serveth oft to hide the worm of corruption. Wherefore labour as one who knoweth not when his master calleth. And, if it be my lot to return to this spot after ye are gone home to your own place, these old withered hands will frame a stone of memorial that your name may not perish from among the people."

Other associations than these are, however, around this place. Along the King's road, which passed close to the door, traveled all those going north or south to various parts of the province, when our State was in its infancy, and the dwellings of the settlers were separated by miles of forest; while here stood the church in a lonely spot, like an oasis in the wilderness, inviting the travelers to rest under the shade of the broad topped oaks that grew near. If it were an ancient burial place of the Indians, none of the tribes but would pause, in going to their hunting grounds, to show their reverence for the graves of their fathers.

Along this highway moved the contending armies during the Revolutionary war, and, no doubt, the doors of the church were open alike to friend or foe. Here, under the protection of the standard of St. George, listened British officers to the preaching of their chaplains, resting on their way to carnage and death, to hear the persuasive eloquence of the teachers of religion. Here, likewise, may the immortal Washington have laid aside his sword, and, kneeling at the little chancel, have partaken of the Holy Communion, after the rector had preached "peace on earth and good will to men." Here, the representatives of the King acknowledged the same religious creed that the early teachings of a mother had left upon the then impressible memory of the great commander.

In this connection, it is gratifying to know that this relic of olden times has been preserved to the present generation, through the liberality of those who regard the days of their ancestors and hold fast to antiquated things. Would that more were like them.

Elizabeth, the widow of the first Samuel Cole, married Griffith Morgan, who was a mariner, and resided in Philadelphia. The license of marriage was granted by the chancellor of Pennsylvania, and bears date December 10th, 1693. In 1697, he purchased a tract of land of William Frampton, situated in Gloucester county near the mouth of Penisaukin creek, whereon he settled, and remained until his decease. He also owned other land in Gloucester county, as, in 1677, he purchased real estate of David Lloyd and Isaac Norris. The issue of this marriage was one son,—Alexander, who married Hannah, the daughter of Joseph and Lydia Cooper, and grand-daughter of William the first settler. Alexander remained on the homestead estate, which, before his death, became valuable. The children of Alexander and Hannah Morgan were Joseph, who married Agnes Evans; Benjamin, who married Jane Roberts; Isaac; Mary, who married Edmund Hollingshead; Elizabeth, who married William Miller; Lydia, who married Nathan Beeks; and Sarah, who married Josiah Burrough. Both the Coles and the Morgans that came from the same maternal ancestors are, at this time, connected with the most respectable families in the country, and have spread through all the United States.

SAMUEL NICHOLSON.

AMONG the few persons who ventured with John Fenwick across the ocean to make the first settlement upon the land in which he had become interested by purchase from Lord John Berkley in 1673, were Samuel Nicholson, his wife Ann, and their children. They came from Wiston, in Nottinghamshire, England, in the ship "Griffith" of London, Robert Griffin, master. They arrived in the Delaware river upon the 9th month, 23d, 1675. Their children were as follows:

Parabol, born second month, 7th, 1659;
Elizabeth, born third month, 22d, 1664;
Samuel, born eighth month, 30th, 1666;
Joseph, born second month, 30th, 1669;
Abel, born fifth month, 2d, 1672.[1]

This little company ended their voyage upon the river Delaware, at Elsinburg, where they found a few Swedes, some Indians, and myriads of mosquitoes, of which last they had heard but little previously, although they now were among the first to make their acquaintance. They were the pioneers of the English colonists, and, but for the sanguine temperament and determined character of their leader, might have allowed the discouragements that surrounded them to induce an abandonment of the undertaking, and a return to their homes. There could be nothing in the prospect before them that was in the least

---
[1] Friends' Records of Salem, N. J.

inviting; to the females, especially, it must have been dark indeed. They could not expect to obtain anything from the soil for more than a year, for it was still covered with timber, and in no condition for raising a crop. The feelings of the Indians towards them were yet to be discovered, and, if their conduct towards those who had preceded them in the Massachusetts colony, was to be an index, they derived but little comfort in that direction.

The Dutch and the Swedes had driven off a colony of emigrants who came from New Haven in 1641, and had made a settlement on "Varken's kill" now Salem creek; and, at the time when Fenwick came, no vestige of their habitations could be found. The jealousy of these people, as well as the suspicions of the Indians, had to be overcome, and no small degree of diplomacy was exercised to steer clear of these difficulties that surrounded them at once.

The High Court at Upland had judicial authority over the Dutch and the Swedes on the eastern shore of the river, and the church at Tinacum was the place whither they all went to attend to their religious duties, and to have their children christened. These were powers and prejudices hard to overcome, and so antagonistic to the theory and practice of those who now proposed to make a settlement, that no compromise could reconcile the differences; and, to a disinterested spectator, this state of affairs would appear likely to lead to difficulty and trouble. Although John Fenwick was impetuous and hasty in much that he did when opposed, especially when his absolute authority over the land of which he claimed to be the owner was questioned, yet the forbearance and good counsel of those who were with him, prevented any trouble with his neighbors, so far as the management of their religious affairs was concerned.

Immediately after, or, perhaps, before they had landed, "the agreements" between the patroon and the planters were drawn up and signed by each of them. These may now be seen in the office of the Secretary of State at Trenton, in a good state of preservation.[2] The document is dated June 28th, 1675; it embodies all the elements of a good government, and upon

---

[2] Salem Records.

this was afterwards established the kind of authority that made the colony a desirable place for settlement. Among the thirty-three persons who put their signatures to this paper, and who were mostly heads of families, may be found the name of Samuel Nicholson, signed by his own hand, which, by its style, shows him to have been a man of some education.

Steps were immediately taken to extinguish the Indian title; this was done for a satisfactory consideration, by three deeds from several chiefs, who held the territory bounded by several large streams, by which the grants were defined therein. This was a proper and just movement, and, although the privileges of the aborigines were not abridged in their hunting and fishing expeditions, yet their ideas of right were met and satisfied, to the avoidance of any trouble in the future.

As soon as abodes were provided for their families, which consisted of the humblest kind of habitations, a religious meeting was established after the order of the Society of Friends, and held at private houses for several years.[3] These meetings took place twice in each week for divine worship, and once in each month for church discipline. It is curious and interesting to examine the records of the Friends meeting at that place, and to notice the various movements taken to secure a locality for public worship.

Upon the fourth month, 2d, 1679, Richard Guy, Edward Bradway, Nathan Smart and Edward Wade were appointed to go on the seventh instant, and select a place for a meeting house and burial ground, and to report at the next monthly meeting. Upon the eleventh month, 5th, 1679, Edward Wade, James Nevil, John Maddox and George Deacon were appointed a committee to *treate* with Samuel Nicholson and William Penton for their houses and plantations in Salem; and, also, to see the widow Salter about her plantation, &c. Upon the twelfth month, 2d, 1679, George Deacon, John Maddox, George Azeheard and Henry Jennings were appointed to take a view of Edward Bradway's house for a meeting house.

At this meeting a minute was made, fixing fourth day and first day as the times for religious worship; the first of which meet-

---

[3] Johnson's History of Salem, 98.

ings was to be held at Robert Zane's house, the next at Samuel Nicholson's house, and the next at Richard Guy's house. This arrangement put at rest, for a short time, the trouble about a meeting house; and not until the seventh of the fourth month, in the next year, does anything further relative to the subject appear. Then the subscription list was entered, showing who contributed, and the amount given by each person.

Upon the ninth month, 1st, 1680, another committee was appointed, to *treate* with Edward Champneys for a lot on which to build a meeting house and a burial lot, and to report at the next Monthly Meeting. Soon after this, some arrangement had been made with Samuel Nicholson for his property, for on the 3d of the eleventh month, 1680, John Thompson and Robert Zane were appointed to look after the repairing of Samuel Nicholson's house (lately by him occupied) for a meeting house, "and forthwith get said house fit for Friends to meet in."

The next year, Samuel Nicholson and Ann, his wife, conveyed to the trustees of the Salem meeting his sixteen acre lot, whereon stood the house aforesaid; and the same committee was directed to enlarge the house by adding "sixteen feet in length, and in height equal to the old frame, with a chimney and pair of stairs." For some reason, this was not done until the next year, when another committee was named for that purpose. Samuel Nicholson's house was, therefore, the first building set apart for public religious worship in West New Jersey. Various alterations were subsequently made in the arrangement of the galleries, and in the mode of heating. This latter was done by large, open fire places built in the ends of the house,—a method which did much to preserve a circulation of pure air in the room, but very little towards making it comfortably warm. Several attempts were made to have the floor constructed of boards; but they failed, as, on the twenty-seventh day of the twelfth month, 1687, Benjamin Knapton and Thomas Woodroose were appointed a committee to have both the old and the new end of the meeting house floored with a "good clay floor," and to have it ready before the yearly meeting. The windows consisted of four panes each, of thick bull's-eye glass, seven inches by nine in size, and set in heavy sash. The doors were clumsy and small, cut horizontally in two parts, and had long iron hinges and wooden latch. Imagine a large open fire place in each end, no ceiling under the roof, and the benches without backs or cushions, and some idea of the inside appearance of this place of worship may be had. Forty-feet in front and sixteen feet in depth, part of frame and part of brick, and, perhaps, ten feet in heighth of story—these items give a fair description of the outside of a building which, at this day, would be looked upon as an odd structure for such uses.

The first Yearly Meeting held at Salem was on the fifteenth day of the second month, 1684; but the Burlington Friends neglected to send a committee,—a matter duly noticed. The next Yearly Meeting there held was on the twelfth day of the second month, 1687; afterwards, the time for such meetings was changed to the twenty-seventh day of the second month, and so yearly, "from inconveniences and impediments being seen in the meeting falling out so early in the spring." These meetings were continued at that place for several years, making it clear that Friends thereabout were able to entertain, and that their place of worship had capacity to receive the strangers thus coming among them.

At the Yearly Meeting held in Salem in the second month, from the twenty-seventh to the thirty-first, 1693, George Keith appeared with his friends, and laid before the meeting their proposals for the settlement of the differences among them. These were in the shape of several propositions, covering the points at issue and discussing the reasons for their adoption. This led to much controversy, and to the final separation of many members from the society. These proposals were signed by Jeremiah Collat, John Penrose, Nathaniel Sykes, Anthony Taylor, Samuel Cooper, Isaac Jacobs, James Shattuck, Samuel Adams, George Keith, Thomas Budd, Henry Furnass, Nicholas Pierce, Robert Granna, William Budd, Benjamin Morgan, Thomas Withers and Andrew Griscom.

Thomas Sharp of Newton was clerk, at that time, of the Yearly Meeting, wherein, no doubt, much excitement existed, and many controversies were had touching the merits of the matters before them, which so sadly vexed the church. The persons who signed the proposals with George Keith were influential in the communities in which they lived, and were well calculated to draw many other valuable members with them to the new dogmas, as laid down by this bold and popular dissenter.

The arrival of new settlers, the frugality and industry of the old ones, and the evident success of the colony, made it necessary that some new and better accommodations should be had for the religious meetings held in that place. The old house met the wants of the society for several years; but, on the twenty-ninth day of the sixth month, 1698, a committee of the Monthly Meeting was appointed to "have a new meeting-house erected." In the same year they agreed with Richard Woodnutt to do the brick work, and Robert Gillman to do the wood work. Matters did not go far, however, before the meeting decided that the house according to the plan would prove too small, and ordered it to be increased to one of forty feet in front by thirty feet in depth. Whether it was erected on the site of the old one does not appear, but the capacity of the new was not very much greater than the old house, nor were its proportion any better.

On the thirtieth day of the first month, 1702, the committee reported the building finished, and that the entire cost was four hundred and twenty-five pounds, thirteen shillings and two pence. The long list of subscribers, and the amount of money severally paid, show how rapidly the neighborhood was being occupied, and the increase of wealth among the inhabitants. Several Friends in other parts contributed; Samuel Carpenter, then a resident of Philadelphia, gave fifteen pounds; Samuel Jennings of Burlington gave five pounds, and many others contributed, who doubtless were frequent visitors, and felt an interest in the comfort and convenience of this religious society.

Next after the patroon, Samuel Nicholson was, perhaps, the wealthiest man in the colony at that time, as he appears to have made several large surveys of land in the county, and also several purchases of real estate. He did not remain in Salem many years, but removed to a plantation which he owned upon

---

4 Salem Records No. 2.

Alloway's creek or Monmouth river, as it was then called, where he died in 1685, intestate.[4] He took an active part in the religious and political advancement of the colony, but does not appear to have participated very much in the difficulties of John Fenwick with the Dutch and the English authorities. They claimed that he was a usurper, and must, consequently, be driven away or imprisoned; this latter misfortune befell him, much to his discomfiture and pecuniary loss. The oath of Samuel Nicholson to show his allegiance to the government of John Fenwick is here copied, it being the same that was taken by most of the planters upon their arrival:

"I, Samuel Nicholson, of the Town of New Salem, in Fenwick Colony, in the Province of New Cæsarea or New Jersey in America, Planter, do hereby declare and promise that I will endeavor to promote the honor of Almighty God in all my undertakings, who is the King of Kings and requires all men to do justly, love mercy, and walk humbly with their God; and, accordingly, I do further declare and promise that I will bear true allegiance to the King of England, his heirs and successors, and also that I will be faithful to the interest of John Fenwick, Lord or Chief Proprietor of the said colony, his heirs, Executors and assigns, and endeavour the peace and welfare of him, them and of his said Colony accordingly. In witness whereof, I have hereunto set my hand, this July 5th, 1676, in the twenty-eighth year of the Reign of King Charles Second, &c."[5]

Samuel Nicholson must have been a favorite of the patroon, for he gave him his choice of lots in the town of Salem, which contained sixteen acres with a tract of marsh fronting on the creek. On this tract of sixteen acres he built his house, which, afterwards, was used by the Friends as the place of meeting before named.

Ann, the wife of Samuel Nicholson, survived him and died in 1694. Of the children, Parabol married Abraham Strand in 1677; Elizabeth married John Abbott; Samuel died in 1694, without family and unmarried; Abel married Mary, a daughter

---

[5] Salem Surveys, 1676.

of William Tyler; and Joseph married Hannah, a daughter of Henry Wood, in 1695.[6]

John Abbott and his wife Elizabeth deceased before Ann Nicholson, leaving three children, Rachel, Mary and Elizabeth. Abel settled in Elsinboro on the homestead property, and died in 1751.[7] His children by his first wife were Sarah, Rachel, Abel, Joseph, William, Mary, John; Ruth, who married John Evans and Samuel Clement; Samuel, who married Sarah Dennis; and Ann, who married John Brick. His second wife, Isabella, survived him.

In the Friends' meeting at Salem there was, perhaps, no more influential and active person than Abel Nicholson. The minutes show that upon almost every important committee he was named. Among the young people he seems to have been a particular favorite, as scarcely a wedding occurred in which his name may not be found among those who attended on behalf of the meeting, to see that everything was conducted in an orderly manner.

Upon the death of Bartholomew Wyatt, he was appointed to fill his place as one of the overseers of the meeting, and, in 1733, was made an elder. In 1729, he married Isabella Daniels, but by this marriage there was probably no issue. Some of his children came into Gloucester and Burlington counties; through whom some of the present generations may trace their lineage.

Henry Wood, whose daughter married Joseph Nicholson, in 1682, purchased one hundred acres of Samuel Cole, in Waterford township, near the mouth of Cooper's creek, fronting on the river, with the buildings put thereon by Cole; to this place he removed, and there remained during his life. He called this place "Hopewell."[8]

The same year in which Joseph Nicholson married his daughter, he removed from Salem county to a tract of land on the north side of Cooper's creek, that he had previously purchased; here he built a house and made a settlement. In 1699, he purchased an adjoining tract of James, a grandson of Henry

---

6 Salem Wills A, 120, 143. Salem Wills No. 5 41.

7 Salem Wills A, 120. Lib. No. 7, 250.

8 Lib. B1, 66.

Wood, which made his landed estate quite large at the time of his death.

Samuel Nicholson, the brother of Joseph, in his will gave him his entire estate; the land of which he sold to George Abbott in 1696. The deed says, "Joseph Nicholson, late of Salem county, now of Gloucester county." This language establishes the identity of Joseph beyond any question, and connects the family hereabout with Samuel, the first comer.

Joseph Nicholson deceased in 1702, intestate,[9] and leaving but two children, George, who married Alice Lord in 1717, and Samuel, who had three wives. These were as follows: in 1722, he married Sarah, a daughter of Samuel Burrough; in 1744, he married Rebecca Saint, and, in 1749, he married Jane Albertson, the widow of William, and daughter of John Engle. The last named female was somewhat remarkable in her marriage relations, having had four husbands and, probably, dying a widow. The husbands were John Turner, William Albertson, Samuel Nicholson, and Thomas Middleton.

As the oldest son, Samuel inherited the landed estate of his father, and had his residence on the tract of land purchased of James Wood in 1699. This he re-surveyed in 1733, which survey discloses the title and the number of acres contained in the same.[10] He was neighbor to the Spicers, the Woods, and Humphrey Day, all of which families and names have long since been lost sight of in that region.

Samuel Nicholson deceased in 1750, leaving the following named children; but how distributed among the several wives, there is no means at this time of discovering.[11] Joseph, the first son, married Catharine Butcher, of Burlington, in 1738; in 1749, he purchased half an acre of land of John Gill in Haddonfield, at which place he at that time resided. This piece of land is situated on the west side of the main street, and is now owned by Joseph B. Tatem. He probably built the house now standing on the lot; but of this there are no certain data. Abel married Rebecca Aaronson, daughter of Aaron; Abigail married Daniel Hillman in 1743, and John Gill in

---

9 Files of Gloucester Wills.
10 Lib M, 159, O. S. G.
11 Lib. No. 7, 02.

1767; Hannah married John Hillman; and Sarah died single in 1756. Abel deceased in 1761, and before his first child was born. This proved to be a son, who was named for his father, and subsequently married Rebecca, a daughter of Isaac Ellis. The widow of Abel married Isaac Burrough, and deceased in 1768. From the last named Abel, the family in this immediate neighborhood has descended. A few of the name reside in Salem county, but the family is not large. In tracing this family, care should be taken not to confound it with that of George Nicholson, who came from Borton Stathers, in Lincolnshire, England, and settled in Burlington county, N. J.[12] His wife's name was Hannah, and their children were Grace, born in 1677; Samuel, born in 1679; George, born in 1680; Joseph, born in 1684, and Mercy, born in 1687. Samuel died at Chester, Pennsylvania, in 1684. Joseph and Mercy were born at the same place, the other children being born before the coming of the parents to America. They probably came among those designing to remain in Pennsylvania under the patronage of William Penn, but finally settling in New Jersey.

---

12 Friends' Records, Cherterfield Meeting, Burlington Co.

THOMAS HOWELL.

THOMAS HOWELL was an Englishman, and lived in Staffordshire previously to his removal to New Jersey.[1] It is somewhat uncertain whether he was a creditor of Edward Byllynge, although the record would seem to show that he was; yet, if so, he did not have his debts discharged directly by that man.

Benjamin Bartlett (or Braclett, as it is sometimes written,) married Gracia, a daughter of Byllynge,[2] through whom many of the sales of proprieties were made, and who, surviving her husband and father, in 1728,[3] sold all the remainder of her interests in New Jersey, derived as the only heir and surviving child of her father, to Daniel Coxe, of London, whose son Daniel came here to look after his father's estate, and made so much trouble in the political affairs of the colony.[4]

The first estate that Thomas Howell acquired in New Jersey, was through Benjamin Bartlett and wife, in 1675, who conveyed him the one-half of one-ninetieth part of one whole share; under which he proceeded in 1685 to sever his interest from the common stock in land.[5] Although his name does not appear among those who first arrived here, yet he, no doubt, came among the earliest adventurers, and brought some considerable personal property, consisting of household goods and

---

[1] Lib. G2, 33.
[2] Lib. A, 24.
[3] Lib. EF, 370.
[4] Lib. A, 24.
[5] Lib. G2, 33.

money. It is probable that his immediate residence in Staffordshire was at Tamworth, a town in the western part of that county,[6] about one hundred and ten miles northeast of the city of London, for, in a division of his estate among his children in 1687, his son Daniel received that property as part of his share.[7-8] In a subsequent agreement between Daniel and Mordecai, the estate passed to the latter, who, in all probability, retained it during his life,[9] it being the ancestral residence of the family, and for this reason deserving his adherence thereto. It does not appear that Thomas Howell was a Friend; if such, he did not participate much in the religious affairs of that society. The short time that he lived after his settlement here may account for this, as he deceased in 1687, only a few years after his arrival. He was, however, a member of the Assembly in 1683, but only served a single year.[10]

The survey he made, fronting on the north side of Cooper's creek, in Waterford (now Delaware) township, included what is generally known as the Jacob Troth farm, on the east, and extended down that stream nearly one mile, and back into "the woods" about the same distance. This tract of land is, at the present day, divided into many valuable farms.[11] It was located for six hundred and fifty acres, but doubtless contained within its bounds a much larger quantity of land. Thomas Howell erected a dwelling on the same, and there resided for the little time that he lived after his settlement. Without any tradition as to where his house stood, the probability is that it was near the creek, and perhaps where the buildings on the "Barton" farm have been erected. He called his place "Christianity."[12]

The will of Thomas Howell has no date, but is undoubtedly a genuine document. It discloses some matters of interest which deserve notice here.[13] Reference is made to his wife's not coming to America, of whom he appeared to know nothing at the time of making his will. He makes provision for her, however, which shows that he had some regard for her comfort, although she did not choose to participate in his adventure.

---

6 Lib. G2, 42.
7 Lib. G2, 62.
8 Lib. G1, 42.
9 Lib. G1, 42.
10 Leaming & Spicer's Laws.
11 Revel's Book, 68.
12 Lib. B, 140.
13 Gloucester Files, 1693.

The will is not signed by the testator, but is subscribed to by three witnesses, who appeared when the same was offered for probate. The court allowed, and the devisees accepted the will as valid. It doubtless conformed to the custom of the Dutch courts in like cases, prevalent in New York at that date and for many years after. He made other locations in Gloucester county, which showed him to be a man with means to buy, and of good judgment in the location of his land. His family consisted of a wife, three sons and three daughters, namely: Samuel; Daniel, who married Hannah Lakin, of Philadelphia, in 1686; Mordecai; Priscilla, who married Robert Stiles; Marion, who married Henry Johnson; and Catharine.[14] Before his death in 1687, Thomas Howell sold Richard Wright one hundred acres of his land on Cooper's creek, where the family of the latter lived for several years thereafter.[15]

Of the son Samuel, nothing appears to indicate that he was in New Jersey as he did not join in any of the conveyances of real estate after his father's death, nor is his name mentioned at all, except in the will of his father. The son Mordecai was one of the witnesses in the controversy between the Penns and Lord Baltimore. In this, he says that he came to America about the year 1682, and ascended the Delaware river in company with the ship that brought William Penn to Philadelphia. This evidence was given by him in 1736, which proves that he did not decease before that date.

After Thomas Howell's death, his son Mordecai returned to the paternal estate at Tamworth, England, and there remained about three years.[16] Afterwards, he returned and lived on the homestead property on Cooper's creek.[17] In 1697, he sold to Henry Franklin, a bricklayer of New York, a part of the original tract, which the latter sold to John Champion, in three years after.[18] Perhaps Franklin never came thither, but sold to Champion, who then resided at Hempstead, in the same state; from which place he removed soon after, remaining until his death. He called his place "Livewell," being situated on that

---

14 Gloucester Files, 1687. Friends' Records, Phila. Lib. G1, 42. Lib. G3, 17.
15 Lib. G1, 14. Lib. G2, 114, 117, 120. 121.
16 Lib. G1, 42. Lib. G2, 42.
17 Lib. G2, 114. Lib. G3, 03, 08.
18 Lib. G3, 122, 465.

part of the estate now known as the "Champion farm," which name has much significance, and perhaps originated with those who enjoyed the hospitality and good cheer of the owner.[19]

Previously to this sale, Mordecai Howell had erected a saw mill on a small branch near the easterly part of the tract, where that stream emptied into Cooper's creek. This mill was kept in use many years after it came into the hands of John Champion. In 1687, Thomas Howell (the father) erected the dam; but he was indicted by the grand jury of the county for stopping the water of the stream contrary to law, and consequently abandoned the work.

It is probable that Catharine, the widow of Thomas Howell, came to America with the son Mordecai upon his return, as she was a resident of Philadelphia in 1693, and conveyed eighty-eight acres of land to Henry Johnson, then about to marry the daughter Marion.[20] This was part of the estate on Cooper's creek, on which the son Mordecai at that time lived. Henry Johnson subsequently took up his abode there with his wife, and through their family, the property passed to other names.

Robert Stiles, who married the daughter Priscilla, settled on the north side of the south branch of Penisaukin creek on land now owned by Samuel Roberts. He deceased in 1728, leaving two sons, Robert and Ephriam; from whom have sprung the family of that name in these parts.[21]

Gabriel Thomas, the first historian of West New Jersey, thus speaks of the head of this family. "The trade of Gloucester county consists chiefly in pitch, tar and rosin, the latter of which is made by Robert Styles, an excellent artist in that sort of work, for he delivers it as clear as any Gum Arabick."

Thomas Howell, in his will, gave his daughter Priscilla one hundred acres of the homestead property. This herself and husband, in 1690, conveyed to her brother Mordecai.[22]

The minute book of the supreme court of New Jersey—still in good preservation, commencing 1681, and now in the vaults of the office of the supreme court, at Trenton—presents a curious trial of Daniel and Mordecia Howell in 1685, for

---

19 Lib. G3, 03.
20 Lib. G3, 17.
21 Lib. G2, 94.
22 Lib. B, 94.

shooting and carrying away the hogs of William Cooper. They were indicted, tried and convicted, the court sitting at Burlington, and were fined five pounds each. The trial, which was a protracted one, discloses the peculiar manner of our ancestors in conducting such cases. The identity of the porkers was the turning point in the case, as the ears had been cut off, and the marks destroyed. But when Daniel Cooper, son of William, testified to having seen a dead hog on the back of one of the defendants, before its ears were cut off, and identified it as one of his father's swine, there was no room for further doubt, and hence the conviction. There was much of that kind of litigation among the old folks hereabout, as the neglect to enter the "ear marks" in the court records was often a means by which persons escaped punishment.

In 1687, Daniel sold his brother Mordecai two hundred and fifty acres of land with the buildings on Cooper's creek, probably the farm on which their father deceased.[23] In 1688, Daniel sold one hundred acres of the homestead to Moses Lakin, bounded by the stream before named.[24] This person was, probably, a brother of his wife; but it does not appear that he ever occupied it. He subsequently disposed of a great amount of proprietory rights to various persons, showing that his landed estate in New Jersey was large and valuable.[25]

In 1690, Daniel Howell sold sixty acres, part of the original tract, to Josiah Appleton, which joined other lands owned by John and Richard Appleton, at a place then called Apple-town. This was a village which stood near the most westerly boundary of the original tract fronting the navigation of Cooper's creek, and, no doubt, deriving many advantages therefrom.[26] What tradition and ancient records have done for the faithful searchers after the curious and the true among the almost forgotten stories and neglected books that attract the attention of antiquarians, has escaped the notice of such seekers, in order to bring down to the present generation the site and history of Apple-town,—a place that had a name and a locality in 1690, but, at the present day, has left no trustworthy memorials.

---

23 Lib. G2, 62.
24 Lib. G1, 83.

25 Lib. G2, 104, 108.
26 Lib. B2, 442.

In the year 1691, he removed from Cooper's creek to a new residence near Philadelphia, which he called Hartsfield; and, after a short stay at that place, he removed thence to "Stacy's Mills," at the falls of the Delaware; around which place now stands the city of Trenton.[27] Mahlon Stacy, who came over with the first emigrants, made a large survey on both sides of the Assunpink creek at this place, and erected a corn mill thereon. A Friends' meeting was established, and the buildings erected thereabouts soon began to assume the proportions of a town. In 1714, Mahlon Stacy, son of Mahlon who deceased in 1703, sold this property, which his father called Bathfield, to William Trent, from whom the present name of the city was derived; previously to this sale, however, considerable of the land had been purchased in small parcels, whereon to erect dwellings.

Among the first and most prominent of the settlers there, the name of Daniel Howell occurs, who may have been a son of Thomas, before named. His religious proclivities were Presbyterian, as he was an active man in that denomination, and resided there when the first church was erected. If these suggestions are correct, then the descendants of Daniel Howell in and about the city of Trenton can make the connection with their emigrant ancestors complete, and can know where he lived the little time in which he remained in the forests of New Jersey, as well as his place of nativity in England, where, no doubt, the lineage of the family can be traced for many generations beyond his departure.[28]

Mordecai Howell was quite a land jobber, and dealt largely in real estate in Gloucester county. In 1702, he purchased the Lovejoy survey of Henry Tredway. This included all that part of Haddonfield, lying east of Main street, as far south as Ellis street, and the "corn mill" built by Thomas Kendall, which stood near the present mill, now owned by the heirs of Josiah B. Evans, deceased.[29] While he held this property, he located fifty acres of land on the opposite side of the stream, bounded on the north by Buckman's run, which falls into Cooper's creek,

---
27 Lib. G2, 138, 140.
28 Lib. No. 3, 382.
29 Basse's Book, 239.

at a short distance below where the present mill stands. By this survey, the place then called Uxbridge, but having long since lost its identity, is clearly defined. It may be said to have been where the Salem road crossed the creek, before the King's highway was laid by law, nearly in its present position. This point was about one-fourth of a mile above the mouth of the run before named, and, no doubt, above the head of the pond as the flow then stood; which pond was a diminutive affair, in comparison to the beautiful sheet of water that now covers the same and much larger premises. The name, however, was not confined to the particular place, but was applied generally to the surrounding neighborhood; yet, as the road was changed and the bridge went to decay, the name, in like manner, was, in the lapse of time, forgotten.

Near the head of the south branch of Cooper's creek in Gloucester township, he purchased several adjoining tracts of land of different persons; part of which was sold to Joseph Thorne in 1706,[30] who sold part to Joseph Bates in the same year.[31] This property adjoined the estate of John Hillman, including several farms around where the White Horse tavern now stands. The deed made by him to Joseph Thorne included the homestead estate on Cooper's creek, and, perhaps, extinguished his title to land in West New Jersey.

At the time of the last sale he had removed to Chester county, Pennsylvania; previously to which he had visited the home of his ancestors in England to look after the interests given to him by his father.[32] His residence being beyond the bounds of New Jersey, there is no means of tracing him to the time of his decease. He was probably a bachelor, as his signatures to the various conveyances made by him stand alone, conclusive that, however large his estate, he did not halve his sorrows and double his joys by taking to himself a helpmate in the days of his youth. Alas, for him!

---

30 Lib. G3, 3.
31 Lib. A, 84.
32 Lib. A, 84.

WILLIAM MATLACK.

"WILLIAM MATLACK of the county of Burlington in the Province of West Jersey, aged about seventy-two years, came before me the underwritten, being his Majesty's Judge of the Common Pleas for said county, and, upon his solemn affirmation, did declare that he, the said William Matlack, about the latter end of October in the year (1677), came to Burlington along with his then master Daniel Wills, who was one of the commissioners for laying out the lands in the Western Division of New Jersey, and several others in the first boate that came there to settle the said Towne of Burlington; and that, as soon as he and the rest were landed, he was present and saw the lots fairly drawn for the nine acre lots mentioned in the next page and on the other side of this leaf in this book; which lots were surveyed by Richard Noble; and that the said lots fell to the ten persons mentioned in said page, and in the three following pages, and in the same order as they are there set down. And further, this deponent says that he is well assured and very well knows that the said Richard Noble was appointed surveyor by the commissioners, and did soon after survey all the remaining part of the Island on the west side of the High street, and bounded by the river and creek; and when it was divided, it was lotted to the said ten persons according as in the said two pages it is particularly described.

"Attested before me, this tenth day of December, in the seventh year of the reign of King George of Great Britain, Anno Domini 1720.   "JOSHUA HUMPHREYS."[1]

---
[1] Basse's Book, 216.

From the foregoing declaration much information may be gathered beside that which pertains to the subject in question. It discloses the age of William Matlack in 1720; it shows that he had attained his majority before his arrival in America. According to an agreement then common among the emigrants, he was to serve Daniel Wills for four years after his coming hither; in which service he worked as a carpenter. They came in the ship "Kent," Gregory Marlow, master; after having touched at Sandy Hook, they found their way into the river Delaware, and, from some unknown cause, the passengers were landed near the mouth of Raccoon creek.[2] Their destination was evidently higher up the stream, as the commissioners soon left the vessel, and proceeded in a small boat to Chygoe's island (afterwards Burlington), and, according to a tradition in the family, William Matlack "was the first person that put his foot upon the shore." It is also shown that the island referred to was not that in the river, but the piece of land on which the city of Burlington stands, nearly surrounded by the Assiscunk creek, which, Samuel Smith says, procured its name from an Indian sachem who lived there. The first "boate" mentioned was the little craft in which the commissioners and a few other persons came from Raccoon creek, and not the ship Kent, which was probably injured, and did not proceed to the end of the voyage. The passengers, after suffering many privations, mostly found their way to Burlington, and settled in the neighborhood.

William Matlack came from a small village in Nottinghamshire, England, called Cropwell Bishop, which lies about seven miles southeast of the city of Nottingham. As a mechanic, he worked upon the first houses built in Burlington, and helped to erect Thomas Olive's corn mill, the first of that kind in West Jersey. He saw a town rise up in the midst of the forest, surrounded by a thriving population, busy in clearing the land and enjoying the reward of their labor. His leisure hours were spent among the natives, watching their peculiarities and striving to win their good will. Following the advice and example of the commissioners, every promise made by him to the aborigines was faithfully kept, and every contract strictly adhered to.

---

[2] Smith's History of New Jersey, 93.

In 1681, there came from Brayles, a small town in the southern part of Warwickshire, a young man named Timothy Hancock, accompanied by his sister, who was about fifteen years of age. Without friends or means, they lived in a very humble manner among the settlers, but the demand for workmen soon found Timothy employment, and the demand for wives did not leave Mary long without a suitor. She was married to the subject of this sketch the next year. They then removed to a tract of land which he had located between the north and south branch of Penisaukin creek in Chester township, Burlington county.[3] Her brother also located a survey adjoining, and, in 1684, married Rachel Firman. These surveys contained one hundred acres each, and were generally known as "head lands," being the quantity to which each male person coming as a servant was entitled under the regulation established by the proprietors. Many young men were styled "servants" and received their one hundred acres of land, who were persons of education, and who afterwards became prominent citizens in the colony.

This was near the Indian town of Penisaukin, where the natives for many years after had a village, and where may yet be seen the remains of the graveyard; which burial places they held in so much reverence and respect, that long journeys were made to visit the remains of their departed friends and connections. Within the memory of those now living, have these burial places been visited by this peculiar people, around which they would remain for a few days, and then mysteriously disappear from the neighborhood. This sacred regard for the dead formed a strange contrast with other characteristics of their savage natures; it showed a tenderness of feeling and a degree of refinement, not always found in civilization.

This stream (Penisaukin creek) bears one of the few Indian names that have come down to the present generation, and, although much corrupted, it has enough remaining to detect its origin.

In 1682, when John Roberts, William Matlack, and Timothy Hancock located the land, they called it Pen-is-au-kin—giving

---
[3] Basse's Book, 35.

the stream the same name as that by which the Indians styled their village then adjoining. This word has been spelled in various ways, with as many definitions, one of which is that William Penn reserved a hawking privilege in the sale of lands there, and thence called the stream Pennshawking creek. This idea is at once demolished upon an examination of the records, for there it may be found as obtained from the natives, and as by them pronounced.

The corruption, or rejection of the Indian names of streams and localities in America, is to be regretted; for their significance and beauty have no parallel in the English tongue, and they are passing away like the people that gave them character and expression, almost without a history or a kindly remembrance. The yielding of the weaker to the stronger race, of savage life to the progress of civilization, has left but a remnant of this people among us. Being without a written history, their legends, their language, and their names, will soon be among the things that have passed beyond the possibility of restoration. It is remarkable that, in the development of literature and the advancement of education, so little has been done to collect and arrange the language of the aborigines of our land. But a single record of their language is known to have been made in West New Jersey, and that by the authorities of Salem county; it is contained in one of their first books, now on file in the office of Secretary of State at Trenton, in which much care has been taken, and from which much information may be had.

William Matlack and Timothy Hancock soon found their neighborhood was a desirable one; for new settlements were made there in a short time, and went on increasing until a meeting of Friends was established at the house of Timothy Hancock by the consent of Burlington Friends in 1685. This was held on alternate first-days with one at the house of John Kay, on the north branch of Cooper's creek, for the accommodation of Friends at Penisaukin and Evesham. These were continued until about the year 1707. At these places many marriages were solemnized during that time, the knowledge of which would add much to the early history of this section of the State.

Thomas Story, an eminent public Friend, who traveled in America in 1700, says that he went from Philadelphia to the Chester meeting (now Moorestown, Burlington county) by water, and upon his return stayed at night at the house of Esther Spicer, the widow of Samuel Spicer, where he was well entertained. This widow lady, who survived her husband several years, then lived near the river shore on the north side of Cooper's creek, now Stockton township, Camden county.

The Matlack family in New Jersey have been remarkably prolific, which peculiarity began with William and Mary; and any attempt to follow the genealogy would lead to endless collaterals, and be attended with much doubt and uncertainty. The children of the first settlers, however, were John, who married Hannah Horner and Mary Lee; George, who married Mary Foster and Mary Hancock; Mary, who married Jonathan Haines and Daniel Morgan; William, who married Ann Antrim; Richard, who married Rebecca Haines and Mary Cole; Joseph, who married Rebecca Haines; Timothy, who married Mary Haines; Jane, who married —— Irvin; and Sarah, who married Carlyle Haines. From these marriages has sprung, one of the largest families in New Jersey, and, one which, at this date, has found its way into every state in the Union.

In 1701, William Matlack purchased about one thousand acres of land of Richard Heritage, situated in Waterford and Gloucester townships, in Camden county (then Gloucester), lying on both sides of the south branch of Cooper's creek, around and near the White Horse tavern.[4]

In 1705, John Matlack purchased two hundred acres of land of Francis Collins in Waterford township. In 1708, he married Hannah Horner, and settled upon his purchase. A part of this estate is now owned by the heirs of John Wilkins, deceased, who there reside. The old house erected by the first owner stood a short distance from the handsome edifice of the present occupants; this old house was pulled down a few years since, for one hundred and fifty years rendered it unfit, both in comfort and style, for further use.

In 1714, William Matlack gave his son George five hundred acres of land in Waterford township, being part of that which

---
4 Lib. G2, 143.

he had purchased of Richard Heritage.[5] George had previously married Mary Foster, and settled on this tract. His house stood near the residence of Israel Riggins, on the south side of the present Haddonfield and Berlin road, near Glendale. He built the saw mill on the south branch of Cooper's creek, formerly known as "Hilliard's" mill, having gone to ruin many years since. This tract of land is now divided among several good farms.

In 1717, William Matlack purchased two hundred acres of land of John Estaugh, as attorney of John Haddon, on which his son Richard settled in 1721—the same year in which he married Rebecca Haines.[6] This tract lies in Waterford and Delaware townships. Upon it is situated the old Matlack graveyard, where lay the remains of nearly all the older branches of the family. Richard (the first settler), who deceased in 1778, was the second person buried here, his son Benjamin being the first. In 1779, this estate passed out of this name to William Todd, but was subsequently purchased by Richard M. Cooper, father of the present owner, and a lineal descendant in the materal line of the first settler.

In 1714, William Matlack gave his son Timothy the remaining part of the tract of land which he had purchased of Richard Heritage in Waterford township. Here Timothy built a house and settled.[7] The house stood on the farm now owned by Ephraim Tomlinson, a short distance from Glendale. In 1720, Timothy married Mary Haines. He remained on the farm only a short time, as, in 1726 he sold the same and removed to Haddonfield, where he erected a house and kept a store.

Among the children of Timothy Matlack, a son Timothy was born in Haddonfield, 1730. He removed to Philadelphia at an early age, and became one of the prominent citizens of that place.[8] During the Revolutionary war, although a Quaker, he held a colonel's commission in the army, and was an active officer throughout that struggle. For this he was dealt with, and lost his membership in that religious body. In connection with Benjamin Franklin, Robert Morris and others, a society was

---

5 Lib. A, 09.
6 Lib. A, 50.
7 Lib. A, 08.
8 Lives of Eminent Philadelphians, &c., 685.

established in Philadelphia, called the "Free Quakers." He was secretary to the Continental Congress for some time, while it sat in that city, and was known as an open and decided advocate for the separation of the colonies from the mother country. His portrait now hangs in the Hall of Independence, among many of his contemporaries of that eventful period. He died in 1829, and was buried in the graveyard of the religious society of which he was a member, in south Fifth street, Philadelphia.

He never lost his interest in the place of his nativity, and, in his declining years, often related the story of his being in one of the apple trees in John Gill's orchard, and listening to John Estaugh preach in the Friends' meeting-house near by. This was when he was a boy. If Friend John had espied him preying upon his fruit, the inclinations of the flesh would have prompted him to visit condign punishment upon the offender; but Timothy understood his habits too well, not to know when to make these predatory excursions, and get safely away, loaded with plunder. This further shows that John Gill's farm extended along the north side of the King's road to the meeting-house; mention of which is made in the deed for the meeting-house lot.

Asa Matlack, now deceased, a descendant of the first settler and formerly residing near Moorestown, Burlington county, New Jersey, on a part of the original estate, collected and preserved a history of the direct and collateral branches of the family, showing how rapidly it spread through the country and became connected with those of the early settlers. Although not arranged for easy reference, yet the collection, as it stands, evidences much labor, and is invaluable to any one in search of genealogical matter connected therewith.

The tract of lands owned by William Matlack and his sons John, Timothy and Richard, extending from the White Horse tavern to the farm of Joseph H. Ellis, both included, and lying on both sides of the Moorestown and Woodbury road, contained some fifteen hundred acres; it passed out of the name more than sixty years since, part by marriage, but much the larger part by sale.

JOHN HINCHMAN.

IN the year 1675, a valuation of the estates of persons resident in Flushing, Long Island, made known that John Hinchman was an inhabitant, and the owner of one negro, twenty-five acres of land, two horses, four oxen, four cows, two colts, four hogs and forty sheep. He was then a well-to-do farmer for the times in which he lived, and much in advance of most of his neighbors. In the year 1698, another list was ordered by the proper authorities of the same town (or township.) This shows the nativity of each; and among the *French* settlers occur the names of John Hinchman and Sarah his wife, and of their children, John, James, Mercy, Mary and Sarah, as well as that of one negro slave called Hector, set down as belonging to the said John Hinchman; also the names of Thomas Hinchman and of Miriam his wife, and two children, Thomas and Sarah. Among the names composing the list of freemen, is that of Robert Hinchman. These assessments evince a degree of care not generally looked for at so early a date, and disclose many valuable and interesting facts not to be obtained through any other channel. The liberality of the Legislature of the State of New York in securing, arranging and publishing all the documentary evidence that relates to the early settlement of that state, cannot be too highly commended; it deserves to be followed by every other commonwealth in the Union. To this liberality are all those indebted that would know anything touching the history of the first comers, of their success and their subsequent movements.

Among the inhabitants of Oyster Bay, Southampton, Hempstead, Flushing and other places on Long Island, may be found the names of many who became the heads of families hereabout, and who did much to clear up and develope the virgin soil in this section of the country.

The inducements held out by William Penn, John Fenwick and others, who were interested in the lands in New Jersey and Pennsylvania, made it to their advantage again to break up their homes and remove hither. Among them were the Hinchmans, the Burroughs, the Clements, the Harrisons and others, whose names are now familiar to every inhabitant in this region of country. In fact, these two sections were so closely connected in this regard, that the history of the one is, to a great extent, the history of the other. In ecclesiastical affairs they were nearly identical, for what in church matters agitated the people of one region was equally exciting among the people of the other.

The name was not confined to Long Island, as Edward Hinchman was a resident of Maryland in 1658, and was fined for refusing to bear arms. This person was a merchant, and had business intercourse with Barbadoes in 1672. He was subsequently banished for his Quakerism, and passed through much bodily suffering therefor. There is nothing, however, to indicate any connection between the last named person and the Hinchmans of Long Island, and any search in that direction might prove fruitless.

On the eighteenth day of May, 1699, John Hugg and Priscilla, his wife, conveyed to John Hinchman of Long Island, one thousand acres of land, situated in Newton township, Gloucester county, New Jersey.[1] Part of this tract was given by Francis Collins to his daughter Priscilla, and other parts John Hugg had purchased of various persons. Parcels of this land still remain in the name, but much the larger portion passed out of the family many years since. According to the best data that can be collected from old maps and indefinite descriptions, in ancient deeds, this estate extended from near the head of the south branch of Newton creek (including the

---
[1] Lib. G3, 279.

Hurley farm on that side), northeasterly toward Haddonfield, taking in the Hinchman estate, the farm of Charles L. Willits and other properties. Much information touching the title to this land may be derived from a re-survey of parts of the tract, made by the third John Hinchman in 1759; which re-survey appears in the records of that year, in the Surveyor-General's office at Burlington. The house of John Hinchman stood on the north side of the stream named, about where the late residence of James S. Hurley, deceased, is erected. Near the house, but on the south side of the water-course, is an ancient burial place, in these days known as "Hurley's" graveyard, but established by the first owner as a place to inter his slaves. Of this kind of property, he was one of the largest holders in the country; their descendants make up many of the families in this region, and these, until a short time since, were buried at the place before spoken of.

Possessing an extensive tract of land, and a large number of slaves, it may be inferred that he was a man of wealth, and lived in somewhat more style than most of those around him. His residence stood near the king's highway, where it crossed King's run, in going from Burlington to Salem; it was a building of some pretension, and one in which a liberal hospitality was dispensed. As a Quaker, his entertainments extended to those traveling Friends who felt it their duty to leave their homes in England to visit the churches in America, at that time scattered over a vast extent of country. The colonies in North Carolina, Virginia and Maryland, to the south, and in East Jersey, Long Island and Connecticut, to the east, were a long distance apart; and the journey to and fro was always attended with many difficulties.

The journals of these missionaries all show that they passed through the same kind of trials, and had the same obstacles to overcome. In his removal from Long Island, John Hinchman doubtless brought with him several slaves, the increase of whom in a few years overcrowded his plantation with laborers, and made a full supply for his children as they settled in life.

Slave property was something more than that of horses or cattle; in the purchase or sale of a slave a deed was executed and delivered, conveying the estate of the owner, and frequently guaranteeing soundness and tractability. One of these indentures is here given in full, explaining in itself the character of the transaction, and the purposes for which it was made.

"KNOW ALL MEN BY THESE PRESENTS, that I, John Hugg, of Gloucester county, New Jersey, for and in consideration of the sum of thirty-five pounds to me paid by John Hinchman, of the same place, before the ensealing and delivery of these presents the receipt whereof is hereby acknowledged; have bargained, sold, and by these presents do bargain and sell unto the said John Hinchman a certain negro boy named Sambo, aged ten years next March or May, as is said. To have and to hold the said negro boy by these presents bargained and sold unto the said John Hinchman, his heirs, executors, administrators and assigns for ever. And I, the said John Hugg, for myself, my executors and administrators, the said negro boy bargained and sold unto the said John Hinchman, against me the said John Hugg and against all and every other person whatsoever claiming or pretending to claim any right or property thereunto, shall and will warrant and forever defend.

"In witness whereof, I have hereunto set my seal, this the third day of July, in the year of our Lord one thousand seven hundred and nine, 1709.

"Sealed and delivered in presence of
THOMAS SHARP,
JOSEPH COLLINS."

"JOHN HUGG. { L. S. }

Noticeable features in many of the last wills of the first settlers in New Jersey are the number of slaves disposed of thereby, and the high value which was attached to them.

With some owners they were badly used, but among Friends they were generally treated with consideration. The unnatural separation of husband and wife, and of parents and children, soon attracted the attention of the more considerate in the Society; and steps were taken to guard against this cruelty, which. eventually led to an open declaration, opposing the institution itself.

These humane influences ultimately extended to the lawmaking power of the State; an act was passed, under which means were adopted for the gradual extinguishment of slavery within its borders. The operation of this law frequently entailed a burden upon families in which slaves had been held; but it was accepted by the people as just to this unfortunate class, and due to their inability to provide for themselves.

The census of 1860 showed but few slaves in the State of New Jersey; these were too old and infirm at that date to carry a vestige of the institution to the present decade.

John Hinchman dealt somewhat in real estate, and located several surveys in Gloucester county. He does not appear to have meddled in politics, or to have joined in the religious bickerings so prevalent in those days. His wife was Sarah, a daughter of Samuel Harrison, whom he married while a resident of Long Island; where also part of his children were born. He deceased in 1721, leaving a will.[2] The inventory of his personal property amounted to two hundred and thirty pounds, sterling, which he disposed of with his real estate among his children. They were John, who married Sarah ———, and Elizabeth Smith (widow); Joseph, who married Phoebe ———; Jacob, who married Abigail Harrison; James, who married Kesiah ———; Sarah, who married Thomas Bispham; Jane, who married ——— Jones; Letitia, who married Thomas Thorne; Ann, who married John Thorne; Abigail, who married John Kaighn and Samuel Harrison; and one child born after the father's decease, named William. John, the oldest son, settled on part of the paternal estate, now mostly owned by Charles L. Willits, Benjamin Cooper, Nathan B. Willits, and others, extending southwardly from an ancient boundary line, west of the old Salem road, to the head of Little Timber creek, adjoining the Jenning's estate. His dwelling house is now part of the residence of Charles L. Willits; it will be remembered by some as a small, hipped-roof, brick building—but now entirely changed in shape and appearance. In its day, it had some pretension to style and comfort, but, at this time, no such claims would be made. In the political affairs of the

---

[2] Lib. No. 2, 198.

colony John Hinchman participated, for, in 1705, he was appointed ensign in one of the military departments of the county; in 1722, he was made coroner, and afterwards acted as sheriff. In 1747, he married Elizabeth Smith (a second wife), the widow of Isaac, only child of Sarah Norris and granddaughter of John Kay, who was the first of the name here.[3] She survived him, and died the owner of considerable real estate in Haddonfield, situated on Potter's street. By this marriage there was no issue. He died intestate in 1754.[4] His children were John, who married —— ————, and died without issue; Hannah, who married Samuel Stokes; Ann, who married —— Bispham; Amy, who married Joshua Stokes; Elizabeth, who married Joseph Bispham, and, after his decease, John Hatkinson.

Joseph Hinchman was a butcher, and lived on part of the original estate in Newton township.[5] He died in 1731, leaving a widow and two sons, James, who married Sarah Bircham, and Isaac, who married Letitia Woolston. James settled in Greenwich township, and Isaac, in Newton.[6] Jacob Hinchman died in 1742, leaving a widow and one child, Mary.[7] James Hinchman took that part of his father's property now partly owned by the heirs of Jeremiah Willits, deceased, and, formerly, by James S. Hurley, deceased; he lived where the last named person died. In 1733, he received a commission from the King appointing him one of the judges of Gloucester county, in which capacity he appears to have acceptably served. He died in 1750, leaving a widow, but no children.[8] The estate is now divided into several valuable farms, any one of which is more productive than the whole tract as then managed. Letitia, who married Thomas Thorne, settled with her husband on land which he purchased of Thomas Cole and James Wild, in Delaware township, bordering on the south side of Penisaukin creek; part of this property is now owned by Asa R. Lippincott. Thomas Thorne also came from Long Island, but several years after John Hinchman. He was a man of large estate, and, like his father-in-law, was the owner of numerous slaves,

---

3 Gloucester Files, 1758.
4 Lib. No. 7, 497.
5 Lib. No. 2, 126.
6 Lib. L, 384.
7 Lib. No. 4, 366.
8 Lib. No. 6, 423.

part, perhaps, the dowry of his wife, and part obtained by purchase. They had three children, namely: Hannah, who married George Turner; Sarah, who married Jacob Burrough, son of Samuel; and Thomas, who married Abigail Burrough, daughter of Samuel. Although the property has not entirely passed out of the blood, yet the name has been lost sight of for many years. Thomas Thorne died in 1757, intestate.[9]

John Thorne, the husband of Ann and brother of Thomas, purchased a tract of land in 1702 of John Reading, lying in Centre township between the south branch of Newton creek and Little Timber creek, including the farm lately owned by J. Stokes Brick, deceased, the estate of John D. Glover, and other properties.[10] By his will, made in 1768, he gave this real estate to his son-in-law, John Glover, in fee.[11] His children were Thomas, who deceased before the making of his will; Mary, who married John Glover; and Sarah, who died single in 1769, but after her father.[12] Ann died a few years after her marriage, and John Thorne married Mary, the widow of John Gill and daughter of Richard Heritage. He died in 1769, having removed to Haddonfield several years before that occurrence. He was a man of considerable estate, and was much respected in the community in which he lived. Thomas, his son, died in 1759, leaving a will.[13] His children were Elizabeth and Abigail, the wife of William Harrison.

William Harrison owned and lived upon the farm south of Mount Ephraim, lately the property of Jesse W. Starr; he was buried in a small family graveyard, near the old brick house— now torn down.

John's last wife survived him six years, as her will was admitted to probate on October 4th, 1775.[14] This instrument of writing puts at rest any doubt of her being the widow of John Gill, and the maternal ancestor of the family of that name in this region. There was no issue by her last marriage. She was in possession of more than a sufficiency of this world's goods, and disposed of them among her children and grandchildren. Of the many articles devised, she gave her son

---

9 Lib. No. 9, 38.
10 Lib. W, 196.
11 Lib. No. 14, 192.
12 Lib. No. 17, 132.
13 Lib. No. 9, 411.
14 Lib. No. 17, 241.

John Gill "a pair of gold studs and a silver spoon," *presented to her by Elizabeth Estaugh;* to which she evidently attached much value, considering it an heir-loom worthy of her especial regard. She lived to see several of her granddaughters married, but the surname of her first husband was limited at her death to two persons, her son, and her grandson, John Gill.

Samuel Thorne also purchased land near Gloucester about the same time, and perhaps took up his abode thereon. In 1706, William Thorne (as the deed says, "late of Long Island, but now of Gloucester county, N. J.,") purchased three tracts of land of Mordecai Howell.[15] Part of this land was near the head of the south branch of Cooper's creek, and the north branch of Timber creek. On one of the tributaries of the last named stream, he erected a saw mill, the site of which may yet be seen; this stream is still known as Thorne's mill branch. At this place he probably settled and reared a large family. For many years the name was a prominent one in that section, but latterly it is scarcely known; as attached to any of the original estate, it is almost forgotten, and, but for the ancient deeds, would not in these days be remembered.

Thomas and John Thorne were the sons of Joseph Thorne of Flushing, Long Island; they came to West New Jersey, after the example of John Hinchman, Jacob Clement, and some others, seeking a home among the newly settled Quakers in these parts.[16]

John Glover also came from Long Island, where quite a number of that name had settled. He was probably a son of Samuel and Sarah Glover, who were residents of Southold as early as the year 1675. In that year, his personal estate was assessed at one ox, three cows, and one horse; but, eight years after that time, his taxable property amounted to one hundred and four pounds, proving him to be a thrifty man. In 1698, he was still an inhabitant of the same place, and was surrounded by a numerous family. His son Samuel, in 1700, was appointed lieutenant in a company of infantry of that town, he having departed from the example of George Fox, doubtless, much to the chagrin of his parents.

---

15 Lib. A, 84.
16 Lib. Q, 451.

With John Glover came two brothers, William and Richard. William settled in Newton township, the creek dividing his estate from that of John's. He was a man of considerable property, for, by his will, he disposed of legacies amounting to more than one thousand pounds, sterling. He was a bachelor, and deceased in the year 1798. Much of the estate in Newton township still remains in the name, as well as that of John Glover, in Centre township, coming to the present owners from John Thorne, as before named.[17] In 1728, Richard Glover married Rachel Clark, and settled in Burlington county, N. J.

John Glover had a numerous family, namely: Thomas, who married Mary Stiles (he dying, she married Peter Thompson); John T., who married Elizabeth, widow of Joseph Ridgway and daughter of —— Olden; Sarah, who married Peter Hanna; Isaac, who married Phoebe, daughter of John Duel; Rachel who married Isaac Stiles; Samuel, who married Hannah Albertson; Mary, who married Thomas Potter; Joseph, who married Sarah Mickle; and Jacob, who married Mary Branson.

Thomas and Sarah Bispham settled in Philadelphia. His business was that of an "inn keeper," but, in what part of the city, it is not known. Thomas died there in 1771, leaving a will.[18] His wife survived him, and the following children: Joseph; Benjamin, who married Hope Fortiner; Thomas; Hinchman; and Elizabeth, who married James Hartley. They held a number of slaves, and owned land in New Jersey. By each marriage the daughter, Abigail, had issue; her descendants may easily trace the maternal blood.

Joseph Hinchman was a brother of the first John, and came also from Flushing, on Long Island, A. D. 1708. Any doubt of the relationship is put at rest by a single passage in the will of John, in which he devised a tract of land to his son John; in the description of one of the boundaries, he says, "to a corner in the line of my brother Joseph Hinchman's land." He was a man of some estate, as he purchased land of John in that part of the original one thousand acres which lay nearest to Haddonfield. His house stood on the west side of the king's

---

17 Lib No. 37, 413.
18 Lib. No. 15, 42.

road, a short distance from where it crossed the "shore" road that passed over Atmore's dam, going towards Philadelphia. It was perhaps nothing more than a log cabin, built of the timber that had stood upon the ground where it was erected. He purchased about fifty acres of Joseph Collins, which brought his property to the stream of the main branch of Newton creek, which still continues one of the boundaries thereof. He also added some other adjoining tracts, dying the owner of a large body of valuable land. His will bears date April 5th, 1737. He made his wife Sarah sole executrix, with power to sell land, to discharge debts, and to manage the estate generally.[19]

His children were Thomas, who married Sarah Clement, a daughter of James of Long Island, and, after her decease, in 1750, Letitia Mickle, widow of Samuel and daughter of Timothy Matlack; Sarah, who married Edward Collins; Hannah, who married James Gill; Mary, who married —— Zane; Deborah; and Emily.

The paternity of Thomas Hinchman's first wife is beyond question, as James Clement names her in his will, dated May 5th, 1724. By this marriage there was no issue.[20] By the will of his father, Thomas was seized of all the real estate, and lived thereon. He deceased in 1758, his wife dying seven years before that time, and perhaps upon the birth of his only child, Joseph, to whom the property, as purchased by his grandfather, passed.

Joseph was born February 18th, 1751, in the old log cabin, for his father died before he had finished the erection of the house now occupied by William C. Hinchman,—a house which, for nearly one hundred years, was the only dwelling on the estate. The broad acres and primitive forests that surrounded him in his youth, his manhood and his old age, came to him through a line of ancestry of which he was the only living representative; and he adhered to them with a tenacity that proved his determination never to break in upon the ancient land marks. His knowledge of the titles, and his familiarity with the boundaries, show that his ownership had afforded him a pleasurable study,—

---

19 Lib. No. 2, 154.
20 Lib. No. 10, New York Wills, 53.

one of great advantage to himself, and to those who were to follow him. He married Sarah Kain, a daughter of William and Charity, and great-granddaughter of Francis Collins, the first settler in this part of Newton township. Of systematic and industrious habits, a close observer, and of good judgment, he combined the farmer and mechanic in a remarkable degree. He was one of the few persons of his day and generation, who deemed it necessary to make a record of events passing under his notice. His journal, commenced in 1811 and continued to 1827 inclusive, is a curious book, and contains much that is valuable. The record of marriages, births and deaths, is of local interest, and it should be preserved for reference to coming generations ; disclosing much that has been already lost sight of, and that, but for such memoranda, could not be restored. Although portions of this book are taken up with his private affairs, yet the larger part refers to matters of increasing value in connection with the families in this region of country ; it will be consulted in future days upon important and material subjects.

It is gratifying to know that more regard is manifested towards old manuscripts, and that an increasing interest now prevails to save such from loss. How much of the history of families and of neighborhoods is now hidden in garrets and neglected, out-of-the-way places, where the hands of such as would appreciate their value may never reach them. The time spent, and the ingenuity exercised in solving an intricate question, may add to its interest ; but to be unable to establish an acknowledged tradition for want of documentary evidence, thoughtlessly destroyed, reflects sadly upon the want of care in this regard among the people.

JOHN SHIVERS.

JOHN SHIVERS appears to have been the first of the name in this neighborhood. He probably came as a servant with some of the first emigrants, and was consequently not named among the lists of passengers; this class of persons being numbered to the individual who entered them as emigrants, a system which secured to each one a certain amount of land upon his arrival. Very many young men who had some estate, and were proficient as mechanics, chose to come out in this way, and, soon after their arrival, acquired more property, and had better positions than those whom they were pledged to serve. Mechanics, in particular, were in great demand, and, if economical, in a few years became classed among the wealthiest of the inhabitants. The subject of this sketch was called a butcher, which occupation he, no doubt, followed at home; but, when he came here and settled in an unbroken forest, with but few families about him, "his occupation was gone." Apart from Philadelphia, there was, within his reach, no collection of dwellings that could be called a town, where he could ply his calling; but, perhaps, with the energy characteristic of these pioneers, he traveled twice each week in his boat to the embryo city, and supplied its people with their meat fresh from the knife. The demand was small, and his means of supply were equally so, for people at that day had no appliances for raising and fattening cattle, except in giving them the range of the woods.

In fact this was so done, as, for many years after the beginning of the colony a law was in force requiring all persons to mark their cattle, and report their mark to the clerk of the county, so that the same might be recorded. An examination of the old books of minutes of the counties will show this; in many instances the mark is illustrated by a fac-simile copy, without any other description than the name of the person who reported it. The similarity of these evidences of ownership often led to disputes and litigation, in which much more money and time were wasted than the cause of the trouble was worth; yet, as is frequently the case at the present day, those who were fierce in the defence of their real or supposed rights, did not stop to inquire whether such a course of policy "would pay."

In 1692, John Shivers purchased a tract of land of Mordecai Howell, in Waterford township, which was bounded on the south side by Cooper's creek and partly by a stream branching therefrom, whereon Mordecai had erected, or was about to erect, a mill;[1] for, in the next year, John Wright, an adjoining owner, released to him the privilege of flooding the meadow for the use of the same. On this tract John Shivers erected a dwelling, and remained until his death.[2] He deceased intestate in 1716, his widow Sarah having been appointed administratrix.[3] He was a man of considerable estate, and owned other lands than the tract here named; among which was one-half of two hundred acres that he had bought of Anthony Sturgiss in 1699, lying in Newton township, fronting on Cooper's creek, and nearly opposite his homestead place.[4] This tract he held in common with Henry Johnson; but at what time it passed out of the family, and who were the subsequent owners, are matters of no interest in this connection.[5]

In 1720, Sarah Shivers, the widow of John, purchased of John Wright before named, the adjoining tract of land which lay between the homestead and Cooper's creek, and which he had, in 1693, bought of Mordecai Howell.[6] This purchase extended the Shivers estate down and along the east side of the pond raised by Howell for the use of his mill, the remains of

---

1 Lib. G3, 8.
2 Lib G3, 513.
3 Gloucester Files, 1721.
4 Lib. GG, 297.
5 Lib. G3, 345.
6 Lib. A, 170.

the dam of which can yet be seen. This was one of the first saw mills erected in Gloucester county, and, if in use at this date, with the primitive forest close around it, as in 1693, it would prove a useful and valuable institution. The site, however, was not a desirable one, being subject to the flow of high tides from the creek, which would frequently check the speed of the wheel; for this reason it was abandoned many years since.

The dwelling on the farm now owned by Richard Shivers in Delaware township is, perhaps, the spot whereon John Shivers erected his first house; and portions of the present building may have been used in the first. His dying intestate leaves some doubt as to the number of his children, their names, and marriages, yet they are judged to have been the following: Samuel, who married Mary Deacon; John, who married Mary Clement; Mary, who married Thomas Bates; Hannah, who married John Matlack; and Josiah, who married Ann Bates.

In 1720, Samuel purchased two hundred acres of Francis Collins, adjoining the homestead property on the north,[7] and, the next year, he conveyed his interest in his father's estate to his brother John, who remained on the old farm, and in whose descendants parts of the same remain to the present day, and in all probability will so remain for many years to come.[8] Samuel settled in Newton township on the property which his father purchased of Anthony Sturgiss in 1699, for, in 1724, he acted as one of the surveyors of highways of that township, as appears by Thomas Sharp's record of the same.

During the life of the second John, the house in which he lived was by him kept as a tavern, standing, as it did, close by the north side of the ferry road leading out of Evesham, and other parts of Burlington county, towards Philadelphia. This was no doubt a favorite stopping place for the market people, where the price of poultry, eggs and butter could be discussed, so that such as were on their way to sell, might know how to deal with their keen and wary customers. There is no tradition, however, that a Jerseyman ever came off second

[7] Lib. T5, Woodbury.
[8] Lib. GG, 297.

best in a bargain, or that he left the market without the worth of his commodities. The quiet, unassuming manner of these folks was sometimes taken for ignorance, and those who considered themselves sharp in trade, only discovered their error when they found the advantage was on the wrong side. The natives of this State are known throughout our land as shrewd dealers,—a trait that may have come down to us from our Quaker ancestors, sharpened by long practice, and deeply instilled by continued example.

Afterwards Samuel removed to Greenwich township, Gloucester county, where he became a prominent citizen, and a wealthy man. He deceased in 1771.[9] Part of his real estate consisted of "Raccoon island," situated at the mouth of the creek of the same name, in Gloucester county, which he purchased of James Lowns in 1747.[10]

A part of this island he leased on the first day of April, 1769, to William Kay for ninety-nine years, which term carried the possession of the estate beyond several generations of his descendants, and rendered it questionable in some instances upon whom the remainders actually fell. This lease was based upon a rental of eighty pounds per annum, and the payment made a lien upon the estate. At that date, and for many years after, the only means of procuring hay and pasture was by improved meadow lands; which rendered the marshes fronting on the tidal streams of West Jersey valuable for such purposes; and the records show that these marshes or flats were sought after, and located at an early date. This lease is, perhaps, the only one in this region that covered so much time, and involved so much valuable real estate. The devise of this was to three of his daughters, involving the fee as well as the rent; one-fourth was given to Sarah Tatem ; one-fourth was given to Martha Booys, and two-fourths were given to Anna Sydonia Shinn, who, perhaps, all enjoyed the income of rent during their lives; but the lapse of years was too great for them to say to whom the possession and fee of the land at the end of the lease would come. Subsequently, the estate passed entirely

---
9 Lib. No. 15, 158.
10 Lib. IK, 423.

out of the family, and some years since other owners had secured the title. The abolishing of the ancient limitations as touching real estate in New Jersey, allows many new owners to this kind of property in the course of one hundred years. Thrift, prudence and economy, are the only guarantees to the long keeping of land in any particular line under the present laws, and a disregard of these often makes room for enterprise and improvement where old fogyism might reign forever.

John Shivers having but two sons, the name is even at this time limited to few families; this circumstance often occurs, although the blood of the ancestors may be found in the veins of many, distributed there by the female descendants, who, upon marriage, lose their names, and, after two or three removes, almost lose their genealogical identity.

JOHN HILLMAN.

JOHN HILLMAN was an husbandman, and the first plantation upon which he lived and which he owned, he purchased of Francis Collins in 1697.[1] It contained one hundred and seventy acres of land, and was situated in Gloucester township (now Centre), adjoining the estate of John Gill, part of which is now owned by William Chapman. Like most of the early settlers, he selected a light sandy soil whereon to clear his farm; this made that operation of much less trouble, and the tilling of it much less laborious. In 1697, agriculture had made but little progress, and had it not been for the timber, then so plenty, which our ancestors worked and sold, the wants of the people would have been but poorly supplied. The leading crops were corn and rye, which followed each other in continued succession, until the return would hardly pay for the seed, and then another piece of land would be cleared and used in like manner, with the same results. Everything was in the most primitive condition, not only the manner of farming, but also the implements wherewith to work. Wooden ploughs, brush harrows, straw collars and grapevine gearing, may be thought to be an overdrawn picture of the farming implements of the early settlers in this region, and one which strikes the farmers of the present day with surprise. Yet these, and still more limited, were the means of the people to eke out a livelihood in the wilderness of New Jersey. With no shelter for

---
[1] Lib. C, 15.

their cattle, no protection for their crops when gathered, and with the rudest of cabins for themselves, their condition can scarcely be appreciated at this day by us, with our many improvements and comforts of every description.

John Hillman's farm lay on both sides of the present road from Haddonfield to Snow Hill; and his house stood near the present residence of William Chapman. Attached thereto was a portion of meadow land, from which were obtained pasture for his cattle during the summer, and hay to keep them alive through the winter. The "old Egg Harbor road" passed near his house, which was in after years kept as a tavern, although not noted as a place of resort. At a short distance south of this place the old road "forked;" the branch was called the Salem road, and crossed Timber creek at or near Clement's bridge.

In 1720, John Hillman, by deed of gift, conveyed this tract of land to his son John, anticipating his will in that particular. The will bore date in 1707, but was not proved until 1729, soon after the decease of the testator. The inventory of his personal property amounted to one hundred and ninety-two pounds.[2] His children appear to have been two sons and two daughters, Daniel, John, Ann and Abigail. Margaret, his widow, also survived him.

After the death of his father, John Hillman sold the homestead; but, by subsequent conveyances, it became the property of Joseph Hillman (a son of the second John), who lived there a short time, and, in 1760, sold the same to Daniel Scull, of Egg Harbor. In a few years after, it became part of the estate of John Gill, who devised a portion of it to his daughter Mary Roberts, during her natural life, and the remainder to her son, John Roberts; the latter sold his share many years before his death. For more than one hundred years the real estate upon which the first John Hillman settled, has been out of the name; it is now partly covered with the town of Snow Hill, and is divided among many owners.

In 1745, John Hillman (the second), who married Abigail, a daughter of Joseph Bates, a resident of that section,[3] pur-

---

2 Gloucester Files, 1731.
3 Lib. No. 3, 432.

chased about five hundred acres of land from Thomas Atkinson. This tract lay near the White Horse tavern, and extended from the south branch of Cooper's creek to the north branch of Timber creek.[4] To this land he removed, and built the house where now resides Hinchman Lippincott, whose farm is part of the original tract. Six years after this purchase, he bought at the sale of John Mickle, sheriff of Gloucester county, one hundred acres adjoining, as the property of Meam Southwick.[5] Included in the first purchase was a saw mill on Timber creek, which was owned by Thomas Webster, Thomas Atkinson, and Meam Southwick, and probably stood upon the site of the grain mill now the property of Ephraim Tomlinson.

These lands were located by Abraham Porter, in 1714, '15 and '16, who settled thereon, having his house near the south side of Cooper's creek, on the farm now owned by Josiah Jenkins, where he, in all probability, kept "bachelor's hall"[6] Of this person there does not appear to be any tradition or history among the people who now own and occupy his estate, nor can he be traced with any certainty through the record beyond his day and generation. It is evident that he was not a Quaker, as he was appointed captain in the military department of the province in 1722,[7] while William Burnett was governor, during the reign of George I of England; he was afterwards promoted to the rank of major.[8] The little military spirit that had been developed among the people at that early day, in a neighborhood where the Quaker element overshadowed every other, would make it supposable that but few soldiers could be found thereabout. It is possible, however, that Capt. Porter did command a company of volunteers of the county of Gloucester, about one hundred and fifty years ago, and acted as the escort of the Governor of the province in his "circuit" from one part of the State to another, to hold the assizes for the crown.

These visits of the governor to the lower counties of the State were quite an event; for, holding their commissions by appointment for the crown, they are exceedingly punctilious

---

4 Lib. K, 85.
5 Lib. K, 83.
6 Basse's Book, 195.

7 Lib. AAA, 182.
8 Lib. AAA, 187.

and exacting in showing their authority, and, to that extent, made themselves obnoxious to our plain and matter-of-fact ancestors. The conduct of Captain Porter must have pleased those who held the reins of government, for he was soon promoted to the rank of major, which position he could not have obtained, unless he had been recommended to the king by those whose prerogative it was to fill all such appointments.

Abraham Porter did not live many years thereafter, as his will bears date 1729. It is a curious document, and discloses that he was a single man, or, if married, had no children.[9] He gave to the churches at Philadelphia, Burlington and Salem, each ten pounds; to the minister at Raccoon, five pounds, and to the meetings at Haddonfield and Salem, five pounds, each. The estate upon which he resided, consisted of some twelve hundred acres, and he, no doubt, had a valuable personal property. Why he should have lived alone so far from the settled neighborhood, and in a place that was some distance from the nearest road, and that one but little traveled, is an inquiry that can not be answered at this late day. After his death, his executors sold the land, and nothing appears to indicate that any of the family have been in that region since. Although a military man and holding his commission from the king, yet he had regard to the advancement of religion and morality in West New Jersey,— a trait that commends his memory to the respect of all, and one well worthy of emulation.

John Hillman lived on this tract of land many years, and, like many others, worked the timber that stood thereon into lumber and cord wood, hauling the same to Chew's Landing on Timber creek, whence it went by water to Philadelphia, to be sold. As his sons grew to be men, they likewise settled within the bounds of his surveys, and made farms for themselves, each of which was surrounded by the primitive forest.

In this, as in some other families, a few favorite names have been adhered to, names which, being attached to two or three living at the same time, mystify the genealogy when examined through a lapse of one hundred years. From this cause a generation is sometimes left out or added; this error it is often impossible to correct.

---

[9] Lib. No. 3, 94.

As before stated, John Hillman had two sons, Daniel and John, and, probably, a son Joseph. Daniel deceased in 1754, leaving his wife Elizabeth surviving him, and four sons, John, Daniel, James and Joseph.[10] John deceased in 1764, leaving his wife Elizabeth surviving him, and five sons, Joab, Josiah, Daniel, James and John.[11] Joseph died in 1768, his wife Drusilla, his sons, Daniel, Samuel, and a daughter, Letitia, surviving him.[12] By this it will be seen that each son had a son Daniel, and two of the sons had, each, a son John. One of these Daniels married Abigail Nicholson, and one of these Johns married Hannah Nicholson, both daughters of Samuel Nicholson, who lived in Waterford township, near the river Delaware. The difficulties of tracing a genealogy like this are at once apparent, and unless the family records are correctly and continuously kept, such difficulties cannot be overcome.

In 1745, John and Daniel Hillman purchased of Timothy Matlack a lot of land in Haddonfield, on the northwest side of the street, where the Methodist church now stands, extending to John Gill's line. Part of this became the property of John Shivers in 1758, although a portion remained in the family for many years after.

As an evidence of the little interest taken in agriculture during the first hundred and fifty years of the settlement of this part of New Jersey, it is worthy of notice that the lands of John Hillman, lying on the south side of Cooper's creek, and the lands of the sons of William Matlack, which lay on the north side of the same stream, were underlaid with green sand-marl, the fertilizing properties of which are now so well understood. The existence of this peculiar deposit must have been known to the dwellers in that region of country, for no well could be dug, or excavation made, in which it would not appear; and yet there is no evidence that this material has been used upon the soil until within the last forty years. These estates taken together and, as originally held, extending from the north branch of Timber creek on the south, to the north branch of Cooper's creek on the north, covered very much

---

[10] Lib. No. 8, 167.
[11] Lib. No. 12, 8.
[12] Lib. No. 12, 495.

of the green sand-marl belt in this region of country,—a deposit which has made it one of the best agricultural districts in the State of New Jersey. Strange as this disregard for a fertilizer so convenient and abundant may seem, it is, nevertheless, true; and it can only be accounted for by the little value of farmers' produce, and the consequent lack of interest in seeking out any means to increase their crops or improve the soil. Commerce and manufacturing had not been sufficiently developed to consume the excess that might have been thus produced; therefore no inducements existed, either to increase the breadth of cleared land, or to advance the fertility of that already in use.

New York and Philadelphia, in that day, made but little demand upon the country for their supplies, while the ashes arising from the consumption of wood, and the debris that collected in the street, were considered worthless, and given to such as would remove them out of reach. The diminitive barns and corn-cribs of the farmers of one hundred years ago would compare strangely with the capacious buildings that now stand upon the same land, filled to their utmost extent with the crops raised upon the same soil.

Within the memory of the older people of the present day, the section of country in question was covered with timber, interspersed with a few half cultivated farms, to which the Gloucester hunting-club looked for the best sport in their manly and exhilarating pastime. The thick underwood growing from the rich soil made the best of cover for game; and no little skill was necessary to drive Reynard forth, the securing of whose brush was the object of the chase. The young men of the neighborhood joined with the club in these hunts, and showed as much horsemanship and daring as those better equipped and more accustomed. Among these was Jonas Cattell, whose knowledge of wood-craft and wonderful endurance made him ever welcome. So much was he liked, that the historian of the club secured his full length portrait, and made it a part of his book.

> "Delightful scene!
> When all around is gay—men, horses, dogs;
> And in each smiling countenance appear
> Fresh blooming health, and universal joy."

Daniel Hillman settled on a tract of one hundred acres given to him by his father in his will, which he had purchased of William Sharp, the locator in 1701; and here Daniel erected a house and cleared his farm.[13] This was situated in what was then Gloucester township, as distinguished from Gloucester town, but is now the township of Centre; it is partly included in the farm of Zophar C. Howell. His dwelling stood near the present farm house on the Howell estate, and, perhaps, was a substantial log cabin, with clay floor and stick chimney. Daniel gradually extended his estate towards the south, while it adjoined the lands of the Clarks on the west, and those of the Albertsons on the east, which are now owned by the heirs of Joseph Davis, deceased, and others in that region.[14]

The Salem road that branched from the Egg Harbor road near the residence of his father, as before named, passed through his land toward Clement's bridge and South Jersey. This road was undoubtedly an Indian trail, and, consequently, was used by our ancestors in traveling through the province, several years before the Legislature established the king's highway; which, although more direct, was objectionable by reason of the many ferries to be passed on the route, found at every stream, where, at the present day, good and substantial bridges supply their places. Perhaps before Daniel, some one of the aborigines had cleared a few acres, upon which the female part of his family could raise their corn and pumpkins, while the head of the house and his able-bodied sons spent their time in hunting and fishing. All representations of Indian life prove that the women performed the drudgery and labor, while the men led a life of idleness and ease. These small spots of land, free from timber, were sought after by the first settlers, and were purchased from the Indians, as they facilitated farming operations, and saved much labor and expense.

In 1754, Daniel Hillman died, and, by his will, gave this tract of land to his four sons, James, John, Daniel and Joseph, who held it for several years in common, and, doubtless, built dwellings for themselves on various parts of it.[15] In 1784, Jacob

---
[13] Lib. D, 50. Basse's Book, 50.
[14] Lib M, 76. Lib. U, 65. Lib. T, 338, O. S. G.
[15] Lib. No. 8, 367.

Jennings became the owner of Joseph Hillman's portion, and, the next year, re-surveyed the same.[16] This included most of the one hundred acres located by William Sharp, and here stood the first dwelling of his father. In 1786, a re-survey was made of other parts of the said land; after which it was sold, and none of the present generation of descendants have any estate therein.[17] James had died before this, and his property was represented by John Gill and his widow, then the wife of Joseph Garwood, as executors thereof.

Samuel and Seth Hillman, sons of the third John, settled on land in Deptford township, Gloucester county, on Almonessing branch; which estate came to them from their grandfather, Daniel, who had purchased of John Ashbrook.[18] This family has now spread itself through nearly all the states of the Union and, directly and collaterally, has a very extensive relationship. Of Daniel Hillman, there is one act worthy of notice, which proves that he was a man of foresight and good judgment, anticipating his wants and those of his children, as farmers. In 1726, in connection with Joseph Lowe, he located the first tract of cedar swamp on Great Egg Harbor river, below where Berlin (Long-a-coming) now stands.[19] It lay south of Blue Anchor, where tradition says that the Indian trail crossed the swamp,—the only trail known to have existed for many years. On the east side stood an Indian wigwam, where travelers were entertained before the white man came, and where a lodging place was kept for such as were going from one part of the State to the other. It is well known that, at Shamong in Burlington county, and at Tuckahoe in Cape May county, resided two powerful tribes of this peculiar people, who, being upon friendly terms, kept up a constant interchange of visits. In going from the one place to the other, they crossed at the point above named, where may yet be seen the remains of a rude bridge. The pathway through the swamp was narrow, crossing an island in its course, but generally going in a straight line. Its position is well defined, as the owners of timber now use it for a wagon road, thus turning to practical purposes the

---

16 Lib. T, 338, O. S. G.
17 Lib. U, 327, O. S. G.

18 Lib. U, 383, O. S. G.
19 Lib. M, 77. O. S. G.

path in which, in olden times, traveled the kings and queens of the aborigines of our land. In going eastward, the trail passed near where Blue Anchor tavern now stands, and where the Indian trail going from the ocean to the Delaware river was intersected, a circumstance which, in all probability, gave rise to this once public place. Near the swamp may yet be seen the spot upon which stood the house of entertainment in which some Indian landlord dispensed cheer to all the passers by, and that without license, restraint or fear of law.

This accounts for Daniel Hillman's selecting his tract of swamp at that place, while larger and more valuable timber stood in profusion, above and below the same. For some reason, this trail was abandoned, and another made about two miles lower down the river, where formerly stood the old Inskeep saw-mill. When the mill was first erected, has passed beyond the memory of man; but, in 1762, when John Inskeep made the survey where stood the building, he put a post as the commencement-corner by the east side of the river, "and where a ford crosseth the same." This was the Indian path going between the points before spoken of, as changed from the old track, and was used by them so long as any remained at both settlements. Here they generally made a resting place for the night, always camping in the open air, without regard to the season, and never remaining after the sun rose in the morning. David Beebe, lately deceased, whose father resided at that place, distinctly remembered that small companies of these people were wont to stop there for the night, and that the females visited the house during the evening.

THE CLEMENTS.

THE name of Gregory Clement is connected with one of the most important events of English history; with one of those convulsions of a nation that destroy its ancient land marks and erect new structures upon their ruins; with one of those eras, the prominence and importance of which make new starting points for the religion, the morals, the habits and the politics of a people; with one of the incidents, the causes of which, the means applied and the ends accomplished, have been a theme for historians, and a subject for moralists, ever since the causes, the means and the end, have had an existence.

He was born when the seeds were being sown that produced oppression, bloodshed and revolution. His early life was spent among the contests for power and the lawful resistance of the people. His manhood brought him into contact with those who knew no limit to royal authority, as well as with those who dared to threaten and accomplish their overthrow. His opinions and his character made him prominent among the men who were foremost in placing the government upon a new basis; among those who sat in judgment upon the conduct of their king, and signed the warrant which brought that king to an ignominious death.

The reign of Charles I. as Sovereign of England, from 1625 to 1649, is crowded with the deeds of a people advancing step by step in civil and religious liberty. It is a period in which the vague and ill-defined outlines of the rights of citizens were coming into contact with the kingly prerogative, and when the latent privileges of the subject, so long abridged, began to show signs of vitality and to bring forth some fruit. In like degree also, the abuse of power became more palpable, and bolder in the accomplishment of its purposes, culminating at last in the overthrow of the government, the execution of the king and the exile of the royal family.

Then followed the Commonwealth, which brought to the surface the extravagance of religious fanaticism and the folly of political bigots, combined with visionary and speculative systems of government, each failing in its turn, and rejected by the people.

The trial of the king brought his judges into notice, who, upon the return of his son to the throne, became the especial objects of punishment. The arrest of Gregory Clement is related in this narrative. It took place about the same time as those of his associates. Then followed the trials of the regicides, the history of which has been faithfully given by Mr. Cobbett in his "State Trials." Portions of these have been herein copied, and may not prove uninteresting to the reader. These trials began at Hick's Hall, Old Bailey, in the county of Middlesex, October 9th, 1660. Twenty-nine persons were indicted by the grand jury; as each was brought to the bar, he was charged. In the case of Gregory Clement, the language was as follows:

Clerk.—"Gregory Clement hold up your hand. How sayest thou? Art thou guilty of the treason whereof thou standest indicted, and for which thou art now arraigned?—or not guilty?"

Clement.—"My Lord, I cannot excuse myself in many particulars; but, as to my indictment as there it is, I plead not guilty."

Clerk.—"How will you be tried?"

Clement.—"By God and the Country."

Clerk.—"God send you a good deliverance."

At this stage of the proceedings much altercation took place between some of the prisoners and the court, in regard to the form and substance of the various charges laid, which occasioned considerable delay and confusion. On the third day

Thomas Harrison, Adrian Scroop, John Carew, John Jones, Gregory Clement and Thomas Scot were brought into court for the purpose of being tried together; but, on account of the trouble in regard to the challenging of jurors, the court determined to try them separately. Near the close of the fourth day's proceedings, Gregory Clement was again brought to the bar, and, being called, retracted his plea of not guilty. Sir Orlando Bridgman, Lord Chief Baron and president of the court, then asked him, as follows:

Lord Chief Baron.—"If you do confess your offence, your petition will be read."

Clement.—"I do, my Lord."

Lord Chief Baron.—"If you do confess (that you may understand it), you must, when you are called (and when the jury are to be charged), you must say, if you will have it go by way of confession, that you may waive your former plea and confess the fact."

Clerk.—"Gregory Clement, you have been indicted of high treason, for compassing and imagining the death of his late Majesty, and you have pleaded not guilty: are you content to waive your plea, and confess it?"

Clement.—"I do confess myself to be guilty, my Lord!"

Clerk.—"Set him aside."

Many of the prisoners followed this example, seeing, as they did, that there was no escape under the ruling of the court and the prejudice of the people. At the close of the several trials, each person convicted received the following sentence:

"That you be led back to the place from whence you came, and from thence to be drawn upon a hurdle to the place of execution; and there you shall be hanged by the neck, and, being alive, shall be cut down and —— —— —— ——, your entrails to be taken out of your body, and (you living) the same to be burnt before your eyes; and your head to be cut off, your body to be divided into four quarters, and head and quarters to be disposed of at the pleasure of the King's Majesty—and the Lord have mercy on your soul."

Barbarous as this sentence may appear, yet it was literally carried out; and many revolting scenes occurred at Charing

Cross, where these sentences were executed, October 17. The next day after being sentenced, Gregory Clement and Thomas Scot were taken on the same sled to the scaffold, disemboweled and quartered in the presence of an immense throng of spectators.

Of the subject of this sketch, it is recorded that "he was very silent both in the time of his imprisonment at Newgate and at the time of his execution at Charing Cross; only it is said that he expressed his trouble (to some of his friends in prison) for yielding so far the importunities of his relations as to plead guilty to the indictment; and, though he spoke little at the place of execution, yet, so far as could be judged by some discerning persons that were near him, he departed this life in peace."

Another historian of the times says, "these victims were hanged, and, before life was extinct, were cut down, and their bowels taken out and burned in their presence. It is said of General Harrison, that, while cutting open his body, he rose up and struck the executioner on the ear."

When Col. Jones, the last victim of that day, was brought to the scaffold, the hangman was so horrified with what was passing around him, that he fell fainting to the ground; while his son, as his assistant, carried out the sentence of the law. Revolting as it was, it reflected the tone of public sentiment at the time, which can only be offered as an explanation, and not as an apology, for such administration of justice.

Ludlow, in his narrative of these dreadful events, says of Gregory Clement: "He was chosen a member of Parliament about the year 1646, and discharged that trust with great diligence; always joining with those who were most affectionate to the commonwealth, though he never was possessed of any place of profit under them. Being appointed one of the commissioners for the trial of the king, he durst not refuse his assistance in that service. He had no good elocution, but his apprehension and judgment were not to be despised. He declared before his death, that nothing troubled him so much as his pleading guilty at the time of his trial to satisfy the importunity of his relations; by which he had rendered himself unworthy to die in so glorious a cause."

Stiles, in his Lives of the Regicides, says: "He was a citizen of London—a merchant, and a trader with Spain. He returned to Parliament in 1646. He sat in the trial of Charles I., on January 8, 22, 23 and 29, 1648. He was expelled from Parliament for some misdemeanor, and did not return until after Cromwell's death. He secreted himself in a house near Gray's Inn, and was detected by better eatables being carried there than generally went into such humble habitations, and, upon search being made, he was discovered and arrested May 26, 1660." There was much difficulty in identifying him, until a blind man, who happened to hear him speak, and then said: "That is Gregory Clement: I know his voice."

The Rev. Mark Noble, in his Lives of the Regicides, Vol. I, page 145, says of Gregory Clement: "It is probable he was a cadet of a knightly family in Kent, and that Major William Clement in the London militia was his son."

Immediately after the Restoration, those in authority set about the trial and punishment of the judges of the king's father, using the greatest vigilence to prevent their escape from England. A strange feature is that so few seemed to anticipate the certain consequence of remaining within the realm, and fell an easy prey to their enemies. The shadows of coming events could not have been mistaken, and the wonder is that all such as participated in the trial of the king, did not flee from their country and avoid what was sure to follow. Much to the credit of Charles II, but six of those who sat in the trial were executed, while the others were placed in the various prisons of the country, and soon passed into obscurity. The estate of Gregory Clement being confiscated, his family was scattered, and one of his sons, James, and his wife Jane, emigrated to Long Island in the year 1670. The family is extensive in England, and can be traced from before the tenth century down through the various political and religious changes that have occurred in the nation since that time. The wife of William Penn was one of the branches of the family; the Historical Society of Pennsylvania has collected and published some interesting correspondence between the widow of that great man and Simon Clement, her uncle.

James could not have been blessed with much of this world's goods at his first coming, for, in the valuation of estates in Flushing in 1675, where he then lived, he is rated with four acres of land, three cows, two young cattle, and two pigs.[1] The inference is that he was a member of the religious Society of Friends, which inference is strengthened by his subsequent conduct. At the time of the erection of the Friends' meeting house at the place last named, (1695), James Clement prepared the deed for the lot upon which the house was to be built, and recorded the same; for which service he received eleven shillings and four pence. He also did some work about the building, and received in payment a small pittance; all of which appears among the papers of the society still in existence. In 1702, he was one of the grand jury of Queens' county, that was directed, in the charge of the court, to find bills of indictment against Samuel Bownas, an eminent Quaker preacher and one known to all readers of the history of that sect. This the grand jury refused to do; and the refusal led to much bitter controversy between the judge and that body. Friend Bownas was then in prison, and so remained for nearly a year, as the judge hoped that the next jury empaneled would listen to his charge with more respect, and obey his commands.[2] He fell into a like mistake the second time, and ultimately released his prisoner and abandoned the prosecution. This proceeding was characteristic of Lord Cornbury towards this class of citizens throughout both provinces, and frequently led to trouble between that officer and the people, especially in West New Jersey.

During the year 1676, and while John Fenwick was a prisoner in the fort at New York, Jacob Clement became one of the witnesses to several deeds executed by Fenwick to purchasers in Salem county, N. J.[3] This person was probably a brother of James, as it was two years before his son of that name was born. He may have been a resident of that city and have remained there, but his descendants are not known in these latitudes.

James Clement was somewhat of a public man in the affairs of the county wherein he lived, and, so far as can be discovered,

---

[1] Doc. His. of N. Y., Vol. 2, p 263.
[2] Thompson's History of Long Island.
[3] Salem Records, No. 1.

discharged his duties acceptably. His second wife was Sarah, a daughter of Benjamin and Elizabeth Field. He died in 1724, leaving a will, his wife dying the same year. The names of his children, and the time of their births were as follows: James, born 1670, who married Sarah Hinchman; Sarah, born 1672, who married William Hall, of Salem county, N. J. (second wife); Thomas, born 1674; John, born 1676; Jacob, born 1678, who married Ann Harrison, daughter of Samuel; Joseph, born 1681; Mercy, born 1683, who married Joseph Bates; Samuel, born 1685, and Nathan, born 1687.[4] The only persons of the family that can be traced to Gloucester county, were Jacob, Thomas, John, Sarah and Mercy, who emigrated from Long Island with the families of Samuel Harrison, John Hinchman and some others, about the year 1700. In a sketch of the history of the Presbyterian Church of West Jersey, made by the Rev. Allen H. Brown, he states that John Clement was employed in 1716, by the Presbytery of Philadelphia, to preach at Gloucester and Pilesgrove; this person was, in all probability, the son of James. If so, he had laid aside his Quakerism and had entered a new field of religious duties, the antipodes of that which he had left. His labors extended over a large territory, which is now occupied by his own and other denominations,— showing by their activity that the religious sentiment of our people has kept pace with their material advancement.

Jacob and Thomas purchased lots at Gloucester and resided there for several years.[5] Jacob was a shoemaker, and plied his calling in the old fashioned style, going to the dwellings of most his employers to do the work for the family. This was called "cat-whipping," and, like the harvests of our forefathers, generally ended in a hard-cider frolic, accompanied with an all night's dance. These times, like the pleasant traditions that surrounded them, have passed away, and, by reason of modern innovations, may never be renewed.

William Hall, who married Sarah, came to Salem county in 1677. His first wife was Elizabeth, daughter of Thomas Pyle. She died in 1699, leaving three daughters. The children of

---
[4] Lib. DD, 449.
[5] Lib. Q, 182.

Sarah were William, born 1701; Clement, born 1706, and Nathaniel, born 1709. From these sons have come some of the most respectable families in West Jersey, at one time holding extensive tracts of real estate. Branches, direct and collateral, may be found in every state in the Union, still retaining the elements of wealth and respectability.

From Jacob, John and Thomas Clement, therefore, must the family name be traced in West New Jersey; which has also spread far beyond the limits of this part of the State since the first coming. In this immediate neighborhood, the children of Jacob and Ann Clement represent the family, from whom have come the direct and collateral branches thereof. They were Samuel, who married Rebecca Collins, daughter of Joseph and Catharine; Thomas, who married Mary Tily; Jacob, who married Elizabeth Tily, daughters of Nathaniel, a cooper, and resident of Gloucester; Ann, who married Joseph Harrison; Sarah and Mary.

In the year 1735, Joseph and Catherine Collins executed a deed to Samuel and Rebecca Clement, for a large tract of land at Haddonfield, extending from the main street southwardly to a line running from Cooper's creek westerly, a line at this day entirely obliterated.[6] The consideration for this was one hundred pounds, and the annual payment of ten pounds so long as the survivor of the said Joseph and Catherine should live,— a circumstance significant of the good feeling existing between the parents and children. Upon this property Samuel Clement lived for many years, a consistent member of the Society of Friends and a participant in the political affairs of his day and generation. Being a practical surveyor, he was intrusted with the running and settlement of the several township lines of the county of Gloucester, and also of the boundaries between that and Burlington and Salem counties. This was done in 1765; it was the first attempt clearly to define these disputed matters, which had caused much quarreling among the inhabitants, and some litigation between the several incorporations. This duty Samuel Clement discharged faithfully, and the papers connected therewith are still in good preservation.

---

[6] Lib. EF, 65.

Jacob Clement was a tanner. He settled in Haddonfield in 1743, where he purchased land of Timothy Matlack and William Miller.[7] His property was opposite the "temperance house" in the village, and joined Sarah Norris's lot on the east; there he carried on considerable trade.[8] In those days, most of the hides were procured from the people living along the sea coast, who took in exchange the leather already prepared for use; thus keeping up a business intercourse, although separated by many miles of dreary forest travel. The people of the present generation, who move with railroad speed, cannot appreciate the patience of our ancestors in performing these journeys, sometimes with teams of oxen, heavy, badly built wagons, and upon the worst of highways.

Mercy Clement, who married Joseph Bates, settled with her husband on land which he had purchased of Joseph Thorne, which lay on the south side of the south branch of Cooper's creek, about where the White Horse tavern now stands. None of the estate has been in the name or family for many years, and it would be difficult to trace the maternal blood in that line at the present day.[9] The family name of Clement is sometimes confounded with that of Edward Clemenz, who purchased a tract of land lying in the forks of the north and the south branch of Cooper's creek, near Haddonfield. There is no question of the distinction; as the first is English, and terminates with *t*, while the last is German and ends with *z*. In 1684, Edward Clemenz, who was called "captain," removed from Long Island to a tract of land which he had purchased in Middlesex county, N. J., on the south branch of Raritan river; whence he came in 1692, and settled on the land first named. He established a landing where the two streams came together, which, at that time, was the head of navigation and, for many years after, a place of much business. In his will he gave the landing and a few acres of land to his daughter Hannah Axford, whose name was attached thereto and has ever after so remained.

Edward Clemenz deceased in 1715, leaving five children,[10] namely: Edward, who married Elizabeth Allen, a daughter of

---
7 Lib. HH, 98.
8 Lib. L, 35.
9 Lib. A, 84.

Judah and Deborah, (which Deborah was a daughter of John Adams, one of the first settlers at Moorestown, Burlington county); Hannah, who married Jonathan Axford; Sarah, who married Thomas Cheeseman; Rachel; and Mary, who married Thomas Bates. Edward removed to Chester township, Burlington county, where he died in 1746, leaving his widow and three sons, Benjamin, Judah, and Ephraim.[11] In 1764, Judah purchased a tract of land of John Burrough, Jr., (late part of the estate of David D. Burrough, deceased,) near Ellisburg, whereon he settled. This was sold from him by the Sheriff in 1785 to Jacob Haines, who conveyed part to Esther Clemenz, the wife of Judah and, *perhaps*, the daughter of the grantor, in 1789. Some portions of this branch of the family still reside in this neighborhood. By the marriage of Jonathan and Hannah Axford there was one child, who deceased before the mother. The landing and surrounding property they sold to John Gill in 1763; these have been out of the name for many years.

The descendants of Thomas and Mary Bates reside in this section of the country, intermarried with many of the old families, but not occupying any of the estate coming from their German ancestor, and having scarcely enough of the native blood to make it traceable.

---

[10] Lib. No. 2, 2.
[11] Lib. No. 5, 283.

HENRY STACY.

ROBERT STACY was one of the persons who came to West New Jersey in 1678, to represent the interests of the Yorkshire owners of the land that they had taken of Edward Byllinge, in consideration of moneys which he owed them, and which he was otherwise unable to pay.[1] Joseph Helmsley and William Emley were his associates, together with Thomas Olive, Daniel Wills, John Penford and Benjamin Scott, who represented the London owners, and who also became seized of these lands from the same person and for the same reasons. Robert Stacy first settled at Burlington in discharge of his duties imposed upon him as commissioner; he here became a leading member in the Society of Friends, and took part in the political affairs of the colony. His occupation was that of a tanner; this business he did not resume until his removal to Philadelphia, which occurred a few years after his arrival; he there remained until his death.[2] Among his children was a son Henry, who, together with his wife Mary, came to New Jersey soon after his father, and also settled at or near Burlington. Besse, in his "Sufferings of Friends," mentions that Henry Stacy was taken, on two different occasions, from religious meetings at Cirencester, in Gloucestershire, to prison, and there detained for some time. This was in 1660 and 1662; the subject of this sketch was, doubtless, the same person.

---
[1] Gordon's History of New Jersey, 39.
[2] Lib. G3, 12 8.

During his stay here he was appointed to a membership in the governor's council, a position at that day given only to persons of talent and strict integrity, and a station which was one of the most responsible and difficult to fill.[3]

In addition to the inducements offered by his father's coming here, he was perhaps tempted to try his fortunes in the new colony by letters sent to him from those already settled, whose representations of the country and its productions were certainly very flattering. A letter from John Cripps to Henry Stacy will show in what light New Jersey was held by those already here, in early times; and how they wrote to their friends still in England, whom they sought to induce to follow them to a country that had so many advantages. It is as follows:

"FROM BURLINGTON IN DELAWARE RIVER,
The 26th of the Eighth Month, 1677.

"DEAR FRIEND:—Through the mercy of God we are safely arrived at New Jersey; my wife and all mine are very well, and we have our healths rather better here than we had in England; indeed the country is so good that I do not see how it can reasonably be found fault with. As far as I perceive, all the things we heard of it in England are very true, and I wish that many people (that are in straits) in England were here. Here is good land enough lies void that would serve many thousands of families, and we think if they cannot live here they can hardly live in any place in the world; but we do not desire to persuade any to come but such as are well satisfied in their own mind. A town lot is laid out for us in Burlington, which is a convenient place for trade. It is about one hundred and fifty miles up the Delaware; the country and air seem to be very agreeable to our bodies, and we have very good stomachs to our victuals. Here is plenty of provision in the country; plenty of fish and fowl, and good venison very plentiful and much better than ours in England, for it eats not so dry, but is full of gravy like fat young beef. You that come after us need not fear the trouble that we have had, for now is land here ready divided against you come. The Indians are very loving to us, except here and

---
[3] Leaming & Spicer's Laws.

there one, when they have gotten strong liquor in their head, which they now greatly love. But for the country, in short I like it very well, and I do believe that this river of Delaware is as good a river as most in the world. It exceeds the river Thames by many degrees.

"Here is a town laid out for twenty proprieties, and a straight line drawn from the river side up the land which is to be the Main street, and a market place about the middle. The Yorkshire ten proprietors are to build on one side, and the London ten on the other side, and they have ordered one street to be made along the river side which is not divided with the rest, but in small lots by itself, and every one that hath any part in a propriety is to have his share in it. The town lots for every propriety will be about ten or eleven acres, which is only for a house, orchard, and gardens; and the corn and pasture grounds are to be laid off in great quantities.

"I am thy loving friend,

"JOHN CRIPPS." [4]

Many such letters as the above were written by the new comers to their friends in England and Ireland, some of which were published as circulars among the people, and aided much in the settlement of the colony. In 1698, Gabriel Thomas published a History of West New Jersey, where, as he says, he "resided about fifteen years;" it is a small book of thirty-four pages, part of which is taken up with a glossary of Indian names and translations. This curious old document was lost sight of and remained out of print for many years, until a copy was secured by Henry A. Brady, of New York city, who had the same faithfully lithographed and a few copies reprinted, most of which found their way into the various public libraries of the country. Gabriel excels all in his praises of the land and climate in New Jersey and Pennsylvania, and is only equaled by some of the papers put forth by sharp land-speculators of the present day, by which many verdant folks are sadly cheated.[5]

Henry Stacy did not remain here many years; he returned with his family to England in 1683, and settled at Stepney,

---

4 Smith's History of New Jersey.
5 Leaming and Spicer's Laws.

near London, where he deceased in 1689.[6] He had four children, namely: Samuel, who died young; Elizabeth, who married William Burge in 1705, and settled in Philadelphia; Mary, who married Jonathan Wilson, and resided in London;[7] and Sarah, who married Robert Montgomery, and lived in New Jersey.[8]

In 1683, and before his departure for England, Henry Stacy made a location of four hundred and ninety acres of land in Newton township, near the head of the middle branch of Newton creek, and east of the Graysbury land.[9] By his will all the real estate was given to his children; and, by division of the same effected in 1711, the tract of land above named became the property of Sarah, the wife of Robert Montgomery.[10] About the year 1715, Robert Montgomery built a house on this tract of land, and removed thither from Monmouth county, where he had previously resided.

On April 1st, 1715, Robert Montgomery and Sarah, his wife, conveyed forty acres of land to Jonathan Bolton and Hannah, his wife, being part of the survey before spoken of. The deed is a curious document, the purpose being to secure some means by which the children of the grantors might have an opportunity for education.[11] Jonathan was a shoemaker, and came from Burlington county together with his wife Hannah, who appears as an important personage in the transaction. The lot conveyed adjoined Thomas Miller's and Joseph Hinchman's land, "to be laid out proportionately in one entire square tract until it amount to forty acres,—to the said Jonathan and Hannah, his wife, for ninety-nine years, if the said Jonathan and Hannah shall so long live, or either of them during their natural lives." The consideration was the "paying of one ear of Indian corn yearly; and that the said Hannah shall, at any time hereafter— as soon as the said Bolton shall get a house built fit to live in— teach or instruct, or cause to be taught or instructed, to read English and to do seamstry work, or any other act or parts of acts that she, the said Hannah, is capable to perform, or inform

---

6 Lib. AAA, 128.
7 Lib. CH, 80.
8 Lib. A, 33.
9 Revel's Book, 37.
10 Lib. A, 33.
11 Lib. A, 90.

or direct all the children of the said Montgomery and Sarah his wife, or either of them, or their children, as it may happen, or any child belonging to their family that they shall think fit to send to learn." Whether the said Hannah possessed any qualifications to discharge the duties thus imposed, does not appear; and whether the said Jonathan was to assist in the intervals of his "making and mending," is also in obscurity; yet it may be assumed that this was the first institution of learning established in the eastermost part of Newton township; and it shows the liberality of the founder to have been applied in a commendable direction. The covenants on the part of the said Jonathan and Hannah were equally curious. They were not to put any other person in their place or stead; were not to take more than one crop of winter corn off the premises in each three years; nor to sell, *steal* or waste any timber, except for rails or fire wood. The agreement on the part of Jonathan and Hannah that they would not steal the timber, would imply that Henry and Sarah questioned their honesty, but were forced to entrust the education of their children to them by reason of the few persons suitable for such a purpose. The contracting parties appear to have understood each other in this matter, and considered it best to use plain terms, not susceptible of double meaning or controversy. On what part of the survey was laid out this proportionately square tract of land, or, on what part of the same, Jonathan and Hannah erected their seminary, no means are at hand to discover; a regret that all must feel, in view of its being the spot where commenced the intellectual development of our country, at least in this particular section. Jonathan and Hannah's house, "fit to live in," was nothing more than a log cabin, of one room. The furniture was in keeping, and the accommodation of the scholars may well be conjectured. Little patience and plenty of birch were part of the system of instruction in those days, and lessons in "reading, writing and cyphering" were frequently enforced in this way, and thus made a lasting impression upon the mind of the pupil. With the approbation of parents, the pedagogue became the terror of the rising generation in general, and of evil-doers in particular.

> "Well had the boding tremblers learn'd to trace
> The day's disasters in his morning face.
> Full well they laugh'd, with counterfeited glee,
> At all his jokes; for many a joke had he;
> Full well the busy whisper, circling round,
> Convey'd the dismal tidings when he frown'd.
> Yet he was kind, or, if severe in aught,
> The love he bore to learning was in fault.
> * * * * * * * * * *
> * * * * * * * * *
> * * * * * * * * *
> But past is all his fame. The very spot
> Where many a time he triumphed, is forgot."

This survey lay east of, and adjoining the Graysbury land, bounded partly by Newton creek and extending to John Haddon's estate; now owned by Rhoda Hampton, the Websters, and others. The house erected by Robert Montgomery stood near the late residence of John M. Whitall, deceased, at a short distance east of the old Philadelphia and Egg Harbor road, which then crossed Newton creek at Atmore's dam. After residing here for a few years, the owners of the land broke up their establishment, and returned to Monmouth county, leaving no one of the name within the limits of Old Newton. Of the Montgomery family, Thomas H. Montgomery, of Philadelphia, has published a valuable genealogical history, showing a commendable industry, of much credit to the author and interest to the reader.

JOHN HUGG.

THERE is no one thing that interferes so much with the connecting of events in the early history of the settlement of New Jersey with the adventurers who originated them, as the loss of the names of the passengers that came over in the first ships. This was one of the difficulties that Samuel Smith sought to overcome in the first history of the State; but the fewness of the names which he secured, and the meagreness of the sketches given in his book, show that he has failed in this particular. In isolated cases a family of emigrants may be traced beyond the sea; but this is the case only when litigated estates find a record among the archives of the Commonwealth, involving the particular family before such emigration took place. It is remarkable that correct and complete records were not kept by the proprietors, in whose interest most of the early settlers came, and from whom the title to their land had to be derived. If such were now in existence, much valuable and interesting information could be obtained. The number and the names of the vessels that arrived here have but a vague and uncertain account rendered of them, while the families and individuals which they brought, in very many instances, have been lost sight of altogether. The first record of Salem colony, in 1675, gives the names of most of the persons that came over with John Fenwick; but there doubtless were many names of heads of families, and of those who afterwards became such, that were left out of these lists; and the connection of such with their settlement at home has thus been entirely destroyed.

The court minutes of Burlington, commenced in 1680—a curious volume in its way, also give the names of most of the freeholders that arrived; but they are silent concerning such as neither held land, nor fell into litigation with their neighbors, constituting a large number, perhaps, a majority of those that made up the community.

Through this kind of neglect, it is impossible to trace the history of persons whose participation in the affairs of the colony rendered them prominent during their day and generation; of whose antecedents as well as those of their ancestors, it would be desirable to know something. The subject of this sketch is in this category.

John Hugg was probably an Irishman, coming from the parish of Castle Ellis, in the county of Wexford, Ireland.[1] Although not a partner in the Newton settlement, he had some dealings with those adventurers, and was acquainted with them in the mother country. He was a Friend, since, in 1669, he was imprisoned for not paying a tax to repair the church at Rosanellis, Queens' county, Ireland.[2] He was a man of considerable estate, but was not a partner in the enterprise that brought his wife's family to New Jersey, neither does his name appear in any of the proceedings in relation to the title of their land. His first residence stood upon the Browning estate, where Little Timber creek falls into Great Timber creek, but a short distance from the river Delaware, commanding a view of both streams, as well as of much of the river before his house. For the purposes of a landing, and for the accommodation of the immediate neighborhood, none better could be procured; this made it a public place for many years after the death of the first owner, as a wharf for wood and lumber to be taken away, and for hay brought thither from the river islands, to be consumed among the farmers in that region.

His first location included five hundred acres, which he purchased of Robert Zane in 1683; the property was bounded by both streams, extending more than a mile up the same, and by a line running nearly south from one to the other.[3] At this writing,

---

[1] Lib. EF, 246.
[2] Friends' Writings.
[3] Revel's Book, 55.

it is probable that very little of the old head-line is in existence, as the exchange and division of real estate adjoining the same, since its first running, have destroyed its identity.[4] For some reason, the owner devised part of said tract of land to his great-grand-son William Hugg, who did not come into possession of the same for nearly a half century,—showing the desire on the part of the donor to keep his estate in the name and family.[5] During that lapse of time, a bridge was built over the Great Timber Creek, and a highway established between Salem and Burlington, which has also been changed and improved since the first laying out. What was then an unbroken forest, has in these latter years been brought into cultivation, and is now among the most valuable of our real estate.

The place where John Hugg's house stood has much of historic interest about it from the fact of its being claimed as the spot where stood Fort Nassau, which was built by the Dutch in 1623, and was the first attempt at settlement by the Europeans on the shores of the river Delaware. This, for many years, has been a mooted question among historians without any approach to a conclusion, and it may always so be. Of the existence of such fort, called by that name, built by the Hollanders and near that place, there can be no doubt; yet the exact spot where it stood will always remain an open question, and a fruitful subject of controversy among antiquarians. On Vanderdonck's map of 1656, it is placed below the mouth of Great Timber creek. The map found in Campanius's history has the fort in the same place, and Gabriel Thomas marks it upon his map as a Dutch fort above the mouth of Cooper's creek. Upon a map of the Dutch and Swedish settlements along the Delaware, attached to Ferris's history, this point of dispute is placed where the city of Gloucester now stands, and is stated to have been erected twenty years before the fort at Elsinburg was built, or a settlement attempted to be made at that place. Other maps made in the interest of the various claimants, extending in date from 1656 to 1702, put the fort in different places, but always within a few miles of the mouth of

---

4 Dividend Book, 21, O. S. G.
5 Bull's Book, 106, O. S. G.

Timber creek; but as none of these were published until after it was destroyed by the natives, such authorities may themselves be questionable upon this subject.

The Historical Society of Pennsylvania, being much interested in the settlement of this question, in 1852 appointed a committee to institute inquiries touching the location of Fort Nassau, in which Edward Armstrong, of Philadelphia, took an active part, and visited several places near Gloucester for that purpose.[6] From what was collected, this gentleman prepared and read a paper before that Society, and also before the New Jersey Association; this paper was exhaustive and interesting, yet he leaves the difficulty about where he found it, to be pursued by some ambitious person determined to accomplish that in which all his predecessors have failed. The attention of Mr. Armstrong was called to the particular spot above named by John Redfield, a gentleman who has for many years resided in the neighborhood, and taken much interest in the discovery of the site of the old fort.

A daughter of this gentleman having upon one occasion brought home a rare flower from the river shore, one which, he suspected, was not indigenous, he visited the spot where it was plucked, and found pieces of Dutch brick and ware near by, and portions of a wall surmounted by a few logs, indicating the remains of a redoubt or building erected for defence. This evidence is certainly very strong, and, in the absence of better, will go far towards settling this much vexed question. The interval of two hundred and forty-six years leaves a wide gap in the history of events; and a careful preservation of intermediate occurrences must happen, or else the corroding hand of time will destroy every trace.

Whether the house of John Hugg stood upon the site of the old fort, partly built of Dutch brick and surrounded by Dutch flowers, cannot be settled at this writing, but it is certain that he remained there until his death, which occurred in 1706.[7] His children consisted of four sons: John, who married Priscilla Collins; Elias, who married Margaret Collins (both daughters of Francis); Joseph, who married Sarah ———; and Charles.

---

[6] Proceedings of N. J. His. Society, Vol. 6, 100, 102, 157, 185.

[7] Lib. No. 1, 166.

He was probably a middle-aged man when he came to New Jersey, and his children of marriageable age, for they soon settled around him and became prominent citizens. Excepting as a member of the colonial Legislature in 1685, he does not appear to have participated in political affairs, and but little is known of him beyond his buying and selling of real estate in the section where he lived.[8] Among that which he disposed of, was a lot in Gloucester, sold to Henry Jennings, of Salem, in 1703.[9]

This is probably the individual about whom so much inquiry has been made, as being the connecting link between a large number of descendants scattered through this region, and a fabulous amount of money held in abeyance in the strong government chest in old England, seeking for an owner through his blood. He was a son of William and Mary Jennings, of the parish of Clemond-deane, in the county of Surrey, England. He was born 7th month, 21st, 1642, and married Margaret Busse, of the parish of St. Bartholomew, London, 1st month, 18th, 1666, a daughter of Paul Busse of York city.[10] Their last abode before emigrating was at Kingston-near-on-the-Thames. They came to Salem in the ship Kent, and arrived 6th month, 23d, 1677. By occupation, he was a tailor. He became the owner of considerable estate in Salem and the neighborhood, where he remained several years after his settlement there.[11] His name frequently occurs among those of the first settlers; but whether he was the prospective heir to the immense estates which his descendants claim for him, may appear in the future. He removed to Philadelphia, where he deceased in 1705, leaving but a small family and a limited amount of property.[12]

His widow survived him, and in her will made mention of his family, and thus did much to connect her husband with those of that name in these parts, with which, with but little trouble, the relation could be made complete.[13] In that writing she gave a portion of her real estate to Isaac Jennings and Sarah Jennings, "*reputed son and daughter of my husband, Henry Jennings,*"—a significant expression, and one that may clear up a long continued difficulty.

---

8 Lib. G3, 470.
9 Basse's Book, 111.
10 Salem Records.
11 Salem Records.
12 Files of Salem Wills.
13 Gloucester Files, 1718.

As a starting point, however, his settlement here is material, and, if accepted as a basis, might lead to valuable developments in both directions. If the half be true that is said of the barrels of coin and square miles of land awaiting the lawful claimants, more persistent efforts may be made to secure their distribution among the patient, yet hopeful owners.

John Hugg, Jr., was one of the most active public men of his day. For six years from 1695, he was one of the judges of the several courts of Gloucester county, and, for ten years, was selected by the governor as one of his council, an evidence of his worth as a just and upright man. In 1703, he was appointed one of the commissioners to purchase land of the Indians, and to adopt a plan with that people to collect them together in certain localities in West Jersey,—a duty which required good judgment and much delicacy, so as to avoid the difficulties that generally attend such undertakings, and frequently led to the shedding of blood. The strong attachment of the Indian to the home of his childhood and the graves of his ancestors, has always been a marked feature in him, and the attempt to break in upon these feelings has seldom ended in peace. In the discharge of these duties, however, the commissioners accomplished everything, and, in after years, the last of this people took their departure for other and better hunting grounds, without a word of censure or reproach towards those who, very soon thereafter, occupied their abandoned possessions.

The last public position that he held, was perhaps that of sheriff, to which he was appointed in 1726, and in which he served for four years.[14] Between 1696 and 1710, he made several locations of land between Great and Little Timber creeks, extending nearly to the head of the latter and across to the former, including what is now known as the Crispin farm, which, taken in connection with the surveys made by his father, brought all that territory within the one family, from whom the title can be traced.[15] He also made surveys on Mantua and Raccoon creeks in Gloucester county, and on Alloway's creek in Salem county.

---

[14] Lib. AAA, 193.
[15] Lib. A. 19 to 110, O. S. G.

In 1703, he conveyed to the church wardens of the Swedish church at Raccoon, in Gloucester county, one lot of land *"where the church was late erected,"* and also another tract on Raccoon creek.[16] The church wardens were Wollo Dalbo, William Cobb, Wollo Peterson and Frederick Hoffman. This church is one of the connecting links of the present with the early history of the settlements of West New Jersey, the history of which deserves preservation.[17] His wife, as the daughter of Francis Collins, had received from her father part of one of his surveys, which John Hugg and wife, in connection with parts of his own land, conveyed to John Hinchman in 1699.[18] This grant extended to the north side of the south branch of Newton creek, including about one thousand acres of land; the remainder of his estate reached southwardly to Great Timber creek, showing his landed property to have been large and, even at that early day, very valuable. The residence of this man was probably near the last named stream, on that part now known as the Crispin estate, which he called "Plain Hope;" where a great breadth of meadow land was secured, and the advantage of navigation enjoyed. He was noted for the great number of slaves in his possession, the descendants of whom now constitute a large part of the colored population among us.

John Hugg deceased in 1730, his death being noticed by Smith in his history of New Jersey, in which reference is made to his services as a public man and a trust-worthy public servant.[19] He was found on the ground near his house, speechless; he died the same day, respected by all who knew him. His second wife (Elizabeth Newbie, whom he married in 1714), and the following named children, survived him: Mary, who married Thomas Lippincott; Hannah, Sarah, Priscilla, Joseph, Gabriel, John, Elias and Jacob. John died under age, and Elias without children.

The old homestead fell to the share of Elias Hugg, who lived in the domicile occupied by his father, where he doubtless kept a store to supply watermen and lumber dealers with such provisions as they found necessary. The occupation and character

---

16 Lib. EF. 126.
17 Lib. A, 183.
18 Lib. G3, 279.
19 Smith's History of N. J., 424.

of his customers made whiskey and tobacco large items in his sales, and his premises furnished the scene of many carousals among them when detained by wind or tide.

The land that Francis Collins conveyed to Margaret, the wife of Elias Hugg,[20] they sold before the death of her father; part of this was purchased by Simeon Ellis, being bounded on the south side by the north branch of Cooper's creek. It included the town of Ellisburg, and several surrounding farms. Other tracts they disposed of to various persons, and, at her death, none of her estate remained in their possession.[21]

Joseph Hugg settled at Gloucester Point, as known in 1722, and kept the ferry for several years after that time. The establishment and maintenance of the ferry from Gloucester to Wickaco can be traced through the records with much accuracy, showing that, although the distance was greater than ordinary, yet the demand for transportation was sufficient to make it remunerative. This, like others of its day, consisted of an open flat-boat, worked with long sweeps and small sails, but controlled very much by the movement of the tide. The first license for a ferry between the points above named, was granted by the county courts to William Royden, in 1688, one year before the town was laid out by Thomas Sharp.[22] Wickaco had also been put in shape by the surveyor sent out by William Penn; and what had been the residence of a few Swedes and Finns, was now the embryo city of Philadelphia, with straight and rectangular streets, meeting-houses and markets. In 1695, John Reading became the owner, and was licensed by the same authority.[23] In 1707, John Spey (whose term of office as sheriff had just expired,) became the proprietor, and so continued until 1722, when Joseph Hugg succeeded him.[24] He maintained it for eight years, and disposed of the same to Richard Wildon, who was followed by John Ladd in 1735. As roads were straightened and improved, bridges built and the country more thickly settled, Cooper's ferries had the preference among travelers, since the distance across the river was much shortened, with less risk and much greater speed. These advantages had

---

20 Lib. G3, 71.
21 Lib. S, No. 6, 338, O. S. G.
22 Gloucester Records.
23 Lib. AAA, 80.
24 Lib. AAA, 182.

their effect, which the public were prompt in discovering, and the Gloucester ferry, with varying fortunes, maintained but a secondary importance, until the introduction of steam and other various improvements on both shores of the river. It need hardly be said here that Gloucester was the county town for many years, where the courts were held and the records kept. In the progress of improvement, it gradually lost its central position and became less desirable for such purposes; it was ultimately abandoned, and soon forgotten as the political and judicial nucleus of the old bailiwick. In the early days of the colony, the records were not considered of much value, and were kept in the dwelling of the clerk, in constant danger of loss by fire or miscarriage. An affidavit of John Reading, made in 1711, in which year he was clerk, has been entered among the books at Burlington, showing that his house was burned in that year, and that many deeds and other valuable papers were destroyed.[25] This accounts for the absence of many title papers often inquired for, but never found, as well as for a break in the records of Old Gloucester, that has led to much trouble among land owners and claimants.

Joseph Hugg deceased in 1757, leaving but two children, Samuel and Joseph.[26] The family at this day is limited, and a continued decrease, for the next half century, may leave none of the name, where, for nearly one hundred years, it was as numerous as any other. The large landed estate once in possession of the second generation has long since passed away from the blood, only to be remembered among the blurred deeds and musty records of the past. Although the collateral branches of the family maintained through the female line, are numerous, yet a fatality seems to have attended the other sex and to have well nigh extirpated it from among us.

---

[25] Lib. BBB, 93.
[26] Lib. No. 9, 66.

SAMUEL SPICER.

SAMUEL SPICER was a son of Thomas and Michal Spicer, and was born in New England, prior to 1640. In 1685, he (Samuel) purchased of Samuel Cole, part of his tract of five hundred acres, situated on the north side of the mouth of Cooper's creek, and fronting on the Delaware river, in Waterford, now Stockton township, Camden county.[1] The deed of conveyance says that he then lived at Gravesend, on Long Island; whence came himself, his wife Esther, and three children, the next year, and settled thereon. Esther was a daughter of John and Mary Tilton of Gravesend; but they were married at Oyster Bay, Long Island, the 21st of the third month, 1665.[2]

Gravesend is one of the towns or townships of King's county, New York; it has an ancient historical record running back to 1640, about which time a few English Quakers came from Massachusetts and joined a number of others who were direct from England. It is situated in the southwestern part of the Island, fronting on the sea, where the "Narrows" open into the Atlantic ocean. Like many other towns of that date, it originated in the persecution of Friends, of whom some had previously settled in America, where intolerance was as vindictive and overbearing as at home; and some had come to seek an asylum free from such evils, in which religious opinions could be developed and enjoyed. Among those who came from Massa-

---
[1] Lib A, 44. Lib. G1, 111.
[2] Friends' Records, Long Island.

chusetts was the lady Deborah Moody, a woman of rank, education and wealth, who entertained opinions in common with the followers of George Fox, and who had become an object of disfavor and ill-treatment among the Puritans of the Bay State.

The patent for the town was obtained from Governor Kieft, in 1645, and among the patentees was the name of the female hereinbefore named, who appears to have been a person of decided opinions; this ultimately led her into difficulty with the elders of the church, and caused her to be expelled therefrom, after which she removed to Long Island. The immediate cause of her excommunication was her assertion that "infant baptism was no ordinance of God," which, together with her adherence to the doctrines of George Fox, made her obnoxious to the rulers of the province of Massachusetts.

Thomas Spicer was one of this little colony, and was the head of a family, for, in 1656, among the freeholders of the town, may be found the names of Samuel Spicer, Jacob Spicer and Thomas Spicer, who were probably his sons, having then grown to manhood and there settled. That Samuel Spicer, the person who bought the land of Samuel Cole in 1685, was a member of this family, there can be no doubt; and, if the records of Friends made at that date were accessible, the family could be traced beyond the sea.[3,4,5]

Tradition says that Samuel Spicer purchased his land one year before he came to settle on the same, from which it may be inferred that he had been in this region, examining the various localities, or perchance on a religious visit among the few who had taken up their residence here, and whose religious notions agreed with his own. Henry Wood, who had purchased a part of the same tract, was already a resident, around whom a few emigrants had made their homes, generally choosing the land fronting on Cooper's creek in preference to that upon the river; which land had been, however, located and somewhat improved before his coming. As the land was occupied, and the inhabitants increased, facilities for travel became necessary, and various means were used to accommodate the public, the first of which

---

[3] Lib. A, 44. [4] Lib. G1, 111. [5] Lib. B1, 66.

appear to have been "ferries," across the smaller streams at various points, to avoid the necessity of fording at places near their source, which would have added much to the distance between certain towns and more thickly inhabited sections.

Burlington county, about the present city of Burlington, had filled up with people more rapidly than any other part of West Jersey; and, as land travel had begun between these parts and the embryo city of Philadelphia, Samuel Spicer soon found that his plantation lay in the most direct route between the two points, and that a ferry over Cooper's creek was needed to maintain this line of travel. Such ferry he established, which was situated near the site of the present bridge, and was always known as "Spicer's ferry". It consisted simply of a flat-boat, sufficiently large, whereon to stand a few horses or cattle, moved by ropes on each shore, and only used when some one wished to go over, provided the ferrymen were in good humor and the pay large enough to compensate for their labor; the demands of the public, or the wishes of travelers, being a secondary consideration.

This ferry was maintained until 1747, when a new straight road was laid from Burlington to Cooper's ferries, and a bridge was erected in its stead.[6] This was a draw bridge, and proves that considerable trade was carried on along Cooper's creek by means of vessels transporting wood and lumber to Philadelphia, which trade had its claims as well as those who traveled by land. The manner in which the funds were to be raised to build this bridge, as provided in the law, is worthy of notice, and shows that the purpose of the Legislature was to make such of the inhabitants pay for its erection as were most to be accommodated therewith. In the act, the commissioners were directed to receive voluntary contributions for six months, and then to assess the remainder of the cost on the inhabitants of all the townships of the county of Burlington except the townships of Nottingham and Egg Harbor, and upon the inhabitants of that part of Waterford township in Gloucester county which extended from the river to the Salem road, and upon Cooper's ferries.[7] This shows how sparse were the settlements in Burlington and

---
[6] Lib. G1, 110.
[7] Laws of 1747.

Gloucester counties at that day, and what part of the territory was to be accommodated by a bridge in the place of a ferry.

Samuel Spicer took a leading part in the religious and political affairs of the colony, and his name may be found in many matters of public interest whereby the development of the country was to be advanced. In religious matters he was a consistent and faithful member of his profession. For a long time meetings of public worship were held at his house; these were continued after his death by his widow, who was also an active member in the same denomination. In 1687, he was appointed one of the judges of the several courts of Gloucester county; he also filled other offices of minor importance. His will was executed in 1692, in which year he probably died.[8]

Esther Spicer, his widow, remained upon the homestead estate, entertaining many Friends, and extending her hospitality to the large circle of acquaintances that surrounded her. On the 24th day of the Seventh month, 1703, she was killed by lightning in her own house, together with Esther Saxby, her servant, and Richard Thackara, son of Thomas, he being about eleven years of age. This event is still preserved among the traditions of the family. The sudden death of this person, at that season of the year, necessitated an early burial. The funeral occurred the night after her decease, the family and friends going in boats down Cooper's creek to the river, and by the river to Newton creek, and thence to the Newton graveyard, the place of interment. Each boat being provided with torches, the scene upon the water must have been picturesque indeed. To the colonists it was a sad spectacle, when they saw one so much esteemed among them being borne to her last resting place. To the Indians, it was a grand and impressive sight. Arasapha, the king, and others of his people attended the solemn procession in their canoes, thus showing their respect for one, the cause of whose death struck them with awe and reverence. The deep, dark forest that stood close down to the shores of the streams almost rejected the light, as it came from the burning brands of pine carried in the boats; and, as they passed under the thick foliage, a shadow was scarcely reflected from the water. The

---

8 Gloucester Files of 1692.

colonists in their plain and unassuming apparel, the aborigines clad in gaudy and significant robes, and the negro slaves (as oarsmen) with their almost nude bodies, must have presented, from the shore, a rare and striking picture. Here—all undesigned—was the funeral of a Friend, in which ostentation and display are always avoided, made one of the grandest pageants that the fancy could imagine, a fertile subject for the pencil of the artist, and one well deserving an effort to portray its beauty.

She left a will and disposed of her estate, which together with that of her deceased husband, as retained by her, passed at that time to their children. The last will of each of them may be found on file in the office of secretary of state at Trenton; these prove them to have been persons of education, and of considerable property.[9] Their children were born at Gravesend, where the names and ages of each may be found entered in the books of the Friends' Meeting of that place.[10] They were as follows: Abraham, born 1666; Jacob, born 1668, who married Judith ———; Mary, born 1671, who married Jeremiah Bates; Martha, born 1676, who married Joseph Brown and Thomas Chalkley; Sarah, born 1677, who married Daniel Cooper; Abigail, born 1683, who married Daniel Stanton; Thomas, born ———, who married Abigail Davenport; and Samuel, born ———, who married ——— ———.

The old graveyard, which is on the land settled by Henry Wood, where many of the Spicers were buried, is still in existence, and some degree of care has been given to it by the descendants of the family. It is on the farm now owned by Lemuel Horner, near the site of the Camden city water works. As in many similar instances, the rule of Friends was observed, and no memorials were placed at the graves of the first settlers of the soil,—a source of unceasing regret with such as care to know the resting place of their ancestors. It is particularly unfortunate for those in search of old things, as much valuable information is often obtained from this source, which, but for this, would be entirely lost.

Samuel Spicer, in his will, gave his son Jacob one hundred and fifty acres attached to the homestead, bounded by the river

---

9 Gloucester Files, 1702.
10 Lib. G3, 257. Proceedings of N. J. His. Society, Vol. IX, 02.

Delaware and Cooper's creek; and to his other sons, Samuel and Thomas, one hundred and seventy-five acres each. Samuel died a minor, and his portion of land passed to his brother Jacob. Subsequently, in 1728, Jacob and Thomas made an exchange of land by which Jacob's amount of acres was increased to two hundred and sixty, and Thomas's, whose plantation fronted the creek, had somewhat less within its boundaries. Thomas remained on this property, and died in 1759, leaving a will.[11] His children were as follows: Jacob, who married Mary Lippincott; Thomas, who married Rebecca Day; and Samuel, who married Abigail Willard and Sarah Potter. From this branch of the family, came those of the collateral issue, who retain the blood in these parts, although the name has disappeared for many years.

In the year 1711, Jacob and Thomas made a division of some other portion of their landed estate;[12] and, in the same year, Jacob sold parts of his share of the paternal property to Samuel Burrough and other persons.[13]

Jacob removed to Cape May county, where he settled as early as 1691. He was a member of the Legislature from 1709 to 1723, and surrogate of that county from the last named year to 1741, and for many years one of the judges of the court. He was born in 1668, and deceased in 1741.[14] The reading of the minutes of the proceedings of the legislature during the time in which he sat as a member, discloses many curious things. One of the troubles was the difficulty of keeping a quorum present to do business; and the sergeant-at-arms was always busy in hunting for absentees. In 1716, this officer went to Gloucester, Salem and Cape May counties in search of delinquents. It was, at that day, a toilsome and difficult journey, even under more propitious circumstances. These representatives heard of his coming, and, suspecting the purpose of his visit, started for Burlington by another road than that usually traveled. Striking their trail, he pursued them with his warrant of arrest nearly to Gloucester, where, again to avoid him, they betook themselves to the water, and crossed the river into Pennsylvania. Here the sergeant-at-arms was completely at fault, and no remedy was

---

11 Lib. No. 9, 306.
12 Lib. A, 45.

13 Lib. A, 205.
14 Lib. No. 4, 318.

left to him but to report to the speaker of assembly. Some of them appeared in a few days and were reprimanded; but Jacob Spicer returned home, and writs were issued for a new election in Cape May county. This did not cure the difficulty, for Jacob was again elected, and still neglected to appear as the representative from that county. Another warrant was issued, and the officer on this occasion, found him sick in bed. Not to be cheated, the sergeant required the honorable member to proceed to Burlington with him, and appear at the bar of the house, according to the requirements of authority in him vested. Jacob pleaded indisposition, and was released until he recovered; at which time he explained his absence, and was allowed to take his seat as a member.

His son, Jacob Spicer, deserves a more particular notice. He was born in 1716, and became a member of the Legislature in 1744; which station he occupied for a period of twenty-one years, first in connection with Henry Young, and afterwards, until his death, with Aaron Leaming. He bore a prominent part in the proceedings and business of the house, and was appointed, in connection with Aaron Leaming, to revise the laws of the State; and "Leaming and Spicer's" collection, the result of their labors, is well known at this day as a faithful exposition of the statutes. He was a man of exemplary habits, of strong and vigorous imagination, and strictly faithful in his business relations with his fellow men.

He married Judith, daughter of Humphrey Hughes, who died in 1747, and afterwards married Deborah Leaming, widow of Christopher Leaming, in 1752.[15] The marriage agreement entered into with the last named female, shows much sound sense and discriminating judgment. In 1756, he purchased the interest of the West Jersey Society in the county of Cape May, constituting what has since been known as the 'Vacant Right.'[16] In 1762, he made his will of thirty-nine pages, the most voluminous and elaborate testamentary document on record in this State.[17] He died in 1765, and was interred in the family burial ground at Cold Spring,—a spot now overgrown with large forest timber.[18]

---

[15] Maurice Beasley's Memo.
[16] Lib. A, 154.
[17] Lib. X, 440 to 461.
[18] Lib. B2, 549.

He kept a diary for many years, in which he not only recorded remarkable events, but also entered in detail the cost of his household and the profits of his business. Strictly honest in all his dealings, plain and decided in all his opinions, prompt and exact in all his agreements, he had, as he deserved, the confidence and regard of his neighbors through all the years of his business life, and served his constituents faithfully as their representative until his death. Many extracts from his diary have been published by the Historical Society of New Jersey, which evince the peculiarities of the man, his views of duty toward himself, and toward those with whom he had intercourse.

THOMAS STOKES.

THOMAS HOOTEN of the Parish of St. Ann, Black Friars, and John Stokes of Wentworth street, in the Parish of Stepney, both of which places are in London, in the county of Middlesex, England, became the owners, as tenants in common, of a certain amount of proprietory rights in West New Jersey. Thomas was a tallow chandler, and John a baker; by these avocations they respectively maintained their families, and gained some extra means to make a venture in the enterprise so much talked of among Friends at that time. The deed conveying this interest was made from William Penn and the other trustees of Edward Bylynge to Thomas Hooten in the year 1676, who immediately conveyed the undivided half-part thereof to John Stokes.[1] It is possible that they were creditors of Edward Bylynge, whose failure in business a short time before involved so many of his creditors in loss, and led to much trouble concerning his estate.

Thomas Hooten and John Stokes were relatives; perhaps their wives were sisters; both were members of the religious denomination of Friends, and were seeking some new place of abode, where their notions of right might be more freely indulged in, with some hope of promulgating their doctrines in peace. Thomas Hooten came immediately to New Jersey to look after their interests, leaving his family in London until he should be heard from, and some conclusion be reached in regard to a permanent removal to the new place. On the 29th day of the 8th month, 1677, he wrote to his wife as follows:

---

[1] Lib. BBB, 191.

"I am this present at the town of Burlington where our land is; it is ordered to be a town for the ten Yorkshire and ten London Proprietors. I like the place well; our lot is the second next the water side. It's like to be a healthful place and very pleasant to live in. I came hither yesterday, being the 28th of October, with some friends that were going to New York. I am to be at Thomas Olive's house until I can provide better for myself. I intend to build a house and get some corn into the ground. And I know not how to write concerning thy coming or not hither; the place I like very well, and believe that we may live here very well. But if it be not made free, I mean as to the customs and government, then it will not be so well, and may hinder many that have desires to come. But if these two things be cleared, thou may take thy opportunity of coming this summer.

THOMAS HOOTEN."[2]

The reference here made about the customs relates to those exacted at New Castle by direction of Governor Andros, they being a percentage upon all the goods brought by emigrants,—an impost which was so much complained of that it was in a short time abandoned. Thomas Hooten's wife soon closed up the affairs of her husband in London, and followed him to America. Thomas Hooten, the son, married Elizabeth Stanley of Philadelphia, in 1686, at which place he then resided, and continued to reside for many years after.[3]

John Stokes, however, remained in London, supplying the people with bread, and husbanding his means to develop his interests here through his brother Thomas. Of this there is undoubted evidence, for, as late as in 1719, in a conveyance of land in this State, he is called John Stokes of Wentworth street, London, biscuit baker, etc.[4]

Thomas married Mary Bernard of Stepney, in 1668, where he remained until the project of removing to America induced him to abandon his home and calling. He and his family came among the first, as they arrived at New Castle about

---

[2] Smith's History of New Jersey, 105.
[3] Friends' Records, Philadelphia.
[4] Lib. BBB, 191.

the middle of the 6th month, 1677, in the ship Kent,—the same that brought the commissioners appointed by William Penn and others—and went immediately to Burlington. He perhaps remained here until the next year, with the others, for mutual defence, and to view the country before he made selection of a place for settlement. This was, however, done in due time, and was chosen from among many on Northampton river, or, as it is now generally known, Rancocas creek. It is probable that three of his children were born in London, and three in New Jersey. They were as follows : Sarah, who married Benjamin Moore ; Mary, who married John Hudson ; John, who married Elizabeth Green ; Thomas, who married Deliverance Horner and Rachel Wright ; Joseph, who married Judith Lippincott and Ann Haines (widow) ; and one other son, who removed to North Carolina, but whose name and family have been lost sight of. Mary, the mother of these children, died in 1699, and Thomas, the father, in 1718, aged 78 years.[5] The obligations of the family are due to Charles Stokes of Rancocas, a descendant, for collecting and arranging much of the history of the same ; who also has taken pains to save from loss many incidents that relate to the early history of West New Jersey. How much might yet be preserved, if more of our citizens would emulate his example. In this region, nothing is known of John Stokes, save what may be gathered from the records in the office of the secretary of state at Trenton. In 1716, an inventory of his estate was made, upon which is the following endorsement : "Came to his end by an unnatural death, in ye lower end of Gloucester county." Too many years have intervened to bring the story of his death to the present generation, however interesting it might now be to his descendants.

In the year 1709, the second Thomas herein referred to, purchased of John Kay of Springwell, three hundred acres of land in Waterford township, (now Delaware,) Camden county, the larger part of which tract is now owned Mark Ballinger, and by the heirs of Jacob Anderson, Nathan M. Lippincott, and Daniel Hillman, deceased. This land is bounded on the

---

[5] Lib. No. 2, 138.

south side by the north branch of Cooper's creek; it extends along both sides of a tributary of the same, and includes what is now some of the best soil in the neighborhood.[6] He settled on this tract, his house standing near the present residence of Mark Ballinger. By his first wife, Delieverance Horner, were the following children: Thomas, who married Abigail Matlack; Deliverance, who married Darling Conrow; Lydia, who married Samuel Haines; and Rachel, who married John Cowperthwaite. By the second wife, Rachel Wright, who was of Oyster Bay, Long Island, N. Y., to whom he was married 7th month, 1st, 1715,[7] were Joshua, who married Amy Hinchman; Hannah, who married Thomas Cole; Jacob, who married Priscilla Ellis; John, who married Ann Champion, (widow) in 1751; Rosanna, who married Samuel Collins and Joseph Browning; and Kesiah. Thomas deceased in 1736, and Rachel in 1747.[8]

This settlement, as made by Thomas Stokes in 1709, was in the midst of an Indian neighborhood, which extended from the north branch southerly to a tributary of the south branch of Cooper's creek, that formed what is generally known as Peterson's mill-pond. On a map left by Thomas Sharp, showing a large survey made to John Willis in 1686, he wrote beside the water course last named, "the stream the Indian King liveth on."[9] This was a survey of some thirteen hundred acres, and lay on both sides of the branch, the original boundaries of which have long since been obliterated.

Judging from the first settlement by the emigrants, the residence of the king referred to by Friend Sharp may be believed to have been on the farm owned by Joseph H. Ellis. Around his palace were collected a few other wigwams, in which lived the retainers of the royal household. This community of aborigines was within the bounds before mentioned, consisting of some families with a few acres of cleared land near the streams; but all were subordinate to the authority named by Friend Sharp. This authority was absolute, dispensing law and equity to the people, regardless of the precedent and without appeal. The wigwam of the king doubtless had

---

6 Lib. BBB, 75.
7 Friends' Records, Long Island.
8 Lib. No. 4, 98.
9 Sharp's Book, 11, O. S. G.

more pretension than others that surrounded it, and was distinguishable by its size and the more outlandish hieroglyphics seen upon the skins that made its covering.

It is unfortunate that our Quaker surveyor, in the multiplicity of his records, did not leave some account of this people who have so entirely passed away from the land; some history of their principal settlements, their form of government, their religion, habits, language and traditions. His intercourse with them in the purchase of land, and his frequent entertainment by them in their own manner of hospitality, while traveling through the country as deputy surveyor, gave him abundant opportunity to study all these peculiarities; and in his own quaint manner he might have saved to future generations that which has been entirely lost. There is evidence that this settlement extended northwesterly, and along Tindall's run, nearly to the main south branch, as the remains of one of their burial places may be seen near Tindall's run, east of the Haddonfield and Berlin road. Within the memory of some now living, a few of these people eked out a miserable existence on part of the land formerly owned by Thomas Stokes, near the residence of Aquilla Hillman and brothers; drunken, lazy, worthless beings, they were a hinderance to a progressive community, and the last of an unfortunate race.

Joshua Stokes occupied the homestead after the death of his father, and there he remained during his life; his brothers and sisters settling in other parts of Burlington and Gloucester counties, whose various descendants have multiplied so rapidly that no attempt to trace them would prove successful. Of the landed estate, as purchased by the second Thomas in 1709, only a small portion is held by his descendants in the direct line. One hundred and sixty years have wrought many changes in the ownership of this property, the beginning and end of several generations, and the gradual extinction of the many land marks by which it was identified. But a single branch of the family is left, that feels any attachment to, or has any knowledge of the localities familiar to the first settlers; that is able to tell where the natives had their wigwams, and where they buried their dead; where the medicine-man dispensed his nostrums, and where the fortune-teller mumbled over her divinations, to the terror of children, the amusement of youth, and the wonderment of all. The descendants of those who were born upon the soil, have passed away; their places have been left to other occupants who, after a like lapse of time, will also be forgotten. A part of this family owned a tract of land in Newton township, lying on the north side of the middle branch of Newton creek, and resided there many years. These were the descendants of Jacob Stokes, who married Priscilla Ellis, a daughter of Joseph, and granddaughter of Simeon and Sarah Ellis of Springwell, the first of the name hereabout. The original estate was conveyed by Isaac Hollingsham to Sarah Ellis, aforesaid, then a widow, in 1717, which afterward became the property of her son Joseph, who deceased in 1757, leaving four daughters, one the wife of Jacob Stokes.[10] He died intestate; and, there being no male issue, the land descended to his children in equal parts, of which Jacob Stokes became the owner about the year 1760, by purchase, and there he deceased. The other daughters of Joseph Ellis were Abigail, who married Caleb Hughes; Sarah, who married John Bubzy and Isaac Mickle; and Kesiah, who married Benjamin Vanlear, M. D.[11]

Portions of the estate remained in the name until 1828, when George Lee, now deceased, became the owner of the homestead; and by his name it is more familiarly known among the people. Of the direct and collateral line of this family much the larger part remained in Burlington county, where they still represent a fair portion of the wealthy and influential inhabitants. The name, however, may be found in many of the states of the Union, and may be traced to John Stokes, biscuit baker, of Wentworth street, in the parish of Stepney, Middlesex, which, at this day, is within the limits of the city of London.

---

10 Lib. A, 56.
11 Lib. C, 241, Woodbury.

GRIFFITH MORGAN.

AFTER Samuel Cole had fixed his abode at New Orchard, across the creek from the little village of Penisaukin, and was laboring diligently to increase the extent of his cultivated acres, so that his farm might yield a comfortable support to his family, he was summoned to his old home in Hertfordshire, England, to arrange some unsettled business at that place. But for the care and attention extended to his wife and children by the few families then living at the town before named, their condition would have been lonely enough in their wild forest home; yet his absence was relieved by this friendly intercourse and protection, as well as by the confidence that had grown up between the emigrants and natives, from whom they had nothing to fear. The deference and respect observed toward the wives and daughters of the emigrants by these untutored children of the forest must always be a redeeming trait in their character, and commend their memories to us for all time to come. Though the emigrants were at their mercy for many years, yet no accusation of tyranny or brutality is recorded against them; although the settlers were without the means of protection or defence, yet no advantage was taken by the natives of their superiority to satisfy a feeling of envy or revenge.

The imperfect knowledge of navigation, and the primitive construction of vessels at that day, rendered a voyage across the ocean dangerous and tedious, and the time occupied was usually more than double that now taken by sailing-vessels. The time of return of Samuel Cole was doubtless fixed upon between himself and wife, always excepting the dangers and delays of the sea, and, as the period of his coming approached, the anxiety of his family to see him again very naturally increased. On the return voyage of the ship in which he came, the island of Barbadoes was taken as a point of stopping; this lengthened the trip, and in a degree added to the uncertainty of arrival. At that place, however, Samuel Cole was attacked by one of the diseases incident to those latitudes, and, before the departure of the ship, had died, and was buried. The extended distance of the voyage, and consequent delay therefrom not being known to the wife, she made frequent visits to Philadelphia to meet her husband and welcome him to his family again. Tradition says that she would stand for hours by the water's edge, looking anxiously down the river for the sail that would bring the father of her children. These visits and watchings at last attracted the attention of a young mariner who frequented the port, and who was not long in discovering the cause of her anxiety. Sympathizing with her, he extended his inquiries in her behalf, and at last discovered that her husband had died on his return, as before named. Her grief for this sad bereavement enlisted his feelings, and, finding that she was about to return home alone in her boat, he offered to accompany her and manage the same. This offer she accepted, and he sailed the craft up the river to Penisauken creek, and thence nearly to her residence, thus bearing the sad news to her children and neighbors.

This man was Griffith Morgan, who, after a proper interval of time, sailed his own skiff up the creek aforesaid to offer his consolations to the widow, and to interest himself about her children and estate. This solicitude soon assumed another shape, and culminated in the marriage of Griffith Morgan and Elizabeth Cole. Many interesting incidents are still remembered in the family touching this courtship and marriage, and will pass from generation to generation by reason of the commendable desire to preserve everything relating thereto. The log house was but lately standing on the farm owned by the heirs of Joseph H. Coles, now deceased, just as left by Samuel Cole on his departure to his native place in England; its limited dimensions and primitive appearance leave no doubt as to its many years of existence.

Griffith Morgan was probably a native of Wales, whence he emigrated to America on account of the religious persecution of Friends in that part of the kingdom of Great Britain. In 1684, he was imprisoned in Haverford West for not attending church, with many others who refused to pay tithes for the support of the rector of the parish wherein they lived, or to attend at the place where he dispensed the gospel to the people. Some years previously to this time, he was arrested in the public road and beaten by the officers, for a similar disregard of the laws and customs of the land in which he lived ; but to these exactions he could not yield, nor could he act in opposition to his religious belief in such matters.[1] Although he appears to have been in this country in 1677, yet he may have visited his old home, and have subjected himself to the outrages above named, as was the case with many of the emigrants. Without assuming that any proof of identity be made out, yet the probabilities are that these facts relate to one and the same person.

The marriage referred to took place in 1693, in Philadelphia, the issue of which was one son, Alexander. Previously to this, however, Griffith Morgan had purchased several tracts of land in Gloucester county, New Jersey. This is evidence that he was a man of considerable estate. The probability is that he continued his sea-faring life, as he does not appear to have participated in the religious or the political affairs of the colony at that time. Upon his marriage, he made a settlement upon a tract of land which he had bought of David Lloyd and Isaac Norris, executors, in 1677, being part of the estate of Thomas Lloyd of Philadelphia, a contemporary and intimate friend of William Penn.[2] This tract was bounded by the river Delaware and partly by Penisauken creek. The old mansion is still standing, but so much enlarged and changed as scarcely to be recognized. This tract of land appears to have been located by Samuel Jennings, the first governor of New Jersey; it was resurveyed in 1717 by Alexander, the son of

---
[1] Besse's Sufferings, Vol. I., 748—759.
[2] Lib. B2, 590.

Griffith Morgan.³ It contained five hundred acres of land, and extended more than a mile up the creek aforesaid, and about one-fourth that distance along the river.⁴ The house is just where a son of Neptune would have it,—near the mouth of the creek, with a clear and uninterrupted view of the river Delaware, where every kind of craft on both streams must pass in sight.

Elizabeth Morgan survived her last husband, and died in 1719. By her will, she bequeathed much personal property among her children.⁵ They were Samuel Cole and Rachel Wild, wife of James Wild (by her first husband), and Alexander Morgan (by her last). This paper indicates beyond question that she was twice married, and also the number of children by each. Her estate was large for the day in which she lived, and was fairly distributed to those nearest of kin.

According to the good order of Friends at the Newton Meeting, in the year 1717 Alexander Morgan was married to Hannah, a daughter of Joseph and Lydia Cooper, and granddaughter of William Cooper, the first emigrant. This marriage connected the Morgan family with the Mickles, the Hopkins, the Ladds, the Coxes, the Coateses and the Clements, of West New Jersey, and with the Rawles, the Riggses, and other families in Pennsylvania,—forming a line of consanguinity which was strengthened by subsequent like connections and in some instances brought down to the present day.⁶ Alexander Morgan settled and remained on the homestead property during his life, making but little change therein, either by purchase or sale. He deceased in 1751, leaving his widow and several children, as follows:⁷ Joseph, who married Agnes Jones; Benjamin, who married Jane Roberts 1761; Isaac; Mary, who married Edmund Hollingshead; Elizabeth, who married William Miller; Lydia, who married Nathan Beeks; Sarah, who married Josiah Burrough; Hannah, Rachel, and Alexander, who died young. Joseph and Agnes Morgan had one child, Griffith, who married Rebecca Clement, daughter of Samuel, in 1766. The first wife of Joseph Morgan deceased, and he married Mary ———.

---

3 Lib. W, 386.
4 Sharp's Book, 39. O. S. G.
5 Gloucester Files, 1718.

6 Lib. No. 4, 77.
7 Lib. No. 7, 165.

Their children were Joseph, who married Mary Evans and Mary Butcher; Hannah, who married —— Saterthwaite; Elizabeth, who married Joseph Reeves; and Sarah, who married James Hinchman. Mary, the second wife of Joseph Morgan, having died, he married Mary, a daughter of Joseph Stokes. Their children were Isaac, who married Sarah Ridgway; Alexander; Mary, who married Joseph Bennett, and Benjamin, who married Mary Champion. Mary, the third wife, deceased, and Joseph Morgan married Elizabeth Atkinson. By the last marriage there was no issue. Benjamin and Jane Morgan's children were Hannah, Benjamin, who died young, and Benjamin R., who never married. He owned part of the paternal estate on Penisauken creek, which, at his death, he gave to his cousin Alexander, of Philadelphia. Edmund and Mary Hollingshead's children were Joseph, who married Alice ——; Edmund, who married Hannah Foster; Morgan, who married Rebecca Matlack; John, Samuel, Hannah, Lydia and Sarah. Nathan and Lydia Beeks had one child, named Morgan. The direct line of connection with the Morgan family of such as are of the blood in the region of Gloucester county, may be traced through Griffith and Rebecca. The issue of this marriage were three daughters: Agnes, who married Enos Eldridge; Rebecca, who married James B. Cooper; and Ann, who married William E. Hopkins. The family connection is very extensive throughout the United States, yet, in many cases, the blood is so much diluted as to be scarcely traceable.

Where the Penisaukin creek falls into the Delaware, and about where the old Morgan house is situated, some two hundred years ago stood Fort Eriwonack, it being one of the centres from which a colony was to radiate and fill the territory that now constitutes Pennsylvania and New Jersey with an industrious and happy people. In 1634, Charles I., king of England, made a title to Sir Edmund Ployden, knight, etc., for all the territory lying between New England and Maryland, with that vague and doubtful kind of description incident to the little knowledge of the estate being conveyed,—a kind of description which in so many instances led to disputes and, sometimes, to bloodshed among the owners and settlers.[8] No

---

[8] Smith's History of New Jersey, 24—60.

regard was paid to the claims of the Dutch or Swedes within the limits of this grant, and, as a consequence, trouble very soon emanated from this source; so, in the same manner, was Ployden's title ignored when the king made a deed to his brother, the Duke of York, for the same section of country.[9] The government was also fully vested in Sir Edmund, and the territory was called "the Province of New Albion, to be and remain a free County Palatine, in no wise subject to any other."[10] Sir Edmund was made Earl Palatine, which gave him regal power in all things save allegiance to the king; and each of his family was also titled, in contemplation of a settlement to be effected in the wilds of America.[11]

Steps were immediately taken to know something of this land; and Beauchamp Plantaganet, a friend of the earl, was despatched to America to make the necessary examinations and report accordingly. This trip was undertaken in 1636; and, after much traveling through the forests, and intercourse with the natives, this adventurer ascended the Delaware river to the mouth of the Penisauken creek, where some of his company had already erected a fort, and where they were waiting for the government of Sir Edmund Ployden to be established. About the same time, another settlement was made near where Salem now stands; but the adventurers were driven away by the Dutch and Swedes, who were jealous of their success, and feared their influence among the natives. The fort at Penisauken creek was occupied for four years by those under the patronage of Earl Ployden, and considerable trade was carried on with the Indians. Subsequently, a small colony of Swedes occupied the place, and doubtless remained until the proprietors assumed the government of West New Jersey and established their title to the land. It is needless to follow the history of this matter, and only necessary to say that none of the brilliant imaginings of the founder of this "palatinate" were realized, and that the whole thing was ultimately abandoned.

A remarkable feature in this attempt at settlement in

---

9 Mickle's Reminiscences, 24.
10 Mulford's History of New Jersey, 72,
11 New Jersey Historical Society Proceedings, Vol. I., 38.

America is that each of the historians of New Jersey, from first to last, has been unsuccessful in collecting and arranging the facts in relation thereto. Each in his turn has explored musty records and consulted new authorities upon the subject, and has extracted something overlooked by his predecessor; yet each became satisfied that other and more reliable knowledge was in existence, but knew not where to find such desirable information.

As late as in 1784, a person named Charles Varlo came to Philadelphia, claiming to have an interest in the palatinate, and enlisted that able jurist, William Rawle, in his behalf, making some stir among the holders of the land in this region by reason thereof. One faithful and industrious antiquarian of that day, John Penington, of the city just named, made this matter a specialty, bringing his knowledge and experience to the purpose, to accomplish what so many others had failed in; but at last, despairing of success, he pronounced the whole matter a fabrication, and Sir Edmund Ployden an imaginary being.

To Isaac Mickle is due the merit of giving this matter a most thorough investigation, and of collecting the reliable authorities in his valuable book, so that the reader may see at a glance the trouble that has always surrounded it, and the doubts that may always attend it. It is, however, one of the incidents of the history of New Jersey, and of this particular neighborhood, that is worth remembering; the truth of which, at some future day, may be brought to light, and may make the first settlement of Griffith Morgan a point of particular attraction to such as care to preserve those myths of historical romance so pleasantly blended through the early settlement of our country.

A gold mine was also said to exist near Fort Eriwonack; and its value was held out as an inducement for persons to come here and settle, unbounded wealth being promised to such as would make the venture. This belief, like the old fort, has passed away with those that occupied the land long before our ancestors came; it being one of the fancies of the brain that promised so much in the New El-dorado, and yet, for those who accepted all as truth, realized so little. This spot is therefore surrounded with much of antiquarian interest; and whether the story of the Palatine of New Albion be true or false, it will always be a fertile subject of inquiry for those that labor without reward and enjoy the search, though nothing be found. To such as have patiently turned from page to page among the dusty tomes that are crowded into the dark corners and out-of-the-way shelves of the various libraries and offices of record in our country, the last lines will be fully understood and appreciated.

THE BURROUGHS.

EDWARD BURROUGH was a distinguished Quaker in England from 1652 to 1661, during the bitterest persecutions that raged against that religious sect. He resided at Underbarro, in Westmoreland. He was convinced through the preaching of George Fox when a young man, and soon became a prominent defender and expounder of his belief. He and a companion, who held the same faith, were the first Friends that visited the city of London, and preached their doctrines to the people. He addressed several letters to Oliver Cromwell, asking his protection for those of his belief, and after his death appealed to his son Richard, but without success.

In 1654, he was mobbed in the city of Bristol for preaching to the people in the streets, and cast into prison in Ireland for a like offence, and finally banished from the island.[1] After Charles the Second came to the throne, he obtained a personal interview with the king, and procured an order from him to prevent the persecution of Friends in New England ; which order the Friends in London forwarded by a ship that they had chartered specially for that duty, at an expense of three hundred pounds. He was an eminent preacher and an influential man. It does not appear that he was ever in this country.

[1] Besse's Sufferings, Vol. I., 39.

John Burrough was imprisoned in Buckinghamshire in 1660, and Joseph Burrough suffered the same injustice the same year in Essex. The son and daughter of William Burrough were maltreated in Warwickshire on their way to Banbury meeting. These facts prove that the family was numerous in England and mostly Quakers. The names are here given to show the probability of their emigrating to America, for the same are found among the inhabitants of Long Island in a few years after the dates above given.

In September, 1675, the assessor's list of the town of Newtown, in Long Island, showed that John Burrough was the owner of forty acres of land, one horse, four oxen, four cows, and twenty-four sheep; and that Jeremiah Burrough was the owner of six acres of land, two horses, two oxen, three cows, and one pig. In 1683, in the same town, Joseph Burrough was assessed with eighteen acres of land, one horse, one ox, and three cows; and John Burrough with ten acres of land, two horses, and one cow. In this year, Jeremiah had increased his territory to twenty acres of land, two oxen, four cows, and two pigs. In the last named year, Edward Burrough was assessed in the town of Jamaica, in Long Island, with five acres of land, and one cow. In 1689, Jeremiah Burrough was lieutenant in one of the "train bands" of Newtown. This is rather strong evidence against his being much of a Quaker; yet he doubtless is the same person hereafter named in this connection.

The inference is but a fair one that the persons named as having suffered in England for their religious opinions, and those named as being residents of Long Island, are the same; and it is only to be regretted that some better account of them has not been left on record, so as to make it conclusive. The first of the name that came in Gloucester county was John Burrough, who settled at Gloucester, and followed the occupation of a weaver.[2] He was here in 1688, as, in the first month of that year, he purchased rights of Robert Turner, and, in the tenth month of the same year, he purchased more of such real estate from Joseph Wood.[3] These rights John Burrough put into one survey on the north side of Gloucester river or Great

---

[2] Lib. G2, 57.
[3] Lib. G1, 129.

Timber creek, extending from Beaver branch on the south, to Little Timber creek on the north.[4] In 1690, he lived on this survey, but the situation of his house is not known. This location is now divided into many farms, among which are the Crispin estate, the property of Isaac G. Eastlack, and others. In 1693, it became the property of Thomas Thackara, and subsequently was owned by the Huggs and the Harrisons. In 1759, this survey and the adjoining lands, extending northwesterly between the branches of Great and Little Timber creek to their junction, were resurveyed ; this re-survey discloses the title of the said lands, and is valuable in this respect.

The next that came was Edward Burrough, who purchased one hundred and seven acres of land of Thomas Atkinson in 1693, it being part of the tract that he had purchased of Francis Collins in 1691.[5] In 1698, Edward bought an adjoining tract of John Martin, the same day that Martin sold another part of the said tract to Joseph Tindall, from whom the stream of water that passed through it takes its name.[6] This land was about one mile south of Haddonfield, in Delaware township, and fronted on the north side of the south branch of Cooper's creek, part of which is now owned by William H. Mason. Edward Burrough built his house beside the old Salem road, a short distance from the stream, and there he resided several years. This old Salem road was not part of that laid out by order of the Colonial Legislature, but was an Indian trail going in the direction of that town, crossing the heads of most of the streams in its way. It has been lost sight of for many years, and no part of it in this neighborhood is now open. It is possible that he removed to Salem before his decease, as, in 1730, letters of administration were granted to Priscilla Burrough upon the estate of Edward Burrough (her husband), deceased. No other reference in regard to his death has been noticed ; and, if this suggestion be true, his descendants may be found in that region of country.

The tract of land before mentioned was held by those of the

---

[4] Lib. G2, 172.
[5] Lib. G1, 01.
[6] Lib. G3, 266.

family name for many years, and until Elizabeth Burrough, a daughter of John, married Samuel Matlack, whose descendants still hold portions thereof. This John, however, was a son of Samuel, hereafter noticed; but in what manner he became the proprietor of this estate is not apparent at this writing, for want of sufficient records and a proper care of family traditions. Of the immediate descendants of John and Edward Burrough, nothing is known at this time, the male branches of the family being but few, and not the owners of much land in this section,—a circumstance which adds to the difficulty of tracing their lineage. Samuel Burrough (frequently spelled Burrows) was the third person of the name that came within the bounds of Old Gloucester. He is first noticed at the little town of Penisaukin, with William Matlack, Timothy Hancock and John Roberts, where he married the daughter Hannah of the last named person. This marriage occurred in 1699, at the house of Sarah Roberts, widow of John. This female was a noticeable character in her day. When the inhabitants of Chester township, Burlington county, in the year 1696, thought proper to assume the responsibilities of a corporation, Sarah Roberts was the only female that signed the agreement as one of the residents and taxpayers therein.

In the year 1700, James Adams, a son of John Adams, conveyed one acre of land to the Friends of Chester, for the purpose of a meeting house and burying place.[7] The grantees consisted of thirteen persons, of whom, Sarah Roberts was one, she being the only instance of a female acting in the capacity of a trustee for real estate in that religious society. These things mark her as a woman understanding and participating in matters generally left for the sterner sex to manage and control, and show that her opinion was regarded, and her influence sought in things of public importance.

The first purchase of Samuel Burrough was made on the 16th of November, 1698; it was one of three hundred acres of land from Joseph Heritage. This tract lay on the south side of the south branch of Penisaukin creek, in Waterford (now Delaware) township, Gloucester county.[8] At that time Samuel was a

---
[7] Lib. GH, 373.
[8] Lib. G3, 285.

resident of Burlington county, and perhaps did not move to his plantation until his marriage in the next year. In 1699, he bought of the same person an adjoining piece of land, and, in 1703, purchased of Richard Bromley two hundred acres, also adjoining, which last was called a farm; and thereon the said Richard Bromley "did lately dwell." To this place Samuel Burrough soon after removed, and there he remained until his decease. The present residence of Edward Burrough, a lineal descendant of Samuel, in Delaware township, stands upon the site of the original dwelling erected by Richard Bromley. Samuel Burrough must have been a man of large means, as he continued to purchase real estate until the year 1730, when he found himself the owner of some two thousand five hundred acres of land, which, at this day, includes many of the best farms in Camden county. He was a careful man in regard to his titles, for they may be found regularly upon record as the purchases were by him made.

One of these tracts was conveyed by Hugh Sharp, in 1715, to Samuel Burrough and Hannah, his wife, and to the heirs of their bodies,—not an ordinary expression in a deed, and one which carried the estate to the survivor of the two persons therein named.[9] In his will, he devised this particular tract to his daughter Sarah, "if she please her mother," doubtless referring to her marriage. The evidence that she pleased her mother in her marriage with Samuel Nicholson is that she made a deed for the same land, in 1732, to Samuel Nicholson and Sarah, his wife, thus carrying out the intention of Hugh Sharp, who designed the estate to remain in the family.[10] Sarah died soon after the last title was executed, but her husband, in good faith, conveyed the same to their son Joseph in 1747.[11] This shows that Joseph Nicholson in the direct line descended from Samuel and Hannah Burrough,— a fact which may be of interest to the present descendants of the said Joseph.

Neither John, Edward nor Samuel Burrough appears to have taken part in the politics of West Jersey, although each lived

---
9 Lib. A, 220.
10 Lib. AD, 242.
11 Lib. AD, 245.

in Gloucester county when there was much trouble among the people in this regard. Samuel Burrough's will bears date June 19th, 1720, but was not proved until 1732, in which year he died.[12] The homestead property he gave to his son Samuel, thus continuing for another generation this part of his estate in his own name. He divided his land among his children, giving his daughters a fair proportion, in opposition to the notion entertained at that day regarding the rights of females, much to his credit, however, and far in advance of his generation. The children of Samuel and Hannah Burrough were Samuel, who married Ann Gray; John, who married Phœbe Haines; Isaac, who married Deborah Jennings and Abigail Hewlings; Jacob, who married Sarah Thorne and Cassandra Ellis; Esther, who married William Bidgood; Kesiah, who married Samuel Parr; and Sarah, who married Samuel Nicholson.

Asa Matlack, in a note made by him of this family, says that Samuel Burrough and his son Benjamin were drowned in the river Delaware; but under what circumstances, or at what particular time, it does not appear. A son Benjamin is mentioned in the will of Samuel Burrough, but no part of the estate passed to him after the father's death, nor does his name occur in any place connected therewith. This would give the story some color of truth, and it may be accepted as reliable, for, Asa Matlack who resided near the old homestead, made himself familiar with all the traditions of the neighborhood. A son Joseph is also named, who probably died after the making of the will, and before his father. After the death of Samuel Burrough, his widow Hannah married Richard Bidgood. There does not appear to have been any issue by this marriage.

Ann Gray, the wife of the son Samuel, was a daughter of Richard and Esther (Gillott), who settled on a tract of land in Newton township.[13] Richard purchased land of Francis Collins in 1701, now mostly owned by Joseph C. Stoy and John E. Hopkins, fronting on the south side of Cooper's creek, where Francis Collins had his landing. Richard Gray deceased in

---

[12] Lib. No. 3, 193.
[13] Lib. G2, 25.

1736, leaving but two children, John and Ann.[14] The second Samuel was born, lived and died at the old homestead, and, in the course of his life, accumulated some other real estate. He adhered strictly to the religious faith of his father, and was a regular attendant at the Haddonfield Meeting. His children were numerous; the following are their names: Hannah, who married Robert Stiles; Sarah, who married Isaac Mickle; Mary, who married Archibald Mickle; Ann, who married Joseph Tomlinson; Joseph, who married Mary Pine, Kesiah Aronson and Lydia Tomlinson; Abigail, who married Thomas Thorne; Bathsaba, who married Jacob Haines; Samuel, who married Sarah Lamb; and Rachel, who married Benjamin Pine and David Davis. The intricacies of this genealogy are very apparent, and will hardly be ventured upon, except by some expert with much patience and little hope of reward. To his son John, Samuel Burrough gave, by his will, four hundred acres of land, lying on the south side of Penisaukin creek, which he increased by purchase from his eldest brother Samuel, in the year 1735. The most of this property passed out of the name and blood many years since.

On a part of this estate John Burrough lived; his children were as follows: John, who married Barbara Fussell; Samuel, who married —— Spencer and Mary Black; Josiah, who married Sarah Morgan; Gideon, who married Phœbe Burnett; Benjamin, who married Phœbe Potter; Esther, who married Juda Clemenz; Martha, who married Benjamin Clemenz; Mary, who married Richard Gibbs; Enoch, who married Deborah Middleton; and Hannah, who married Joshua Gibbs. Among these may be recognized the ancestors of several families of Gloucester and Burlington counties, at this day unknown through the little care paid to the preservation of family bibles with their continued memoranda of births, deaths and marriages.

The John last named, who married Barbara Fussel, was a blacksmith; he owned and lived on part of the farm lately David D. Burrough's, deceased, in Delaware township, near Ellisburg, where yet may be seen the remains of his shop. His residence was a tavern, standing near where the Eves-

---
14 Lib. No. 4, 84.

ham road crossed the King's highway leading from Salem to Burlington. This position made it one of the most public places in the county. This was part of a survey made by William Cooper; it came into the Burrough family about the year 1720, and became the property of John Burrough in 1735. Subsequently, however, it passed out of the name by sale, but, like much other real estate, has again come to be owned by one of the name and family who held the fee nearly a century and a half since. The house stands on the west side of the old road; it is built of brick and has every evidence of having been erected many years ago. How long, and from what time it was kept as an inn, there is no means of knowing at this late day, as those who received its hospitality and enjoyed the many sports that centered there, have gone to

"That undiscovered country from whose bourne no traveller returns."

Apart from its use to the traveling community and to the neighborhood as a resort for business and gossip, it was a place where many of the out-door manly pastimes were enjoyed, and where collected those who in them participated. In front of and to the north of the house, was a level, straight piece of road, kept smooth and used as a race-course, where the "quarter-nags" from far and near were brought to compare their mettle and speed, and where their owners and admirers would back their opinions with a bowl of punch or a bottle of metheglin. Horses, like politicians, unless successful, soon wear out in public estimation, and the animal that baulked, shied or bolted, lost his friends and had no place upon the turf. In those early days, small purses and short races were the fashion, and thimble-rig or faro-bank were unknown. This amusement with our ancestors was a genuine sport, clear of all the evil tendencies which now cling to it. The improvement of the stock of horses was not set up as an apology, neither was jockeying then reduced to a science; but they engaged in it for the "fun of the thing," and faced the censure accordingly.

Fox hunting was also an out-door recreation. There was no scarcity of game; the country was free from fences; good dogs and practiced hunters abounded. Every farmer and farmer's son had his steed and saddle, ready (after the crops were safe)

to engage in the exciting sport. Being acquainted with the haunts and familiar with the habits of the animal, there was no uncertainty of a day's sport whenever they took the field, and frequently more than one "brush" was secured during the hunt. The assembling was generally by arrangement near the ground where game was plentiful; but, by common consent, the day's sport ended at a country inn, where the incidents and mishaps could be talked over before the open wood-fire of the bar-room, and while surrounding a bowl of egg-nogg, "called in" by the man who carried the brush in his hat. This old way-side tavern was, in its palmy days, often the scene of the last of a hard day's hunt, where the boldest rider and the luckiest sportsman would receive the rude gratulations of his companions in the chase; while others, who were unhorsed or thrown out in some of the many ways incident to the sport, would arrive singly, only to be jeered and laughed at for their ill luck, and made to drown their chagrin by drinking deep from the bowl before them. But, like the old tavern, their sports have passed away; the inroads of agriculture upon the forests, and the filling up of the country with a thrifty and industrious people, have left no shelter for reynard in this part of New Jersey.

John Burrough rented the tavern and his shop, and removed to Haddonfield, where he plied his calling for several years before his death.

Isaac Burrough, upon his marriage with Deborah Jennings, settled in Waterford township, near the Delaware river, but, after his second marriage, removed into Newton township, where he deceased. His first wife was a daughter of Isaac Jennings, reputed to be a son of Henry, and claimed as the person who connects the large property in England with so many expectants in the United States.[15] The collateral branches of the family are numerous in New Jersey. Their genealogy has been carefully digested and arranged in anticipation of the call for the heirs of Isaac Jennings to receive the property which has so long been without an owner. The children were Isaac, who married Rebecca Nicholson (widow of Abel and daughter of Aaron Aaronson); Priscilla, who married James Cooper;

---
15 Lib. No. 9, 157.

Jacob, who married Elizabeth Gill; Hannah, who married Joseph Mickle; and Reuben and Jacob, who both died young.

Samuel and Hannah Parr settled on part of the "Burrough" estate, in Waterford township, where Samuel deceased in 1753, leaving the following children:[16] John, Mary, Samuel and James. Hannah, his widow, died in 1750. Samuel was a prominent person in the Society of Friends, and, perhaps, a preacher.[17] None of the name reside in this region at the present time.

William and Esther Bidgood, in a few years after their marriage, removed to Pennsylvania, where they both deceased.[18] Nothing is known of the family.

Sarah, the wife of Jacob Burrough, died soon after her marriage in 1751, as, in 1753, Jacob married Cassandra, the widow of Jacob Ellis and daughter of Josiah and Ann Albertson. The Burroughs are among the ancient Quaker families of the neighborhood of Haddonfield, and belong to those that originated and sustained the society hereabout for more than one hundred years. In the name has been held some of the most valuable real estate in the county of Gloucester; but, in the progress of time, this has passed to other owners, strangers to the blood. The collateral branches of the family are numerous as well as those in the direct line; and much trouble and uncertainty attend the effort to collect and arrange them correctly.

---

16 Lib. No. 7, 312.
17 Lib. No. 8, 345.
18 Lib. Z, 297, 481.

THE WOODS.

THERE were more persons of this name among the first English emigrants who came to New Jersey than of any other. They must have been pleased with the scheme of settlement as laid down by the commissioners and proprietors, and must have considered its success as certain from the beginning. They were men of some estate, for they purchased their proprieties before they left their native land; and men of education, for they at once participated in the management and control of the new government, as novel in its operations as were the people and the scenery that surrounded them in their adopted country. Men of decided characteristics, they were well calculated to develop any new system; and, acting from a proper motive, they would soon draw around them those who naturally sought such guides in this adventure. They were all Quakers, and a perusal of Besse's History of that sect will show the reason why the members of this family were so ready to break up their homes in England and seek others in the wilds of America, regardless of the privations and troubles that attend such an undertaking. From 1654 to 1683, persons of this name were imprisoned in the Hertfordshire, Lancashire, Yorkshire, Durham, or Cumberland jails, for attending the meetings of Friends, no matter how quietly or secretly the same were held. Frequently some of these were kept for two years in these loathsome places, without any means of redress or opportunity to attend to the wants of their families. The acts against conventicles, as passed by the parliament, and the little reliance to be placed in the promises of the king, left no hope for an end of the persecutions which this religious body suffered. As late as in 1681, the House of Commons rejected the following resolution:

"That in the opinion of the House, the persecutions of the Protestant dissenters upon the penal laws, is at this time grevious to the subject, a weakening of the Protestant interest, an encouragement to Popery and dangerous to the peace of the Kingdom."

Those who observed this reflex of public sentiment could not be mistaken in regard to the rigorous enforcement of the laws; and such as suffered thereby were forced to look to some other place where this kind of intolerance could not reach them.

William Wood arrived at Burlington in the "Willing Mind," John Newcomb, commander, in November, 1677; and, in the records of the first court held at that place in 1680, William and Thomas Wood appear as grand jurymen, when that part of the government was put in motion.[1] William was the first to change his place of settlement and take up his abode in New Jersey. In the year last named, he located thirty-six acres within the town bounds of Burlington, where he, no doubt, built himself a log cabin, perhaps emulating his neighbors in its style and finish. He married Mary Parnell in 1682.[2]

In the year 1677, John Wood of Attercliffe in the parish of Sheffield, Yorkshire, purchased of George Hutchinson a quantity of proprietary rights, to be used by him on his arrival in West New Jersey;[3] and the ship book of the "Shield" has an entry which says, "that John Wood of Attercliffe, in the parish of Sheffield, Yorkshire, was a passenger in that vessel, and arrived in the Delaware in the tenth month, 1678."[4] His family consisted of five children, who came with him, and whose names also appear on the said book.[5] They were John, Joseph, Esther, Mary, who married Thomas Coleman, and Sarah.[6] Thomas Wood, a brother of John, came in the same ship; he located a lot of land in Burlington and built a house

---

1 Smith's History of New Jersey, 102.
2 Revel's Book, 12
3 Lib. B1, 98.
4 Historical Society of Pennsylvania.
5 Smith's History of New Jersey, 109.
6 Revel's Book, 79.

thereon.[7] He married Mary Howle in 1685, but of his family nothing is known.[8]

This was the first English vessel that passed up the river as far as Burlington.[9] It was moored to a tree, and the next morning the passengers went ashore on the ice. A "godlie companie" of Friends came in this boat, and doubtless were well received by those who had preceded them.

In 1682, John, Constantine and Jeremiah were residents of the town of Bury in Lancashire, and in that year they each bought of the trustees of Edward Byllynge proprietary rights in anticipation of their removal to America.[10] This town lies about forty miles northeast of Liverpool, and has, since their departure therefrom, become a place of considerable proportions.

It may be safely concluded that the first John herein named is not the John herein secondly mentioned; but, when spoken of in other connections, the distinction does not appear so clear.

Jonathan Wood (husbandman), a resident of the parish of Maltby in Yorkshire, England, also became the owner of rights about the same time; but he abandoned the idea of moving to the "Plantations in America," and sold his acres to Christopher Snowdon in 1684, who came over and settled in Burlington county about the time of his purchase.[11]

John, Constantine and Jeremiah Wood came to New Jersey the same year in which they made their purchases. On September 4th, 1682, Henry Wood bought of Samuel Cole a tract of land on the north side of Cooper's creek, bounded by the land which Samuel Cole subsequently sold to Samuel Spicer and extending to the river Delaware.[12] This appears from maps of the Woods' and Spicers' lands in the office of the Surveyor-General at Burlington, N. J., as re-surveyed in 1723 and 1728. The deed says: "situate at Arwawmosse, in West Jersey, also the dwelling house or tenement which he, the said Samuel inhabiteth, with the folds, yards, &c., excepting one cow house, &c." This farm fronted on both streams, and was part of the survey returned to Samuel Cole a few months before this sale, upon which the improvements were all new. The

---

7 Revel's Book, 27.
8 Lib. B1, 123.
9 Smith's History of New Jersey, 108.
10 Lib. G1, 01, 03, 05.
11 Lib. B1, 248.
12 Lib. B1, 66.

Indian name of this plantation does not appear to have been retained through many generations, as no mention of it is made in any of the papers after that time.[13]

The Henry Wood last named was not of the family first noticed. He with his wife and children came from Newport, Rhode Island, as appears by the records of the Friends' Meeting of Newton; but not until a year or so after the purchase, as his certificate of removal is dated twelfth month 5th, 1687. He was probably a son of William Wood, author of a much read Quaker pamphlet, called "New England's Prospect," published in 1634; he returned to England in 1635 with his brother John in the ship Hopewell, from which Henry named his homestead property.

John, Constantine and Jeremiah selected their land at the mouth of Woodbury creek, also in Gloucester county, where had already settled a few Swedes. In 1683, John Wood located three hundred acres at that place, within the bounds of which these persons erected their habitations.[14] This hamlet is deserving of more than a passing notice, for from it radiated all the settlements in that part of Gloucester county, as well in the unexplored forests as along the river shore. In John Wood's house a meeting was established after the order of Friends, to which place those in that section resorted for religious worship.[15] It was known among the people at that day as "The Shelter," although the name does not often occur, neither does it appear to have any significance. This meeting was so kept until 1696, in which year John Wood conveyed to Thomas Gardiner, William Warner and Joshua Lord, a lot of land for a graveyard, and upon this a meeting house was erected the same year.[16] No vestige of the old building remains, but the spot in which were laid the bodies of those hardy pioneers is still held sacred. So may it always be.

Those who were contemporary with John, Constantine and Jeremiah Wood in this little colony, and who joined in the meeting at John's house, were Joshua Lord, Henry Tredway, Thomas Gardner, Thomas Mathews, John Ladd, George Ward, William Warner and others. The several locations of these

---

13 Revel's Book, 63.
14 Revel's Book, 43.

15 The Friend, Vol. 4, 206.
16 Lib. G3, 214.

persons extended along the river shore as far as Eagle Point, up the creek to about where Woodbury now stands, and also on Mathew's branch, a tributary of the last named stream. Previously to the settlement by the English, these localities were called "Long Harris's creek" and "Batchelor's bank;" but these names were soon lost sight of after their coming.[17] In what way they were derived does not appear.

There were a few Swedish families about the mouth of Woodbury creek previously to the coming of these colonists. This may have been an inducement for stopping at that place.[18] The Dalboos had land thereabout, and Walla Swanson of Wickaco was likewise an owner of two hundred acres.[19] In his will dated in 1692, he gave these to his children, John, Peter, Swan, Mary, wife of William Warner, Lydia, wife of Josiah Harper, Bridget, Catharine, wife of James Laconey, and Judith.[20] They divided the same in 1729.[21]

In 1715 John Swanson conveyed to John Ladd, Henry Wood and John Cooper, one acre of land on the west side of the creek and on the south side of the King's road, no doubt to be used for a burial place, and thereon to erect a meeting house.[22]

John Wood sat as a member of the Legislature in the year 1685, was appointed one of the commissioners for dividing land in the same year, and, in 1687, one of the judges of the courts of Gloucester county. From 1695 to 1700, he was continuously appointed one of the coroners, and in 1701 made king's attorney. In 1687, he was, with William Warner, presented by the grand jury for assisting two "notorious criminals" to go out of the county. John Wood appeared at the bar of the court, made proper explanation of the matter and acknowledged his error; and the case was abandoned.[23] It was, perhaps, through his influence that the courts were held at Red Bank for a few years; but this was soon found to be an out-of-the-way, inconvenient place, and accordingly abandoned.

John Wood deceased in 1705, having a large landed estate,

---

17 Revel's Book, 68.
18 Lib. Z, 454.
19 Lib. E, 423.
20 Lib. X 177.

21 Revel's Book, 61.
22 Lib. A, 145.
23 Minute Book of Gloucester County Courts, Woodbury.

which he disposed of by his will.[24] The homestead property fronting on the creek and the river, he gave to his son John. In this devise he excepted the graveyard and meeting house property, doubtless to avoid any trouble after his death in regard to the boundaries and rights of the society to the same. His wife Sarah and the following named children survived him: John, Joseph, Esther, Constantine, who married Alice —— and died in 1734. Mary, Henry, Sarah, who married Joshua Lord, and Alice.

It is probable that the daughter Sarah died before her father, as mention is made of her four children in his will. Portions of this estate remained in the name and family for many years after his decease.

Henry Wood remained on the premises which he purchased of Samuel Cole, and there died in 1691, having been a member and constant attendant of the Newton meeting. He was somewhat of a public man, as he was a member of the Assembly in 1683 and 1684; but in the last year did not attend.[25] In 1684, he was appointed one of the commissioners for laying out land and purchasing from the Indians; and, in 1685, he acted as a commissioner for opening highways and keeping the same in repair. He rendered service in many other minor positions, and was a useful man in his time. All his traveling was done by water, and the daughters as well as the sons were experts in managing a boat. No fishing excursion was defeated for want of a man to work the skiff, nor sailing party put off because the beaux were not there to manage the helm. To be equal to every emergency in this means of locomotion, was part of an education not to be neglected; and no little table talk originated in the rivalry of those who prided themselves upon their nautical ability, and who were always ready to test their knowledge by a race on the water.

Newton creek (perchance, before the tide was checked by dam, or the stream narrowed by banks,) has been the scene of many such trials. The merits of every new craft must needs be tested, and, with a good breeze, the temptation was too great not to know the strong and the weak points thereof. Some

---

24 Lib. No. 1, 173.
25 Leaming and Spicer's Laws.

public friend, upon his return from meeting, may have unwillingly found himself in the midst of one of these contests, and, while having fast hold of his hat, may have yielded for the moment to the excitement that surrounded him, forgetting that the force of example always strengthened precept. In our day, horse flesh supplies this means of travel, and the followers of George Fox have now as keen an eye for the good points of a roadster as our ancestors had for the sailing qualities of their water craft.

Early and constant training will control the bent of our nature, yet its latent propensities may occasionally crop out in a direction not consistent with our education, or with the examples that sometimes surround us. The line that separates a commendable purpose from that which leads to error, may, in our zeal, be overlooked, and, unless experience and ripe judgment be regarded, the dangers of a wrong direction are much increased.

In 1683, Henry Wood located three hundred and fifty acres of land on the north side of and fronting Cooper's creek; this he afterward sold to Matthew Burden in 1686, who probably settled on the same.[26] This grantee was a resident of Portsmouth in Rhode Island at the time of the purchase, and in some way connected with the grantor.[27] The name of Burden does not often occur among the early settlers hereabout. Richard, a son of Matthew Burden, conveyed this land to John Cox in 1711; much of it is now included in the Browning estate, and divided into various farms. He was the owner of much other land in West New Jersey, but he disposed of the greater part before his death.[28]

Henry Wood's will bears date April 2d, 1691, and was admitted to probate in June of the same year.[29] Samuel Carpenter of Philadelphia and George Smith of West New Jersey were made trustees, and Walter Clark and Benjamin Newberry of Rhode Island were appointed executors. In this writing, he says that he was a resident of Hopewell, in Gloucester county, West New Jersey, which name has, however, been lost to the estate for many years. Although much

---

[26] Basse's Book, 150.
[27] Lib. BB, 67.
[28] Lib. BBB, 68.
[29] Lib. No. 13, 518.

real estate passed under this document, yet it does not appear of record for more than half a century after its probate,—an occurrence that but seldom happens, and that remains uuexplained. The appointment of persons residing in Rhode Island as executors, is accounted for by his having left friends and, perhaps, relatives in that colony upon his removal hither. His children were Henry, James (a shipwright, who lived in Philadelphia and married Mary Pellor in 1715); Richard; Judith, who married Thomas Willard in 1689; Abigail, who married Daniel Cooper in 1693; Hannah, who married Joseph Nicholson in 1695; Elizabeth, who married Stephen Newbie in 1703; and Benjamin, who married Mary Kay, daughter of John, in 1707.

His widow Hannah survived him several years. In 1754, the son Henry died a single man, and by his will disposed of the real estate given to him by his father among his brothers and sisters.[30] Thomas and Judith Willard settled on a plantation near that of her father's. Thomas died there in 1734, intestate, leaving three sons, James, Henry and Thomas.[31]

Abigail, the wife of Daniel Cooper, died in a short time after her marriage, and without children. Joseph Nicholson, a son of Samuel, and the first of the name that settled in Gloucester county, became the owner of the homestead in 1699, by deed from James Nicholson, and with his wife made that his home.[32] Joseph deceased in 1702, intestate, leaving but two children, George, who married Alice Lord in 1717, and Samuel, who married Sarah Burrough in 1722, Rebecca Saint in 1744, and Jane Albertson, widow of William and daughter of John Engle, in 1749.[33]

Stephen and Elizabeth Newbie settled in Newton township on part of the land taken up by Mark, the father of Stephen. He died in 1706; his widow and two children survived him. Of these, Mark died single in 1735, and Hannah married Joseph Thackara.

After the decease of Joseph Nicholson, Benjamin Wood purchased the homestead estate, and thereon he resided until

---

30 Gloucester Files.
31 Lib. W, 386.
32 Lib. G3, 214.
33 Gloucester Files.

his death in 1738. Like his father, he called the old place Hopewell, the original Indian name of Arwawmosse, as mentioned by Samuel Cole when he conveyed to Henry Wood, having been abandoned at an early date in their ownership. Benjamin Wood's plantation fronted on the river. His wife Mary survived him, and the following children: Mary, who married Joseph Cole and Richard Matlack; Elizabeth, who married Elias Toy; Hannah, who married Joseph Heulings; Abigail, who married Robert Hunt; Benjamin, who married —— ——, the latter dying in 1750; John, Judith and Jane.[34] By his will, the real estate of which he died seized, passed to his children; but in that generation much thereof was alienated, and, at this writing, no part of the soil is held in the name.[35]

The graveyard commenced by the Woods and Spicers, which stands upon the original tract of land as surveyed to Samuel Cole, is still in existence. Some of those in whose veins flows the blood of the first English settlers, have with commendable care preserved its boundaries, and saved it from encroachment. In later years memorials have been raised to show where lie the remains of some of the younger branches of the families; but, of the first there interred, no tradition or record has been left to point out their particular resting place.

The majestic oaks that stood around, and upon whose bark had been rudely traced the names of many of the occupants, are gone. These marks, which, to the heedless axeman, were without meaning, bore in themselves a history, full of interest to the descendants of those whose memory they were designed to preserve. No trace of these old, living monuments is left, and with them passed away the only remembrance of the first settlers in that part of the colony. Where stood the primitive forests, as owned by Henry Wood one hundred and eighty years since, the soil is now divided into valuable farms, and, before another like lapse of time, will be included in the city of Camden and be covered with the dwellings of its inhabitants.

34 Lib. No. 7, 367.
35 Lib. No. 4, 135.

RICHARD MATHEWS.

IN 1699, Richard Mathews was a "factor," and resided in Stokenewington, in the county of Middlesex, England.[1] He had previously resided in the city of London, but had probably been driven from that place on account of the persecution of Friends. He was largely interested in the proprieties, and, through his agents in West New Jersey, made several surveys in Gloucester county. In 1683, a survey of five hundred acres was returned in his name as made in Newton township; upon which now stands the larger part of the village of Haddonfield.[2] In 1691, he, through Elias Farr, his attorney, conveyed one hundred acres of the same to William Lovejoy, it being that part of the survey which lay east of the main street of the town, at that time nothing more than a bridle path or Indian trail.[3-4] The remainder of the tract was by him sold to John Haddon, in whose family it was held for many years.[5] The blacksmith shop, which is marked on a map of the same made in 1700, and is the only building thereon represented, was, in all probability, placed there by William Lovejoy, who attended to the wants of the small community around him in his particular line. It is supposable that his business included the duties of a tinker, a gunsmith and a clock maker also, and that he looked after all the hardware of the housekeepers near his place; kept all the fowling-pieces and muskets in good order; and regulated

---

[1] Lib. G3, 458.
[2] Revel's Book, 38.
[3] Basse's Book, 237. [4] Lib. G3, 93.
[5] Lib. G1, 07.

the clocks thereabout when the sun shone and his dial was properly adjusted.[6]

In 1684, Edward Byllynge appointed Thomas Mathews as his attorney, with the consent of George Hutchinson, to sell thirty shares of propriety of West New Jersey. This shows that he had the confidence of the patroon.[7] It would appear that William Lovejoy was an apprentice to Thomas Mathews, for, in 1696, Thomas Gardiner, as administrator, conveyed to Lovejoy fifty acres of land for services rendered.[8] These services were those of a blacksmith; but this calling he abandoned after a few years.

In 1686, a survey was made to Richard Mathews on a branch of Woodbury creek, called Mathew's run, containing four hundred and fifty acres, whereon his son Thomas and Thomas Gardiner, who married his daughter Hannah, settled. Another survey was made near Red Bank of three hundred and fifteen acres, which, together with all his other real estate, passed out of the name many years since. There is nothing to show that Richard Mathews himself ever came to America; while but part of his family came, consisting of one son, Thomas, and a daughter, Hannah, who married Thomas Gardiner, Jr., in 1684, at Friends meeting in Burlington.[9] The probability is, however, that these were his only children, and that, like Elizabeth Estaugh, they came hither to look after the estate of the parent.

Thomas Mathews, the son, settled on the tract of land near Woodbury creek, and, if he was not a bachelor, he died without children, and intestate, as his entire landed property passed to his sister Hannah Gardiner, through whose blood at this time there remains no connection with this particular family in New Jersey.[10] Richard Mathews died about 1696, and the son Thomas about 1702.

In the year 1683, Thomas Mathews made a proposition to the Legislature to exchange one thousand acres of land for a site to build a saw mill in the forks of Rancocas creek. The matter was referred to commissioners, and, perhaps, was con-

---

6 Lib. B, 129.
7 Lib. G1, 139.
8 Lib. G2, 176.

9 Lib. S, 465.
10 Basse's Book, 52, 123.

summated ; but where the saw mill stood, and whether it has been maintained to the present time, do not appear.

In 1685, he was returned as one of the members of the Legislature from the fourth tenth; at which time he resided at Woodbury creek. In the same year, he represented Benjamin Bartlett, Robert Squib and Robert Squib, Jr., as their proxy in the disposal of proprieties, and in voting for members of the council of proprietors; this privilege, from some irregularity, the Legislature revoked, and passed a resolution to meet the trouble. The Legislature was jealous of the power and action of the council, and much diplomacy had to be used by the more conservative members of each body to prevent difficulty between them. The interest of many members of the Legislature in the soil, and their desire to encourage emigration and settlement, prevented the clashing of the two bodies, which, otherwise, would have led to disastrous results.

ROBERT TURNER.

THIS person was never a resident of New Jersey. Being a man of large estate, he became interested in the various speculations going on in England, touching the settlements in America, and rendered much service to such as desired to remove, but had not the means wherewith to accomplish that end. He was an Irish Quaker, engaged in merchandise. He resided in the city of Dublin, where he much advanced the spread of the religious doctrines which he had espoused; and this brought upon him an equal measure of persecution from those who conceived their authority to be absolute.[1] In 1662, he, with many others, was taken from a religious meeting of Friends, and confined in the Bridewell prison. Two years before he had been locked up in Newgate for a like offence. In 1665, he was imprisoned and despoiled of his goods, and, in 1669, had his property again taken for the reason that he had refused to pay tithes. His estate seems to have had an attraction for such as, in those days, went about with religious zeal to punish those who differed with them in opinion.

Immediately upon the consummation of the grant of territory in America by the king to William Penn, he closed his business in Ireland, and removed to Philadelphia. He came in the ship "Lion" of Liverpool from Dublin, with the certificate of the Men's Meeting of Friends from the last named place, and arrived in Philadelphia on the 14th of the eighth month, 1683. He brought with him his family and some twenty

---
[1] Lib. B1, 52.

persons as servants. With William Penn he was on the most intimate terms, having been associated with him in his various religious difficulties; and he was frequently his companion in his travels in England. From among the extensive correspondence that occurred between them, it may not be uninteresting to copy a letter, in which an explanation is given of the way in which the appellation that his territory now bears, was fixed, showing how fearful he was that the same might appear egostistical. It runs as follows:

"To ROBERT TURNER. 5 of 1st Mo, 1681.

Dear Friend: My true love in the Lord salutes thee, and dear friends that love the Lord's precious truth in those parts. Thine I have, and for my business here. Know that after many waitings, watchings, solicitings and disputes in Council, this day my country was confirmed to me under the great seal of England, with large powers and privileges by the name of Pennsylvania—a name the King would give it, in honour of my father. I chose New Wales, being as this is a pretty hilly country, but Penn being Welsh for *a head*, as Penaumoire in Wales, and Penrith in Cumberland, and Penn in Buckinghamshire, the highest land in England, he called this Pennsylvania, which is *the high* or *head Woodland*; for I proposed, when the secretary, a Welshman, refused to have it called New Wales, *Sylvania*, and they added *Penn* to it; and though I much opposed it and went to the King to have it struck out, and altered, he said it was past, and would take it upon him. Nor could twenty guineas move the under secretaries to vary the name, for I feared least it should be looked on as a vanity in me, and not as a respect in the King as it truly was to my father, whom he often mentions with praise. Thou mayst communicate my grant to friends, and expect shortly my proposals. It is a clear and just thing, and my God that has given it to me through many difficulties, will, I believe, bless and make it the seed of a nation. I shall have a tender care of the government, that it will be well laid at the first. No more now, but dear love in truth. Thy true friend,

WILLIAM PENN."

In this letter are disclosed the real sentiments of the writer upon the subject in question, as well as the history of a matter now of much interest to all. In a money point of view, this grant discharged a debt which the creditor feared never would be paid, and about which there had been much controversy and dispute. The influence of William Penn with the king was a cause of jealousy among those who surrounded him, and who sought the same position that he undoubtedly held at court. This was the secret of all the opposition to the settlement of the claim, and the fact that hindered its consummation.

The charter, which contained "large powers and privileges," has become a venerable document. It has been framed, and it now hangs in the office of the secretary of the commonwealth at Harrisburg. It is ornamented with heraldic devices on strong parchment, and, at the top of the first page, displays a finely executed likeness of Charles the Second, king of England, &c.

The letter contains one other sentiment worthy of note, which is that this grant of land, and the laws that he proposed to establish there, would make the colony *"the seed of a nation."* Whatever may have been the expectations of this great man in regard to the people that should spring up on his new acquisition, or whatever he hoped that time would develop, in the resources and advantages of the soil within its bounds, he never could have contemplated any such advancement as the present generation beholds at this day. He only knew it as it lay upon the river Delaware; which stream would offer all the water communication that was necessary for the wants of the people. The immense forests, the inexhaustible mineral resources, the advantages of water power for manufacturing purposes and inland transportation, as well as the extensive agricultural districts that lay within the bounds of his purchase, were things beyond his view, and beyond the scope of his imagination. The "tender care" which he had for the government, that emigrants might be assured of justice to all, marked him as a man of foresight and deserving merit, and in this he certainly planted the "seed of a nation."

Many difficulties occurred in regard to titles to land made by Penn, some concerning the boundaries, and others, the right of possession; these troubles were frequently referred to Robert Turner, who mostly settled them to satisfaction. As Thomas Sharp, and those other adventurers who settled at Newton, came from Dublin, and took their land within the bounds of the Irish tenth, as laid forth in West Jersey, there can be no doubt that Robert Turner knew them before they came, and continued the acquaintance after their arrival here. In the memorial left by Sharp touching this part of their history, reference is made to the adjustment of a difficulty by Robert Turner in relation to land taken up by George Goldsmith. In this settlement he showed his good feeling toward Goldsmith, by conveying him a portion of the survey whereon he had made his improvements. The remainder of this survey he sold to Isaac Hollingsham.

The Graysburys purchased a tract of land lying in Newton, which he had located on the south side of the main branch of Newton creek. He made other surveys in the township, some of which were bounded by Cooper's creek, and some by the river front, now included in the city of Camden.[2] For the five years immediately after the first settlement, he perhaps owned more land in this township than any other individual, and no doubt took much interest in its advancement and progress. In the sales of land, as made in Pennsylvania by William Penn to those who were settling there, and to many residents in England, and Scotland, and Ireland, who never came thence, the name of Robert Turner often occurs; and, at his death, his landed estates must have been large and valuable. In the city, he owned several squares of ground, which he, no doubt, used for farming purposes, but which are now in the centre of the metropolis.

The wife of Robert Turner was Susanna, daughter of William Welch, and their children were Edward, who married Catharine Carter. (He dying, she married John Baldwin.[3] She also survived him and married —— Cloud of Chester county, Pa.);[4] Martha, who married Francis Rawle; and Mary, who married Joseph Pidgeon.[5] Mary Rawle, a daughter of Francis, married William Cooper in 1732, a son of Daniel and grandson of the

---

[2] Sharp's Book, 03. O. S. G.
[3] Lib. G3, 379.
[4] Lib. E, 69.
[5] Lib. BB1, 352.

first William.[6] Her husband settled with her in Philadelphia, where he remained until his death.[7] He was the owner of much land in Camden, coming to him from his paternal ancestors. Mary Pidgeon deceased in 1733, leaving one son, Joseph. Francis and Martha Rawle had other children than Mary, as follows: Robert, Francis, William, Joseph, John, Benjamin, Jane, Rebecca, and Elizabeth. Robert Turner died intestate.

Although not a resident of the colony, yet, in 1685, he was returned as one of the representatives of the third tenth in the Legislature of West New Jersey; but he did not appear at the first sitting thereof.[8] At the second session, his name appears, at which time he was appointed as one of the commissioners to regulate the sale of land, and to contract with the Indians for the purchase of their right in the soil. He was also appointed one of the committee to examine proxies sent by the proprietors residing in England, since some difficulty had arisen concerning their legality, the manner in which they were obtained, and the way in which they were being used.

The exercising of these privileges by Robert Turner would seem to show that he lived in West New Jersey for a short time, although nothing beside would lead to such conclusion; or that the custom prevailing in England at that time, and still, to some extent, followed there, of electing persons of one section of the realm to represent those of another, in this single instance obtained here. Supposing such to be the fact, the rule was much strained in this case, for he then resided in another commonwealth, based upon a different constitution and governed in many particulars by different laws. That he had large interests here is well known. He was also as desirous as the inhabitants were that wholesome regulations should be provided for the growing colony, in order that new comers could be induced to settle; for, as a consequence, the value of the land held for sale would be greatly increased. It would appear that Robert Turner's interest in New Jersey was not confined to the western division, for, in 1683, as one of the owners of East New Jersey,

---

6 Lib. F, 03, Philadelphia Records.
7 Vol. IX., 19, New Jersey Historical Society Proceedings.
8 Leaming & Spicer's Laws of New Jersey.

he, by his proxy, voted to confirm Gawen Lawrie as deputy governor of that province under the appointment of Robert Barclay, he being empowered so to do by the original covenant entered into with the proprietors.[9]

He was also one of the signers of the letter from the proprietors to the planters in that province, about the same date; in which is expressed a desire that equity and justice may rule, and that right shall be done to all who may transport themselves into that country. But little is said of him in the many histories and narratives of those early times; which is surprising in view of the large estates which he held in Pennsylvania, East and West New Jersey. He did not participate very much in the political affairs of these colonies, and is not known in any of the troubles that occurred in those times. His place seems to have been that of umpire in the settlement of personal troubles to the avoidance of law suits and other like scandal.

---

9 Leaming and Spicer's Laws of New Jersey.

SAMUEL CARPENTER.

THE business relations of William Penn with Edward Byllynge and his creditors, and the disposal of the latter's landed estate in West New Jersey to settle their claims against him, as well as his troublesome diplomacy with John Fenwick, are said to have been the first motives that attracted his attention toward the establishment of a colony in America. The indebtedness of the crown to his father for valuable naval services, which remained unpaid at the time of his decease, and, in the financial condition of the government treasury at that period, were likely so to remain, was an additional incentive for the son to petition for a grant of land in liquidation of the claim.

This petition was strongly opposed in the privy council; some of whom, on the subject of civil and religious liberty, were hostile to his views. He succeeded, however, after much importunity, in securing a charter for the territory of Pennsylvania, and at once took steps to transport emigrants thereto. His position in the Society of Friends, his known honesty and singleness of purpose, soon drew around him very many persons who were willing to "make the adventure," a greater part of whom had sufficient of this world's goods to make their outfit comfortable, with enough, after their arrival, to protect them from want. His form of government and code of laws were especially acceptable to such as were thus suffering from the intolerance that surrounded them in England; and of these they took advantage by joining the various companies of emigrants coming to Pennsylvania. One important principle involved was set forth in these words: "That all persons living in this province, who confess and acknowledge the one Almighty and Eternal God to be the Creator, Upholder and Ruler of the world, and that hold themselves obliged in conscience to live peaceably and justly in civil society, shall in no wise be molested or prejudiced for their religious persuasion or practices in matters of faith and worship; nor shall they be compelled at any time to frequent or maintain any religious worship, place, or ministry whatever."

All these things took place within three years after the arrival of the first emigrants at Burlington. The settlements of the English on both sides of the Delaware river, were thus made almost identical. The same enlarged views in the form of government, and the same liberality in the sale and disposal of land, were as faithfully observed in the one colony as in the other; and whatever was considered as advantageous to the one was certain to be adopted by the managers of affairs on the other side of the river. The social and religious intercourse that was constantly kept up between the settlements introduced many business transactions, some of which involved the sale and purchase of real estate on one side of the stream to persons residing upon the opposite side; and it was frequently the case that persons in Pennsylvania owned considerable tracts of land in New Jersey; many of which were held for terms of years, and sometimes descended through several generations of the same family. Of these persons, Samuel Carpenter was one. The first purchase of land made by him in Gloucester county was of Samuel Jennings in 1684. It was one of six hundred acres, lying on the south side of Timber creek, and having considerable front on the river Delaware.[1] This included what has since become the valuable fisheries at Howell's Cove, though, at the time of purchase, they had no worth in the eyes of the contracting parties. These lands remained in the family for many years, passing to the son Samuel, whose widow, Hannah, sold part thereof, as executrix of her husband, to

---

[1] Lib. B1, 43.

Samuel Ladd, through whom they descended to his daughter, Deborah West.[2]

In 1689, Samuel Carpenter bought fifty acres of William Royden, situated in Newton township, with a front on the river. This was part of the survey that Royden had previously made, extending from the river easterly to Cooper's creek.[3] Upon this now stands the principal part of the city of Camden, which, after several conveyances, became the property of William Cooper. The fifty acres extended down the edge of the stream from near Cooper street, and back from the shore sufficiently far to obtain the full quantity, as called for in the deed. This, however, he sold the same year. He did not make any subsequent purchase of land in the township. In Bowden's History of Friends, may be found a short sketch of Samuel Carpenter. This says:

"He emigrated to Pennsylvania a few years after its settlement. He had previously resided in Barbadoes, when, in 1673, and again in 1685, he suffered considerably in distraints, for his faithful testimony in bearing arms. Next to William Penn, he was considered the most wealthy person in the province, for, besides large mills at Bristol, Darby and Chester, and dwelling houses, warehouses and wharves in Philadelphia, he also held nearly twenty thousand acres of land in different parts of the province, and was largely engaged as a merchant. In 1693, he became a member of the Assembly, and, a few years later, one of the council, and ultimately treasurer of the province. Through a great variety of business, he preserved the love and esteem of a large and extensive acquaintance. His ability, activity and benevolence of disposition in divers capacities, but more particularly among his friends, the Quakers, are said to have distinguished him as a very useful and valuable member, not only of that religious society, but also of the community in general. He died in 1713."

He took an active part in the political affairs of the city of Philadelphia, being, for several years previous to 1712, one of the members of council, and, in 1701, also sitting as a

---

2 Lib. AL, 496.
3 Lib. C, 128. Lib. G, 108.

member of the Assembly, representing a larger constituency than any other person elected. Beside the real estate which he held within the city bounds, he was also the owner of large tracts of land in the interior of the State, the grant for which was made directly to him by the patroon. Near the mouth of the Schuylkill he had considerable marsh land, which he improved into meadow, and which for many years was called Carpenter's island.

Whether he was a native of the Island of Barbadoes, or was banished from England on account of his religious principles, does not appear; but that he was a consistent and active member of the Society of Friends, cannot be questioned. On that island there were many of this religious pursuasion, and to this place nearly all the ministers of this Society that visited America resorted before their return to England. This was before settlements were attempted in Pennsylvania or New Jersey; and the island was looked upon as a place of banishment for those who fell under the displeasure of the government, and whose adherence to their creed and practice could not be abated by any of the punishments inflicted at home. A few years corrected much of the misery and destitution that was intended by those in power, who not only imprisoned such as became subject to their tyranny, but robbed them of their property, and transported them without any means of future support; for, in a short time, those who had been previously sent for like offences, had, by thrift and economy, secured enough to assist others who came under similar circumstances, and to render their condition comparatively comfortable.

By the industry and perseverance of this class of citizens, the agricultural advantages of the island were soon developed; and the increase of revenue to the home government, as well as large exportations of the products to England for trade, appeared as a reproach upon those who had so shamefully driven these people from their home and estates for opinion's sake.

The purchase of New Jersey and Pennsylvania by Friends, whose liberal form of government was so attractive, opened an asylum for such as remained under persecution. Hither they soon directed their footsteps, and here they laid the foundation for the institutions that now surround us, "where none should make them afraid."

Samuel Carpenter married Hannah Hardiman in 1684. She was of South Wales, and came to Pennsylvania with her parents.[4] Their children were: Hannah, who married William Fishburn in 1701; John, who married Ann Hoskins in 1710; and Samuel, who married Hannah Preston in 1711. Samuel removed to Gloucester county, New Jersey, where he deceased in 1747, leaving a widow and children.[5] Many of the name are now residents of this State, and the direct and collateral branches are numerous throughout the United States. As the record of the family of Samuel Carpenter is uncertain, by reason of the early branches thereof residing in another state, it is perhaps proper that a conveyance of land made by Robert Turner to Abraham Carpenter, a mariner, and Joshua Carpenter, a brewer, both of Philadelphia, in 1693, should be referred to.[6] This tract contained four hundred and twelve acres, and lay in Newton township, fronting on Cooper's creek and adjoining the lands of Archibald Mickle, Edward Newbie and others.

In 1697, the Carpenters sold the whole to Joseph Cooper, who, in 1714, gave the same to his eldest son, Joseph.[7] This tract of land now constitutes the most easterly part of the Cope estate, lying between Haddonfield and Camden. These men were brothers of the first Samuel, and resided in Philadelphia. Joshua was a man of considerable real estate in the city, and acted as commissioner for William Penn in the sale of his land in Pennsylvania.

That the subject of this sketch was always a resident of Pennsylvania, and came to Philadelphia before it had shape as a town, has generally been accepted as historic truth. Yet there is doubt upon this point, as will appear from the following references. In the year 1685, he was a member of the Friends' Meeting at Salem, as, on the 30th day of the 9th month, he was one of a committee to visit a member for some shortcoming. In the next year, he discharged a similar duty, and was also a contributor (he subscribing the largest sum) to finish the new end of the meeting house. On the 25th of 5th month, 1687, he

---

[4] Vol. IX, 19, N. J. Historical Society proceedings.
[5] Lib. No. 5, 433.
[6] Lib. A, 148.
[7] Lib. A, 08, Gloucester Deeds.

was appointed one of a committee to attend the Quarterly Meeting at Newton.

In the year 1700, when the Yearly Meeting was held in Salem, he took an active part in the proceedings, and was one of the committee to receive money for the support of the Yearly Meeting, on behalf of the Salem Meeting. In Leaming and Spicer's revision of the laws of New Jersey, which also contains full lists of the members of the Legislature, may be found the name of Samuel Carpenter, as returned to represent the Salem tenth. This was in May 1685; and the inference would naturally follow that he resided within the limits of that division of the province at that time, and was selected to look after the interests of the people in those parts. A note, however, appended to the list says, "Robert Turner and Samuel Carpenter appear not." A curious feature of this session was that the Legislature sat but a single day, and, in the words of the resolution, agreed "to continue things upon the same foot and bottom as formerly, until things shall be controverted in England, or the king's pleasure be further known therein." The day was spent in appointing justices, commissioners, treasurers, clerks, sheriffs and constables for the several divisions, and in assessing a general tax upon the people.

On the 25th of the ninth month in the same year, this body again assembled, at which time Samuel Carpenter appeared and took his seat, representing the Salem tenth, and was appointed one of the council. The sitting on that occasion was for nine days, in which time a number of salutary laws were passed, and several resolutions acted upon, concerning the duties devolving upon them. All this looks as if Samuel Carpenter had been a resident of West New Jersey until about the year 1702, as, in that year, he gave fifteen pounds to erect the new meeting house at Salem, in which contribution he is mentioned as residing in Philadelphia, where he soon grew into the confidence of the patroon and rendered him valuable services in the government of the colony and the selling of his land. In reference to the laws of New Jersey passed while he was a member of the Legislature, the first act recorded may interest many persons at the present day, as it shows how our

Quaker ancestors avoided the inconsistency that is generally charged upon them, in regard to the military establishment attached to the province, which they saw the necessity of maintaining thereafter. It is as follows:

"That whereas the purchasers and chief inhabitants for the generality in this province of West New Jersey, are a people whose principles for conscience-sake cannot bear arms nor be found in the exercise of war: Nevertheless and notwithstanding, that such their principles may not be found or judged injurious to the King's and Queen's service, (under whose protection we now live, and heartily receive them as such, as by our Proclamations thereof may appear); Be it enacted by the Governor, Council and Representatives now in General Assembly met and assembled, and by the authority of the same, that such our principles and practices as aforesaid, shall be no ways binding or obliging to restrain such of the inhabitants of this province whose freedom and principles induce them to serve the King in the defence of the Province in such posture and form as the Governor and Council shall seem meet, being the liberty that we claim to ourselves, may not justly be denied to them, least we should do as we would not be done unto. Any act or law made to the contrary heretofore notwithstanding."

In the framing and passage of this act, Samuel Carpenter, no doubt, took part. It bears the marks of great concession on behalf of Friends in this particular, and shows that no trouble would arise on their part with the executive of the government, touching a matter at that time considered so essential to its dignity and existence. Andrew Hamilton was then governor; he differed with the representatives of the people in many matters relating to the laws, and in their observance and enforcement; yet, in this enactment, he could not but see the yielding of this religious sect to his wishes, and their desire to avoid trouble among the people.

THOMAS GARDINER.

THOMAS GARDINER came to Burlington in 1678 with his wife and children, bringing also considerable estate. His house was the first dwelling erected within the limits of the town. Although of logs, it was of larger dimensions than any other among his neighbors, and was finished with more care and expense; in it was held the first Yearly Meeting of Friends in New Jersey. He probably came from the city of London, as some real estate owned by him there became the property of his grandchildren, who were, at the time, residents of Burlington. This is an inference only, and may prove erroneous.

James Bowden, in his History of Friends, says: "At Burlington Monthly Meeting in the third month, 1681, it was concluded to establish a Yearly Meeting, the first to be held in the sixth month following. A notice of this conclusion was circulated among Friends of the provinces of East and West Jersey, and on the 28th of the sixth month, 1681, the meeting assembled at the house of Thomas Gardiner, of Burlington. But very little information of the proceedings of this Yearly Meeting, which occupied four days, has been preserved."

In one of the manuscripts of Samuel Smith, the historian, has been found the following passage: "1685. This year erected a large and commodious meeting house. Samuel Jennings, Thomas Budd, John Gosling, Richard Guy, William Brighton and Thomas Gardiner were the principal promoters and contributors." The authority from which this is derived cannot be questioned, and is conclusive as to the building of the "great meeting-house at Burlington."

The Monthly Meeting, as above named, was regularly established three years previous to this time, the original records of which have been preserved, and from which the first minute there entered is here copied, as follows:

"Since, by the good Providence of God, many Friends with their families have transported themselves into this province of West Jersey, the said Friends in the upper parts have found it needful, according to the practice in the place we come from, to settle monthly meetings for the well ordering of the affairs of the church. It was agreed that accordingly it should be done the 15th of the fifth month, 1678."

This Monthly Meeting consisted of Friends settled about the Falls (now Trenton), and of the particular meetings of Rancocas, in New Jersey; Shackomaxon, and Chester in Pennsylvania. From all of these places, Burlington could be reached by water; and of this easy mode of transportation those attending the Monthly Meeting, no doubt, took advantage. It also shows that the Friends who had settled on the west side of the river had not as yet organized their meetings, and were not yet in a position to assume the business relations necessary to a proper intercourse with kindred associations. In fact, the yearly meetings were, for several years, alternately held at Burlington and Philadelphia, which included all the meetings in New Jersey and Pennsylvania.

The history above referred to also contains a copy of the first epistle of Friends at Burlington to the Yearly Meeting of London, written in 1680, and signed by the most prominent Quakers then resident in the province. It alludes to their present prosperous and hopeful condition, shows their attachment to the doctrines which they had espoused, and the zeal with which they adhered to their religious belief. To such as are interested in the early history of this religious denomination, the work above quoted is especially attractive, the author having had access to much of the correspondence of the first emigrants, and free use of the books of records of Friends in England,

and in America, from which he has collated a reliable and interesting history of Friends in America.

Among the records of the Salem Friends' Meeting are several entries in regard to William Bradford, the first printer in West New Jersey, which may prove interesting in this connection. At the Yearly Meeting held at Burlington in 1690, several Friends agreed to raise a sum of money, if he would continue his press there, and publish Friends' books as heretofore. Each particular meeting belonging to that Yearly Meeting was solicited to assist in raising money, and the request was responded to accordingly. This shows how well the new comers understood the free circulation of the doctrines and opinions held by them, in the shape of printed pamphlets; and, as William Bradford was the only artisan of that kind in these parts at that time, it was necessary to hold out certain pecuniary advantages to have him remain. In England, this policy had been pursued with much advantage, and there was no reason why an equal benefit should not be derived here. As showing who was the first printer in West New Jersey, his name and residence, this particular record has much interest and is worth preservation.

The first meetings of Friends in Burlington were held in a tent made of the sails taken from the vessels in which they crossed the ocean; in it they assembled for the first year after their arrival, and until Thomas Gardiner's house was finished: thus proving that they allowed no difficulties or hindrances to prevent them from discharging their duty, as sincere and consistent Christians. In all the doings of this little colony, both religious and political, Thomas Gardiner took an active and prominent part, and appears to have commanded the confidence and respect of the community around him. He was a tailor, and the chances are that he had the whole business to himself, free from competition and with no one to differ with him about the fashions, as, with singular tenacity, the society of Friends, for nearly two hundred years, has adhered to the same form of dress.

He was a member of the first provincial legislature of West New Jersey, that sat at Burlington in 1682 ; was one of the first commissioners for dividing and regulating land ; and was one of the committee of ways and means, who represented the London tenth, to provide money to defray the expenses of the government, appointed at that sitting of the assembly.[1] At the same time, he was appointed one of the judges of the courts of Burlington county. As such he served the people acceptably for several years.[2] The next year he was appointed one of the governor's council, and made one of the treasurers of the province. Some of these appointments were continued through several years, and until refused. This shows in what estimation he was held by the people of his county and province.[3] He deceased in 1694, leaving a widow and several children,[4] namely: John, who deceased the same year as his father, unmarried;[5] Mathew, who settled at Raritan previous to 1716, but died without children;[6] Esther, who married John Wills; and Thomas, who married Hannah Mathews.[7]

Without any certain data to prove it, the probability is that Thomas Gardiner was a brother to Peter Gardiner, a public Friend, who resided near Castle Hedingham, in Essex, England. Peter Gardiner was an active man in the ministry during the persecutions of Friends in England, and suffered in person and estate, as did the most of those who dared to preach and practise the doctrines of George Fox and Robert Barclay in those times. Upon his return from a gospel mission to Scotland, he was taken ill of small-pox at Carlisle, in Cumberland, and there died in 1695. Although Thomas Gardiner was the first of the name that came to New Jersey, yet he was not the first in America.

In 1658, there resided at Newport, Rhode Island, a woman named Hored Gardiner, who left her family of several children to go on a religious visit to Weymouth, in the province of Massachusetts, distant some sixty miles, mostly through the wilderness. She carried with her an infant, and was accompanied by a small white girl only. At that time Governor Endicott was much embittered against the Quakers, who deemed it proper to make religious visits among the colonists, and whom he punished severely for so doing. Upon this female's arrival at

---

[1] Leaming & Spicer's Laws.
[2] Leaming & Spicer's Laws.
[3] Lib. BBB, 82.
[4] Smith's History of New Jersey.
[5] Lib. 2, 717.
[6] Burlington Files of Wills.
[7] Basse's Book, 164, 280.

Weymouth, she was arrested and taken before the Governor, who used abusive language to her, and ordered that she and her young attendant should receive ten lashes each upon their naked bodies. This punishment was inflicted upon the woman while she held her infant, which was only protected from the lash by the arms of the mother. As repulsive as this kind of punishment was to the more conservative class of citizens, yet the authorities indulged their malice and bigotry in many instances toward the people, and continued so to do until at last restrained by the home government, before which many complaints were laid by those of like persuasion in England. Imprisonment in loathsome and filthy dungeons, dragging at the cart's tail, and sitting in the pillory, were some of the inflictions visited upon the Quakers in New England in the first colonizing of that part of America.

In examining and reviewing the actions of the first English settlers in West Jersey, it is often inquired why they passed so far up the river in selecting a site for a town, leaving behind them so many suitable places, where greater depth of water could have been had, and the settlement would have been many miles nearer the sea. The Swedish settlements did not extend far above the mouth of Raccoon creek, with the exception of a small number of colonists at Woodbury creek; and the next point at which they found any inhabitants besides the natives, was where a few Hollanders had settled, and where one kept a tavern for the accommodation of travelers, on the river's shore above the mouth of the Assiscunk creek, and near where these adventurers selected their site for "Bridlington." The records of Upland Court as held at Chester, Pa., at the date heretofore given, will prove conclusively that such a tavern was there kept; at which place a ferry was also maintained for the use of the few persons passing from New York to Virginia by the way of land, it being the only place below the falls where persons could cross with horses in going from the one point to the other. The record runs as follows:

"Peter Yegou, Plaintiff,	In an action of trespass
vs.	upon the case.
Thomas Wright and Godfrey Hancock, Def'ts.	9 mo. 25, 1679.

"The plaintiff declares that in ye year 1668 he obtained a permit and grant of Governor Philip Carteret to take up ye land called Leasy Point, lying and being over against Mattinagcom Island, now Burlington, to settle himself there and to build and keep a house of entertainment for the accommodation of travelers, all which ye plaintiff accordingly hath done and moreover hath purchased of Cornelis Jorissen, Jurirus Macelis and Jan Clarssen, each their houses and land at Leasy Point aforesaid, which was given them by the Dutch Governor in the year 1666, for all which Governor Carteret promised your plaintiff a patent, all which said houses and lands ye plaintiff had in lawful possession until the year 1670, at which tyme your plaintiff was plundered by the Indians, and by them utterly ruined, as is well known to all the world, so that your plaintiff then for a time was forced to leave his land and possessions aforesaid and to seek his livelihood and to repair his loss in other places and to leave his land as aforesaid with intention to return when occasion should present. But so it is, may it please your worships, that with the arrival of these new comers called Quakers out of England, these defendants, Thomas Wright and Godfrey Hancock, have violently entered upon your plaintiff's said land and there have by force planted corn, cut timber for houses, mowed hay and made fences. Notwithstanding they were forewarned by your plaintiff's friend, Henry Jacobs, in your plaintiff's behalf in the presence of Capt. Edmund Cantwell and afterwards by your plaintiff summoned before your magistrates at Burlington, who making no end of it, the case was with said magistrates' and these defendants' consents removed by him before your worships. Wherefore your plaintiff craves your worships to order the defendants and all others not to molest ye plaintiff in the quiet possession of the said land, &c.

"The defendants in court declared themselves to be very willing to stand ye verdict and judgment of this court. Whereupon the court (having heard the debates of both parties, and examined all the papers) are of opinion that since Mr. Peter Yegou had Governor Carteret's grant, and was in quiet possession of ye land before the said land was sold by John Lord Berkley unto Edward Byllinge, and that he, ye said Peter Yegou, hath also bought the land and payed ye Indians for ye same,—that therefore Mr. Peter Yegou ought peaceably and quietly, to enjoy ye same land and appurtenances according to grant and purchase."[8]

The Legislature of the province in 1683 made restitution to Thomas Wright on account of the difficulty which he had thus fallen into, by giving him one hundred acres of land in another place, to be surveyed according to the rules. In 1697, another act was passed in relation to this piece of land, to confirm the title to John Joosten and John Hamel, who held, after several conveyances, under Peter Yegou; this settled the possession and estate of said land, so that, after eighteen years of litigation, the purchaser could hold it in peace. It is easy to discover by this how the name of Yegou, or Cheygou, attached to the island, which is really that part of the fast land surrounded by the creek where the city of Burlington now stands, the name being of Dutch origin, and not that of an Indian chief, as generally considered. The truth of history often destroys the romance and beauty that surround an object, yet a faithful adherence to facts ought not to be disregarded.

George Fox, in traveling from Middletown harbor to New Castle, lodged at this place in 1672, and at this point he crossed the river. He says it had been deserted from fear of the Indians. This statement is confirmed by the before-copied record, and also explains why the first emigrants sailed so far up the river, before they landed; for, at this place, the only inhabitants above Raccoon creek were found.

An extract from his journal may not prove uninteresting upon this point; it will show how well the history of this place is corroborated. "Next day we traveled fifty miles as we computed, and, at night, finding an old house which the Indians had forced the people to leave, we made a fire and lay there at the head of Delaware Bay. The next day we swam our horses

---

[8] Publications of the Historical Society of Penna.

over the river, about a mile, twice, first to an island called Upper Dinidock and then to the main land, having hired Indians to help us over in their canoes."

During the first ten years that elapsed between the marriage of Thomas Gardiner, Jr., and the death of his father, he resided on part of the estate owned by his wife at Woodbury creek, where also her brother lived on part of the same property. At that time he was one of the trustees of the Friends' Meeting at that place, and participated somewhat in the political affairs of the province. He was a practical surveyor, and acted as one of the judges of the court of Gloucester county, when they were held at Red Bank.[9] After the death of his father, he removed to Burlington, and, in a short time, was appointed surveyor-general of the western division of New Jersey, by the council of proprietors, which office he appears to have filled with satisfaction for several years.[10] The duties of this position at this time were onerous and responsible; he was required to review all the maps and locations of land made by the several deputy surveyors, to examine the calculations as to the quantity of acres named, to test the several bearings as marked upon the maps, and to certify to the council that they were correct in all these particulars. If any disputes occurred among the claimants (which often happened), he became the executive officer, and went upon the land, so that he could report where the real difficulty existed. During the term of his office, which extended from 1701 to 1717, (in which last year he died,) there was much trouble among the proprietors in the taking up of land where the Indian title had not been extinguished.[11] In this particular, the council was careful to prevent surveys from passing this board beyond the bounds of any "purchase" already consummated with this simple-minded people. It may not be uninteresting to copy here an advertisement published by the council touching one of these purchases; it shows the manner in which the assessments were made, so that from such funds all the contracts should be faithfully carried out.

---

9 Leaming & Spicer's Laws.
10 Basse's Book
11 Minutes of the Council of Proprietors, O. S. G.

ADVERTISEMENT.

"These are to give notice to the proprietors of the Western Division of New Jersey, that, the Council chosen to negotiate the affairs of the said division having resolved to proceed to a fourth dividend, in order thereunto, have treated with the Indians and bargained with them for a very large quantity of land for which divers payments are to be made them in a short time. All persons that have rights to take up on a fourth dividend, or any part or parts of their first, second or third dividend are desired to meet the council of proprietors on the 20th day of October next, at Burlington, to enter the quantities which they have a right to, as also to provide, as speedy as may be, their proportion of the purchase money, which will amount by computation to six shillings of the currency of New York per hundred; for the collection of which money with the least loss of time that may be (and converting it into goods to be paid to the natives), Peter Fretwell at Burlington, Richard Bull at Gloucester and John Budd at Philadelphia, are appointed to receive the same, and the agents of such proprietors as are abroad, are desired to take notice hereof that due care may be taken of their constituents' interests.—May, 1717."[12]

This paper explains the manner in which the title of the natives to the soil was extinguished, and proves that the council of proprietors would not consent to the occupation of their lands until a contract had been made and carried out. Many of these "Indian" deeds are still in existence; some among the owners of the estate conveyed, and many on file in the office of the secretary of state at Trenton, with all sorts of hieroglyphics attached as the signatures of the grantors, which are quite as unexplainable as the names which they stand to represent. Under these grants no attempt was made by the settlers to interfere with the privileges of the Indians, or to remove them from their places of abode; and, only as they deceased, and from time to time abandoned their towns, were these places occupied by the whites. Through West Jersey there are still many places remembered as Indian settlements,

---
[12] Minute Book of the Council of Proprietors, O. S. G.

and some of their burial grounds are known; but the gradual falling off in numbers, and the collecting of families into the more thickly settled neighborhoods, which ended at Shamong, or Brotherton, in Burlington county, gave the purchasers, under the rules of the proprietors, full and complete possession, without any dispute or difficulty: thus were avoided the bloodshed and murders that attended the advance of civilization in the Western States at a subsequent period.

With the framing of these titles fixing the boundaries of the sections of land to be conveyed, the surveyor-general had much to do. It was afterward his duty to watch the progress of the locations, and see that they were kept within the limits of the purchase. During the term of Thomas Gardiner, the greatest of these troubles existed; and, having to contend with avarice and unjust dealing in opposition to what was his sworn and palpable duty towards those whom he represented, he was often the subject of complaint to the council, and of misrepresentation and abuse among the people. Under his administration, new and more rigid rules were established in defining the boundaries of locations, making them plainer and more definite; and thus much contention and trouble were avoided in the future. In one instance, he found it necessary to prevent his deputies from making locations in the new Indian purchase until some existing dispute should be arranged; again, in making surveys, he ordered that they should be laid adjoining each other, and as near as possible in parallel lines. These, with other like regulations, were necessary and useful, and showed him to be a man that understood and looked after the interests of those whom he represented.[13] In 1710, Thomas Gardiner sold part of his real estate at Woodbury creek to James Whitall, and subsequently disposed of all the land owned by his wife at that place.[14] He died, seized of considerable landed property about Burlington, some of which he previously conveyed in trust for the use of his children.[15] His family consisted of two sons, Thomas and Matthew, and of two daughters,—

---
[13] Lib. A, 194.
[14] Lib. E, 418.
[15] Lib. GH, 51, 53.

Elizabeth, who married Abraham Bickley, and Hannah, who married Isaac Pearson.[16,17,18].

Abraham Bickley was a distiller; he lived in Philadelphia, and died about 1747. Ten years before his death, he located a tract of land in Gloucester county, N. J., generally known as the Blue Anchor tract; whereon was the tavern that bore the same name, so long and favorably known by the traveling public in this section of the State. The old house stood upon the Indian trail that went from the coast to the Delaware river, and at about an equal distance from each. This location made it, for more than a century, a place of rest for persons crossing this part of the State. The building of the Camden and Atlantic railroad has destroyed its usefulness, and the next generation will have no remembrance of it.

Isaac Pearson was a silversmith, and resided in the city of Burlington, where some of his descendants still remain. The male branch of the Gardiners being limited, the name is not very extensive in West New Jersey, although the collateral connection is numerous.

---

16 Lib. BBB, 195, 318. 17 Lib. B2, 717. 18 Lib. BB, 318.

JOHN CHAMPION.

AS early as in the year 1673, John Champion and Thomas Champion and their families were residents of the town of Hempstead, on Long Island, in the State of New York. Ten years after that date, the constable and overseers of the said town made a valuation of the estates of the inhabitants; but, for some reason, John Champion was not included in the list. His name, however, appears among those who were in default, and had neglected or refused to give the officers the proper information. That paper was attached to the first, and is headed as follows:

"These under-written are ye remainder of ye inhabitants of ye said towne, which, having not brought in their valuation, are guest att by ye Constable and Overseers of ye towne aforesaid."

In this the name of John Champion is seen, and his estate is "guest" to be worth one hundred pounds, sterling. The family was probably English, and was among the first that occupied that part of Long Island, where the hardy pioneers soon made themselves comfortable homes. As soon as John Fenwick had effected a landing at Salem, in 1678, and the Yorkshire and London Friends had fixed upon Burlington as the place for a town, the settlers about Long Island established direct and frequent intercourse with them, which lasted for many years thereafter.

Matthew Champion, who lived in Burlington about the year 1690, and purchased land of John Tomlinson, at Onanickon, in Springfield, the next year, does not appear to have been of this immediate family. Neither is connected with it the family of the same name which emigrated to Tuckahoe, in Cape May county—a family which was among the first settlers in that section, and which has now become numerous along the sea shore of this State.

On May 13, 1700, Henry Franklin conveyed to John Champion, of Hempstead, Queen's county, Long Island, a tract of land lying on the north side of Cooper's creek, in Waterford, (now Delaware) township, Camden county, New Jersey, to which place the said John removed.[1] This tract contained three hundred and thirty acres of land; it was the same as that which Henry Franklin had purchased of Mordecai Howell three years before, and which in that deed is described as being situated at "Livewell."[2] Henry Franklin was a bricklayer. He resided at Long Island at that time, but perhaps never removed to this purchase. Part of this estate is what has, for many years, been known as the "Barton" farm, and thereon stood the residence of John Champion. This was near where one of the roads crossed Cooper's creek in going from Burlington to Philadelphia, and where travelers had much trouble in crossing the stream. It is recorded in one of the minute books of Old Gloucester, that "John Champion makes great complaint of his great charge in setting people over Cooper's creek at his house; whereon ye Grand Jury propose that in case ye said John Champion will find sufficient convenience to put people over at all seasons, the said Champion may take for ferriage as follows: For two persons together, two pence per head; for one single person, three pence, and for a man and horse, five pence. To which ye bench assents."

In connection with this, Isaac Mickle says: "It will be observed that no mention is made in any of these regulations of carriages. Such refinements were not introduced generally, even in Philadelphia, until the Revolution. In West Jersey, most journeys were performed on horse-back, and the marriage

---

[1] Lib. G3, 465.
[2] Lib. C, 122.

portion of the daughters of the most wealthy men consisted of a cow and a side-saddle."[3] Funerals were frequently attended in boats, and the bodies of the deceased taken from Cooper's creek to the old Newton graveyard by water.

The coming of John Champion from Long Island to New Jersey may be accounted for by the marriage of his daughter Elizabeth to John Wright, a son of Richard Wright, who had purchased land of Thomas Howell, on Cooper's creek and settled there.[4] The minutes of the Gloucester county courts of 1687, show a dispute between Richard Wright and Thomas Howell about the conveyance of this land.[5] The verdict of the jury was in favor of Wright, and Howell was required to carry out his contract. In 1691 and in 1693, the son John increased his possession by purchases of adjoining tracts from Thomas Howell's heirs, which lands lay near to those of his father-in-law. This marriage is additional proof of the intercourse existing between the sections named, and shows that families removing from one place found easy means to preserve their intimacies with friends living at the other.

The application of John Champion for a ferry license is evidence that he came hither soon after his first purchase; and here he resided during the remainder of his life. Living, as he did, near a navigable stream, his intercourse with the city of Philadelphia was frequent, and he knew it long before sufficient of the timber had been removed to show even the direction of the streets. The bank fronting the river Delaware, being filled with caves and rude huts, where the citizens lived and where stood much of the primitive forest, must have presented a strange appearance in approaching it from New Jersey. Opposite the mouth of Cooper's creek was the most populous part of the town; and perhaps he did not live to see it enlarged beyond the limits of Shackomaxon. The many troubles through which William Penn had passed, and the difficulties which he had in regard to the sale and settlement of his lands in Pennsylvania, were a hinderance to the enlargement of the city, and prevented the rapid settlement that he had anticipated.

---

[3] Mickle's Reminiscences of Old Gloucester, 42.
[4] Lib. G, 14. Lib. G2, 114.
[5] Lib. G3, 5.

In the year 1718, John Champion divided his landed estate between his sons Robert and Nathaniel, by a line running from the creek "into the woods," and made each a deed bearing the same date (April 24).[6] His other children were Thomas and Phœbe. He died in 1727, leaving a will, and, by that, disposing of the remainder of his estate. The son Robert was made executor. He had removed to the city of Philadelphia, where he deceased soon after his father, and before the will was offered for probate.[7] The second son Nathaniel proved the writing, and as administrator settled the estate.[8]

On September 13th, 1720, Robert Champion sold his part of the real estate given to him by his father, to Tobias Halloway, but the latter re-conveyed the same to him on the 24th day of July, 1723.[9] At the date of the deed (1720), Robert lived on the property at Cooper's creek, and, as no female joined with him in the conveyance, he was probably unmarried at that time. Like a large majority of the settlers hereabout, he could not write his name; which inability was also the case with his father. He afterwards married, and had one child,—a son, Peter, who, in the year 1740, married Hannah Thackara, a daughter of Benjamin. She deceased, and, in 1746, he married Ann, a daughter of Simeon Ellis (the son of Simeon). By the last marriage there was one child, Joseph. Peter Champion deceased in 1748, and his widow, Ann, became the administratrix to the estate, he leaving no will.[10]

A short time before his death, he conveyed a piece of meadow land to John Shivers, being part of the homestead. He was therefore the owner thereof after his father's demise. In 1751, Ann, the widow, married John Stokes, and, after his demise, she married Samuel Murrell, 1761.[11] By each marriage she had children, thus rendering it difficult to trace the descendants of Ann Ellis, and to know the paternal line. Joseph Champion, the issue of the second marriage of Peter, married Rachel Collins, a daughter of Samuel and Rosanna (Stokes). Samuel was a blacksmith and plied his calling at Colestown, then in Waterford township. This Samuel Collins was a son

---

6 Lib. A, 165—166.
7 Lib. No. 2, 437.
8 Lib. No. 2, 441.
9 Lib. A, 236.
10 Lib. No. 6, 76.
11 Lib. AH, 385.

of Samuel and Abigail (Ward), who was the youngest son of Francis and Mary, the last wife of Francis, the widow of John Goslin, M. D. and daughter of Thomas Budd. Ann Ellis inherited, through the blood of her ancestors, a tract of land in Delaware township, lying on both sides of the Haddonfield and Moorestown road, now mostly owned by William M. Cooper and the heirs of Batheuel Heulings, deceased.

In 1723, Nathaniel Champion sold his lands on Cooper's creek to James Parrock, who, soon after the death of Nathaniel, conveyed the same to Mary, his widow, she remaining the owner thereof during her life and devising it to John Barton by her will.[12-13] Nathaniel died in 1748, leaving the following children: Nathaniel, who married —— ———; Benjamin, who married Ann Hewitt; Thomas, who married Deborah Clark, daughter of William; Elizabeth, who married John Barton; and Sarah.[14]

The widow of Nathaniel remained on the estate for many years after her husband's decease. Her will bears date ———, 1772. In this paper she names her children and several of her grandchildren. She gave the farm on Cooper's creek, "where she then dwelt," to her son-in-law before named.

Thomas, the son of Nathaniel, was a tailor, and resided in Haddonfield, where some of his descendants were known to the older inhabitants now living. He probably owned the lot whereon stood the mansion built by Matthias Aspden, now the property of the heirs of Benjamin W. Blackwood, M. D., deceased. This house was one of the largest in the village, and, when erected, was more commodious and expensive than most of those around it. Upon the death of Samuel, the son of Thomas, it passed out of the name; and that branch of the family removed from the village.

John Wright, husband of the daughter Elizabeth, made his home on part of the Howell estate before John Champion purchased his land. In the grant to him by Mordecai Howell, in 1693, Howell reserved the right to overflow the meadow and use the water in the stream for his corn-mill, which he built about that time. In 1702, he purchased two hundred and eight

---
[12] Lib. A, 166. [13] Lib. GG, 356.
[14] Lib. No. 5, 524.

acres of Martin Jarvis, in Newton township.[15] This tract lay near the mouth of Newton creek, and extended up that stream to Fork branch, and also up that on the north side for a considerable distance. It now includes several valuable farms in that part of the old township of Newton.[16] The estate on Cooper's creek passed out of the name and blood many years since, even beyond the memory of the oldest inhabitant in that section. Only such as have occasion to examine the ancient deeds or records relating to the land here spoken of, will know that such owners ever there resided; and, unless some defect in the title should appear in passing through the heirs of Richard Wright and of his son John, no inquiry may ever be started in regard to their genealogy.

Richard Wright died in a few years after his coming hither, leaving a widow named Constance, and three children, John, Sarah and Hannah.[17] It is remarkable that so few of the name of Champion are now living in the neighborhood of the old estate; and a few more decades may remove it entirely.

The mutation of families is an interesting and instructive study, deserving labor and attention. Some go on increasing for generations, while others fall away and altogether disappear. While one family may be found for a century where the first settlers placed it, another has been scattered, and the old homestead forgotten. Where one family adheres to the land of its forefathers with an admirable tenacity, another has no regard for ancient things, and parts with them without a regret. The laws regulating the descent of lands in New Jersey makes it of importance that a correct knowledge in this regard should be had; but, in the absence of legislative action, it must always be surrounded with trouble and doubt.

---

15 Basse's Book, 38.
16 Lib. A, 111.
17 Lib. G2, 177.

JOHN EASTLACK.

AMONG the Friends who settled in the island of Bermuda, some of whom were banished by the British authorities, while others followed to be near their families, was one Francis Eastlack, or Eastlake, as sometimes spelled, who appears to have been a prominent man in that place. He was persecuted in like manner by the rulers of the island for the course which he pursued in religious matters, and was frequently imprisoned and sometimes beaten and put in the stocks. In 1660, he was taken from a religious meeting and tied, hand and foot, so that he could not move; in 1666, he was beaten and fined, and, in other ways, maltreated in person, and despoiled of his goods. He was a public Friend, and proclaimed his views and doctrines among the people. This made him obnoxious to those in power, and the object of dislike to such as differed with him in opinion. During his stay at that island he fell into a religious controversy with one Sampson Bond, a leading man in some other persuasion. This ended in the printing of a book on each side, some few copies of which have been preserved by the curiosity-hunters in the literary line, and may be found hidden away in the libraries of such, being shown as typographical wonders though but seldom read. These books made their appearance in the year 1683, and, like all such, were only of interest to those who knew the parties and resided in that particular locality.

The early Quakers were prolific in the production of pamphlets and books in defence of their doctrines and mode of worship; these led to replies from their opponents, and, consequently, added much to the printed matter of those times, and now give a very fair reflex of the controverted points, as well as of the manner of maintaining and rebutting them. The book of which Francis Eastlack was the author bears the title of "The truth in Christ Jesus with the Professors thereof in the Island of Bermuda, (Commonly called Quakers,) cleared from the three ungodly false charges. Charged upon them by Sampson Bond (teacher in said Island); in a Book entitled 'The Quakers in Bermudas tryed,' &c., by a Friend and Lover of the Truth in the same Island, called Francis Eastlacke."

This was printed in London in 1683 and no doubt had considerable circulation in the island, as well as among Friends in London and thereabout. Much pains has been taken of late years to collect and preserve all such publications; which has brought to light many that had been lost sight of and, in the lapse of years, entirely forgotten. About the date last named, Francis Eastlack came to West Jersey and settled in Newton township; but the exact locality of his habitation cannot be discovered, as he does not appear to have been the owner of any real estate. He was probably advanced in years, and did not participate much in the religious or political matters of the colony. Those of his own religious persuasion doubtless sympathized with him in the trials and persecutions through which he had passed, to show the world his attachments to the doctrines which he had espoused. So far as can be discovered, he had four children, namely: John, who married Sarah Thackara, daughter of Thomas; Hepsibah, who married Thomas Thackara; Jemima, who married William Sharp; and Elizabeth, who married Joseph Mickle. Taking this as the starting point, and assuming it to be correct, the surname was confined to one person even in the second generation, and the family, as a whole, limited to but few persons.

The first settlement of John Eastlack was, in all probability, upon fifty acres of land conveyed to him by his brother-in-law, Benjamin Thackara, in 1706, who thus carried out the intentions of the father of his wife, not consummated during his life.[1] This adjoined another tract given to the daughter Han-

---

[1] Lib. A, 107.

nah, the wife of John Whitall, who, with her husband, had also thereon erected a dwelling. The exact locality of this fifty acres would be difficult to trace at this time, but it lies in the estate late of John C. DaCosta, deceased, near the head of the Fork creek, in old Newton township. The building was doubtless a substantial log cabin, and, with the exception of a few cleared acres for farming purposes, surrounded by the primitive forest. The creek, at that time open to the flow of the tide, provided a means of travel, and a source whence food also could be procured; thus removing all anxiety from the minds of these adventurers in regard to a full supply for the inner man.

Among the many inducements held out by these pioneers to their friends still in the old country, none were made more prominent than the abundant supply of food always at hand in the rivers and forest; and the fact that the danger of starvation could not by any possibility surround them. From Gabriel Thomas to the last correspondent on record, this assurance is faithfully held out and was always found good by such as chose to test it.

Thomas Sharp shows on his map of the lands in Newton township, made in 1700, one hundred acres owned by John *Easly*, being part of Thomas Matthew's survey, afterwards owned by John Haddon,—at this writing held by the heirs of James Stoy, deceased. This title is so obscured by various conveyances and the tautology of English deeds, that no intelligent explanation can be arrived at; and whether John Easly (Eastlack) had an indefeasible estate therein, and disposed of it by the regular channel, is yet to be discovered.

John Eastlack was a man of some estate, and dealt in land, even in those early times.[2] In 1716, he purchased a plantation of one hundred and seventy-five acres, of Benjamin Richards, situated on the north branch of Timber creek, and three years after sold the same to Thomas Smallwood. This probably lay west of Chew's Landing, and parts of it may yet be in the name of the last named grantee. In 1718, he purchased a lot of meadow land of John Wright, in Newton township on

---

2 Lib. A, 109, 118.

Fork creek, near to or adjoining the fifty acres before named. This much enlarged his boundaries thereabout.[3]

The old documents say that John was a weaver, a worker in wool; which calling occupied his long winter evenings in a useful and commendable manner. Buckskin breeches, with coat and vest to match, supplied in a great measure the demand for cloth; and our worthy ancestors could often have been seen in the gallery of the meeting house, or in the halls of legislation, clad in this array, making a very presentable appearance. Buttons for vests, and buckles for the knees of breeches, were, for several generations, considered an heir-loom; and the son who found himself the possessor thereof was always marked as the favorite of the paternal head of the family. John Whitall, the brother-in-law of John Eastlack, died in 1718, having, by his will, directed his land to be sold. John Eastlack was the executor, and with the widow made a deed for said lands to Isaac Willowby in 1724. Isaac Willowby re-conveyed the same to John Eastlack the same year. These were sixty acres given by Thomas Thackara to John Whitall in 1696 upon his marriage; they adjoined John Eastlack's fifty acres. These two tracts passed to the second John by will, who re-surveyed said lands in 1760.[4] As before hinted, these tracts lie in the estate late of John C. DaCosta, deceased.

In 1729, John Eastlack purchased another property in Newton township, fronting on Cooper's creek, of which James Whitall died the owner. He conveyed the same to John Estaugh in 1735.[5] By the will of John Estaugh, all his landed estate passed to his wife, who deeded the said farm to her nephew, Ebenezer Hopkins, in 1747.[6] John Eastlack bought and sold much other land in Gloucester county, showing himself to have been a business man with an eye to thrift and care taking. He died in 1736, leaving a will by which, after a few legacies, he gave the remainder of his estate to his sons, John and Samuel.[7] He was a resident of Newton township, but of what part does not appear. An inventory of his personal effects discloses their value to be two hundred and sixty-three pounds. His children

---

3 Lib. A, 110.
4 Lib. H, 484, O. S. G.
5 Lib. GG, 09.
6 Lib. S6, 124, O. S. G.
7 Lib. No. 5, 131.

were Sarah, who married James Mickle; Samuel, who married Ann Breach; John, who married Mary Bolton and Patience Hugg; Daniel, who married Mary Cheesman; Esther, Elizabeth and Hannah. Samuel died intestate in 1744; Elizabeth remained a single woman and deceased in 1757, also without a will.[8-9]

James Mickle, the husband of Sarah, deceased in 1736, about four years after his marriage, leaving a will.[10] His wife survived him with two children, Rachel and Jacob.

The husband of Jemima was probably a grandson of Thomas Sharp, the surveyor, and one of the first emigrants to Newton. Of the descendants of this daughter nothing can be at this date discovered.

Daniel Eastlack settled in Greenwich township now Gloucester county, and is the ancestor of the family in that region of country. John Eastlack settled in Newton township on the land by him re-surveyed; part of which came to him in a direct line from his maternal ancestor, Sarah Thackara, and part from Hannah Whitall, the widow of John. He also purchased a tract of land in Newton township of Gabriel Newbie, in 1742. His two sons, John and Samuel, were also grantees with him in the title as joint tenants, and the son John, being the survivor, conveyed the whole to Joseph Mickle in 1752. He became the owner of much other real estate in Gloucester county, some by the will of his father, and some by purchase. None of these acres, now so valuable, have been in the name or family for many years, and, but for the time-stained deeds that carry the title from one purchaser to another, the name would long since have been forgotten. The little increase in the male line will account for the small number of the name now left, and the blood must in a few years be sought for among the female descendants.

---

8 Lib. No. 5, 86. 9 Lib. No. 8, 437.
10 Lib. No. 4, 65.

THE LIPPINCOTTS.

(Contributed by James S. Lippincott of Haddonfield, New Jersey.)

    Sons of the Quaker sires,
      And daughters of a noble race of old,
    List! while a love of olden time inspires
      The simple story in these pages told!
    Here shall ye find the faith that must prevail,
      Mighty, through God, o'er every evil thing;
    The faith that scorned the scaffold and the jail
      Could, e'en in dungeons, hallelujahs sing.
    A love of liberty their souls possessed;
      Nor sought they freedom for themselves alone;
    The truth they brought, their hearts had truly blessed;
      And broad and deep their charity had grown.
    No servile sycophants to worthless kings,
      No semi-Jewish ritualists, were they;
    But Christ's true light was their illumining,
      And led their spirits by a better way.
    The native of the wilds, whose lands they bought,
      The swarthy Afric borne across the main—
    To those the law of love and truth they taught;
      From these they struck the weight of slavery's chain.
    No fairer scene can history's page unfold,
      No more Arcadian age shall time display,
    Than Jersey annals in our "age of gold,"
      Ere pure Astræa took her heavenward way.
    Sons of the Quaker sires,
      And daughters of those worthy ones of old,
    Re-kindle, then, the pure and heavenly fires
      That warmed your fathers in our "age of gold!"

THE name of Lippincott is one of the oldest English surnames of local origin. It has been traced to Lovecote of the "Domesday book" of William the Conqueror, compiled in 1080. Lovecote still bears its ancient name. It is an estate lying near Highampton, Devonshire, England. The earliest known name derived from Lovecote is found in the rolls of the king's court of the time of king John, 1195, in which that of Roger de Lovecote is recorded. In the time of Edward I, 1274, the names of Jordamus de Loginggetot and Robertus de Lyvenescot and Thomas de Lufkote appear in the Hundred Rolls. The manor of Luffincott, now the parish of that name, on the west border of Devonshire, twenty miles distant from Lovecote, comprising nearly 1,000 acres, was the property of Robert de Lughencot in 1243, and remained in the family until 1415. This property is also described as having pertained to Robert de Lyvenscot in 1346. The above mentioned names, and many more which we could recite in a modified spelling, are evidently the same upon which the early scribes tried their skill and tested the plasticity of the English language.

Another branch of the family resided at Webworthy, pronounced "Wibbery," in northwestern Devon, where they held extensive estates for three hundred and fifty years. Their name was spelled Luppingcott and Luppincott. The last of the line, Henry Luppincott, resided at Barcelona, Spain, and died in 1779. A branch of this family removed to Sidbury in East Devon, about the middle of the sixteenth century, from which descended Henry Lippincott, a distinguished merchant of Bristol, who was made a baronet in 1778 by George III; also his son Sir Henry Cann Lippincott, baronet, whose descendants, Robert Cann Lippincott and his sons, Robert C. Cann Lippincott and Henry Cann Lippincott, are probably the only living male representatives of this ancient branch of the family now residing in England. The residence of the last named is at Overcourt near Bristol. The Lippincotts of England held a good position in the world, as is shown by the numerous coats-of-arms granted to them. No less than eight coats appear to have been bestowed upon gentlemen of the name; some of them probably as early as in 1420, when John Lippingcott of Wibbery is found bearing his, from which several others were derived by modification. One style, granted to one whose name was spelled Luffyngcotte, diverges widely from the others, and was probably granted at the time of the Crusades. "A black eagle, sprinkled with drops of blood, and displayed upon a field of silver," is the description of this remarkable shield.

Richard Lippincott, the ancestor of the family in America, emigrated from Devonshire, England. He was probably nearly connected with the branch settled near Sidbury, which early inclined towards Puritanism. He associated with the settlers of the colony of Massachusetts Bay, and was made a freeman by the court of Boston, May 13th, 1640. In 1641, Richard and his wife Abigail resided in Dorchester, near Boston, when their eldest son Rememberance was born and baptized in the seventh month of that year. They removed to Boston, where a son John was born in 1644; also a daughter Abigail, who died in infancy, in 1646. In 1651, having become influenced by other Christian views, he withdrew from the Church and was excommunicated therefrom, fifth month 6th, 1651. Thus this conscientious man, having obtained a deeper insight into the nature of the gospel of Christ, was preparing to accept the views held by the Friends, though no books by the teachers of that sect had yet been issued. In 1652, he returned to England, and in the next year his son, Restored, or Restore, was born at Plymouth. This name was, no doubt, bestowed in commemoration of his restoration to his native land and to the communion of more congenial spirits. With these he early associated, was a partaker with them in suffering for his faith, and was imprisoned in the jail near the castle of Exeter in February, 1655. His offence appears to have been his assertion, "that Christ was the word of God and the Scriptures a declaration of the mind of God." His home was now at Plymouth, where he was not a quiet spectator of the wrongs inflicted upon the Friends, for, in May, 1655, as stated in Sewell's history of the Quakers, he, with others, testified against the acts of the mayor and the falsehood of the charges brought against them. In the same year a son, Freedom, was born, doubtless, so named in commemoration of his release from "durance vile." A daughter, Increase, was added to his family while residing at Stonehouse, near Plymouth, in the tenth month, 1657; and a son Jacob in the year 1660, at the same place, who died in 1689. In the latter year, he was again imprisoned by the mayor of Plymouth for his faithfulness to his religious convictions, having been taken from a meeting in that city. His release was brought about by the solicitations of Margaret Fell and others, who influenced the newly restored king (Charles II.) to grant the liberation of many Friends. The colony of Rhode Island offering to the Friends freedom in the exercise of their mode of worship, Richard Lippincott again removed to New England, where he sojourned for a time. Having been preserved from persecution and the perils of the sea, he named his son Preserved, who was born here upon Christmas day, 1663, but who died in infancy. The names of the surviving children of Richard and Abigail form the words of a prayer, which needed only the addition of a son, Israel, to have been complete; thus: *Remember John, Restore Freedom, Increase Jacob* and *Preserve (Israel)!* This arrangement was doubtless accidental, having never been premeditated by the parents, though inclined to ways in fashion among the Puritans at that day.

A new charter having been granted by the king (Charles), incorporating the Rhode Island and Providence plantations, in 1663, and the New Netherlands having come into possession of the English in 1664, and a patent having been granted to a company of Friends from Long Island in 1665, who first bought the land of the natives, Richard Lippincott was induced, with others from Rhode Island, to become a patentee with the residents on or near Shrewsbury river. He thus became a member of the first English colony in New Jersey, in which he was the largest shareholder. He was an active officer of the colony. In 1669, he was a deputy and overseer, and, in the next year, an overseer of Shrewsbury town. In 1670, the first meeting for worship was established by the Friends, which was visited by George Fox in 1672, who was entertained by Richard Lippincott. His residence was on Passequeneiqua creek, a branch of South Shrewsbury river, three-fourths of a mile northeast of the house of his son-in-law, Samuel Dennis, which stood three-fourths of a mile east of the town of Shrewsbury.

It is probable that Richard Lippincott made another voyage to England, and was there in 1675, when John Fenwick was preparing to remove to West New Jersey; and that he then obtained a grant of 1,000 acres of land in Fenwick colony, having advanced the purchase money to aid that colonist. In 1676, the title was conveyed, the consideration being twenty pounds with a royalty, or quit rent, of two bushels of wheat, annually. This tract of land Richard conveyed to his five sons in 1679, but it was never occupied by them. Having at length found a fixed place of residence, Richard Lippincott lived an active and useful life in the midst of a worthy family, in the possession of a sufficient estate, and happy in the enjoyment of religious and political freedom. Here he passed the last eighteen years of his life of varied experience, and here he died on the 25th of the ninth month (November, old style), 1683.

The Dutch proprietors of New Amsterdam had long been engaged in the slave trade, and, at the surrender in 1664, the colony contained many slaves; some of whom were owned by the Friends. As early as in 1652, members of this society at Warwick, Rhode Island, passed a law requiring all slaves to be released after ten years' service, as was the manner regarding English servants. The court of Shrewsbury colony also made a law against trading in slaves, in 1683. These are the earliest instances of legislation in behalf of these oppressed bondsmen. Richard Lippincott was owner of several slaves, some of whom were set free under the will of his widow Abigail, who deceased in 1697, leaving to her children and grandchildren much real estate and considerable bequests in money.

Rememberance of Shrewsbury, eldest son of Richard, married Margaret Barber of Boston, and died in 1722, aged eighty-two years. He was a prominent man in the affairs of the colony, and an opponent, as were his brothers, of George Keith, in his attempt to seduce the Society of Friends from its faith. He had received a gift in the ministry which was usefully exercised. His friends sum up his life in a few words: "Rememberance Lippincott was a clerk of our Monthly and Quarterly Meetings many years, a diligent attendant of our meetings for worship; his labour was acceptable to Friends." He had four sons and eight daughters, four of whom died in infancy; they were Joseph and Elizabeth (twins), Abigail, Richard, Elizabeth, Joseph, William, Abigail, Sarah, Ruth, Mary and Grace.

The descendants of Rememberance through his sons, Richard and William, were numerous. Some of these who derive their descent from Jacob, son of Richard, have resided in Chester township, Burlington county, N. J., and have inter-married with the families of Clemenz, Rudderow and Matlack. Those derived from William, son of Rememberance, claim their blood through Wilbur, Samuel and Darius. Richard, one of the sons of Wilbur, removed to Philadelphia, and married Mary Scull, daughter of Jasper of Reading, Pa. From Samuel a numerous posterity has descended: first, through his son Joseph, who married Elizabeth Engle and lived for several years at Haddonfield, where he practiced the art of a silversmith, and acted as town clerk from 1777 to 1788. His children were Mary, born 1769, and married to Turner Risdon; Elizabeth, Hannah; and Samuel, born 1778, who married Elizabeth Edwards. Samuel resided in Philadelphia and Mauch Chunk, Pa., and was, for thirty-three years, associated with the business of the Lehigh Navigation Company.

Samuel, the son of William, the son of Rememberance, had several sons, some born after he removed to Westmoreland county, Pa. Many of their descendants now reside in Pittsburg and other western cities.

John Lippincott, yeoman, of Shrewsbury, second son of Richard, was born 1644, and married Ann ———. She dying in 1707, he married Jennett Austin, three years after, and died in 1720. His first wife left him eight children,—John, Robert, Preserved, Mary, Ann, Margaret, Robert and Deborah. Their numerous descendants reside chiefly in Monmouth county, N. J.; Green county, Pa., and in the city of New York.

Restore Lippincott of Shrewsbury, afterwards of Northampton, Burlington county, New Jersey, third son of Richard, was born in 1653, and married Hannah Shattock of Boston, in 1674. She deceased, and he married Martha Owen in 1729, and died in 1741. By his first wife there were three sons and six daughters; namely: Samuel, Abigail, Hannah, Hope, Rebecca, James, Elizabeth, Jacob and Rachel. Restore Lippincott was a useful citizen, exemplary in all the relations of life, and much respected by the community on account of his regard for truth and justice. In 1703 and 1705, he was a member of the governor's council of West New Jersey, to which he had removed in 1692. In that year, he bought of Thomas Olive five hundred and seventy acres of land in Northampton, Burlington county, N. J., upon which he settled. About 1698, he made, in company with John Garwood, a further purchase of 2,000 acres, lying to the east of the present town of Pemberton. Restore had many descendants. Of those from his own son Samuel and the latter's son Samuel, who married Mary Arney, some now reside upon the first purchase, between Mount Holly and Pemberton. Among the most active have been James, the Rev. Caleb A., a methodist preacher, and his son the Rev. Joshua A., now professor of mathematics in Dickinson College, Pa., and Isaac K. of Freehold and Philadelphia, deceased.

The descendants of James, who married Anna Eves, have resided in Northampton, in Evesham and in Philadelphia. Among the latter and most noteworthy, are Joshua B., the distinguished publisher, Benjamin H., for many years a public man in Burlington county, and Aaron S., a successful cotton manufacturer in Philadelphia.

The descendants of Jacob, who was born in 1692, and married Mary Burr, daughter of Henry, in 1716, are numerous, living chiefly in Gloucester and Salem counties. Among them, however, was Joshua of Philadelphia, at one time a director of the Bank of the United States and president of the Schuylkill Navigation Company.

Freedom Lippincott, fourth child of Richard, described as a tanner, lived by Rancocas creek, where the king's highway crossed the same, about where Bridgeboro now stands. Having sold his Salem land, he located two hundred and eighty-eight acres in 1687, whereon he settled. To the trade of a tanner he probably added that of a smith, and could shoe a horse or "upset" the axes of his neighbors with some skill. However that may have been, we find that, in the summer of 1697, while shoeing a horse, he was killed by lightning. His widow and five children survived him, the oldest being but thirteen years of age. The children's names were Samuel, who married Hope Wills; Thomas, who married Mary Haines; Judith, who married Joseph Stokes; Mary, who married Edward Peake; and Freedom, who married Elizabeth Wills.

The descendants of Freedom, through his sons, Samuel, Thomas and Freedom, are most numerous in the western townships of Camden and Burlington counties. Judith, who married Joseph Stokes, became the ancestor of many of that name. The descendants of Samuel, through his youngest son Aaron and the latter's son Samuel, who married Theodosia Hewlings, have resided in Evesham, near Marlton, Burlington county. Those now living and bearing the Lippincott name claim their descent through Samuel's sons, Samuel and Jacob.

Thomas, second son of Freedom, purchased in 1708 a tract of one thousand and thirty-four acres, extending from Penisaukin creek to Swedes' run, joining the No-se-ne-men-si-on tract, reserved to the Indians; from which the name, Cinnaminson, is derived. The village of Westfield stands upon the northern border of the Lippincott tract. The name was originally given to the meeting-house which was erected in 1800, in Thomas Lippincott's western field.

Thomas Lippincott was an active and useful man in the business affairs of Chester township, in which his lands were then included. The first house, built by him about 1711, stood where Samuel L. Allen now (1877) resides; and his descendants occupied the same and a second, built upon its site in 1800, for one hundred and thirty years. The first meeting of Friends in this district was held in his house, and there continued to be held until 1800. He married Mary Haines in 1711. Their children were Nathaniel, who married Mary Engle in 1736; Isaac, who married Hannah Engle; Thomas, who married Rebecca Eldridge in 1745; Abigail, who married Thomas Wills; Esther, who married John Roberts; Mary, who deceased; and Thomas, who married Mercy Middleton. Thomas had three daughters, namely: Patience, who married Ebenezer Andrews in 1742; Phœbe; and Mercy, who married Ephraim Stiles.

Nathaniel Lippincott, son of Thomas, settled in Goshen, Chester county, Pa., about the year 1737, where his two eldest children were born. Thence he removed to a farm on the road leading from Haddonfield to Milford, now owned by Aquilla S. Hillman and brothers, in Camden county, N. J. The descendants of Nathaniel, through his sons, John, Caleb and Seth, are numerous. Those from John, through his son Thomas, settled in Chester township, Burlington county, N. J., in Philadelphia, and in the State of Illinois; General Charles Ellet Lippincott, now auditor of the latter State, being the most distinguished. Caleb and Seth have representatives living in the vicinity of Moorestown and Haddonfield.

The descendants of Thomas through his son, Isaac of Westfield, are also numerous through the latter's sons, Thomas, Isaac and Samuel; all of whom settled on part of their grandfather's tract in Cinnaminson and Chester townships, Burlington county, and in Philadelphia. Among them may be noticed Joshua, a cloth merchant, and Samuel R., a director of the National State Bank of Camden, N. J.

Although Freedom, youngest son of the first Freedom Lippincott, settled early in Cropwell, Burlington county, N. J., but few of his descendants are now found there. His son Solomon, born in 1720, removed to Upper Greenwich, Gloucester county, N. J. His name is commemorated by "Solomon's Meeting," which he built in that township. Another son Samuel, a member of Pilesgrove Meeting, Salem county, N. J., was a minister among Friends. Descendants of the younger children are now living in Evesham and Haddonfield.

Increase, only daughter of Richard and Abigail Lippincott, married Samuel Dennis, and removed from Shrewsbury and settled in Salem county, N. J. Some of their children married among the Mickles and Tindalls, and were members of the old Newton Meeting in Gloucester county, N. J. The name of Dennis has not been known hereabout for many years, and no trace now remains of this branch of the family.

MARRIAGES.

The following lists of marriages, collected from various sources, are defective in many particulars. Although the dates and the names given may be considered as correct, yet there are errors as to the meetings to which they are assigned; moreover they are not the whole record, nor are they arranged in chronological order. They may, however, as here presented, assist in tracing family descent, and aid in settling many doubtful questions.

BURLINGTON.

Marriages of Friends at the Burlington Meeting in Burlington county, N. J., who were connected with the families belonging to, or settled within the limits of, the Newton Meeting in Gloucester county, N. J.

1679   Robert Zane to Alice Allday.
1680   William Heulings to Doratha Eves.
1682   William Wood to Mary Parnell.
1686   Francis Collins to Mary Gosling, widow.
1698   Thomas Bryant to Rebecca Collins.
1701   Thomas Sharp to Elizabeth Winn.
1704   Thomas Stokes to Deliverance Horner.
1707   John Matlack to Hannah Horner.
1709   George Matlack to Mary Foster.
1710   John Kaighn to Elizabeth Hill.

1711 Tobias Griscom to Deborah Gabitas.
1713 William Matlack to Ann Antrim.
1716 John Wood to Susanna Furness.
1721 Joshua Lord to Sarah Wills.
1721 Bartholomew Horner to Elizabeth Wills.
1723 Samuel Shivers to Mary Deacon.
1730 John Hugg to Mercy Middleton.
1731 William Tomlinson to Rebecca Wills.
1732 Thomas Webster to Sarah Vinacom.
1732 Thomas Lippincott to Mercy Hugg.
1734 Isaac Decou to Hannah Nicholson.
1738 Joseph Nicholson to Catharine Butcher.
1738 Hugh Clifton to Mary Wood.
1740 Thomas Smith to Rebecca Wood.
1741 John Mickle to Mary Stockdale.

Marriages solemnized in open court at Burlington, N. J., as recorded in the Minute Book thereof, on file in the office of the Secretary of State at Trenton, N. J.

1682 Charles Buggley to Elizabeth Stephens.
1682 Thomas Sherman to Frances Ward.
1682 Walter Reeves to Ann Howell.
1682 William Barnes to Martha Bromley.
1682 Francis Boswick to Priscilla Parrock.
1683 William Lee to Joan South.
1683 Richard Boyes to Mary Dodson.
1683 John Woolstan to Latitia Newbold.
1683 George Elkinton to Mary Bingham.
1684 Peter Jennings to Anne Nott.
1684 Jodia Higgins to Mary Newbold.
1684 Robert Ingalls to Joan Home.
1684 Jonathan Stephenson to Mary Allen.
1684 Timothy Hancock to Rachel Firman.
1685 Seth Hill to Mary Grubb.
1685 Edward Ingleton to Sarah Hoult.
1685 John Snape to Anne Clark.
1685 John Smith to Elizabeth Ball.
1685 Thomas Wood to Mary Howle.

MARRIAGES.

1685 Thomas Kendall to Mary Elton.
1685 Henry Tredway to Anne Driver.
1685 George Willhouse to Mary Hill.
1685 Samuel Smith to Mary Appleton.
1686 John Renshaw to Mary Stacy.
1686 Thomas Knight to Elizabeth Brown.
1686 John Langford to Isabella Bowman.
1686 Daniel Wills to Margaret Newbold.
1687 William Bustill to Elizabeth Tonkin.
1688 Daniel Sutton to Agnes Carr.
1688 John Chadwick to Elizabeth Light.
1688 James Creek to Frances Churther.
1688 Robert Rigg to Jane Bayliff.
1688 Anthony Elton to Elizabeth Revell.
1689 Thomas Peachee to Mary Miller.
1690 Thomas Kendall to Ann Jennings.
1690 Eleazor Fenton to Elizabeth Stacy.
1690 Joseph Houldin to Hannah Jonson.
1691 Gilbert Murrell to Judith Hancock.
1691 Edward Smout to Jane Abbott.
1691 Edward Hunlock to Mary Bassett.
1692 John Tuelie to Judith Murrell.
1692 Thomas Clark to Margarett Duhurst.
1692 John Bowne to Frances Bowman.
1692 Thomas Wilson to Ann Silvers.
1693 Thomas Bibb to Ruth Kettle.
1693 Bartholomew Minderman to Jane Joyner.
1693 Henry Marjerman to Jane Rigg.
1694 John Meridith to Elizabeth Lambert.
1694 Joseph White to Ann Revell.
1694 Richard Francis to Mary Major.
1694 Edward Andrews to Sarah Ong.
1694 Nathaniel Cripps to Grace Whitten.
1695 Benjamin Maplin to Elizabeth Lee.
1695 Thomas Dugles to Mary Odonoghas.
1695 John Reeve to Ann Bradgate.
1695 William Heulings to Mary Lovett.
1695 William Righton to Sarah Biddle.

1695 Charles Sheepy to Elizabeth Davis.
1695 James Newbold to Elizabeth Powell.
1695 Daniel Wills to Mary Shinn.
1695 Richard Dell to Elizabeth Decou.
1696 John Baker to Mary Peachee.
1696 Robert Powell to Mary Perkins.
1698 Thomas Potts to Mary Record.
1698 Richard Dell to Elizabeth Basnett.
1698 William Ogborn to Mary Cole.
1699 James Harpen to Sabilla Clayton.
1699 John Paine to Abigail Curtis.
1699 Joshua Ely to Rachel Lee.
1699 Jacob Decou to Elizabeth Newbold.
1699 Robert Dummer to Martha Warren.
1699 Abinelock Hudson to Pricilla Beswick.
1700 Andrew Sim to Margaret Hutchinson.
1701 Jacob Gibbs to Elizabeth Casson.
1701 Hugh Huddy to Martha Hunlock.
1701 Thomas Smith to Elizabeth Hibbard.
1701 John Briggs to Sarah Smith.
1701 James Verier to Valbert Williams.
1701 Robert Edwards to Sarah Bennett.

SALEM.

Marriages solemnized in open court at Salem New Jersey, as recorded in the Minute Book thereof, No. 2., on file in the office of the Secretary of State, at Trenton, N. J.

1682 January 11, Anthony Dixon to Elizabeth Camel.
1682 January 19, John Paine to Elizabeth Wotton.
1683 July 16, John Fuller to Ellenor Lewis.
1683 August 23, Anthony Windsor to Elizabeth Adams.
1683 February 19, John Walker to Mary Smith, daughter of John Smith.
1684 May 21, William Hall to Elizabeth Pyle.
1684 November 6, John Worledge to Ann Leupuvre.

MARRIAGES.

1686 August 10, William Price to Ann Croutcher.
1686 August 10, John Allen to Mary Huthings, daughter of Roger Hutchings.
1686 September 7, Mark Reeve to Ann Hunt.
1686 November 24, Thomas Jones to Hannah Prior.
1686 February 3, Hugh Hutchings to Mary Adams, daughter of John Adams.
1687 June 14, William Shute to Mary Clark.
1687 August 18, Fenwick Adams to Ann Watkins.
1687 August 18, Alexander Smith to Hannah Ashbury.
1688 October 17, John Bacon to Elizabeth Smith, daughter of John Smith.
1688 January 1, Bernard Hedge to Elizabeth Prague.
1689 June 18, William Wilkinson to Mary Nicholson.
1690 April 24, John Hughes to Martha Buckley.
1690 October 5, Charles Angello to Katharine Noer.
1691 March 18, Charles Peterson, widower, to Ann Kerrt, widow.
1691 March 23, Joseph Burgin to Jane Silver.
1693 March 26, William Remington to Mary Woodhouse.
1693 August 7, Joseph Bacon to Elizabeth Pancoast.
1694 July 19, Ebenezer Ashbury to Margaret Depfos.
1694 January 22, Samuel Woodhouse to Ann Hudson.
1695 October 31, Samuel Hunter to Katharine S. Keene.
1699 January 16, Nicholas Winton to Doratha Davis.
1702 July 2, William Braithwaite to Ann Worlidge, widow.
1702 November 24, William Pope to Mary Hersley.

Marriages of Friends at the Salem Meeting in Salem county, N. J., who were connected with the families belonging to the Newton Meeting, in Gloucester county, N. J., or who settled within the limits of the meeting.

1677 Abraham Strand to Rachel Nicholson.
1687 William Bradway to Elizabeth Wood.
1692 William Cooper, Jr., to Mary Bradway.
1693 Bartholemew Wyat to Sarah Ashton.
1693 Abel Nicholson to Mary Tyler.
1704 Isaac Sharp to Margaret Brathwill.

1710 William Tyler to Mary Abbott.
1722 Hugh Clifton to Elizabeth Tindall.
1723 Robert Smith to Elizabeth Wyat.
1729 John Brick to Ann Nicholson.
1729 Abel Nicholson to Isabella Daniels.
1730 John Evans to Ruth Nicholson.
1734 Joseph Tomlinson to Lydia Wade.
1737 Erastmus Fetters to Rebecca Thompson.
1740 William Griscom to Sarah Davis.
1740 John Nicholson to Sarah Powell.
1741 John Gill to Anne Davis.
1743 Samuel Nicholson to Sarah Dennis.
1744 Othniel Tomlinson to Mary Marsh.
1746 Jacob Spicer to Mary Lippincott.
1747 Thomas Redman to Mercy Davis.
1748 Isaac Ellis to Mary Shivers.
1749 William Haines to Sarah Lippincott.
1749 Joshua Ballanger to Naomi Dunn.
1753 Andrew Griscom to Mary Bacon.
1756 Richard Haines to Elizabeth Test.
1758 Joseph Kay to Ann Thompson.
1761 Joseph Clement to Ann Brick.

NEWTON.

Marriages of Friends who were members, or who married members, of Newton Meeting, Gloucester county, N. J.

1684 James Atkinson, of Philadelphia, to Hannah Newbie, widow of Mark, of Newton.[1]
1685 John Ladd to Sarah Wood.[2]
1686 Walter Forrest to Ann Albertson.[3]
1686 Thomas Shable to Alice Stalles.[3]
1686 Samuel Toms to Rachel Wood.[3]
1687 Joshua Frame, of Pennsylvania, to Abigail Bates.[2]
1687 William Clark to Mary Heritage.[3]

---

[1] At Hannah Newbie's house.
[2] At James Atkinson's house.
[3] At Newton Meeting.

MARRIAGES.

1688 John Hugg, son of John, to Pricilla Collins, daughter of Francis.[1]
1688 Joseph Cooper to Lydia Riggs.[2]
1689 Thomas Thackara to Hepsibah Eastlack.[3]
1689 Thomas Willard to Judith Wood, daughter of Henry.[4]
1691 John Butcher to Mary Heritage.[8]
1692 Simeon Ellis to Sarah Bates, daughter of William.[5]
1693 Daniel Cooper to Abigail Wood, daughter of Henry.[6]
1695 Daniel Cooper to Sarah Spicer, daughter of Samuel.[7]
1695 William Sharp to Jemima Eastlack, daughter of Francis.[5]
1695 Joseph Nicholson, son of Samuel, to Hannah Wood, daughter of Henry.[6]
1695 Isaac Decou to Rachel Newbie, daughter of Mark.[5]
1699 Thomas Thackara to Ann Parker, of Philadelphia.[5]
1701 Joseph Bates to Mercy Clement, daughter of James.[8]
1702 John Estaugh to Elizabeth Haddon.[9]
1703 Stephen Newbie to Elizabeth Wood, daughter of Henry.[5]
1704 John Mickle, son of Archibald, to Hannah Cooper, daughter of William, Jr.[2]
1705 Josiah Southwick to Elizabeth Collins, daughter of Francis.[10]
1706 Joseph Brown to Mary Spicer, daughter af Samuel.[5]
1706 Edward Newbie to Hannah Chew.[5]
1707 Benjamin Wood to Mary Kay, daughter of John.[11]
1707 Benjamin Thackara to Mary Cooper, daughter of William, Jr.[11]

AT NEWTON MEETING.

1707 John Hallowell, of Darby, to Elizabeth Sharp, daughter of Thomas.
1707 John Kay, son of John, to Sarah Langstone.
1708 Samuel Mickle to Elizabeth Cooper, daughter of Joseph.
1708 Ezekiel Siddons, son of John, to Sarah Mickle.

---

1 At Francis Collins' house.
2 At William Cooper's house.
3 At James Atkinson's house.
4 At Henry Wood's house, Hopewell.
5 At Newton Meeting.
6 At Hannah Wood's house.
7 At Samuel Spicer's house.
8 At John Hinchman's house.
9 At Elizabeth Haddon's house.
10 At Joseph Collins' house.
11 At John Kay's house.

1709 Simeon Breach to Mary Dennis.
1709 John Harvey to Sarah Hasker.
1709 Robert Braddock to Elizabeth Hancock, daughter of Timothy.
1710 Thomas Bull to Sarah Nelson.
1710 William Harrison to Ann Hugg, daughter of John.
1710 Thomas Middleton to Mercy Allen.
1710 Joseph Stokes, son of Thomas, to Judith Lippincott, daughter of Freedom.
1710 Thomas Sharp to Catharine Hollingsham.
1711 Thomas Smith to Sarah Hancock, daughter of Timothy.
1711 Jonathan Haines, son of John, to Mary Matlack, daughter of William.
1711 Daniel Mickle to Hannah Dennis.
1711 Samuel Dennis to Ruth Tindall.
1711 Thomas Lippincott, son of Freedom, to Mary Haines, daughter of John.
1712 Abraham Brown to Hannah Adams, Jr.
1714 Joseph Dole to Hannah Somers.
1714 John Hugg to Elizabeth Newbie.
1714 John Cox to Lydia Cooper, daughter of Joseph.
1716 John Adamson to Ann Skew.
1716 Francis Richardson to Sarah Cooper.
1716 Thomas Robinson to Sarah Lowe.
1716 William Sharp to Mary Austin, daughter of Francis.
1717 Alexander Morgan, son of Griffith, to Hannah Cooper, daughter of Joseph.
1718 Benjamin Cooper, son of Joseph, to Rachel Mickle.
1718 Thomas Rakestraw to Mary Wilkinson, daughter of Thomas.
1718 Samuel Sharp to Martha Hall.
1718 John Gill to Mary Heritage.
1719 John Sharp to Jane Fitchardall.
1719 Thomas Eyere to Pricilla Hugg.
1719 Joseph Gibson to Elizabeth Tindall.

MARRIAGES.

AT HADDONFIELD MEETING.

1720 Timothy Matlack to Mary Haines.
1720 Jedediah Adams to Margarett Christian.
1720 Joshua Raper to Sarah Cooper, daughter of Joseph.
1720 Thomas Adams to Hannah Sharp.
1722 Samuel Nicholson to Sarah Burrough, daughter of Samuel.
1722 Thomas Ellis to Catharine Collins.
1723 Samuel Burrrough to Ann Gray.
1723 Joseph Mickle to Elizabeth Eastlack.
1724 James Wills to Sarah Clement.
1724 Thomas Sharp to Elizabeth Smith.
1725 John Hudson to Hannah Wright.
1725 Robert Jones to Sarah Siddon.
1725 Isaac Albertson to Rachel Haines.
1726 John Burrough, son of Samuel, to Phœbe Haines, daughter of John.
1726 John Wills, son of Daniel, to Elizabeth Kaighn.
1727 Joseph Kaighn to Mary Estaugh, daughter of James.
1727 Ephraim Tomlinson, son of Joseph, to Sarah Corbit.
1727 James Cattle to Mary Engle, widow of John.
1728 John Haines to Jane Smith.
1728 Isaac Knight to Elizabeth Wright.
1729 Thomas Wright to Mary Thackara.
1729 John Turner to Jane Engle.
1730 Timothy Matlack to Martha Haines.
1730 Samuel Sharp to Mary Tomlinson.
1730 John Kay to Sarah Ellis.
1730 Bartholemew Wyat to Elizabeth Tomlinson.
1730 David Price to Grace Zane.
1731 Daniel Morgan to Mary Haines, widow.
1732 William Mickle to Sarah Wright.
1733 Samuel Abbott to Hannah Foster.
1733 Thomas Egerton to Sarah Stephens.
1733 Richard Bidgood to Hannah Burrough, widow.
1734 Peter White to Rebecca Burr.
1735 Nathan Beaks to Elizabeth Hooten.

1736 Edward Borton to Margarett Tomlinson.
1736 Thomas Bishop to Rachel Matlack.
1736 Nathan Lippincott to Mary Engle.
1736 Walter Faucett to Margarett Rillings.
1736 David Stratton to Mary Elkinton.
1737 Jacob Taylor to Ann Andrews.
1737 Thomas Redman to Mercy Gill.
1737 Jacob Howell to Mary Cooper.
1737 Thomas Thorne to Mary Harrison.
1738 Thomas Egerton to Esther Bates.
1739 James Whitall to Ann Cooper.
1739 Charles French to Ann Clement.
1739 Robert Stevens to Ann Dent.
1739 Isaac Lippincott to Hannah Engle.
1739 Thomas Rakestraw to Mary Mason.
1740 Jacob Hinchman to Abigail Harrison.
1741 Samuel Stokes to Hannah Hinchman.
1741 Thomas Stokes to Abigail Matlack.
1741 William Albertson to Jane Turner.
1741 Joshua Stokes to Amy Hinchman.
1742 Isaac Burrough to Deborah Jennings.
1742 John Ashard to Mary Middleton.
1742 Thomas Hooten to Mercy Bates.
1742 Samuel Mickle to Latitia Matlack.
1743 Henry Wood to Ruth Dennis.
1743 Daniel Fortiner to Rebecca Smith.
1743 Joseph Wilkins to Sarah Hartshorn.
1743 Daniel Hillman to Abigail Nicholson.
1744 Abraham Haines to Sarah Ellis.
1744 Samuel Nicholson to Rebecca Saint.
1744 John Warrington to Hannah Ellis.
1744 Job Siddon to Achsa Matlack.
1746 James Cooper to Deborah Matlack.
1746 John Hillman to Hannah Nicholson.
1746 Samuel Noble to Lydia Cooper.
1747 William Miller to Elizabeth Woodward.
1747 Jacob Clement to Hannah Albertson.
1748 Joseph Snowdon to Rebecca Howell.

MARRIAGES.

1748 Michael Lents to Rachel Richardson.
1748 Samuel Clement to Ruth Evans.
1748 Benjamin Champion to Ann Hewitt.
1748 William Matlack to Mary Turner.
1748 Samuel Collins to Rosanna Stokes.
1749 Samuel Nicholson to Jane Albertson, widow.
1749 James West to Mary Cooper.
1749 Jacob Stokes to Pricilla Ellis.
1749 John Jaffereys to Mercy Butcher.
1749 Archibald Mickle to Mary Burrough.
1750 Thomas Hinchman to Latitia Mickle, widow.
1750 Jacob Ellis to Casandra Albertson.
1750 John Branson to Sarah Sloan.
1750 John Thorne to Mary Gill, widow.
1750 John Barton to Elizabeth Champion.
1750 Jonathan Fisher to Hannah Hutchison.
1750 Simeon Breach to Mary Shores.
1751 Jacob Burrough to Sarah Thorne.
1751 Enoch Burrough to Deborah Middleton.
1751 John Glover to Mary Thorne.
1751 Joseph Bispham to Elizabeth Hinchman.
1752 Samuel Hugg to Elizabeth Collins.
1752 Thomas Bates to Sarah Pancoast.
1752 Restore Lippincott to Ann Lord.
1752 Charles West to Hannah Cooper.
1752 James Hinchman to Sarah Bickam.
1753 Joshua Evans to Pricilla Collins.
1753 Nathan Beaks to Lydia Morgan.
1753 Robert Stevens to Mary Kaighn.
1753 Jacob Burrough to Casandra Ellis.
1754 Samuel Burrough to Hannah Spence.
1755 John Hillman to Mary Horner.
1755 Isaac Ballinger to Patience Albertson.
1756 William Bates to Elizabeth Hooten.
1756 Isaac Horner to Elizabeth Kay.
1757 Josiah Burrough to Sarah Morgan.
1757 Caleb Hughes to Abigail Ellis.
1758 Samuel Clement to Bulah Evans.

1758 Daniel Tomlinson to Mary Bates.
1758 John Buzby to Sarah Ellis.
1758 Samuel Tomlinson to Ann Burrough.
1758 Joseph Morgan to Mary Stokes.
1759 Thomas Thorne to Abigail Burrough.
1759 Samuel Webster to Sarah Albertson.
1759 John Branson to Sarah Sloan.
1760 John Starr to Eunice Lord.
1760 John Brick to Abigail French.
1760 Thomas Champion to Deborah Clark.
1760 Chatfield Brown to Hannah Andrews.
1760 Constantine Lord to Sarah Albertson.
1761 John Sharp to Sarah Andrews.
1761 Simeon Zane to Sarah Hooten.
1761 Elnathan Zane to Bathsaba Hartly.
1761 Jacob Jennings to Mary Smith.
1761 Richard Gibbs to Mary Burrough.
1762 Jacob Cozens to Esther Zane.
1762 John Mickle to Elizabeth E. Hopkins.
1762 James Brown to Catharine Andrews.
1762 John E. Hopkins to Sarah Mickle.
1762 Stephen Thackara to Elizabeth Sloan.
1762 David Davis to Martha Cole.
1762 James Gardiner to Mary Tomlinson.
1763 Job Kimsey to Elizabeth Eastlack.
1764 James Whitall to Rebecca Matlack.
1764 Caleb Lippincott to Ann Vinacomb.
1764 James Starr to Elizabeth Lord.
1764 James Cooper to Mary Mifflin, widow.
1764 Ebenezer Hopkins to Ann Albertson.
1765 Jonathan Knight to Elizabeth Delap.
1765 William Cooper to Abigail Matlack.
1765 Joseph Burrough to Mary Pine.
1766 Griffith Morgan to Rebecca Clement.
1766 Constantine Jeffreys to Patience Butcher.
1766 Isaac Townsend to Katharine Albertson.
1767 John Wilkins to Rachel Wood.
1767 Josiah Albertson to Elinor Tomlinson.

MARRIAGES.

1767 Caleb Cresson to Sarah Hopkins.
1767 John Redman to Sarah Branson.
1767 Aquilla Jones to Elizabeth Cooper.
1767 Joshua Lippincott to Elizabeth Wood.
1767 Robert Cooper to Mary Hooper.
1767 Mark Miller to Mary Redman.
1767 John Gill to Abigail Hillman.
1768 Jacob Haines to Bathsaba Burrough.
1768 Samuel Brown to Rebecca Branson.
1769 Job Whitall to Sarah Gill.
1770 Joshua Cresson to Mary Hopkins.
1770 James Sloan to Rachel Clement.
1770 Jonathan Iredell to Elizabeth Hillman.
1771 Joseph Gibson to Sarah Haines.
1771 Isaac Buzby to Martha Lippincott.
1772 Joseph Mickle to Hannah Burrough.
1772 Thomas Wright to Mary Branson.
1772 Benjamin C. Cooper to Ann Black.
1772 Amos Cooper to Sarah Mickle.
1773 Samuel Allison to Martha Cooper.
1773 George Ward to Ann Branson.
1773 John Barton to Amy Shivers.
1774 Joseph Reeve to Elizabeth Morgan.
1774 Benjamin Catheral to Esther Brown.
1774 Joshua Stretch to Lydia Tomlinson.
1774 William Zane to Elizabeth Hillman.
1774 William Kneas to Sarah Pederick.
1774 James Stuart to Mary Ballanger.
1774 Enoch Allen to Hannah Collins.
1775 Joab Wills to Amy Gill.
1775 William Edgarton to Tabitha Herison.
1775 John Haines to Hipparchia Hinchman.
1775 Caleb Lippincott to Zilpah Shinn.
1776 Nathaniel Barton to Rachel Stokes.
1776 John Clement to Hannah Griscom.
1776 Jonathan Brown to Sarah Ballinger.
1777 Samuel Tomlinson to Martha Mason.
1777 Joshua Evans to Ann Kay.

FIRST EMIGRANT SETTLERS.

1777 Job Cowperthwaite to Ann Vickers.
1777 David Branson to Elizabeth Evans.
1778 Joseph Burrough to Lydia Stretch.
1778 Marmaduke Cooper to Mary Jones.
1778 William White to Ann Paul.
1779 Samuel Stokes to Hope Hunt.
1779 Joshua Paul to Mary Lippincott.
1779 James Hinchman to Sarah Morgan.
1779 Jededia Allen to Ann Wilkins.
1779 Benjamin Test to Elizabeth Thackara.
1779 Richard Snowdon to Sarah Brown.
1780 Benjamin Hooten to Sarah Snowdon.
1780 William Lippincott to Elizabeth Folwell.
1780 Samuel Tomlinson to Mary Bates.
1781 Peter Thompson to Mary Glover.
1781 John Gill to Sarah Pritchett.
1781 Robert Zane to Elizabeth Butler.
1781 Daniel Hillman to Martha Ellis.
1781 Isaac Ballinger to Mary Bassett.
1781 John Webb to Amy Wills.
1781 Edward Gibbs to Hepsibah Evans.
1782 Joshua Cooper to Abigail Stokes.
1782 John Barton to Rebecca Engevine.
1782 John Reeves to Beulah Brown.
1782 David Ware to Sarah Shinn.
1782 Restore Lippincott to Deborah Ervin.
1782 Joshua Harlan to Sarah Hinchman.
1783 Zacheus Test to Rebecca Davis.
1783 Isaac Stiles to Rachel Glover.
1783 Jacob Jennings to Ann Hopkins.
1783 Asher Brown to Mary Ward.
1784 James Thackara to Jane Guant.
1784 Charles Fogg to Ann Bates.
1784 William Knight to Elizabeth Webster.
1784 James Hopkins to Rebecca Clement.
1784 Darling Haines to Mary Lippincott.
1784 James Mickle to Hannah Lord.
1784 Jonathan Morgan to Elizabeth Fisher.

MARRIAGES.

1785   Daniel Roberts to Hannah Stokes.
1785   Abraham Warrington to Rachel Evans.
1785   Peter Thompson to Sarah Stephenson.
1785   John Stuart to Deborah Griscom.
1785   John Evans to Elizabeth Browning.
1788   Isaac Jones to Sarah Atkinson.
1788   Caleb Atkinson to Sarah Champion.
1788   Francis Boggs to Ann Haines.
1789   William Rogers to Mary Davis.
1789   Joseph Davis to Mary Haines.
1789   William Saterthwaite to Mary Prior.
1789   Samuel Glover to Hannah Albertson.
1789   John Thorne to Mary Duberee.
1790   Thomas Knight to Hannah Branson.
1790   Thomas M. Potter to Mary Glover.
1790   James Wood to Ruth Clement.
1790   Josiah Kay to Elizabeth Horner.
1791   George Abbott to Mary Redman.
1791   Samuel Abbott to Martia Gill.
1791   Jeremiah Wood to Mary Horner.
1792   Joseph Burrough to Martha Davis.
1792   John Gill to Susanna Branson.
1793   Jesse Lippincott to Mary Ann Kay.
1793   Joseph Cooper to Sarah P. Buckley.
1793   Marmaduke Burr to Ann Hopkins.
1793   Jacob Glover to Mary Branson.
1793   Abraham Silver to Sarah Knight.
1793   Joshua Roberts to Sarah Cole.
1794   Obediah Engle to Patience Cole.
1794   John Albertson to Ann Pine.
1795   Isaac Ballanger to Esther Stokes.
1795   Job Bishop to Lardle Jones.
1795   Joseph Kaighn to Sarah Mickle.
1795   Jesse Smith to Mary Paul.
1795   William E. Hopkins to Ann Morgan.
1796   Joseph Glover to Sarah Mickle.
1796   Aaron Pancoast to Ann Cooper.
1796   Joseph Bennett to Mary Morgan.

1796 Reuben Braddock to Elizabeth Stokes.
1797 Jonathan Knight to Elizabeth Kaighn.
1797 Peter Hammit to Mary Duel.
1797 Joseph C. Swett to Ann H. Clement.
1798 Richard M. Cooper to Mary Cooper.
1798 Joseph Burr to Mary Sloan.
1798 Abel Ashard to Ann Jennings.
1799 Robert Rowand to Elizabeth Barton.
1799 William Roberts to Ann Brick.
1799 Isaac Thorne to Rachel Horner.
1799 Samuel Hooten to Sarah Ballanger.

CHESTER.

Marriages of Friends who were members of Chester Meeting, (Moorestown), Burlington county, N. J.

1692 William Hollingshead, son of John, to Elizabeth Adams, daughter of John.[1]
1696 Edward Buzby to Susanna Adams, daughter of John.[1]
1696 Francis Austin to Mary Borton.[2]
1697 Joseph Heritage to Hannah Allen, daughter of Juda.[3]
1699 Thomas Eves, son of Thomas, to Mary Roberts, daughter of John.[4]
1699 Samuel Burrough to Hannah Roberts, daughter of John.,
1701 Juda Allen to Deborah Adams, daughter of John[5]
1702 Hugh Sharp to Rachel Allen, widow of Mathew.[6]
1705 Enoch Core to Sarah Roberts, daughter of John.[4]
1706 John Heritage, son of Richard, to Sarah Slocum[7]

AT CHESTER MEETING.

1712 John Roberts to Mary Elkinton.
1714 Henry Allen to Abigail Somers.
1714 John Antrim to Amy Andrews.

---

1 At John Adams's house.
2 At Thomas Wilkins's house.
3 At Richard Heritage's house.
4 At Sarah Roberts's house.
5 At Chester Meeting.
6 At Rachel Allen's house.
7 At John Heritage's house.

MARRIAGES. 403

1719	Abraham Haines to Grace Hollingshead.
1719	John Hancock to Mary Gurnell.
1719	Henry Warrington to Elizabeth Austin.
1721	Richard Haines to Agnes Hollingshead.
1722	Joseph Matlack to Rebecca Haines.
1724	Benjamin Clark to Mary Hooten.
1724	John French to Sarah Wickawan.
1724	John Lewdell to Hannah Ward.
1724	Henry Willard to Elizabeth Ballanger.
1725	Thomas Bickam to Elizabeth Hooper.
1727	Derrick Tyson to Ann Hooten, daughter of Thomas.
1728	Henry Warrington to Elizabeth Bishop.
1729	John Swain to Mary Buzby.
1729	Richard Heritage to Sarah Tindall.
1729	George Ward to Margarett Bennett.
1730	Hasker Newberry to Mary Heritage.
1730	William Hooten to Ann Sharp, widow.
1731	John Buzby to Hannah Adams.
1731	Anthony Sharp to Mary Dimack.
1731	Thomas Clark to Mariba Parker.
1734	Hugh Hollingshead to Ann Eves.
1734	Samuel Haines to Lydia Stokes.
1734	John Cowperthwaite to Rebecca Stokes.
1736	Thomas Bishop to Rachel Matlack.
1737	Jonathan Ellis to Mary Hollingshead.
1737	William Sharp to Elizabeth Risdon.
1737	Andrew Griscom to Susanna Hancock.
1737	Benjamin Moore to Mercy Newberry.
1737	Edward Hollingshead to Mary Morgan.
1737	John Maxwell to Hannah Matlack.
1737	Nathan Allen to Martha Stokes.
1737	Ebenezer Brown to Elizabeth Ives.
1737	Robert French to Hannah Cattel.
1738	John Tanner to Susanna Alcott.
1738	John Higbee to Mary Barton.
1738	Amos Wilkins to Susan ———.
1739	Isaac Warren to Pricilla Matlack.
1740	Samuel Butcher to Mercy Newberry.

1740 Abraham Iredale to Sarah Coffin.
1740 Daniel Packer to Ruth Warrington.
1740 Michael Mills to Sarah Moore.
1741 Habakuk Ward to Hannah Lord.
1741 William Barton to Abigail Lord.
1741 Joshua Roberts to Rebecca Stokes.
1742 John Roberts to Esther Lippincott.
1742 Thomas Hooten to Mercy Bates.
1743 Benjamin Heritage to Kesiah Matlack.
1743 George Matlack to Rebecca Hackney.
1744 James Delzel to Elizabeth Hancock.
1744 Edward Barton to Elizabeth Middleton.
1744 John Rowand to Sarah Matlack.
1745 Richard Matlack to Mary Cole.
1745 Hudson Middleton to Christian Hopwell.
1746 William Allen to Judith Stokes.
1746 John Brown to Sarah Cooper.
1746 Joseph Stokes to Ann Haines, widow.
1746 Richard Ward to Hannah Warrington.
1746 George Ward to Martha Bates.
1747 Thomas Warrington to Mary Roberts.
1748 Ebenezer Andrews to Mary Warrington.
1749 Robert Hunt to Martha Ward, widow.
1749 Ezekiel Lindsey to Rachel Shores.
1750 William Middleton to Ann Barton.
1750 Thomas Eyres to Sarah Mills.
1750 Nathaniel Brown to Mary Bircham.
1750 Benjamin Matlack to Susanna Hewitt.
1750 Thomas West to Deborah Wills.
1750 Daniel Bassett to Mary Lippincott.
1750 John Risdon to Sarah Turner.
1750 Isaac Mason to Sarah Price.
1750 William Cushin to Phoebe Young.
1750 Joseph Browning to Kesiah Stokes.
1751 Thomas Evans to Hannah Roberts.
1754 William Rogers to Sarah Warrington.
1754 William Snowden to Margarett Ballanger.
1754 Joseph Buzby to Hannah Warrington.

MARRIAGES.

1754 Samuel Andrews to Phœbe Cowperthwaite.
1754 William Wilkins to Elizabeth Swain.
1754 Amos Haines to Mary Conrow.
1755 John Hankinson to Elizabeth Bispham, widow.
1755 William Cathcart to Mary Orin.
1755 Joseph Hackney to Agnes Haines.
1756 John Lippincott to Ann Matlack.
1756 John Newbold to Mary Cole.
1756 Caleb Evans to Abigail Hunt.
1757 David Saterthwaite to Mary Wright.
1757 Robert Stiles to Mary Ellis, widow.
1757 Hudson Middleton to Sarah Haines.
1757 Joseph Stokes to Atlantic Bispham.
1757 Jacob Wilkins to Ann French.
1758 Isaac Haines to Deborah Roberts.
1758 Aaron Wills to Rachel Warrington.
1758 Ephraim Haines to Sarah Cheesman.
1759 George Turner to Hannah Thorne.
1759 John Moore to Hannah Eyre.
1759 John Mason to Mary Moore.
1759 Lewis Darnell to Grace Thomas.

EVESHAM.

Marriages of Friends who were members of Evesham Meeting, Burlington county, N. J.

1703 Henry Newberry to Sarah Boyes, daughter of Richard.
1703 Henry Clifton, of Philadelphia, to Jane Engle, widow.
1705 William Newberry to Mary Hasker, daughter of William.
1707 John Engle to Mary Ogborn.
1713 Mark Stratton to Ann Hancock, daughter of Timothy
1713 Emanuel Stratton to Hannah Hancock, daughter of Timothy.
1715 Thomas Evans to Esther Haines.
1717 William Hudson to Jane Evans, daughter of William.
1721 Richard Matlack to Rebecca Haines.

1721	Luke Gibson to Sarah Clark.
1721	Jacob Coffin to Hannah Wilkins.
1721	Carlisle Haines to Sarah Matlack.
1721	Zachariah Pritchett to Mary Troth.
1722	John Darnell to Hannah Borton.
1723	John Ratherwell to Mary Ballanger.
1723	Jonathan Ladd to Ann Wills.
1723	John Pim to Lydia Briggs.
1724	William Garwood to Jane Troth.
1725	Nathan Haines to Sarah Austin.
1725	Amaziah Ballanger to Elizabeth Garwood.
1726	Nathan Crosby to Elizabeth Garwood.
1727	Josiah Albertson to Ann Austin.
1727	Thomas Wilkins to Mary Core.
1728	Richard Clark to Elizabeth Flanagan.
1728	Edward Richardson to Mary Richardson.
1729	William Foster to Hannah Core.
1729	Thomas Pederick to Rebecca Bickam.
1731	William Borton to Deborah Hedge.
1731	Thomas Jennings to Ann Borton.
1731	John Cripps to Mary Eves.
1731	Samuel Cole to Mary Lippincott.
1731	Amos Haines to Rebecca Troth.
1732	Philip Pederick to Hannah Bickam.
1732	Thomas French to Mary Cattel.
1732	John Wills to Abigail Lippincott.
1733	Joseph Hopwell to Sarah Briggs.
1733	Thomas Garwood to Mary Ballanger.
1733	Francis Dudley to Rachel Wilkins.
1733	David Davis to Mary Musgrove.
1734	Brazilla Newbold to Sarah Core.
1734	Josiah White to Rebecca Foster.
1734	Samuel Hopper to Mary Johnson.
1734	John Haines to Ann Ashard.
1737	Daniel Garwood to Susanna Collins.
1737	Isaac Decou to Mary Cripps.
1738	William Evans to Sarah Roberts.
1739	William Earl to Mary Sharp.

MARRIAGES.

1739 Thomas Budd to Rebecca Atkinson.
1739 Freedom Lippincott to Hannah Rakestraw.
1740 Joseph White to Martha Lippincott.
1740 Joseph Lippincott to Elizabeth Evans.
1740 John Lippincott to Elizabeth Elkinton.
1740 Jonathan Haines to Hannah Sharp.
1740 Thomas Middleton to Esther Barton.
1740 David Elwell to Mary Haines.
1740 Timothy Middleton to Elizabeth Barton.
1741 Joshua Ballanger to Martha Stratton.
1741 Sylvester Sharp to Mary Mills.
1741 William Austin to Mary Robeson.
1741 Samuel Wickward to Sarah Buzby.
1742 Jonathan Davis to Esther Haines.
1742 Ebenezer Andrews to Patience Lippincott.
1743 Freedom Lippincott to Elizabeth Ballanger.
1743 Eber Decou to Sarah Eves.
1743 Gabriel Davis to Sarah Ballanger.
1743 William Pinyard to Mary Young.
1743 Robert Stiles to Hannah Burrough.
1744 Solomon Lippincott to Sarah Cozens.
1744 Amaziah Ballanger to Ruth Collins.
1745 John Green to Catharine Hustead.
1745 Isaac Evans to Bathsaba Stokes.
1745 Thomas Lippincott to Rebecca Eldridge.
1745 Jacob Shinn to Hannah Lippincott.
1746 Aaron Lippincott to Elizabeth Jennings.
1746 Samuel Atkinson to Esther Evans.
1746 John Garwood to Charity Wright.
1746 Enoch Stratton to Amy Elkinton.
1746 Francis Collins to Ann Haines, widow.
1747 Samuel Hammock to Esther Sharp.
1747 Joseph Butcher to Prudence Rogers.
1747 John Fisher to Grace Mason.
1747 Jonathan Austin to Rebecca Mason.
1748 William Haines to Elizabeth Ballanger.
1749 Jacob Evans to Rachel Eldridge.
1749 Job Haines to Esther Hammitt.

1749 William Austin to Hannah Thomas.
1749 John Pinyard to Martha Wilkins.
1749 Aaron Silver to Ann Hall.
1749 Obediah Borton to Mary Driver.
1751 Amaziah Ballanger to Mary Ashbrook.
1751 James Lippincott to Elizabeth Lippincott.
1752 Thomas Eyre to Catharine Moore.
1752 John Eves to Jane Evans.
1752 Abner Woolman to Mary Aronson.
1752 Joseph Lowe to Rebecca Waite.
1752 Joseph Wilcox to Sarah Iredell.
1752 Thomas Andrews to Catharine Webster.
1752 Caleb Lippincott to Hannah Wilkinson.
1752 Julius Ersan to Sarah Middleton.
1752 Richard Saterthwaite to Elizabeth Wright.
1752 William Sharp to Mary Haines.
1753 John Ballanger to Mary Andrews, widow.
1753 Henry Burr to Elizabeth Foster.
1753 Aaron Lippincott to Elizabeth Tomlinson.
1753 Thomas Middleton to Jane Nicholson, widow.
1753 Joseph Johnson to Mary Ellis.
1753 Thomas Cummings to Mary Craig.
1754 Edward Darnell to Jane Driver.
1754 Joseph Sleeper to Hannah Haines.
1756 Edward Andrews to Tabitha Richardson.
1756 Ezekiel Lippincott to Bathsaba Matlack.
1756 Jacob Evans to Mary Cherrington.
1756 Joshua Lippincott to Rachel Dudley.
1756 Benjamin Gaskill to Sarah Heustead.
1756 William Montgomery to Mary Ellis.
1757 Joshua Gibbs to Hannah Burrough.
1757 William Troth to Esther Borton.
1757 Abraham Eldridge to Mary Lippincott.
1758 John Brackney to Mary Cheesman.
1758 John Peacock to Susanna Ballanger.
1758 Jacob Pritchett to Elizabeth Philips.
1758 Caleb Austin to Lydia Mason.
1758 Abel Lippincott to Jemima Evans.

MARRIAGES.

1758 William Sharp to Elizabeth Lippincott.
1758 John Haines to Mary Shreeve.
1758 John Miller to Sarah Andrews.
1758 Isaac Halloway to Mary Haines.
1759 Brazilla Pritchett to Sarah Sharp.
1759 Samuel Sharp to Rosanna Pritchett.
1759 Clayton Newbold to Mary Foster.
1759 John Painter to Susanna Stratton.
1760 Joseph Engle to Mary Borton.
1760 Thomas Rogers to Elizabeth Craig, Jr.
1761 Isaac Borton to Mary Hooten.
1764 Thomas Stokes to Sarah Inskeep.
1765 William Wills to Ann Craig.
1766 John Jessup to Elizabeth Ballanger.
1766 Joseph Gibson to Mary Ballanger.
1769 Jesse Thomas to Sarah Beckett.

WOODBURY.

Marriages of Friends who were members of Woodbury Creek Meeting, Gloucester county, N. J.

1689 Joshua Lord to Sarah Wood, daughter of John.
1709 Joshua Lord to Isabella Watts.
1710 James Dilks to Ann Barker.
1710 John Wood to Mary Whitall.
1713 Samuel Ladd to Mary Medcalf.
1714 Thomas Hackney to Rebecca Wilkins.
1715 Henry Wood to Hannah Whitall.
1716 Job Whitall to Jane Siddon.
1717 Abraham Chatten to Grace Mills.
1717 William Wickawan to Sarah Mason.
1717 George Nicholson to Alice Lord.
1718 James Whitall to Sarah Rakestraw.
1718 John Hill to Sarah Whitall.
1721 John Lord to Mary Tindall.
1721 Luke Gibson to Sarah Clark.

1722 John Haines to Hannah Wood, widow.
1722 James Caffery to Margarett Zane.
1725 Richard Bickam to Mary Wood.
1725 James Smith to Jane Whitall, widow.
1727 William Clark to Phillis Ward.
1728 Moses Ward to Mary Clark.
1730 John Borton to Elizabeth Lord.
1730 Thomas Wilkins to Joanna Wood.
1730 Joseph Parker to Mary Ladd.
1731 John Saunders to Elizabeth Wilkins.
1732 John Ladd to Hannah Mickle.
1733 Francis Eastlack to Phœbe Driver.
1733 Richard Chew to Abigail Wood.
1733 John Wilkins to Sarah Wood.
1733 Obediah Gibson to Mary Lord.
1733 Thomas Saunders to Ann Hopper.
1734 William Wood to Hannah Wood.
1734 John Howell to Catharine Ladd.
1734 Abraham Moss to Ann Ladd.
1734 Edmund Lord to Elizabeth Wood.
1737 Ebenezer Hopkins to Sarah Lord.
1737 John Jessup to Margarett Whitaker.
1737 James Wood to Sarah Kinsey.
1739 James Whitall to Ann Cooper.
1739 William Wood to Rachel Stockdale.
1740 Thomas Kinsey to Hannah Ward.
1740 Habakuk Ward to Hannah Lord.
1741 William Barton to Abigail Lord.
1742 Robert Downs to Catharine Ladd.
1743 John Mitchner to Sarah Wilkins.
1743 Robert Zane to Martha Chatten.
1745 Abraham Chatten to Mary Wood.
1746 Joseph Gibson to Sarah Lord.
1747 Jacob Wills to Deborah Ladd.
1748 John Heustead to Sarah Lord.
1748 Joseph Cowgill to Ann Arnold.
1751 Isaac Wilkins to Elizabeth Bliss.
1751 Ebenezer Cook to Elizabeth Zane.

MARRIAGES.

1752   Thomas Robeson to Sarah Chatten.
1752   Francis Wood to Rachel Zane.
1752   John Lawton to Elizabeth Stevens.
1753   James Wood to Sarah Bickam.
1753   Nathan Lord to Ruth Snowdon.
1758   James Wood to Rebecca Wilkins.
1760   James Wilkins to Mary Ward.
1760   Samuel Mifflin to Mary Jessup.
1762   John Tatem to Sarah Ward.
1768   Jeremiah Andrews to Ann Wood.
1768   Thomas Saunders to Rachel Stevens.
1771   Phineas Lord to Mary Gibbs.
1772   William Mickle to Sarah Lord.
1777   William Wood to Hannah Ladd.
1780   John Tatem to Elizabeth Cooper.
1780   Richard Wood to Ann Cooper.
1782   George Ward to Edith Wood.
1794   George Ward to Deborah Saunders.
1794   Benjamin Hopkins to Rebecca Ward.

LICENSES OF MARRIAGE.

A copy of the licenses of marriage granted by the Governor of the State of New Jersey, as taken from the license books and from the files relating thereto, in the office of the Secretary of State at Trenton, N. J., of Burlington and Gloucester counties.

1727.

Benjamin Wood, of Gloucester county, to Mary Ashton, of Philadelphia.
Thomas Thorne, of New York, to Laticia Hinchman, of Gloucester county.
Robert Bishop to Mary Hall, of Burlington county.
Thomas Briant to Sarah Dunn, of Gloucester county.
Richard Buckle to Sarah Johnson,   "   "
Thomas Cheesman to Sarah Coleman,   "   "
William Ward to Mary Ann Warder,   "   "
Jonathan Wood to Doratha Dogsflesh.

1728.

William Budd, of Burlington county, to Susanna Cole, of Gloucester county.
Joseph Inskeep to Mary Matlack, of Burlington county.
Richard Glover to Rachel Clark, " "
Jonathan Bolton to Mary Champion, of Gloucester county.
Gabriel Hugg to Patience Ervin, " "
Amos Ashard to Cecelia Cheesman, " "
George Gilbert to Hannah Fish, " "
Benjamin Ingersoll to Hannah Dole, " "

1729.

Benjamin Cooper, of Gloucester county, to Hannah Carlisle, of Philadelphia.
Edward Hurley to Frances Warrick, of Burlington county.
Thomas Briant to Martha Middleton, of Gloucester county.
Isaac Tindall to Ann Harland, " "
Josiah Shivers to Ann Bates, " "
Henry Roe to Hannah Cheesman, " "

1730.

Samuel Harrison, of Gloucester county, to Mary Preston, of Philadelphia.
Benjamin Cheesman to Kesiah Lawrence, of Gloucester county.
John Testor to Hannah Briggs, " "
Joseph Heritage to Sarah Whitall, " "
William Holmes to Rebecca Jones, " "

1731.

Jacob Albertson to Patience Chew, " "
Joseph Thackara to Hannah Albertson, " "
Ebenezer Jones to Mary Hampton, " "
Joseph Cole to Mary Wood, " "

1732.

Edward Gaskill to Elizabeth Lippincott, of Burlington county.
Aaron Ward to Phœbe Holmes, of Gloucester county.
John Ashbrook to Esther Hamilton, " "

MARRIAGES.

John Holmes to Esther Fawsett, of Gloucester county.
Thomas Cole to Hannah Stokes, " "
John Kaighn to Abigail Hinchman, " "
Remembrance Lippincott to Hannah Bates, " "
James Mickle to Sarah Eastlack, " "
Thomas Bates to Mary Shivers, " "
Tobias Holloway to Mary Ladd, widow, " "

1733.

Edward Tonkins, of Burlington county, to Mary Cole, of Gloucester county.
Samuel Parr, of Burlington county, to Hannah Burrough, of Gloucester county.
Robert Hunt, of Burlington county, to Abigail Wood, of Gloucester county.
Jacob Matlack to Ruth Woodathall, of Burlington county.
Isaac Matlack to Rebecca Bates, of Gloucester "
Isaiah Ross to Ruth Tindall, " "
John Preston to Margarett Macintosh, " "
John Kentee to Hannah Sharp, " "
Samuel Eastlack to Ann Breach, " "
William Kent to Sarah Powell, " "
John Wright to Ruth Mapes, " "
John Maher to Edith Jones, " "

1734.

Benjamin Cooper to Elizabeth Burdsall, widow, of Gloucester county.
Abraham Siddon to Mary Cooper, widow, of Gloucester county.

1735.

George Vaughn, of Gloucester county, to Hannah Smith, of Burlington county.
Abraham Sharp to Mary French, widow, of Burlington county.
William Sharp to Ann Austin, " "
Henry Cooper to Elizabeth Curtis, " "
Thomas Budd to Jemima Leeds, " "

Benjamin Collins to Ann Hedger, of Gloucester county.
Thomas Potter to Rachel Wainwright, " "
John Eastlack to Margarett Hillman, " "
George Ellis to Sarah Wild, " "
William Heppard to Deborah Hinchman, " "
Andrew Morton to Emily Somers, " "
William Guess to Christiana Archard, " "
Elias Champion to Mary Steelman, " "
Benjamin Holmes to Hannah Roberts, " "
John Kain to Mary Worriman, " "
Charles Axford to Rebecca Beeks.
Reuben Eldridge to Susanna Perkins.
Samuel Reeves to Mary Hill.

1736.

Charles Taylor, of Burlington county, to Rachel Horner, daughter of Isaac, of Gloucester county.
Jeremiah Wood, of Long Island, to Catharine Lloyd, of Salem county.
Blackinstone Ingledon, of Philadelphia, to Mary Mickle, widow, of Gloucester county.
John Chambers, of Philadelphia, to Mary Mickle, of Gloucester county.
Nathan Middleton to Mary French, of Burlington county.
Amos Austin to Esther Haines, " "
John Goslin to Sarah Budd, " "
Hugh Caldwell to Jane Cox, of Gloucester "
John Shivers to Mary Clement, " "
Samuel Morton to Lydia Cox, " "
Henry Willard to Ann Wetherill, " "
George Flanagan to Sarah Jennings, " "
John Matlack to Hannah Shivers, " "
Jeremiah Birch to Mary Jones, " "
Samuel Butcher to Susanna Marple, of Philadelphia.
Charles Hopkins to Ann Green, of Salem "
John Hampton to Ann Deval, " "
Abraham Lord to Amica Mullica, " "

MARRIAGES.

1737.

John Collins, of Gloucester county, to Elizabeth Moore, daughter of Benjamin of Burlington county.
William Hugg to Sarah Harrison, daughter of Samuel, of Gloucester county.
William Kaighn to Abigail Cooper, daughter of Mary Siddons, of Gloucester county.
Samuel Few to Susanna Collins, daughter of Edward, of Gloucester county.
Abraham Albertson to Hannah Medcalf, widow, of Gloucester county.
John Bishop to Rebecca Matlack, of Burlington county.
Roger Hartley to Rebecca Packer, " "
John Hooten to Sarah Kay, " "
Thomas Clement to Mary Tylee, of Gloucester "
Archibald Jolly to Deborah Cheesman, " "
Joseph Albertson to Rosanna Hampton, " "
John Eastlack to Mary Bolton, " "
John Green to Elizabeth Browning, " "
John Norton to Hannah Eastlack, " "
Ephraim Norton to Sarah Mickle, " "

1738.

Isaac Kay to Mary Ann Gregory, daughter of Joseph, of Gloucester county.
Benjamin Donnoly to Susanna Collins, daughter of Elizabeth Kent, of Burlington county.
Henry Siddons to Elizabeth Sharp, daughter of Samuel, of Gloucester county.
Henry Jones to Naomi Cheesman, of Gloucester county.
Jonathan Thomas to Sarah Ellis, widow, " "
Daniel Barber to Margarett Hampton, " "
Robert Turner to Abigail Burne, " "
David Roe to Elizabeth Taber, " "
John Wiltshire to Elizabeth Williams.
John Johnson to Mary Redman.

1739.

John Chew to Ann Jennings, daughter of Isaac, of Gloucester county.
Isaac Smith to Elizabeth Norris, of Gloucester county.

1740.

Abraham Inskeep to Sarah Ward, daughter of George, of Gloucester county.
Jones Cattel to Mary Pratt, of Burlington county.
Philo Leeds to Sarah Shinn, " "
William Wallace to Dorathy Connolly, of Gloucester county.
James Ward to Mary Hackney, " "
Daniel Eastlack to Mary Cheesman, " "
Nathaniel Paul to Deborah Vaneman, " "
Clement Russel to Sarah Purdy, " "
Peter Champion to Hannah Thackara, " "
John Wild to Sarah Chew, " "
Thomas Spicer to Rebecca Day, " "
Jacob Horner to Zabatha Wright, " "

1741.

Gabriel Newbie, of Gloucester county, to Elizabeth McCoppering, of Cumberland county.
John Heritage, of Burlington county, to Ann Hugg, daughter of Joseph, of Gloucester county.
Edward Fennett, of Gloucester county, to Margarett Smith, widow, of Burlington county.
William Bates, of Gloucester county, to Rebecca Tomlinson, of Burlington county.
John Githens to Rebecca Frame, daughter of Joshua, of Gloucester county.
Jacob Clement to Elizabeth Tylee, daughter of Ann Ellison late Tylee.
James Shivers to Rebecca Doster, of Burlington county.
Michael Bowker to Mary Collins, " "
Thomas Kingston to Sarah Cripps, " "
Edward Hampton to Sarah Breach, of Gloucester "
John Eastlack to Patience Hugg, widow, " "

Joseph Cooper to Deborah Taylor, of Monmouth county.
Thomas Simpson to Abigail Burleigh, of Pennsylvania.
Ephraim Albertson to Kesiah Chew, daughter of Thomas.
Joseph Heulings to Hannah Wood, daughter of Benjamin.

1742.

Casper Fish, of Gloucester county, to Sarah Collins, daughter of Edward, of Philadelphia.
Owen Carty, of Gloucester county, to Esther Watson, of Burlington county.
Abraham Albertson to Sarah Dennis, daughter of Esther Cowgill.

1743.

John Franklin to Mary Graysbury, daughter of James, of Gloucester county.
Francis Kay to Jemima French, daughter of Charles, of Gloucester county.
William Kay to Barbara Smith, of Burlington county.
Samuel Spicer to Abigail Willard, of Gloucester county.

1744.

John Cox, of Burlington county, to Abigail Ellis, of Gloucester county.
Hugh Middleton to Mary Fairly, of Burlington county.
Laban Langstaff to Ann Hewitt, of Gloucester   "
Joseph Morgan to Sarah Mickle,   "   "

1745.

James Wood, of Philadelphia, to Rachel Cooper, of Gloucester county.
John Hammit to Sarah Hilliard, of Gloucester county.
Jeremiah Chew to Hannah Ashbrook,   "   "

1746.

Daniel Bates, of Gloucester county, to Sarah Higbee, of Burlington county.
Joseph Heritage to Ruth Haines, of Burlington county.
Abraham Hess to Elizabeth Hammit,   "   "

Vespasian Kemble to Rachel Haines, of Burlington county.
Thomas Bates to Mary Clemenz, of Gloucester "
John Erwin to Mary Bellows, " "
Richard Cheesman to Hannah Cheesman, " "
Peter Cheesman to Ann Ellis, " "
Edward Castle to Ann Norton, " "
Thomas Clark to Ruth Hooten, " "
Isaac Mickle to Sarah Burrough, " "
Samuel Champion to Sarah Dilks, " "

1747.

John Bates, of Burlington county, to Sarah Collins, of Gloucester county.
Jonathan Wright to Mary Inskeep, of Burlington county.
James Inskeep to Mary Patterson, " "
James Gill to Hannah Hinchman, of Gloucester "
Abraham Hammit to Mary Hilliard, " "
William Albertson to Hannah Harrison, " "
John Hinchman to Elizabeth Smith, widow, " "

1748.

Charles Collins to Ruth Starkey, of Burlington county.
Joseph Nicholson to Rachel Livzey, of Gloucester "
Daniel Fortiner to Bathsaba French, " "
Edward Hollingshead to Susanna Shivers, " "
Samuel Packer to Elizabeth Hawkes, " "
John Holmes to Esther Carty, " "
Joel Hillman to Laticia Cheesman, " "
Isaac Kay to Hope French, " "

1749.

William Southerly Cooper to Mary Cheesman, of Gloucester county.
Joseph Harrison to Ann Clement, of Gloucester county.
Charles Hubbs to Mary Eastlack, " "

1750.

William Dwyer to Sarah Ellis, " "
Josiah Ward to Kesiah Albertson, " "

MARRIAGES.

1751.

John Eastlack, of Gloucester county, to Elizabeth Read, of Salem county.
Richard Lippincott to Hannah Clemenz, of Burlington county.
John Stokes to Ann Champion, widow, of Gloucester "
Edward Browning to Grace Oldale, " "

1752.

Jacob Spicer to Deborah Leaming, widow, of Cape May county.

1753.

Isaac Hinchman to Laticia Woolstan, of Gloucester county.

1754.

Thomas Bispham, of Burlington county, to Sarah Hinchman, of Gloucester county.
John Mullen to Hannah Collins, of Burlington county.
James Brown to Alice Wood, of Gloucester "
Henry Crawford to Elizabeth McCullock, " "
James Hillman to Mary Smallwood, " "

1756.

Levi Albertson, of Gloucester county, to Kesiah Roberts, of Burlington county.
Joseph Inskeep, of Salem county, to Hannah McCullock, of Gloucester county.
Joseph Heulings to Elizabeth Hammit, of Burlington county.
Aaron Albertson to Elizabeth Albertson, of Gloucester "
Elijah Clark to Jane Lardener, " "
William Ellis, Jr., to Amy Matlack, " "
Jonathan Knight to Elizabeth Clement, " "

1757.

Abraham Heulings to Sarah Perkins, of Burlington county.
Thomas Rakestraw to Elizabeth Zane, " "
James Mulock, M. D., to Pricilla Collins, of Gloucester county.
David Hurley to Sarah Branson, of Monmouth county.

1758.

John Buzby, of Burlington county, to Sarah Ellis, of Gloucester county.
John Budd, of Salem county, to Rosanna Shivers, of Gloucester county.
Abraham Heulings to Mary Ann Kay, widow, of Burlington county.
John Inskeep to Elizabeth Buckman, of Burlington county.
Joseph Hillman to Sarah Shivers, of Gloucester "
William Rudderow to Abigail Spicer, " "

1759.

Benjamin Cooper, of Gloucester county, to Elizabeth Hopwell, of Burlington county.
Thomas Ellis, Jr., to Hannah Albertson, widow, of Gloucester county.
Richard Collins to Sarah Griffith, of Burlington county.
Samuel Gaskill to Sybilla Collins, " "
Titan Leeds to Hope French, " "
Charles Day to Laticia Albertson, of Gloucester "
Hugh Creighton to Mary French, widow, " "
William Harrison to Abigail Thorne, " "
John Parker to Elizabeth Kay, " "
Biddle Reeve to Anne Clement, " "

1760.

Capt. Joseph Ellis to Mary Hinchman, " "
Simeon Ellis to Pricilla Bates, " "

1761.

Isaac Albertson to Deborah Thorne, " "
James Cooper to Sarah Ervin, " "
Thomas Heppard to Rhoda Zane, " "
Joseph Hugg to Sarah Smith, " "
Joseph Harrison to Kesiah Tallman, " "
Josiah Hillman to Elizabeth Pancoast, " "
Joab Hillman to Mary Matlack, " "
Samuel Hugg to Elizabeth Thorne, " "

MARRIAGES.

Samuel Murrel to Ann Stokes, of Gloucester county.
John Cane to Hannah Tice, " "
Robert Friend Price to Mary Thorne, " "

1762.

Thomas Gill, of Gloucester county, to Mary Wallis, of Burlington county.
Samuel Boggs to Margaret Halloway, of Gloucester county.
Benjamin Hartley to Mary Bates, " "
John Kay to Rebecca Hartley, " "
Joseph Holmes to Elizabeth Guthridge.

1763.

Joseph Hillman to Drusilla Cheesman, " "

1764.

Nathan Albertson to Jane Thorne, " "
Abraham Albertson to Sarah Albertson, " "
Samuel Hugg to Mary Collins, " "

1765.

Thomas Ellis, of Gloucester county, to Anna Humphries, of Burlington county.
Aaron Albertson to Margarett Wells, of Gloucester county.

1766.

Moses Branson to Sarah Borrodale, of Burlington county.
Haddon Hopkins to Hannah Stokes, of Gloucester "
Benjamin Bates to Sarah Hugg, widow, " "
Robert Friend Price to Lizzie Hugg, " "
Isaac Tomlinson to Elizabeth Shivers, " "

1767.

Isaac Burrough to Rebecca Nicholson, " "
Benjamin Graysbury to Lydia Matlack, " "
Joseph Kaighn to Prudence Butcher, " "

1768.

William Bakely to Elizabeth Albertson, widow, of Gloucester county.
Samuel Kaighn to Mary Gerard, of Gloucester county.
Joseph Bates to Judith Albertson, " "

1769.

George Flanagan to Patience Collins, widow, of Gloucester county.

1770.

John Lippincott to Abigail Collins, of Burlington county.
Jacob Albertson to Elizabeth Flanagan, of Gloucester "
Samuel Nicholson to Elizabeth Haines, " "
John Blackwood to Hannah Stretch, of Salem "
Joseph Blackwood to Rebecca Moss, " "
John Eastlack to Jerusha Parks.

1771.

Isaac Burrough to Abigail Marshall, of Gloucester county.
Brazilla Hugg to Mary Wood, " ".
Jacob Rowand to Anne Heppard, " "

1772.

Benjamin Holmes to Phœbe Heulings, " "
Aaron Haines to Pricilla Collins, " "

1773.

Joseph Albertson to Mary Albertson, " "
Job Kay to Rachel Adams, " "

1774.

Vespasian Kemble to Esther French, widow," "
Silas Lord to Elizabeth Bates, " "

1775.

Ephraim Albertson to Elizabeth Warrick, " "
Jacob Burrough to Elizabeth Gill, " "
Samuel Ellis to Hannah Gilbert, " "

Henry Thorne to Elizabeth Tice, of Gloucester county.
Benjamin Graysbury to Laticia Shivers, " "
William Zane to Alice Chatten, " "

1777.

Benjamin Bates to Mary Thackara, " "
Thomas Burrough to Rebecca Fish, " "
Benjamin Bates to Sarah Hammel, " "
William Davidson to Elizabeth Eastlack, " "
William Kaighn to Mary Cole, " "

1779.

William Buzby to Sarah Burrough, " "
John Kay to Kesiah Thorne, " "

1782.

Isaac Evans to Esther Collins, of Burlington "
Isaac Albertson to Sarah Thackara, of Gloucester "
Ephraim Albertson to Charity Langley, " "
Abraham Bennett to Mercy Bates, " "
Thomas Kay to Mary Mattson, " "

1783.

Benjamin Burrough to Hannah Wilkins, " "
Levi Ellis to Elizabeth Hillman, " "

1784.

Samuel Risley to Abigail Somers, " "

1785.

Isaac Ellis to Sarah Hillman, " "
Alexander Rowand to Phœbe Clement, " "

1786.

Abel Nicholson to Mary Ellis, " "

1791.

Nathan Eyres, of Philadelphia, to Sarah Kay, of Gloucester county.
John Roberts to Hannah Bassett, of Gloucester county.

INDEX.

A

ABBOTT, Elizabeth, 220.
    George, 221.
    John, 219, 220.
    Mary, 220.
    Rachel, 220.
    Samuel, 136.
ABORN, Jonathan, 53.
ADAMS, James, 318.
    John, 276, 318.
    Samuel, 217.
ADVERTISEMENT of Council of Proprietors, 361.
ALBERTSON, William, 50, 69, 101, 103, 104, 105, 106, 123, 152, 221, 332.
    Aaron, 106.
    Abraham, 104, 106.
    Ann, 104, 108, 123, 324.
    Benjamin, 104.
    Cassandra, 56, 104, 108.
    Chalkley, 107.
    Derric, 102.
    Elizabeth, 106, 108.
    Ephraim, 106.
    Esther, 106.
    Hannah, 64, 104, 108, 247.
    Hans, 102.
    Isaac, 106.
    Jacob, 106.
    Jane, 106, 221, 332.
    John, 106, 153.
    Jonathan, 106.
    Joseph, 106.
    Josiah, 104, 107, 108, 198, 324.
    Katurah, 108.
    Levi, 106.
    Mary, 106, 108.
    Patience, 108.
    Rebecca, 104, 106.
    Sarah, 108.

ALLDAY, Alice, 14.
ALLEN, Deborah, 276.
    Elizabeth, 276.
    Enoch, 82.
    Hannah, 132.
    Juda, 276.
    Mary, 123.
    Samuel, 384.
ANTRIM, Ann, 235.
ANDERSON, Jacob, 303.
ANDREWS, Ebenezer, 384.
APPLETON, John, 227.
    Josiah, 227.
    Richard, 227.
ARASAPHA, 89.
ARNEY, Mary, 383.
ARONSON, Aaron, 221, 323.
    Rebecca, 221.
    Kesiah, 321.
ARMSTRONG, Edward, 286.
ARNOLD, Richard, 147.
ARWAWMOSSE, 75, 327, 333.
ASHARD, George, 215.
ASHBRIDGE, Aaron, 199.
ASHBROOK, John, 264.
ASHTON, Sarah, 197.
ASPDEN, Mathias, 20, 369.
ATKINSON, Elizabeth, 311.
    James, 45.
    Thomas, 259, 317.
ATMORE, Caleb, 161, 164.
    "Dam," 163, 166.
    Thomas, 164.
AUSTIN, Ann, 104, 107.
    Francis 107, 169.
    Jennett, 382.
AXFORD, Hannah, 275, 276.
    Jonathan, 178, 276.
    "Landing," 131.

B

BALDWIN, John, 342.
BALLINGER, Elizabeth, 82.
   Henry, 169.
   Isaac, 108, 120, 153.
   John, 183.
   Mark, 303, 304.
BANK, Mark Newbie's, 40.
BARBER, Margaret, 381.
BARCLAY, Robert, 344, 356.
BARTLETT, Benjamin, 202, 223, 337.
   Gracia, 223.
BARTON, John, 224, 369.
BASSE, Jeremiah, 139.
"BATCHELOR'S Bank," 329.
BATES, William, 17, 24, 25, 32, 38, 40, 47, 48, 49, 50, 51, 52, 53, 54, 55, 56, 57, 130, 183.
   Abigail, 51, 52, 53, 64, 258.
   Ann, 253.
   Benjamin, 53.
   Elizabeth, 53.
   Jeremiah, 51, 52, 64, 297.
   Jonathan, 53.
   Joseph, 51, 52, 55, 56, 229, 258, 273, 275.
   Mary, 52, 199, 276.
   Martha, 52.
   Sarah, 51, 52, 56, 189.
   Samuel, 81.
   Thomas, 53, 55, 253, 276.
BEEKS, Lydia, 311.
   Morgan, 311.
   Nathan, 212, 310, 311.
BENNETT, Joseph, 311.
BERNARD, Mary 302.
BERKLEY, John, 359.
BETTLE, Edward, 161.
   William, 162.
BEVERLY, 106.
BICKLEY, Abraham, 363.
BIDGOOD, Esther, 324.
   Richard, 320.
   William, 320.
BILDERBACK, Francis, 46.
BILLINGTON, James, 131.
BIRCHAM, Sarah, 244.
BISHOP, Hannah, 82.
BISPHAM, Benjamin, 247.
   Elizabeth, 247.
   Hinchman, 247.
   Joseph, 244, 247.
   Thomas, 243, 247.

BLACK, Mary, 321.
BLACKWELL, Robert, 209.
BLACKWOOD, Benjamin W., 369.
BLUE Anchor tract, 363.
BOGG, Judith, 108.
BOLTON, Jonathan, 129, 280, 281.
   Hannah, 280, 281,
   Mary, 66, 375.
BOOYS, Martha, 254.
BORRADALE, Ruth, 82.
BORTON, Edward, 90, 197.
   Sarah, 97.
BOWDEN, James, 353.
BOWNAS Samuel, 272.
BRADFORD, William, 355.
BRADWAY, Edward, 91, 215.
   Mary, 91.
BRADY, Henry, 279.
BRAITHWILL, Margaret, 35.
BRANSON, John, 163.
   Mary, 247.
   Sarah, 137.
BREACH, Ann, 66, 375.
   Simeon, 77, 161.
BREARLEY, Alexander, 18.
BRICK, John, 220.
   J. Stokes, 245.
BRIDGMAN, Orlando, 269.
BRIGHTON, William, 353.
BROMLEY, Richard, 319.
BROOKS, Stephen, 136.
BROTHERTON, town of, 362.
BROWN, Allen H., 273.
   John, 120, 146, 153, 180.
   Joseph, 297.
   Prudence, 147.
BROWNING, Joseph, 54, 304.
BRYANT, Abraham, 79, 179.
   Ann, 79.
   Benjamin, 79.
   Elizabeth, 79.
   John, 79.
   Rebecca, 79.
   Sarah, 79.
   Thomas, 76, 79,
BUDD, Ann, 204.
   George, 147.
   James, 81.
   John, 78, 361.
   Thomas, 40, 41, 80, 98, 217, 353, 369.
   William, 204, 217.

INDEX. 427

BULL, John, 72.
    Richard, 361.
BUNTING, Mary, 97.
    Samuel, 91.
BURCHAM, Elizabeth, 92, 147.
    Jacob, 147, 204.
BURDEN, Matthew, 331.
    Richard, 331.
BURLINGTON, town of, 84, 86, 88, 90, 91, 170.
BURLINGTON and Gloucester County lines, 32, 33, 203.
BURR, Ann, 21, 123.
    Henry, 383.
    Marmaduke, 123.
    Mary, 383.
BURROUGH, Abigail, 245, 321.
    Ann, 199, 321.
    Bathsaba, 321.
    Benjamin, 320, 321.
    David, 189, 276, 321.
    Edward, 315, 316, 317, 318, 319.
    Elizabeth, 318.
    Enoch, 321.
    Esther, 320, 321.
    Gideon, 321.
    Hannah, 319, 320, 321, 324.
    Isaac, 222, 320, 323.
    Jacob, 108, 136, 245, 320, 324.
    James, 324.
BURROUGH, Jeremiah, 316.
    John, 170, 276, 316, 318, 320, 321, 324.
    Joseph, 153, 316, 320, 321.
    Josiah, 212, 310, 319, 321, 322, 323.
    Kesiah, 320.
    Martha, 321.
    Mary, 321, 324.
    Priscilla, 317, 323.
    Rachel, 321.
    Reuben, 324.
    Samuel, 141, 221, 318, 319, 320, 321, 324.
    Sarah, 141, 319, 320, 321, 324, 332.
    William, 316, 324.
BURNETT, Phœbe, 321.
    William, 259.
BURGE, William, 280.
BUSSE, Margaret, 287.
    Paul, 287.
BUTCHER, Catharine, 221.
    Mary, 311.
    Prudence, 156.
BUZBY, John, 190, 306.
BYLLYNGE, Edward, 13, 27, 44, 48, 58, 72, 74, 90, 98, 112, 132, 202, 223, 277, 301, 327, 336, 345, 359.
    Gracia, 223.

C

CAMPBELL, John, 61.
CANTWELL, Edmund, 358.
CAREW, John, 269.
CARPENTER, Samuel, 18, 218, 331, 345, 346, 347, 349, 350, 351.
    Abraham, 92, 349.
    Hannah, 347, 349.
    John, 349.
    Joshua, 92, 349.
CARTER, Catharine, 342.
CARTERETT, Philip, 358, 359.
CASSIMER, Fort, 102.
CATHCART, John, 53.
CENSUS of Gloucester County, 96.
CHALKLEY, Thomas, 297.
CHAMPION, John, 225, 226, 365, 366, 367, 368, 369.
    Ann, 304.
    Benjamin, 369.
    Elizabeth, 367, 369.
CHAMPION, Joseph, 82, 185, 368.
    Mary, 311, 369.
    Matthew, 200, 366.
    Nathaniel, 368, 369.
    Peter, 64, 185, 368.
    Phœbe, 368.
    Robert, 368.
    Samuel, 36, 38, 46, 369.
    Sarah, 369.
    Thomas, 365, 368, 369,
CHAMPNEYS, Edward, 216.
CHARLES I., King of England, 267, 271.
CHARLES II., 219, 271, 315, 341, 380.
CHAPMAN, William, 257, 258.
CHATTIN, Mary, 19.
CHAUNDERS, Thomas, 146.
CHEESMAN, Mary, 66, 375.
    Thomas, 276.

CHEW, Hannah, 45.
    Kesiah, 106.
    Patience, 106.
    Richard, 106.
CHILD, Mrs. Maria, 116.
CHRISTIANITY, 224.
CHURCH at Swedesboro, 289.
CLARK, Ann, 91.
    Deborah, 369.
    Rachel, 247.
    Walter, 331.
    William, 132, 169, 369.
CLARSSEN, Jan, 358.
CLEMENT, Ann, 274.
    Gregory, 267, 268, 269, 270, 271.
    Jacob, 108, 246, 272, 273, 274, 275.
    James, 52, 248, 271, 272, 273.
    Jane, 52, 271.
    John, 133, 273, 274.
    Joseph, 273.
    Mary, 253, 274.
    Mercy, 51, 273, 275.
    Nathaniel, 273.
    Rebecca, 310.
    Samuel, 59, 78, 220, 273, 274, 310.
    Sarah, 248, 273, 274.
    Simeon, 272.
    Thomas, 273, 274.
    William, 271.
CLEMENZ, Edward, 131, 275, 276.
    Benjamin, 276, 321.
    Ephraim, 276.
    Esther, 276.
    Hannah, 276.
    Juda, 276, 321.
    Mary, 276.
    Rachel, 276.
    Sarah, 276.
CLEWS, William, 174.
CLOUD, ———, 342.
COATES, Hannah, 92.
COBB, William, 289.
COFFING, Jacob, 145, 147.
COLLAT, Jeremiah, 217.
COLLINS, Francis, 20, 32, 68, 70, 72, 73, 74, 75, 76, 78, 79, 80, 81, 82, 83, 95, 114, 140, 168, 170, 177, 182, 183, 235, 240, 242, 249, 253, 257, 286, 289, 290, 317, 320, 369.
    Abigail, 82.
    Benjamin, 78, 185.

COLLINS, Catharine, 78, 79, 184, 274.
    Charles, 82, 185.
    Charity, 81.
    Edward, 71, 248.
    Elizabeth, 71, 76, 80, 81.
    Hannah, 82.
    Job, 82, 83.
    John, 81, 82, 83.
    Joseph, 76, 78, 79.
    Joshua, 82.
    Lizzie, 81.
    Margaret, 76, 286, 290.
    Mary, 71, 80, 81, 82, 83, 369.
    Mercy, 82.
    Priscilla, 76, 78, 79, 81, 82, 188, 240, 286.
    Rachel, 82, 185, 368.
    Rebecca, 76, 78, 79, 274.
    Samuel, 81, 82, 304, 368.
    Sarah, 56, 76, 78, 81, 82, 184.
    Susanna, 81.
    Sybilla, 81.
COLLINGS, Richard, 20.
    Edward Z., 15, 17.
COLE, Samuel, 147, 201, 202, 203, 204, 205, 212, 220, 293, 294, 307, 308, 310, 327, 330, 333.
    Elizabeth, 203, 204, 212, 308.
    Joseph, 178, 204, 308, 333.
    Kendall, 204.
    Mary, 204, 235.
    Rachel, 204.
    Sarah, 203.
    Susanna, 204.
    Thomas, 82, 204, 244, 304.
COLEMAN, Thomas, 326.
CONROW, Darling, 304.
COOPER, William, 19, 39, 62, 63, 64, 85, 86, 87, 88, 89, 90, 91, 92, 93, 96, 97, 98, 140, 141, 147, 152, 173, 185, 201, 212, 226, 310, 322, 342, 343, 347, 369.
    Abigail, 95, 332.
    Ann, 91.
    Benjamin, 92, 97, 141, 146, 147, 153, 175, 204, 243.
    Daniel, 52, 85, 92, 93, 94, 95, 96, 97, 114, 226, 297, 332, 342.
    David, 92, 120, 153.
    Elizabeth, 92, 141, 147.
    Hannah, 85, 90, 91, 92, 93, 141, 212, 310.
    Isaac, 41, 92, 97, 147.

COOPER, James, 85, 91, 120, 147, 153, 311, 323.
    John, 91, 97, 98, 120, 329.
    Joseph, 85, 92, 93, 97, 98, 120, 129, 130, 141, 147, 151, 152, 156, 168, 212, 310, 349.
    Lydia, 92, 310.
    Margaret, 85, 86.
    Mary, 64, 91, 93, 169.
    Richard, 236.
    Samuel, 96, 97, 147, 217.
    Sarah, 91, 92, 96.
COPE Estate, 92.
CORBIT, Sarah, 197.
CORNBURY, Lord, 39, 96, 175, 176, 196, 272.
COWPERTHWAITE, John, 137, 204, 304.
COX, Abigail, 185.
    John, 92, 136, 185, 331.
    Lydia, 97.
    Samuel, 185.
    William, 185.
COXE, Daniel, 173, 174, 175, 223.
CRESSON, Caleb, 123.
    Joshua, 123.
CREWS, Eve, 89.
    Richard, 89.
CRIPPS, John, 278, 279.
CRISPIN, William, 317.
CROMWELL, Oliver, 315.
    Richard, 315.
CUTHBERT, Joseph, 81.

D

DAGGER, John, 24.
DALBO, Walla, 289.
DANIELS, Isabella, 220.
DARKIN, Richard, 18.
DAVENPORT, Abigail, 297.
    Francis, 18, 76, 177.
    Rebecca, 177.
DAVIS, Amy, 133.
    David, 133, 321.
    Joseph, 263.
    Mercy, 137.
    Sarah, 152.
DAY, Humphrey, 210, 221.
    Jane, 210.
    Rebecca, 298.
    Stephen, 210.
DEACON, George, 215.
    Mary, 253.
DECOSTA, John, 65, 184, 373, 374.
DECOU, Isaac, 45.
DENNIS, Hannah, 141.
    Samuel, 380, 385.
    Sarah, 106, 220.
    Thomas, 155.
DENT, Ann, 156.
    Hannah, 92, 93.
DIMSDALE, John, 77.
    Robert, 76, 78, 183.
    Sarah, 76, 77.
    William, 77.
DOLE, John, 149, 151.
    Joseph, 151.
    Hannah, 151.
    Mary, 151.
    Rebecca, 151.
    Sarah, 150, 151.
DONALSON, Arthur, 156.
DUEL, Phœbe, 247.
DUFFIELD, Phœbe, 185.
DUYRE, William, 189.
DYLWYN, Ann, 185.

E

EASTLACK, John, 21, 61, 64, 65, 66, 371, 372, 373, 374, 375.
    Daniel, 66, 375.
    Elizabeth, 66, 141, 372, 375.
    Esther, 66, 375.
    Francis, 63, 371, 372.
    Hannah, 66, 375.
    Hepsibah, 63, 372.
EASTLACK, Isaac G., 317.
    Jemima, 372.
    Samuel, 66, 153, 374, 375.
    Sarah, 66, 141, 375.
EDWARDS, Elizabeth, 382.
    Richard, 157.
    Samuel, 157.
    Sarah, 157.

ELDRIDGE, Enos, 311.
   Joseph, 50.
   Rebecca, 384.
ELFRETH, Joseph, 46.
ELKINTON, Amy, 136.
   Ann, 136.
   Elizabeth, 136.
   Francis, 136.
   George, 79, 136.
   Joseph, 135.
ELLIS, Simeon, 51, 56, 69, 78, 168, 180, 182, 183, 184, 186, 187, 189, 290, 306, 368.
   Abigail, 185, 190, 306.
   Ann, 185, 368, 369.
   Benjamin, 189.
   Catharine, 185.
   Cassandra, 320, 324.
   Elizabeth, 180.
   Isaac, 189, 222.
   Jacob, 56, 108, 324.
   John, 189.
   Jonathan, 56, 184, 190.
   Joseph, 56, 69, 183, 184, 189, 237, 304, 306.
   Josiah, 183.
   Kesiah, 190, 306.
   Mary, 184.
   Priscilla, 190, 304, 306.
   Rebecca, 222.
   Sarah, 56, 59, 183, 184, 189, 190, 306.
   Thomas, 56, 78, 180, 182, 184.
   William, 56, 180, 184, 185, 189.

ELMER, L. Q. C., 42.
ELSINBURG, 11, 24.
EMLEN, Sarah, 185.
EMLEY, William, 277.
ENGLE, John, 221, 332.
   Elizabeth, 382.
   Hannah, 384.
   Mary, 384.
ERIWONACK, Fort, 311, 313.
ERVIN, George, 93.
   Sarah, 147.
ESTAUGH, Elizabeth, 21, 33, 77, 84, 109, 117, 119, 120, 121, 122, 123, 125, 127, 128, 129, 130, 132, 133, 134, 155, 236, 246, 336.
   James, 155.
   John, 29, 112, 113, 114, 116, 117, 118, 120, 121, 128, 133, 134, 155, 170, 236, 237.
   Mary, 155.
EVANS, Agnes, 212.
   Elizabeth, 169.
   John, 153, 220.
   Joshua, 81, 178.
   Josiah, 171, 228.
   Mary, 311.
   Nathaniel, 208.
   Thomas, 169.
   William, 120, 169.
EVES, Anna, 383.
   Thomas, 169.

F

FAIRMAN, Thomas, 89.
FAIRLAND, Catharine, 197.
   Mary, 197.
FARR, Elias, 335.
FENWICK, John, 11, 48, 107, 213, 214, 219, 240, 272, 283, 345, 365, 380.
FELL, Margaret, 380.
FENIMORE, John, 79.
FERRY License, 94, 96.
FIELD, Benjamin, 175.
   Elizabeth, 273.
FIRMAN, Rachel, 222.
FISHBURN, William, 349.
FISHER, John, 19, 146.
FOLWELL, Ann, 147.
FORTINER, Hope, 247.

FORREST, Ann, 106, 149.
   Francis, 106.
   John, 106.
   Walter, 104, 106, 107, 149, 152.
FOSTER, Josiah, 120.
   Hannah, 311.
   Mary, 235, 236.
   William, 120.
FOWLER, Andrew, 209.
   Rennels, 133.
FOX, George, 48, 57, 70, 84, 90, 128, 135, 168, 205, 247, 294, 315, 331, 356, 359, 380.
   James, 18.
FRAME, Joshua, 51, 53.
FRAMPTON, William, 212.

INDEX. 431

FRANKLIN, Benjamin, 121, 237.
    Henry, 225, 366.
    John, 162.
FRENCH, Hope, 177.
    Jemima, 179.
FRETWELL, Peter, 361.
FRIENDS' Meeting, Chester, (Moorestown), 318.
FRIENDS' Meeting, Burlington, 353, 354.
FRIENDS' Meeting, Haddonfield, 119, 120.
FURNASS, Henry, 217.
FUSSEL, Barbara, 321.

G

GABITAS, Deborah, 151.
GARDINER, Thomas, 17, 328, 336, 353, 355, 356, 360, 362.
    Elizabeth, 363.
    Esther, 356.
    Hannah, 363.
    Hored, 356.
    James, 198.
    John, 356.
    Matthew, 356, 362.
    Peter, 356.
GARWOOD, Joseph, 264.
    Daniel, 81.
    John, 383.
    Joshua, 151.
GASKILL, Samuel, 81.
GERARD, Mary, 157.
GIBBS; Joshua, 321.
    Richard, 321.
GILL, John, 33, 73, 84, 120, 121, 127, 128, 129, 130, 131, 132, 133, 134, 135, 136, 138, 152, 168, 190, 221, 237, 245, 246, 257, 258, 261, 264, 276.
    Amy, 136, 137.
    Elizabeth, 136, 324.
    Hannah, 133, 137.
    Henry, 127.
    James, 248.
    Mary, 133, 134, 245.
    Mercy, 134.
    Sarah, 136.
    William, 136.
GILLMAN, Robert, 218.
GILLOTT, Esther, 320.
GLOUCESTER, county of, 27, 75, 92, 138.
GLOUCESTER and Burlington counties, line of, 32, 33, 203.

GLOVER, Isaac, 247.
    Jacob, 247.
    John, 120, 153, 245, 246, 247.
    Joseph, 153, 247.
    Mary, 247.
    Rachel, 247.
    Richard, 247.
    Samuel, 246, 247.
    Sarah, 246, 247.
    Thomas, 247.
    William, 247.
GOLDSMITH, George, 24, 25, 26, 49, 61, 65, 67, 69, 70, 342.
GOODEN, Isaac, 29.
GORDON, Thomas, 180.
GOSLIN, John, 80, 353, 369.
GRANNA, Robert, 217.
GRAY, Ann, 320.
    Esther, 320.
    Richard, 73, 320.
GRAYSBURY, James, 50, 159, 160, 161, 162, 163.
    Abigail, 163.
    Ann, 160, 162.
    Benjamin, 159, 160, 161, 162, 163.
    Elizabeth, 160.
    Joseph, 159, 160, 161, 162.
    Margaret, 160.
    Mary, 160, 162, 163.
GREEN, Elizabeth, 303.
GREGORY, Mary Ann, 176.
GRISCOM, Andrew, 149, 151, 152, 217.
    Mary, 152.
    Samuel, 152.
    Sarah, 149, 151.
    Tobias, 151, 152.
    William, 152.
GUANT, ——, 197.
GUY, Richard, 215, 216, 353.

H

HADDON, Elizabeth, 111, 112, 113, 114, 116.
   John, 65, 110, 112, 113, 115, 118, 120, 121, 127, 128, 130, 134, 236, 282, 335, 373.
   Sarah, 112.
HADDONFIELD, Old and New, 74, 77, 80, 115, 116, 118, 119, 120, 125, 133, 134, 135, 136, 137, 142, 170, 171, 173, 177, 335.
HAINES, Amos, 19.
   Ann, 81, 303.
   Carlisle, 235.
   Daniel, 79.
   Elizabeth, 82, 147.
   Jacob, 276, 321.
   Jonathan, 235.
   Mary, 235, 236, 384.
   Phœbe, 320.
   Rebecca, 235, 236.
   Ruth, 133.
   Samuel, 304.
   Solomon, 82.
HALL, Clement, 274.
   Martha, 35.
   Nathaniel, 274.
   Sarah, 274.
   William, 273, 274.
HALLOWAY, Tobias, 36, 152, 368.
HALLOWELL, John, 35, 36.
HAMEL, John, 359.
HAMILTON, Andrew, 351.
HAMMOND, Rebecca, 16.
HAMPTON, Rhoda Ann, 282.
   Rose, 106.
HANNA, Peter, 247.
HANCOCK, Godfrey, 358.
   Mary, 233, 235.
   Susannah, 152.
   Timothy, 169, 202, 233, 234, 318.
HARDIMAN, Hannah, 349.
HARPER, Josiah, 329.
HARRISON, Abigail, 157, 243.
   Ann, 273.
   Ellen, 70.
   Joseph, 188, 209, 274.
   Rebecca, 209.
   Samuel 157, 243, 273.
   Thomas, 269, 270.
   William, 145, 173, 245.
HARRY, William, 52.

HARTLEY, Bathsaba, 19.
   James, 247.
   Rebecca, 19, 177.
   Roger, 19, 20.
HATKINSON, John, 244.
HATTEN New Garden, 132.
HEATH, Levi, 209.
HEDGER, Ann, 78.
HELMSLEY, Joseph, 277.
HEMPSTEAD, 19.
HENRY, David, 106.
   Sarah, 106.
HEPPARD, Thomas, 20.
HERITAGE, Benjamin, 133.
   Hannah, 133.
   John, 132, 133.
   Joseph, 132, 133, 318.
   Mary, 132, 133, 169.
   Naomi, 132.
   Richard, 132, 133, 235, 236, 245.
   Sarah, 132.
HEULINGS, Abigail, 320.
   Abraham, 178.
   Batheuel, 185, 369.
   Joseph, 178, 333.
   Martha, 157.
   Theodocia, 384.
   William, 205.
HEWITT, Ann, 369.
HIBBARD, Samuel, 199.
HIGBEE, Daniel, 209.
HIGGS, William, 128.
HILL, Elizabeth, 154.
HILLMAN, John, 53, 221, 229, 257, 258, 260, 261, 264.
   Abel, 55.
   Abigail, 137, 258.
   Ann, 258.
   Aquilla, 305, 385.
   Daniel, 137, 221, 258, 261, 263, 264, 265, 303.
   Drusilla, 261.
   Elizabeth, 261.
   James, 261, 264.
   Joab, 261.
   Joseph, 258, 260, 264.
   Josiah, 261.
   Letitia, 261.
   Margaret, 258.
   Samuel, 261, 264.
   Seth, 264.

INDEX.

HINCHMAN, John, 52, 77, 80, 156, 161, 178, 239, 240, 241, 242, 243, 244, 246, 248, 273, 289.
  Abigail, 156, 243.
  Amy, 244, 304.
  Ann, 243.
  Deborah, 248.
  Edward, 240.
  Elizabeth, 244.
  Emily, 248.
  Hannah, 244, 248.
  Isaac, 244.
  Jacob, 243, 244.
  James, 77, 145, 239, 243, 244, 311.
  Jane, 243.
  Joseph, 77, 243, 244, 247, 248, 280.
  Letitia, 243.
  Mary 239, 244, 248.
  Mercy, 239.
  Miriam, 239, 243.
  Robert, 239.
  Sarah, 239, 243, 248, 273.
  Thomas, 142, 239, 248.
  William, 248.
HOFFMAN, Frederick, 11, 289.
HOLMES, Thomas, 41.
HOLLINGSHEAD, Edmund, 212, 310, 311.
  Hannah, 311.
  John, 120, 311.
  Joseph, 311.
  Lydia, 311.
  Mary, 56, 184, 311.
  Morgan, 311.
  Samuel, 311.
  Sarah, 311.
HOLLINGSHAM, Catharine, 35.
  Isaac, 61, 69, 184, 342.
HOOTEN, Sarah, 19.
  Thomas, 301, 302.
  William, 97.
HOPEWELL, Elizabeth, 147, 220.
HOPKINS, Ann, 123.
  Benjamin, 112, 121, 128.
  Ebenezer, 21, 73, 108, 122, 123, 124, 130, 374.
  Elizabeth, 123.
  Haddon, 123.
  John E., 73, 120, 123, 153, 320.

HOPKINS, Mary, 123.
  Sarah, 121, 123, 128.
  William E., 311.
HORSLYDOWN, 110, 191.
HORNER, Bartholomew, 131.
  Deliverance, 303, 304.
  Hannah, 46, 235.
  Isaac, 131, 179.
  Jacob, 82, 131.
  Lemuel, 297.
  Nathan, 131.
HOSKINS, Ann, 349.
HOWELL, Thomas, 223, 224, 225, 226, 367.
  Catharine, 225, 226.
  Daniel, 224, 225, 226, 227, 228.
  Jacob, 93.
  Marion, 225, 226.
  Mordecai, 224, 225, 226, 227, 228, 246.
  Priscilla, 225.
  Samuel, 225.
  Zophar, 263.
HOWLE, Mary, 327.
HUDSON, John, 303.
  Mary, 92.
HUDDLESTON, Catharine, 76.
HUGG, John, 18, 45, 76, 79, 80, 240, 242, 283, 284, 285, 286, 288.
  Charles, 287.
  Elias, 76, 183, 286, 289, 290.
  Gabriel, 289.
  Hannah, 289.
  Jacob, 289.
  Joseph, 178, 287, 289, 290, 291.
  Margaret, 80, 183, 290.
  Mary, 289.
  Patience, 66, 375.
  Priscilla, 79, 80, 240, 289.
  Samuel, 81, 83, 291.
  Sarah, 133, 289.
  William, 285.
HUGHES, Caleb, 190, 306.
  Humphrey, 299.
  Judith, 299.
HUMPHREYS. Joshua, 231.
HUNT, Robert, 178, 333.
HUNTER, Robert, 173, 175.
HURLEY, James S., 162.
HUTCHINSON, George, 180, 326, 336.

I

INGLEDON, Blackinstone, 145.
INGERSOLL, Daniel, 151.
INSKEEP, John, 109, 265.
ISLE of Man, 150.

IVES, William, 144, 145.
IVERSON, John, 69.
IVINS, Margaret, 69.

J

JACOBS, Henry, 358.
    Isaac, 217.
JARVIS, Martin, 147, 370.
JENKINS, Josiah, 259.
JENNEY, Robert, 207, 208.
    Thomas, 41.
JENNINGS, Deborah, 320, 323.
    Henry, 215, 287, 323.
    Isaac, 287, 323.
    Jacob, 108, 178, 264.
    Mary, 287.

JENNINGS, Samuel, 40, 74, 98, 183, 218, 309, 346, 347, 353.
    Sarah, 287.
    William, 287.
JESSUP, Mary, 151.
JOHNSON, Henry, 225, 226, 252.
JONES, Agnes, 310.
    John, 269.
    Joseph, 46.
JOOSTEN, John, 359.
JORISSEN, Cornelius, 358.

K

KAIGHN, John, 104, 107, 149, 150, 151, 152, 153, 154, 156, 157, 190, 243.
    Abigail, 157.
    Amos, 170.
    Ann, 149, 156.
    Charles, 150.
    Elizabeth, 154, 156, 157.
    Ellen, 150.
    Isaac, 156.
    James, 156.
    Jane, 150.
    Joseph, 120, 153, 154, 155, 156, 157.
    Mary, 156.
    Prudence, 156.
    Samuel, 157.
    William, 156.
KAIN, Charity, 81, 249.
    Charles, 81.
    Sarah, 249.
    William, 249.
KAY, John, 26, 56, 64, 91, 152, 167, 168, 169, 170, 171, 172, 173, 174, 175, 176, 177, 183, 184, 234, 244, 303, 332.

KAY, Ann, 178.
    Benjamin, 177.
    Elizabeth, 169, 179.
    Francis, 177, 179.
    Garvis, 167, 168.
    Hope, 178.
    Isaac, 163, 176, 177, 178, 179.
    Joseph, 177, 178, 179.
    Josiah, 176, 177, 179.
    Mary, 176, 178, 332.
    Mathias, 177.
    Rebecca, 178.
    Sarah, 176, 179.
    William, 177, 254.
KEITH, George, 63, 205, 206, 209, 217, 218, 381.
KELLY, Richard, 160.
KENDALL, Mary, 82, 203.
    Thomas, 82, 131, 171, 203, 228.
KENT, Ishmael, 81.
KIRLEE, John, 164.
    Joseph, 164.
KINSEY, John, 173.
KNAPTON, Benjamin, 216.
KNIGHT, Edward C., 184.

L

LACONEY, James, 329.
LADD, Hannah, 29.
    John, 142, 143, 144, 145, 291, 328, 329.
    Samuel, 347.
    Sarah, 142, 143, 145.
LAKIN, Hannah, 225.
    Moses, 227.
LAMB, Sarah, 321.
LANGSTONE, Sarah, 176.
LANE, Daniel, 150.
LARGE, Ebenezer, 77.
LAURIE, Gawen, 344.
LEAMING, Aaron, 299.
    Christopher, 299.
    Deborah, 299.
LEE, George, 306.
    Mary, 235.
LEEDS, Daniel, 24, 60.
LIPPINCOTT, Aaron, 198, 383, 384.
    Abigail, 53, 378, 380, 381, 382, 384, 385.
    Ann, 382.
    Asa, 244.
    Benjamin, 383.
    Caleb, 383, 385.
    Charles, 385.
    Deborah, 382.
    Elizabeth, 53, 382.
    Esther, 384.
    Freedom, 53, 380, 383, 384, 385.
    Grace, 382.
    Hannah, 382.
    Henry, 378.
    Hinchman, 259.
    Hope, 382.
    Increase, 379, 380, 385.
    Isaac, 383, 384, 385.
    Jacob, 52, 379, 380, 382, 383, 384.
    James, 377, 382, 383.
LIPPINCOTT, John, 136, 378, 380, 382, 385.
    Joseph, 53, 382.
    Joshua, 53, 383, 385.
    Judith, 303, 384.
    Margaret, 382.
    Mary, 204, 298, 382, 384.
    Mercy, 53, 384.
    Nathan, 303, 385.
    Nathaniel, 120, 153, 384.
    Patience, 384.
    Phœbe, 384.
    Preserved, 380, 382.
    Rachel, 382.
    Rebecca, 382.
    Rememberance, 378, 380, 381, 382.
    Restore, 379, 380, 383.
    Richard, 378, 380, 381, 382, 383, 385.
    Robert, 378, 382.
    Ruth, 382.
    Samuel, 53, 382, 383, 384, 385.
    Sarah, 382.
    Seth, 385.
    Solomon, 385.
    Thomas, 384, 385.
    William, 382.
LLOYD, David, 212, 309.
    Thomas, 309.
LONDON Commissioners, 12, 87.
LONG Harris's Creek, 329.
LORD, Alice, 221, 332.
    James, 120, 122.
    John, 198.
    Joshua, 120, 153, 328, 330.
    Sarah, 122.
LOVEJOY, William, 131, 132, 171, 335, 336.
LOWE, Joseph, 140, 161, 264.
LUCAS, Nicholas, 76.
LURTIN, Thomas, 24, 67.

M

MACELIS, Jurirus, 358.
MADDOX, John, 215.
MARLOW, Gregory, 232.
MARSH, Mary, 197, 199.
MARTIN, Daniel, 160.
    John, 317.
MASON, Hannah, 156.
    William H., 317.
MATHEWS, Hannah, 336, 356.
    Richard, 65, 112, 118, 120, 333.
    Thomas, 328, 336, 373.

MATLACK, William, 202, 231, 232, 234, 235, 236, 237, 261, 318.
   Abigail, 304.
   Amy, 189.
   Asa, 206, 209, 237, 320.
   Benjamin, 236.
   George, 130, 235, 236.
   Jane, 235.
   John, 162, 235, 237, 253.
   Kesiah, 133.
   Letitia, 141, 248.
   Lydia, 162.
   Mary, 235.
   Rebecca, 311.
   Richard, 178, 235, 236, 237, 333.
   Samuel, 318.
   Sarah, 235.
   Timothy, 120, 130, 136, 142, 235, 236, 237, 248, 261, 275.
MAYHAM, Sarah, 71.
MEDCALF, Hannah, 104.
   Jacob, 155.
MEW, Noel, 169.
   Richard, 72, 169.
MICKLE, Archibald, 139, 140, 141, 145, 147, 321, 349.
   Daniel, 141, 145.
   Elizabeth, 97.
   Hannah, 97, 142.
   Isaac, 16, 27, 28, 140, 141, 147, 148, 190, 306, 313, 321, 366.
   Jacob, 145, 375.
   James, 66, 141, 145, 147, 375.
   John, 91, 120, 123, 141, 259.
   Joseph, 141, 147, 156, 324, 372, 375.
   Letitia, 248.
   Mary, 141.
   Rachel, 92, 141, 145, 146, 375.
   Samuel, 92, 123, 141, 142, 157.
   Sarah, 123, 141, 145, 156, 247.

MICKLE, William, 123, 141.
MIDDLETON, Deborah, 321.
   Mercy, 384.
   Thomas, 221.
MILLER, Henry, 209.
   Mark, 137.
   Thomas, 280.
   William, 212, 275, 310.
MONTGOMERY, Robert, 280, 281, 282.
   Sarah, 280, 281.
   Thomas, 282.
MOODY, Deborah, 294.
MOORE, Aaron, 82.
   Benjamin, 81, 303.
   Elizabeth, 81.
MORGAN, Griffith, 212, 307, 308, 309, 310, 311, 313.
   Agnes, 311.
   Alexander, 92, 204, 212, 309, 310, 311.
   Ann, 311.
   Benjamin, 212, 217, 310, 311.
   Daniel, 235.
   Elizabeth, 212, 310, 311.
   Hannah, 310, 311.
   Isaac, 310, 311.
   Jane, 311.
   Jonathan, 162.
   Joseph, 212, 310, 311.
   Lydia, 212, 310.
   Mary, 212, 310, 311.
   Rachel, 310.
   Rebecca, 311.
   Sarah, 212, 310, 311, 321.
MORRIS, Ann, 129.
   Anthony, 18.
   John, 309.
   Robert, 236.
MORTON, Ann, 162.
MOUNTWELL, 73, 74, 78, 79, 84, 114.
MULLEN, Isaac, 82.
MULOCK, James, 82, 187, 188.
MURRELL, Samuel, 185, 368.

N

NASSAU, Fort, 285, 286.
NEVILL, James, 215.
NEWTON, 9, 11, 16, 24, 66, 74, 84, 87, 89, 92, 103, 115, 170.
NEWBIE, Mark, 24, 25, 37, 38, 39, 40, 42, 44, 45, 46, 49, 61, 62, 64, 90, 332.
   Edward, 41, 45, 349.

NEWBIE, Elizabeth, 289, 332.
   Gabriel, 41, 45, 375.
   Hannah, 40, 45, 64, 332.
   John, 41, 45.
   Nathan, 41, 45.
   Rachel, 45.
   Stephen, 38, 45, 64, 68, 332.
NEWBOLD, Letitia, 90.

NEWCOMB, John 326.
NEWBERRY, Benjamin, 331.
    Hasker, 132.
NICHOLSON, Samuel, 77, 137, 213,
    215, 216, 218, 219, 220, 221,
    222, 319, 320, 332.
    Abel, 153, 213, 219, 220, 221,
        222, 323.
    Abigail, 221, 261.
    Ann, 213, 216, 219, 220.
    Elizabeth, 213, 219.
    George, 90, 221, 222, 332.
    Grace, 222.
    Hannah, 97, 221, 222, 261.
    Isabella, 220.
    James, 332.
    John, 220.

NICHOLSON, Joseph, 213, 219, 220,
    221, 222, 319, 332.
    Mary, 220.
    Mercy, 222.
    Parabol, 213, 219.
    Rachel, 220.
    Rebecca, 323.
    Ruth, 220.
    Sarah, 220, 221, 319.
    William, 220.
NOBLE, Richard, 231.
NORRIS, Elizabeth, 178.
    Isaac, 18, 212, 309.
    James, 176, 178.
    Samuel, 151.
    Sarah, 177, 179, 186, 244, 275.

O

OLIVE, Thomas, 44, 90, 232, 277,
    302, 383.

OWEN, Martha, 382.

P

PAINE, Elizabeth, 35.
PARKER, Ann, 64.
———, 179.
PARR, Hannah, 324.
    James, 324.
    John, 324.
    Mary, 324.
    Samuel, 320.
PARNELL, Mary, 326.
PARROCK, James, 369.
PEARSON, Hannah, 363.
    Isaac, 152, 363.
    Sarah, 90.
PEAKE, Edmund, 384.
PELLOR, Mary, 332.
PENISAUKIN creek, 12, 33, 82.
PENN, William, 11, 13, 37, 48, 49,
    76, 89, 90, 98, 102, 112,
    137, 139, 143, 155, 171,
    225, 234, 240, 271, 290,
    301, 303, 309, 339, 340,
    341, 342, 345, 347, 367.
PENNINGTON, John, 313.
PENROSE, John, 217.
PENTON, William, 215.
PENFORD, John, 277.
PERKINS, Widow, 87.
PETERSON, Priscilla, 189.
    Wallo, 289.

PHILADELPHIA, 84, 143.
PHILIPS, Robert, 159.
PIDGEON, Joseph, 342, 343.
    Mary, 343.
PIERCE, Nicholas, 217.
PINE, Benjamin, 321.
    Mary, 321.
PLANTAGENET, Beauchamp, 312.
PLOYDEN, Sir Edmund, 311, 312, 313.
PORTER, Abraham, 198, 259, 260.
POTTS, Judith, 35.
POTTER, Phœbe, 321.
    Sarah, 298.
    Thomas, 247.
POWELL, Arthur, 19, 141, 146.
    James, 146.
    Margarett, 146.
    Mary, 146.
    Rachel, 146.
    Richard, 146.
PRESTON, Hannah, 349.
PRITCHETT, Diana, 81.
    Josiah, 137.
    Sarah, 137.
PRICE, Robert Friend, 81, 187, 188.
PUSSEY, Samuel, 209.
PYNE Point, 86, 88, 89, 91, 96.
PYLE, Elizabeth, 273.
    Thomas, 273.

R

RAKESTRAW, Grace, 19.
RANDOLPH, John, 54.
RAPER, Joshua, 92.
    Sarah, 97.
RAWLE, Benjamain, 343.
    Elizabeth, 343.
    Francis, 342, 343.
    Jane, 343.
    John, 343.
    Joseph, 343.
    Martha, 343
    Mary, 96, 342.
    Rebecca, 343.
    Robert, 343.
    William, 313, 343.
READING, John, 29, 95, 143, 245, 290, 291.
READ, Charles, 145.
REDMAN, Hannah, 137.
    John, 137.
    Mary, 137.
    Thomas, 133, 137, 138.
REDFIELD, John, 286.
REEVES, Abraham, 46.
    Joseph, 311.
RICHARDS, Jeremiah, 202.
    Benjamin, 373.

RICHARDSON, John, 113, 114.
RIDGWAY, Catharine, 197.
    Jeremiah, 50.
    Joseph, 247.
    Sarah, 311.
RIGGS, Lydia, 92.
RIGGINS, Israel, 236.
RISDON, George T., 82.
    Turner, 382.
ROBINSON, Richard, 69.
ROBERTS, Enoch, 204.
    Jacob, 136.
    Jane, 212, 310.
    John, 133, 142, 234, 258, 318, 384.
    Kesiah, 106.
    Mary, 258.
    Samuel, 226.
    Sarah, 318.
ROBESON, Andrew, 95, 106.
ROTHERHITHE, 110, 113.
ROYDON, Robert, 89.
    William, 12, 88, 94, 95, 290, 347.
RUDDEROW, Abigail, 206, 209.
    John, 206.
    William, 206.

S

SAINT, Rebecca, 221, 332.
SALEM, 12, 24, 116, 170, 198.
SALTER, Ann, 215.
SATERTHWAITE, Joseph, 104, 311.
SAUNDERS, Hannah, 147.
SAXBY, Esther, 296.
SCOTT, Benjamin, 277.
    John, 76.
    Thomas, 269, 270.
SCROOP, Adrian, 269.
SCULL, Daniel, 258.
    Jasper, 382.
    John, 151.
    Mary, 382.
SHABLE, Thomas, 75, 170.
SHACKOMAXIN, 13, 89, 354, 367.
SHATTOCKS, Hannah, 382.
    James, 217.
SHELTER, The, 328.

SHARP, Thomas, 11, 13, 18, 23, 25, 26, 27, 28, 29, 33, 34, 35, 38, 39, 49, 58, 61, 65, 67, 68, 70, 73, 74, 115, 119, 129, 141, 145, 152, 162, 191, 192, 194, 217, 242, 253, 290, 304, 342, 373, 375.
    Anthony, 23, 25, 59, 191.
    Elizabeth, 35, 162.
    Hugh, 319.
    Isaac, 35.
    John, 35.
    Joseph, 35.
    Mary, 35.
    Samuel, 35, 36, 162, 197.
    Sarah, 35.
    William, 263, 264, 372.
SHINN, Anna, 254.
    John, 76.

INDEX.

SHIPPEN, Edward, 18.
SHIVERS, John, 251, 252, 253, 255, 261, 368.
    Hannah, 253.
    Josiah, 253.
    Latitia, 162.
    Mary, 189, 253.
    Richard, 253.
    Samuel, 21, 155, 253, 254.
    Sarah, 252.
SIDDON, Ezekiel, 141, 145.
    Jane, 65.
SLEIGHT, Joseph, 49.
SLOCUM, Sarah, 132.
SLOAN, Joseph, 153.
    James, 153.
SMALLWOOD, Thomas, 373.
SMART, Nathan, 215.
SMITH, Anna, 136.
    Barbara, 178.
    Daniel, 81.
    Elizabeth, 35, 243, 244.
    Francis, 91.
    George, 331.
    Isaac, 178.
    Mary, 178.
    Nicholas, 69.
    Rebecca, 97.
    Richard, 77.
    Robert, 197.
    Samuel, 79, 86, 180, 232, 353.
    Sarah, 178.
    Thomas, 69.
    Joseph Few, 161, 162.
SNOWDON, Christopher, 327.
SOMERS, Hannah, 151.
    Richard, 151.
SOUTHWICK, James, 80.
    Josiah, 76, 80.
    Meam, 80, 259.
    Ruth, 80.
SPARKS, Henry, 144.
SPENCER, ——, 321.
SPEARMAN, Thomas, 140.
SPEY, John, 290.
SPICER, Samuel, 91, 95, 202, 293, 294, 296, 297, 298.
    Abigail, 207, 297.
    Abraham, 297.
    Esther, 95, 235, 293, 294.
    Jacob, 294, 297, 298, 299.
    Martha, 297.
    Mary, 51, 297.
    Michel, 293.
    Rebecca, 206.
    Sarah, 95, 297.

SPICER, Thomas, 206, 293, 294, 297, 298.
SPICER'S Ferry, 295.
SPRAGUE, Caleb, 77, 161.
    Samuel, 209.
SPRINGWELL, 182.
SQUIBB, Robert, 337.
STALLES, Alice, 75.
STANTON, Daniel, 297.
STANLEY, Elizabeth, 302.
STAFFORD, Joseph C., 130.
    John, 83.
STAMPER, Francis, 113.
STARKEY, Ruth, 82.
    Thomas, 25, 26, 66, 67.
STARR, Jesse W., 245.
STACY, Elizabeth, 280.
    Henry, 202, 277, 278, 279, 280, 281.
    Mahlon, 228.
    Mary, 280.
    Robert, 277.
    Samuel, 280.
    Sarah, 280, 281.
STEVENS, Robert, 156.
ST. MARY'S church, Colestown, 205.
STILES, Ephraim, 226, 384.
    Isaac, 247.
    Mary, 247.
    Priscilla, 226.
    Robert, 184, 225, 226, 321.
STOY, James, 373.
    John, 65.
    Joseph C., 73, 320.
STORY, Thomas, 235.
STOCKDALE, Jarvis, 104, 106.
    Mary, 141.
STOKES, Thomas, 120, 301, 302, 303, 304, 305.
    Charles, 303.
    Deliverance, 304.
    Hannah, 123, 204, 304.
    Jacob, 190, 304, 306.
    John, 185, 301, 302, 303, 304, 306, 368.
    Joseph, 303, 311, 384.
    Joshua, 120, 123, 152, 244, 304, 305.
    Kesiah, 304.
    Lydia, 304.
    Mary, 303, 311.
    Rachel, 304.
    Rosanna, 82, 304, 368.
    Samuel, 244, 368.
    Sarah, 303.
STRAND, Abraham, 219.

STRATTON, David, 136.
STURGEON, William, 208.
STURGISS, Anthony, 252, 253.
SURKETT, John, 91.
SWANSON, Bridget, 329.
    Catharine, 329.
    John, 329.
    Judith, 329.

SWANSON, Lydia, 329.
    Mary, 329.
    Peter, 329.
    Swan, 329.
    Wallo, 329.
SWEDESBORO church, 289.
SWETT, Benjamin, 93, 130.
SYKES, Nathaniel, 217.

T

TALLMAN, ——, 185.
TATEM, Joseph B., 221.
    Sarah, 254.
    William P., 184.
TATHAN, John, 76.
TAYLOR, Anthony, 217.
    Samuel, 142.
THACKARA, Thomas, 12, 17, 24, 25, 45, 49, 52, 57, 58, 60, 61, 62, 63, 64, 65, 66, 153, 296, 317, 372, 374.
    Abigail, 46.
    Ann, 46.
    Benjamin, 45, 46, 61, 64, 65, 91, 152, 169, 368.
    Christopher, 57.
    Daniel, 57.
    Elizabeth, 46.
    Hannah, 46, 57, 64, 65, 97, 368.
    Hepsibah, 64.
    Isaac, 46.
    Jacob, 45, 46.
    James, 45, 62.
    Joseph, 45, 61, 62, 64, 65, 332.
    Margaret, 46.
    Mark, 46.
    Mary, 46, 64, 97.
    Rachel, 46.
    Richard, 296.
    Sarah, 64, 372, 375.
    Stephen, 45, 61, 65.
    William, 46, 65.
THOMAS, Gabriel, 226, 279, 285, 373.
    Hannah, 82.
    Jonathan, 204.
    Mercy, 82.
    Samuel, 82.
THOMPSON, Ann, 179.
    John, 216.
    Peter, 247.
THORNE, Abigail, 245.
    Elizabeth, 245.

THORNE, Hannah, 245.
    John, 133, 243, 245, 246, 247.
    Joseph, 52, 229, 246, 275.
    Mary, 245.
    Samuel, 246.
    Sarah, 245, 320.
    Thomas, 243, 244, 245, 246, 321.
    William, 246.
TILTON, Esther, 293.
    John, 293.
    Mary, 293.
TILY, Nathaniel, 274.
    Elizabeth, 274.
    Mary, 274.
TINDALL, Joseph, 317.
    Sarah, 133.
TODD, William, 236.
TOMS, William, 102.
TOMLINSON, Joseph, 120, 191, 192, 193, 194, 195, 197, 200, 321.
    Ann, 197.
    Catharine, 198.
    Daniel, 199.
    Ebenezer, 197.
    Eleanor, 108, 198.
    Elizabeth, 197, 198.
    Ephraim, 120, 197, 198, 236, 259.
    Hannah, 198.
    Isaac, 198.
    John, 162, 197, 198, 200, 366.
    Joseph, 197, 198.
    Lydia, 321.
    Margaret, 197.
    Mary, 197, 198, 199.
    Othniel, 197, 199.
    Richard, 197.
    Samuel, 198, 199.
    William, 197, 198, 199.
TONKINS, Edward, 204.
TOWNSEND, Isaac, 108.
TOY, Elias, 52, 178, 210, 333.

INDEX.

TRAFFORD, Thomas, 48.
TRENT, William, 228.
TREDWAY, Henry, 228, 328.
TROTH, Jacob, 224.
TUFT, John, 46.
TURNER, Robert, 13, 26, 38, 49, 50, 54, 57, 58, 59, 67, 68, 69, 107, 140, 146, 147, 150, 159, 161, 316, 339, 340, 342, 343, 349, 350.

TURNER, Edward, 342.
    George, 245.
    John, 221.
    Martha, 342.
    Mary, 342.
    Susanna, 342.
TYLER, Mary, 219.
    William, 219.

U

UPPER Dinidock, 360.

UXBRIDGE, 131, 132, 229.

V

VANLEAR, Benjamin, 190, 306.

VARLO, Charles, 313.

W

WADE, Edward, 215.
    John, 209.
    Lydia, 197.
WALLACE, Philip, 209.
    Mary, 209.
WALL, James, 52.
WARD, Abigail, 82, 369.
    George, 328.
WARNER, William, 162, 328, 329.
WARRICK, Beulah, 163.
WATKINS, Christopher, 95.
WATTS, Sarah, 140.
WEBSTER, Josiah, 153.
    Samuel, 108, 120, 153.
    Thomas, 259.
WELCH, William, 342.
WEST New Jersey Society, 139, 174.
WEST, Deborah, 347.
WHARTON, John, 93.
    Tract, 93.
WHITALL, Hannah, 65, 372, 375.
    James, 19, 21, 362.
    Job, 65, 136.
    John, 61, 64, 65, 66, 282, 374, 375.
    Mary, 65.
    Sarah, 133.
WHITE, John, 17, 18, 373.
    Joseph, 15, 18.
    William, 18.
WICKACO, 329.

WILD, Elizabeth, 204.
    James, 203, 204, 244, 310.
    John, 204.
    Jonathan, 204.
    Rachel, 204, 310.
    Samuel, 204.
    Sarah, 204.
WILDON, Richard, 291.
WILKINS, Arsuba, 19.
    John, 235.
WILLARD, Abigail, 298.
    Henry, 332.
    James, 332.
    Judith, 332.
    Thomas, 332.
WILLIS, Esther, 104.
    Henry, 19, 104.
    John, 112, 115, 130, 161, 163, 164, 304.
    Thomas, 112, 115, 130.
WILLITS, Charles L., 241, 243.
    Jeremiah, 77, 244.
    Nathan B., 243.
WILLS, Daniel, 79, 91, 203, 231, 232, 277.
    Elizabeth, 97, 384.
    Hope, 384.
    James, 169.
    Joab, 136.
    John, 91, 356.
    Rebecca, 197.

WILLS, Thomas, 384.
WILSON, Jonathan, 280.
WINN, Elizabeth, 35.
WISTAR, Richard, 198.
WITHERS, Thomas, 217.
WOOD, Abigail, 94, 178, 332, 333.
    Alice, 330.
    Benjamin, 169, 176, 178, 332, 333.
    Constantine, 120, 327, 328, 330.
    Elizabeth, 45, 178, 332, 333.
    Esther, 326, 330.
    Hannah, 94, 178, 332, 333.
    Henry, 32, 65, 91, 94, 202, 219, 220, 294, 297, 327, 328, 329, 330, 331, 332, 333.
    Isaac, 118.
    James, 220, 221, 332.
    Jane, 333.
    Jeremiah, 327, 328.
    John, 65, 95, 326, 327, 328, 329, 330, 333.
    Jonathan, 327.
    Joseph, 194, 316, 329, 330.
    Judith, 332, 333.
    Mary, 178, 204, 326, 330, 333.
WOOD, Richard, 332.
    Sarah, 326, 330.
    Thomas, 326.
    William, 326, 328.
WOODNUTT, Richard, 218.
WOODROSE, Thomas, 216.
WOOLSTAN, Elizabeth, 91.
    Hannah, 90, 91.
    John, 87, 90, 91.
    Jonathan, 90, 91, 97.
    Joshua, 91.
    Latitia, 244.
    Mary, 90,
    Michael, 91.
    Rebecca, 91.
    Samuel, 90, 97.
    Sarah, 90.
WRIGHT, Constance, 370.
    Hannah, 370.
    John, 252, 367, 370, 373.
    Rachel, 303, 304.
    Richard, 225, 367, 370.
    Sarah, 370.
    Thomas, 64, 358, 359.
WYATT, Bartholemew, 197, 198, 220.
    Elizabeth, 197, 198.
    Sarah, 198.

Y

YEGOU, Peter, 358, 359.
YEGOU'S Island, Burlington, 359.
YORKSHIRE Commissioners, 12, 87.
YOUNG, Henry, 299.

Z

ZANE, Robert, 11, 12, 13, 14, 15, 16, 17, 18, 20, 21, 22, 25, 49, 59, 60, 61, 146, 215, 216, 284.
    Abigail, 19.
    Ebenezer, 19, 21.
    Elizabeth, 19.
    Elnathan, 19, 146.
    Esther, 19, 20.
    Hannah, 19.
    Isaac, 19, 21, 22.
ZANE, Jonathan, 19, 21, 52.
    Joseph, 19, 20.
    Margaret, 19.
    Nathaniel, 19, 20.
    Rachel, 19.
    Rebecca, 19.
    Sarah, 19.
    Silas, 21.
    Simeon, 19.
    William, 19.

CORRECTIONS.

Page 73, second paragraph; for "south," read "north." Page 89, second paragraph; for "lead," read "led." Page 110, foot-note; omit "O. S. G." after 458. Page 161, last paragraph; for "Low," read "Lowe." Page 170; for "Shackle," read "Shable." Page 184, last paragraph; for "being formerly," read "and." Page 202; in foot-notes 5 and 7, read "B1," &c. Page 213, first paragraph; transpose the words "Griffith" and "Griffin." Page 226, first paragraph; for "saw-mill," read "corn-mill." Page 253, near the top; for "saw-mill," read "corn-mill." Page 303, near the bottom; insert the word "by" between "owned" and "Mark Ballinger." Page 304, top line; for "south side by," read "north by the south side of." Page 345, last line; for "thus," read "then." Page 357, near the bottom; for "heretofore," read "hereafter." Page 384, third paragraph, seventh line; insert "subsequent meetings" before "continued."

EXPLANATION

OF THE NUMBERS FOUND UPON THE ACCOMPANYING MAP.

No. on Map.	Name of the Locator.	Reference to Record.
1	1,600 acres to Mark Newbie, Thomas Thackara, Robert Zane, George Goldsmith and Thomas Sharp.	Revel's Book, 25.
2	250 acres to William Bates.	" 53.
3	100 acres to Mark Newbie, Thomas Thackara, Robert Zane, William Bates, Thomas Sharp and Robert Turner.	" 25.
4	300 acres to William Cooper.	" 32.
5	450 acres to William Roydon (also the island).	" 95.
6	350 acres to Mark Newbie.	" 42.
7	500 acres to Francis Collins.	" 39.
8	450 acres to Francis Collins.	" 39.
9	490 acres to Henry Stacy.	" 37.
10	500 acres to Richard Mathews.	" 38.
11	28 acres to John White.	" 39.
12	400 acres to Robert Turner.	" 44.
13	500 acres to Robert Turner.	" 51.
14	1,500 acres to Samuel Norris.	" 52.
15	250 acres to Thomas Carlton.	" 53.
16	900 acres to Robert Turner.	" 51.
17	18 acres to John Ashton.	" 25.
18	500 acres to John Willis.	Lib. A, 12, 80.
19	117 acres to Francis Collins.	Revel's Book, 39.
20	220 acres to William Albertson.	Lib. T, 355, O. S. G.
21	220 acres to Robert Turner.	Revel's Book, 51.
22	200 acres to Richard Arnold.	Basse's Book, 27.
23	500 acres to Robert Turner.	Revel's Book, 51.

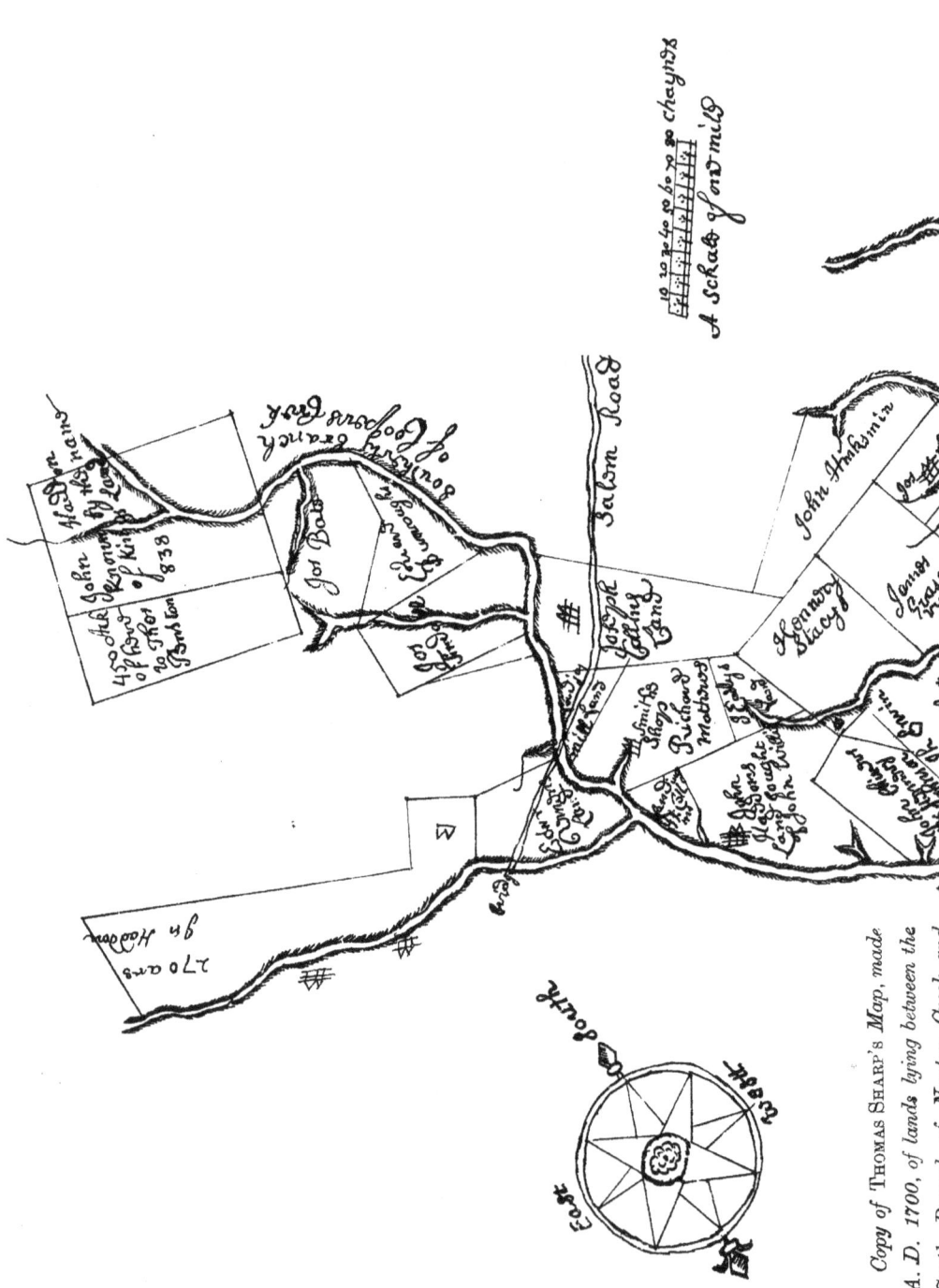

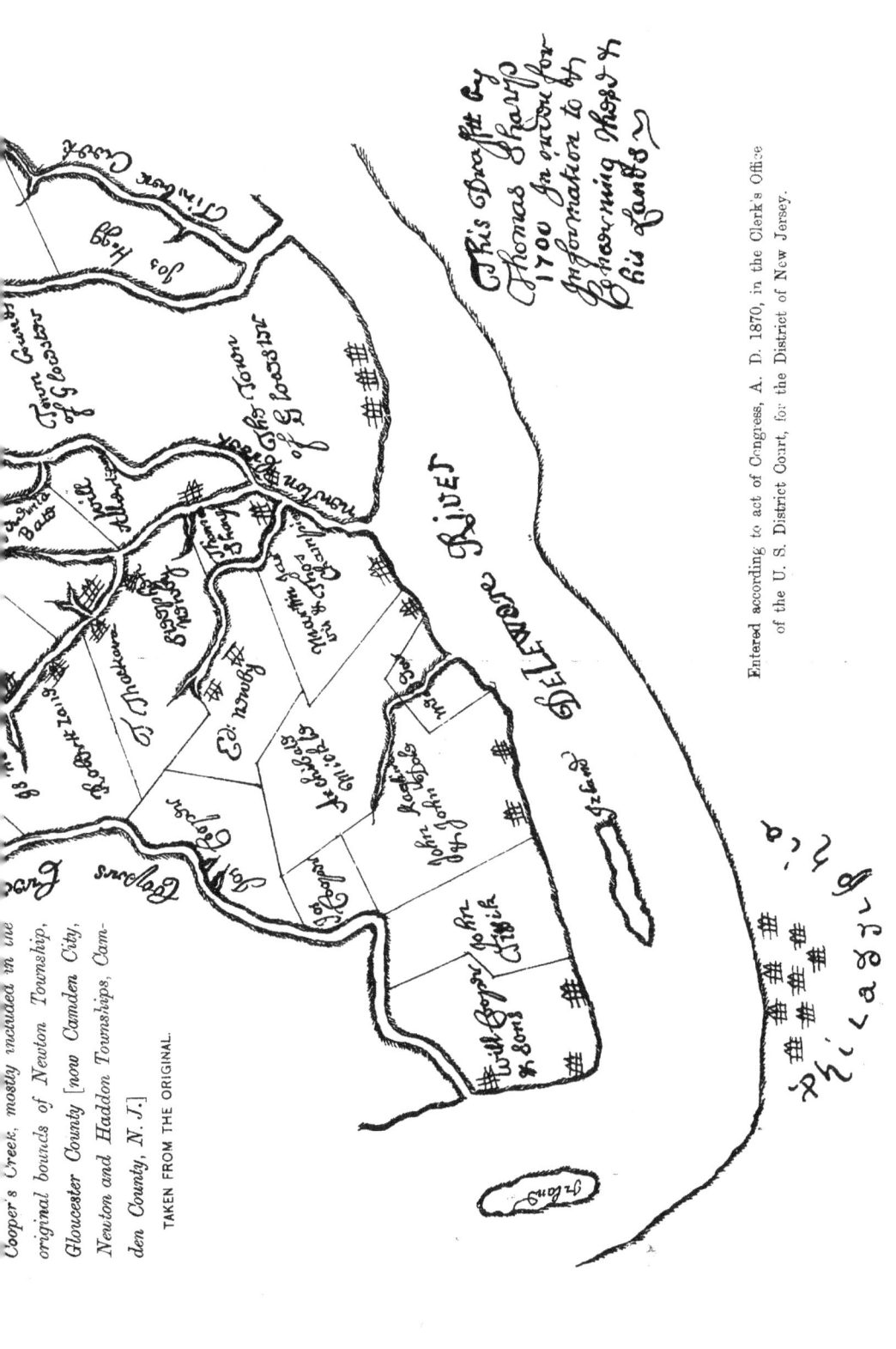

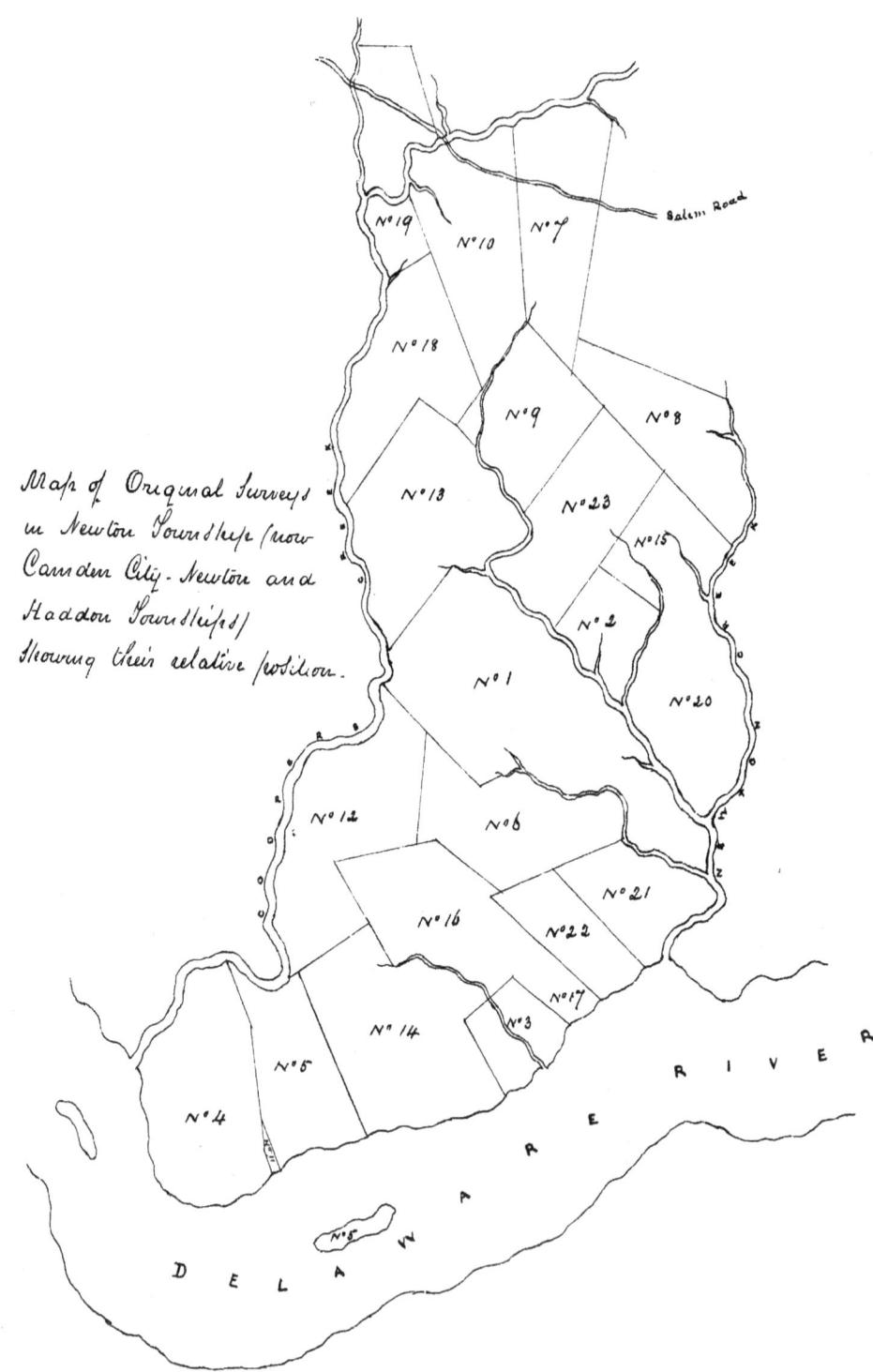

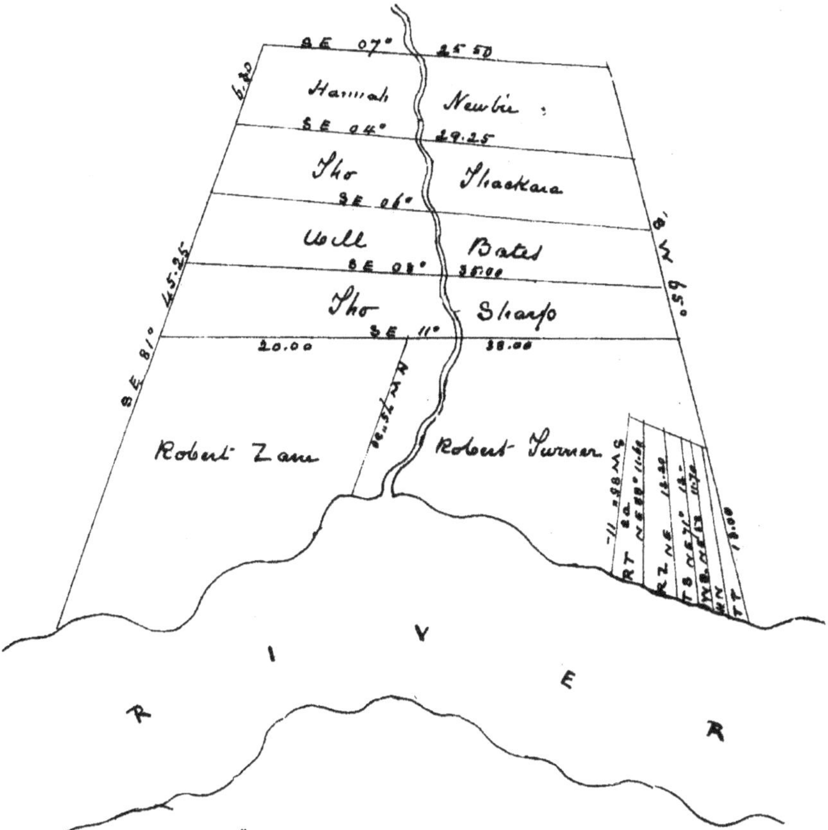
SE 07° 25.50
6.80
Hannah Newbie
SE 04° 29.25
Tho Thackara
SE 06°
Will Bates
SE 08° 35.00
Tho Sharp
SE 11°
20.00
38.00
SE 81° 45.25
Robert Zane
Robert Turner
R I V E R

"The Meadow which belongs
to the Towne of Newton" (Copy)

100 Achors unto William Aalliot

100 Achors Unto John Ah[...]

200 Achors were surveyed unto Anthony Sturges this 2[...] of 4 mo 98

John Jonsons Land

Jsack hollingams Land

Coopers Creek

Newton Creek

Robertt Zanes Land

Tho Thackras Land

Map of Land in Newton Township by Thomas Sharp 1698

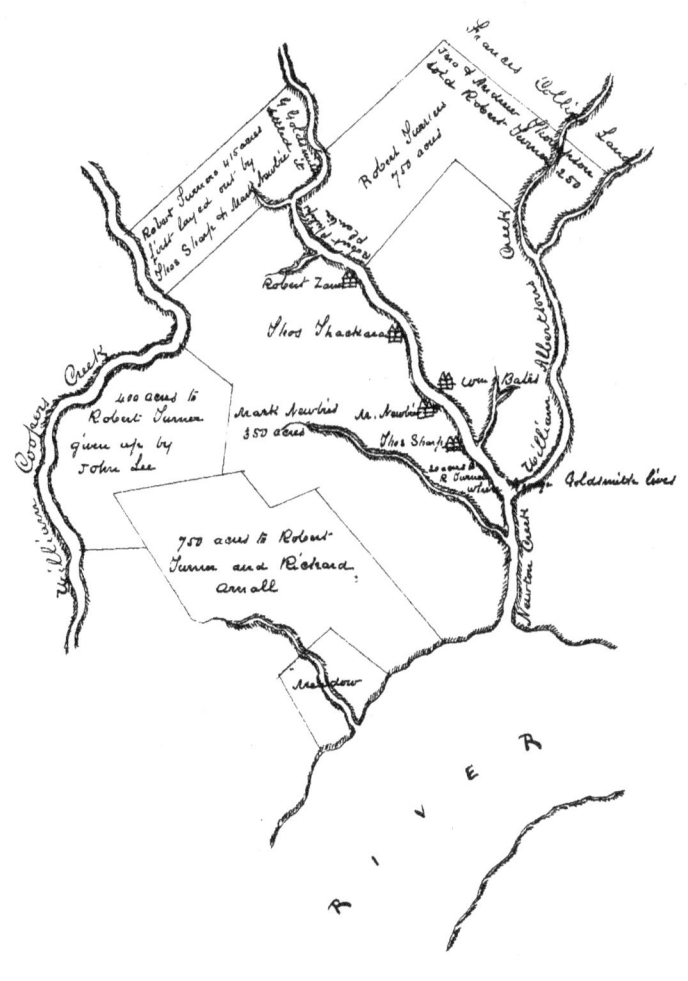

Copy of a Map (reduced from the Original) of
Robert Turners Land in Newton Township
Gloucester County NJ

www.ingramcontent.com/pod-product-compliance
Lightning Source LLC
Chambersburg PA
CBHW060348080526
44583CB00012B/216